High Culture Fever

High Culture Fever

Politics, Aesthetics, and Ideology
in Deng's China

Jing Wang

UNIVERSITY OF CALIFORNIA PRESS
Berkeley · Los Angeles · London

972938

University of California Press
Berkeley and Los Angeles, California

University of California Press, Ltd.
London, England

© 1996 by
The Regents of the University of California

Wang, Jing, 1950–
   High culture fever : politics, aesthetics, and
ideology in Deng's China / Jing Wang.
     p. cm.
   Includes bibliographical references and index. '
   ISBN 0-520-20294-5 (alk. paper).—
   ISBN 0-520-20295-3 (pbk. : alk. paper)
    1. China—Intellectual life—1976– I. Title.
   DS779.23.W36 1996
   001.1'0951—dc20   96-5580

Printed in the United States of America
9 8 7 6 5 4 3 2 1

For Hitomi, Tani, Miriam, and Ling-hsia

Contents

Acknowledgments

I owe a great deal to Kent Mullikin and his staff at the National Humanities Center, where I worked on this book between September 1992 and May 1993. This project was also supported by funds awarded by Duke University Research Council and the Asian/Pacific Studies Institute of the University.

I am grateful to Howard Goldblatt and David Der-Wei Wang for reading the manuscript and offering invaluable suggestions for revision. No less an acknowledgment of appreciation is due to colleagues with whom I conversed at different stages of writing: Tani Barlow, Christopher Connery, Arif Dirlik, Prasenjit Duara, Judith Farquhar, Edward Gunn, Ted Huters, Fredric Jameson, Li Tuo, Victor Mair, Lisa Rofel, Mark Selden, Darko Suvin, Marilyn Young, Zhang Longxi, and Zhang Xudong. I also wish to thank Edward Martinique, the head of the East Asian Section at the Davis Library of the University of North Carolina at Chapel Hill, for building the collection of contemporary Chinese literature and intellectual history at such a phenomenal pace. My thanks, also, to Leo Ching for brainstorming with me about subtitles, and to Gail Woods for her assistance in reformatting the notes.

Sheila Levine's exquisite professionalism and support of this project made the final preparation of the manuscript a delightful task. My gratitude extends to Carolyn Hill, my copy editor, Scott Norton, my project director, and Wen-hsin Yeh, who connected me to the Press.

I remain indebted to friends near and far. And as always, no book could have been written without Candy's generous understanding of her mother's indulgence in scholarship.

I dedicate this book to Hitomi Endo, Tani Barlow, Miriam Cooke, and Ling-hsia Yeh, for the generosity of their hearts.

Introduction

Future historians will remember the 1980s in China as a period of utopian vision on the one hand and an era of emergent crises on the other. Euphoria and great expectation swept over the nation as the Party's economic reform completed its first initiative of promoting household-based agriculture. A much-anticipated urban reform had just begun, spreading far and wide the catchword "commodity economy." As a finishing touch toward utopian closure, the Party organ *People's Daily* churned out in quick succession speeches given by Deng Xiaoping, Wan Li, and other high-ranking officials about the urgency of political reform. At the juncture of 1985, the metaphor of consummation could well have captured the apex of national jubilance.

China's postrevolutionary utopia, in its feverish progression toward socialist modernization, continued the legacy of Maoism in spirit—replete with its anti-imperialist rhetoric. But such a vision stood a better chance of being fulfilled precisely because the state ideology of Deng's China underwent a paradoxical phase of collaboration with capital and an intricate process of de-alienating intellectuals at home. Thus began a ten-year history of the complex and contradictory relationship between the cultural elite and their political counterpart in the Party.

Of particular importance were 1985 and 1986, two memorable years that witnessed the intensification of the intellectuals' "methodology fever" on the nation's cultural agenda, the massive propagation of the formula for a market economy, and the reiteration of the imperative that the Party discuss political reform. Excessive nationwide expectations of a more enlightened and wealthier future escalated dramatically. Therefore, the early signs of thwarted economic reform in the cities, the difficulties of negotiating the transformative relationship between the vertical bureaucratic command system and the horizontal market coordination based on the laws of supply and demand, and the ensuing inflation in 1987 and 1988 as the result of an aborted price reform were all taken as ominous setbacks that baffled the previously impassioned public.[1] Successive political events of a dramatic nature—a university students' demonstration in Beijing in late 1986, Party Secretary Hu Yaobang's immediate ouster as a result, the launching of yet another campaign against "bourgeois liberalism" in early 1987—further deepened the disillusionment that culminated in a pervasive dystopian mentality, which was exacerbated when Premier Zhao Ziyang announced at the Thirteenth Party Congress in 1987 that the nation lingered at the threshold of the *"primary* stage of socialism."[2]

By June 1988, when the television miniseries *Heshang* (Yellow river elegy) sent waves of sensational impact across the country, the crisis consciousness had finally overtaken the utopian mood and sunk deeply in the national psyche. *Heshang* was the last milestone in the intellectual history of the 1980s that marked the cultural elite's illusion that their enlightenment project could not only go hand in hand with, but also steer, the state's project of modernization in the right direction. Indeed, throughout the decade, since the inception of the controversy over "socialist alienation" in 1983, the collaboration of the cultural elite with the state's reconstruction of a socialist utopia coincided with the elite's making of their own utopian discourse of enlightenment, which, more often than not, took the Party as its contestant. The uneasy coexistence of those two utopian projects did not last long. Their inevitable collision came on June 4, 1989.

Nothing much can be said at this moment (although a great deal of raw emotion has been expressed) about the abortive closure of the decade. The historical verdict on the Tian'anmen Square crackdown has yet to come. Although poetic justice has already passed sentence on the victimizers, the agenda of the martyrs themselves (and one may add, that of Western media) is by no means immune to inquiries and criticisms.[3] At home, public opinion about the crackdown has undergone a subtle change in the post-Tian'anmen era of affluence. In the mid-1990s, it is much more difficult for mainland Chinese citizens to conclude which historical course would better empower the masses politically, culturally, and materially: the victory of the enlightenment intellectuals, were the students to succeed in their revolt, and hence the continual monopoly of an elitist cultural agenda, or Deng Xiaoping's political survival, the ensuing economic boom, and the perpetuation of Chinese socialism (no matter how ideologically corrupt it turns out to be) as a challenge and alternative to Western liberalism.

The ambiguous meaning of the epochal closure notwithstanding, the June Fourth crackdown accentuated the irreconcilability of the state utopian project with that of the intellectuals. Although the Western media predicted that the failure of the enlightenment utopia would lead Communist China to a political and economic bankruptcy in the immediate wake of June 1989, history delivered a scenario much to the surprise of China watchers: the demise of one utopian project gave rise to the success of the other. Despite the controversy surrounding the issue of ideological purity, China's post-1989 economic boom illustrates for its average citizen the near-completion of socialist modernization, and, better still, the possibility of an economically and geopolitically greater China than ever before.

The Chinese success story of the 1990s is a controversial topic that lies beyond the immediate historical configuration of this book. What the following pages present is the cultural and literary elite's utopian discourse of the 1980s in its various manifestations—their decade-long ideological negotiations with the Party and their engagement in the debates over the aesthetics through which broader issues of cultural politics were addressed.

No critic or historian who attempts to depict Deng's China of the 1980s can claim that her study of the last decade covers every territory of inquiry. History can only create its meaning by selection and exclusion. The seven essays collected in this volume do not provide a detailed chronicle of the cultural and literary events that took place in the 1980s in China. I am less interested in painting a detailed portrait of what transpired year in and year out than in depicting in broad strokes those ideological moments that broke the comfortable circuit of continuity and chronology. To do so, I focus on seven major topics that foreground the geneses of polemics and moments of transition in the cultural politics of postrevolutionary China. Together, the essays form a diachronic order that reenacts before our eyes moments of crises and transformation, breakdowns and irruptive events, explosive controversies whose repercussions crossed the boundaries of cultural domains and the literary field. In other words, to restage that theater of ideas, I dwell on disruptive events that created space for ideological contestations and highlighted, in Paul Rabinow's expression, the "successive coagulations of power and knowledge" that form the heart of the epochal discourse of the 1980s.[4]

Each of these seven essays focuses on a historical moment of danger and indeterminacy: the outbreak of the debate over socialist alienation and Marxist humanism in 1983; Culture Fever in 1985; the controversy over the TV series *Heshang* in 1988; the proposition of "pseudo-modernism" during the same year; the emergent problematic of subjectivity from 1985 onward; the rise of the pseudoproposition of postmodernism in the late 1980s; and the dialogue of "the Wang Shuo phenomenon" with a rampant popular culture in the early 1990s.

One can indeed delineate the 1980s by more than seven different perspectives. What is presented in this book by no means exhausts the subject. There are many significant topics—literary movements and prominent writers in particular—that I leave out. In order to fix our gaze on the 1980s as a decade of change in the realm of ideas, I choose to speak more in the capacity of a cultural critic than a literary historian. Topics such as reportage literature and "neorealism" (*xin xieshi zhuyi*) that would have taken up much room in any official literary history of the 1980s are to be found only at the margins of this book. Realism has a marginal status in this book because it played a lesser role as a catalyst for the deep structural change of the epochal discourse. In comparison, the problematics of modernism and postmodernism, which I treat at greater length, are significant precisely because they were embroiled in the larger issues of the ideology of resistance and strategies of sinicization and were thus figured in the broad configuration of indigenous and global cultural politics. The degree of the intensity of the liaison that a particular literary phenomenon (whether realism or modernism) forged with cultural politics decided the attention that each literary figure or movement received in this book.

I take this triple focus as a given. It seems inconceivable that any literary historian can render the history of Chinese postrevolutionary literature independent of the decade's intellectual and cultural history. By the same token, it is equally insufficient to write a treatise on the rise or resurgence of ideological debates (on Marxist humanism or modernity, for instance) without bearing in mind that the postrevolutionary literature of the 1980s corresponded intimately to the succession of ideas that swept over the ideological field. In modern and contemporary China before 1989, literature was always "self-conscious of its own historical mission of thought enlightenment."[5] From humanism to the topos of *fansi* (introspection) and on to their fervent search for "roots" and simultaneous inquiries into *xiandai yishi* (modern consciousness), creative writers kept close pace with insurgent ideologists in their propagation of major epochal themes and partook in the postrevolutionary discourse of rational critique and utopianism.

What this book delivers is an abridged, ten-year, entwined history of Chinese intellectuals, writers, and literary and cultural critics. Most of the time, needless to say, the boundaries between these roles were fluid. The literary, cultural, critical, and intellectual histories of the 1980s—each commanding its own discursive regimes—merged to form one epochal discourse that was distinctly elitist.

We can better understand the utopianism embedded in such an elitist discourse only in hindsight. There is no better way of bringing into relief the utopianism of the 1980s than closing the book with a discussion of the post-topian mood of the 1990s. To highlight this ironic contrast, I conclude the story of the 1980s with a chapter on the pop cultural syndromes of the post-Tian'anmen era. Only through such a juxtaposition—pitting the intellectuals' lament in the 1990s about their *social* alienation against their earlier discourse on *socialist* alienation—can we perceive and appreciate the tragicomic drama of the history of post-Mao China.

Chinese intellectuals are entering a new phase of self-reflection in the 1990s. A cycle has just been completed. We must remember that the decade of the 1980s began with the onset of the elite's introspective look at Mao's era that kicked off the epochal theme of thought emancipation. What took form then as a congratulatory self-reflection of their historical role in the program of modernization returns now in the 1990s as a genuine self-examination devoid of the confidence and optimism that once characterized each of their earlier introspective campaigns. Ironically, as the 1990s spurns the vision of enlightenment, the long overdue process of the elite's somber self-criticism has just begun. It is through this probing post-1989 self-critique that the once vainglorious architects of China's destiny (and we as spectators) learn more about the decade of the 1980s.

The honest acknowledgment of their own dilemma and the search for post-topian redemption gave birth to many soul-searching testimonies in the early years of the 1990s.[6] Even the most relentless critic of Chinese intellectuals must marvel at their nascent practice of critiquing, perhaps for the first time in Chinese history, what elitism and intellectualism stood for. Those scathing self-critiques bring into sharp relief some of the characteristic vicious cycles to which the discourse of the 1980s was susceptible: the writer-intellectuals' unqualified condemnation of

Mao Zedong and his utopian vision,[7] the tendency of postrevolutionary literature toward "pan-ideologization," the increasing inaccessibility of elite literature to ordinary people, the intellectuals' "public square consciousness" (the self-inflationary picture of an intellectual savior standing in Tian'anmen Square commanding a crowd who awaited enlightenment), and the hidden utilitarian drive underlying the notion of enlightenment.[8]

The most optimistic among those critics resisted the temptation to denounce the decadence of the 1990s but learned to problematize the elevated (kangfen) mood of the 1980s instead.[9] Depletion was now viewed by them as progress,[10] far superior to the Age of Abstinence, and in a certain sense, a more natural condition than the continual erection that the 1980s put the entire nation through. In the wake of the crackdown in 1989, an acute self-consciousness was in the making: the historical opportunity had arrived for intellectuals to let go of their centuries-old public-sphere persona and carve a solitary niche for themselves. This may not signify a return to academia—academia understood in the sense of total withdrawal from immediate sociopolitical reality—but the maintaining of distance from society instead of making strides with it in the same direction and at the same tempo (an old mental habit of Chinese intellectuals, which Li Zehou could not decide whether to characterize as the "tragedy" or the "formal drama" of Chinese history).[11]

The intellectuals' reassessment in the 1990s of the utopianism that the 1980s inspired and aspired to reopens many questions that a modernity caught in its own temporal vision could not afford to ask. Whether Chinese intellectuals can achieve a historical breakthrough in the 1990s remains to be seen. But they have certainly delivered to us a unique perspective that is simultaneously critical of and nostalgic for the decade whose ideological agendas I explore in the following chapters.

Many major themes of the 1980s recur throughout the book. Although each essay forms a self-sufficient unit, the complex theme of modernity and cultural subjectivity spans several chapters. So does the depiction of the literary school of "modernism" (xiandai pai), the root-searchers (xungen pai), and the experimentalists. The mention and cross-examination of each school in different chapters serves as an apt illustration of what Wallace Stevens conveys with such poetic economy in "Thirteen Ways of Looking at a Black Bird": we can never consume the plurality of a sign. The most we can do is examine it in the changing context that yields different, and perhaps conflicting, vantage points.

The 1980s is a decade to be celebrated, critiqued, and reminisced about all at once. As Chinese intellectuals undergo the difficult task of coming to terms with commercial culture and with the "hedonistic view of life" that permeates the social mores of the 1990s, it is high time to look back at a decade that exalted the politics of resistance and the emancipatory capacity of knowledge.[12] The 1990s may mock the 1980s for the large stake its engineers placed on the accumulation of symbolic capital, but revisiting that utopian moment in history may yet teach a long overdue lesson to those Chinese intellectuals now mired in legitimation crisis: knowledge is not power, but a mere tool of critique.

ONE

"Who Am I?"

Questions of Voluntarism in the Paradigm of Socialist Alienation

Any significant chronicle of post-Mao Chinese literature must start with the emergence of the problematic of humanism in the early 1980s. No matter how contemptuously Chinese avant-garde writers and critics now regard those earliest specimens of exposé literature that promote the value and dignity of human beings in crude confessional realism, it is precisely the literature's complicitous relationship with the postrevolutionary politics of humanism that accounted for its quick popularity both at home, albeit for a very short while, and abroad for a decade and beyond. Such an asymmetrical reception of the literature of humanism tells us worlds about the discrepancy between China's ever changing agenda grown out of an increasingly unstable self-identity and the stagnant frame of reference known as postcolonial Orientalism, in whose terms the West fabricates the representation of China. The image of Chinese writers defying the communist regime in the name of humanity will continue to feed into the Western fabrication of "Oriental despotism" long after the Chinese themselves have gone far beyond their preoccupation with human rights issues.[1] That the Chinese social imaginary could be cleansed so soon of the memory of summer 1989 and be filled anew with the fetishism of consumerism is a reality that Westerners, especially liberal democrats, confront with mixed emotions.[2] Although they welcome the Communist Party's unabashed promotion of consumerism as an unambiguous sign of the victory of Western capitalism, advocates of human rights in the West at the same time deplore the alacrity with which the Chinese shed their mourning apparel to slip into attire designed for the nouveau riche.

Historical amnesia may be a malady that plagues the Chinese populace in the age of boom economies, for better or for worse. But back in the late 1970s and early 1980s, active remembrance was an exercise in which intellectuals and writers engaged with unrelieved piety. For nearly half a decade, confessions and self-introspection not only pervaded literary discourse, but also emerged as a dominant trope in political discourse. The Chinese Marxists' unorthodox acknowledgment that Marxism is conscious of its own self-alienation is characteristic of the soul-searching mood poignantly and theatrically presented in the political arena and in creative writers' sentimental homage to "Ah, Human Beings! Human Beings!" (Ren a ren) (1980).[3] Neither state ideology nor one's personal history was exempt from the intense epochal call to remember the past. What was remembered was not only personal wounds inflicted upon each individual by the Revolution and the Gang of Four—a cliché that outlived its appeal by the mid-1980s—but also the repressed memory of the early history of Marxism, specifically, the humanist epistemology of the young Marx epitomized in his *Economic and Philosophic Manuscripts of 1844*. In the immediate wake of the defeat of ultra-leftism, what stood in need of rehabilitation (a postrevolutionary "fever" blazing with the same intensity as that of class struggle in Mao's time) was certainly not simply the so-called individual victims of the Revolution, but Marx himself: the historical past of Marx the philosopher whose outcry against alienation now provided to disillusioned Party intellectuals a new possibility to reinvent Chinese Marxism.[4]

Needless to say, the stakes were exceedingly high for those who dared to venture the theoretical proposal of "socialist alienation" at the turn of the early 1980s. Future historians will commend the enormous moral courage and personal risk that Wang Ruoshui and Zhou Yang took in challenging Maoism-Marxism and in pioneering the theoretical critique of the Cultural Revolution. Without the intervention of the alienation school in the Chinese intellectual and political debates at that historical moment, the issue of humanism would not have occupied such a prominent place on the national agenda and the liberatory vision would not have been so deeply engraved on the intellectual history of the 1980s. New terrains of inquiry opened up in the following years precisely because the alienation theorists proved that transgression into forbidden ideological domains provided a possibility for self-introspection.

But what Wang Ruoshui, Zhou Yang, and their collaborators set out to achieve in the early 1980s was much less the condemnation of dogmatic Marxism than the seizure of the historical opportunity to rejuvenate an ossified ideology by reconstructing a genuine ethics of humanism within the ideological confines of Marxism. Thus, although the abundant political literature on the controversy of alienation integrated, more often than not, the introduction and critique of Sartre and existentialist humanism, the alienation school took particular care to dispel any suspicion that it might be Sartre rather than the young Marx who served as the theoretical point of departure for their advocacy of a Marxist humanism.

The Chinese discourse on Sartre during the debate was intriguingly double-edged. This is an issue that has not attracted much attention from scholars abroad. But precisely because indigenous scholars cannot afford to probe into it without inviting intervention from Party ideologues, I suggest that we take a closer look at theorists' strategic approach to Sartre vis-à-vis the young Marx. The problem I wish to address is the theoretical limitations of the construct of socialist alienation, limitations closely related to Chinese intellectuals' attitude toward the voluntarist aspect of Sartre's humanism (that is, the "greater valorization of subjective forces") that underlay the emotive content of the thesis for socialist alienation.[5] And yet, to critique the alienation school and to recognize the limitations of its perspective is not to downgrade both the importance of such a paradigm and the intellectual integrity of its propagators. Can we recognize the urgency of the problem of socialist alienation and at the same time critique the terms in which it was framed?

Before such a critique can be undertaken, we need to review the short history of the controversy surrounding the alienation school. Such a history has been recounted by Western political scientists and historians on various occasions.[6] To compose another similar chronicle of all the important episodes that led to the Anti–Spiritual Pollution Campaign (fall 1983 to spring 1984) is beside the point here. My purpose is not to analyze the political machinery that first triggered and then ended a fruitful debate. Nor will I reiterate in detail the sequence of events that unfolded between Zhou Yang's talk presented on the occasion of Marx's centenary and Hu Qiaomu's authoritative counterarguments published on January 27, 1984.[7] The rehearsal of the major arguments of the debate will only be meaningful if it serves as the point of departure for a critique of the theoretical construct of socialist alienation that has been taken for granted by many Western commentators.

ALIENATION

Most theorists of the Chinese alienation school were tacit about, or slow to acknowledge, Georg Lukács' contribution to the exegesis of the Marxist theory of alienation (*yihua*). There seemed to be a conscious and concerted effort among alienation theorists not to remind their powerful opponents that it was Lukács "the idealist" who brought Marx's theme of alienation into the limelight with his extensive explication of the term "reification" (*wu hua/yihua*; *Verdinglichung*) in *Geschichte und Klassenbewusstsein* in 1923. It is certainly intriguing that although many Chinese theorists insisted on distinguishing the Hegelian notion of "objectification" (*duixiang hua*; *Vergegenstandlichung*) from that of alienation, they involuntarily glossed over the issue of the conceptual affiliation or distinction between reification and alienation.[8] The interchangeability of these two terms in post-Mao China serves as a meaningful comment on the Chinese theorists' silent acknowledgment of the "rational elements in Lukács' thought."[9]

Though the term "alienation" has become a ubiquitous cliché since the mid-1940s in the West, its resurfacing in post-Mao China rang as fresh as ever following the immediate demise of the reign of the Gang of Four. As early as 1980, Wang Ruoshui, the deputy editor of *People's Daily*, raised the theoretical issue of socialist alienation and delineated its three major manifestations in China, a viewpoint reiterated almost verbatim by Zhou Yang in his speech commemorating Marx's centennial in 1983. Wang identified the three categories of alienation as "the alienation of thought attributed to the cult of Mao Zedong," "political alienation," and "economical alienation," but clearly foregrounded political alienation instead of economical alienation as the origin and culmination of socialist alienation in China.[10]

It is worth noting that it was not the Soviet but the Polish, Hungarian, Czech, and Yugoslavic communists who emerged as the intellectual forefathers of the Chinese alienation school. The works of Adam Schaff, a member of the Central Committee of the Polish Communist Party, and those of the Yugoslav Gajo Petrovic appeared in great abundance in *Zhexue yicong* (Translations of philosophical texts) between 1979 and 1982.[11] Stringent critiques of socialism by Eastern European communists circa 1965 sounded no doubt like bombshells when they were first translated into Chinese in 1979. Schaff's assertion that "in all forms of a socialist society different forms of alienation occur" and Petrovic's declaration that the "de-alienation of economic life also requires the abolition of state property" reverberated in Wang Ruoshui's and his colleagues' inquiries into the problematic of socialist alienation in Mao's China.[12]

Adam Schaff's perspective was particularly crucial to the development of Wang Ruoshui's theoretical framework. The major questions Schaff addresses—"Is it true that private property is at the basis of all alienation? And consequently, does the end of capitalism mean the end of all alienation?"—were transported verbatim into the agenda of Chinese theorists.[13] Wang Ruoshui was nonetheless selective of Schaff's arguments. Though Schaff deplores continued existence of the state as a coercive machinery, he recognizes that the state bureaucracy "will not wither away" and that labor on "an assembly line is inherently the same regardless of government."[14] This view, which asserts that labor should not have been identified as a category of alienation in the first place, is a point of contestation that Wang Ruoshui chose not to pursue because it subverted his effort to revalorize the alienation paradigm proposed by the young Marx. In the early 1980s, what intrigued Wang Ruoshui was not Schaff's subtle critique of the original Marxian paradigm but Schaff's open censure of communism. Wang found particularly inspiring Schaff's discussion of the relationship between the "cult of personality" and the communist state as an alienating force. In his defense of humanism, the Chinese theorist echoed the position of the Polish communist regarding the controversy over the young versus the mature Marx; he emphasized the unity in the development of Marx's theory and, as a result, the possibility of integrating the "scientific motivation of Marxism with an ethical, humanist one."[15]

Underlying all the communist critiques of socialism is the ominous accusation that whereas capitalist alienation is economical, therefore partial, communist alienation is political and total. The implication of such an ideological twist was by no means lost on Hu Qiaomu and his orthodox Marxist comrades. If, as Wang Ruoshui proclaimed, alienation, now in the guise of political estrangement of the people from the Party, had by no means disappeared with the implementation of public ownership of productive materials, then the old Marxist category of "private property" as the root cause of alienation had to give way to a new category of "power."[16] And what did Wang Ruoshui involuntarily propagate here, according to his Party critics, if not the total elimination of bureaucratic power—a position that could only reflect the ideological fallacy of anarchism?[17]

If the complaint about the anarchist tendency of the alienation school still maintained the fragile semblance of an academic exchange, a more underhanded recrimination discharged by the Party against Wang Ruoshui followed an unmistakably political course. At issue was Wang's alleged relapse into the ideology of permanent revolution advocated by the ultra-leftists during Mao's era. Those familiar with the subtle strategies of criticism and countercriticism at which the Chinese (both politicians and commoners alike) have been adept throughout history know how to decipher this treacherous device of counterattack. They take the Party's indictment of Wang Ruoshui's "leftism" with a grain of salt. Those speaking for the Party knew only too well that Wang's subscription to Mao's popular thesis of permanent revolution amounted to nothing more than a defensive gesture adopted for the purpose of camouflaging his own theoretical premise about continuous alienation under socialism: if Mao Zedong could talk about an endless series of social contradictions and struggles, then surely Wang Ruoshui's vision of a socialist society suffering from continual reification could not be immediately judged heretical. However, this conceptual coalition backfired. Wang Ruoshui was so preoccupied with making a preemptive strike against his imagined critics by quoting Mao as the theoretical underpinning for his own proposition of everlasting alienation ("Human history is a history of the continual development from the realm of necessity to the realm of freedom. This history will never come to an end.")[18] that he forgot the Party could beat him at his own game at any time by simply accusing him of re-allying with the now stigmatized Left. The subtle mechanism underlying this psychological warfare has undoubtedly obscured the initial hidden agenda of both the accused and the accuser. Yet given the fact that both Wang Ruoshui and his attackers (Deng Liqun among them)[19] were using roundabout rhetoric, the quick conclusion drawn by some Western observers about the close resemblance between the alienation school and the leftists of the Cultural Revolution should be reexamined carefully.[20]

Regardless of either charge (the school's ideological affiliation with anarchism on the one hand and with leftism on the other), the collision between alienation theorists and their opponents reveals that the subtext for the debate over the three specific forms of socialist alienation was none other than critique of the Cultural Revolution and, by extension, the Great Helmsman himself. Though officially the Party now criticized Mao strongly on some occasions (Hu Qiaomu, the veteran Party historian, saved some harsh words for the Chairman), it still insisted that an all-out critique of the Revolution could only culminate in a categorical condemnation of the socialist system in general. Thus despite Zhou Yang's assurances that the causes of alienation did not lie in the socialist system itself and that the Third Plenum of the Eleventh Central Committee had already taken measures to overcome each of the three forms of alienation,[21] Hu Qiaomu still adamantly clung to a position that would make any further discussion of socialist alienation ideologically suspect. To achieve this end, he resorted to the most powerful weapon of ideological battles: everything, including the prestige of Mao Zedong and the historical standing of the Revolution, could be compromised except the sacred aura of socialism itself. Wang Ruoshui and Zhou Yang, his indictment charged, had wittingly stepped into this forbidden territory by merely suggesting that alienation, a category integral only to capitalism, exists in socialism too. For what had the two theorists breached if not the faith in the utopian capacity of socialism to eliminate all forms of alienation? By a simple speculative move, Hu Qiaomu succeeded in equating the proposition of alienation with the incriminating heresy that "socialism might be negated by dynamics internal to itself."[22] All of a sudden, Party ideologues harped relentlessly on the same accusation: alienation theory "would necessarily lead to the assertion that socialism itself is the root cause of 'socialist alienation.'"[23]

Such an irrevocable indictment could only lead to one possible outcome. After Hu's talk was published in January 1984, not only was the debate wrapped up officially, but another political campaign was clearly in the making. Wang Ruoshui was dismissed from his editorial post of the *People's Daily;* Zhou Yang was forced to compromise his views; Deng Liqun, who had spoken like an enlightened Party official in April 1983 against the political persecution of humanist advocates in the name of "adhering to the 'Two Hundreds' policy,"[24] now quickly reversed his position and joined a major campaign against the alienation school; and Deng Xiaoping himself raised the slogan of "anti–spiritual pollution" at the Second Plenum of the Twelfth Central Committee in October 1983. A full-fledged campaign targeting both pornography and early Marxism—strange bedfellows indeed—was unleashed.

Whether Hu Qiaomu and his collaborators overestimated the subversive potential of the alienation school remains to be investigated. I should perhaps rephrase the issue as follows: Had the alienation critique actually identified anything more than a formulaic root cause of ultra-leftism to explain the petrification of socialist praxis? Did any of the advocates of the alienation school ever say, in the same daring fashion as Albrecht Wellmer, "We must start from the assumption that . . . if not the nucleus then at least a theoretical correlative for the decline in [socialist] practice must be available in the theory itself"?[25] And if to question Marxism proved to be too much a political gamble, then did Wang Ruoshui, Zhou Yang, and all those intellectuals who claimed to be victims of the system ever genuinely contemplate the possibility that domination and alienation might have been reproduced with the complicitous cooperation of the oppressed themselves?

A closer look at the three fundamental forms of socialist alienation reveals the school's limited understanding of the nature of oppression and the necessary means of de-alienation. Whether they were expounding the meaning of the "fetishism of politics" (*zhengzhi baiwu jiao*) or speculating about the various factors that triggered economical alienation, none of the theorists succeeded in breaking away from the epistemological constraint that dictates a clear-cut dichotomy of the oppressor and the oppressed.[26] Nor did anyone contest China's postrevolutionary wisdom that the origin of oppression is located externally. Alienation was viewed as an alien machinery, imposed upon one and therefore an aberration that could only be eliminated from the outside, whether it was designated as the repressive bureaucratic party-state, identified specifically with Lin Biao and Jiang Qing, or labeled as Mao Zedong's voluntarism, or even as residual feudalism.

The theoretical possibility of internalized oppression—after all, why had the whole country responded to the fanaticism of the Great Leap Forward?—was equally absent from the theorists' discussion of economical alienation. Although Wang Ruoshui attributed China's economic backwardness to voluntarism, he stopped short of exploring the intriguing issue of collusion and internalized tyranny; indeed, he halted in the face of the entire dimension of subjectivity to which the term "voluntarism" refers. Instead, he opted for an easy exit by reverting to the old position of scapegoating exterior machineries, namely, "bureaucratism," the "polity or institutional structure" (*tizhi*), and the Party's failure to understand the "objective law of economics."[27]

Theoretically, Wang Ruoshui's proposition of economical alienation under socialism is much more subversive than that of political alienation. Whereas the latter addresses a specific case of socialist praxis gone astray, the former addresses the theoretical core of Marxism's fundamental tenets. This could be the point of entry for a vigorous critique of Marx.

Yet what could Wang Ruoshui do given the intense ideological climate but utter a tentative and laconic commentary: "Didn't [they] say that once the system of public property is established, all problems will be resolved? According to Marx and Engels' original conception, it seems that all forms of alienation originate from private property. It seems as long as and as soon as society gains control over productive materials, alienation will be exterminated."[28] This remark, inconclusive as it may sound, probably constitutes Wang Ruoshui's most radical statement during the debate in terms of its potential to undermine the political economy of Marxism itself.

Wang's silence on the issue of the relationship between public ownership and economic exploitation under socialism led to other gaps in his discourse on socialist alienation. It seems predictable that his critique of the Great Leap Forward would fail to open up a critical space for a comparative study of functional capitalist exploitation vis-à-vis the authoritarian socialist system of institutionalized exploitation. No seasoned politician would make the mistake of undertaking such a task. And the closest Wang Ruoshui ever came to such a dangerous comparison was his veiled complaint that in the realm of productive relations in socialist China, primacy was given to production rates and development indices, and that bureaucratic economic planning objectives were pursued at the systematic expense of human labor.[29] What remained to be pursued, of course, was the burning issue of the exclusive state ownership of the means of production and how such a mode of ownership had given rise to exploitation that may be qualitatively, but not quantitatively, different from the mode of exploitation that resulted from private ownership. Needless to say, in the early 1980s the political climate for such a discussion had not yet matured. It was not until 1987 that the emergence of the term *guandao* (governmental corruption) succeeded in sharpening the people's consciousness that the Party had been the sole entrepreneur under state socialism who possessed the exclusive right of control over the materials and process of production. But in Wang Ruoshui's time, it would have been impious to suggest that the Party entrepreneurs were nothing other than the socialist counterparts of capitalists.

Wang Ruoshui's criticism of *tizhi* conjures up other forms of systematized alienation that he could not address openly. One such form arises with the institutionalization of a new revolutionary class structure that the humanists swore to dismantle with their impassioned slogan that "human nature is not equal to class nature." Just as in the Soviet Union, social inequalities were institutionalized through the oligarchical system of *nomenklatura*:[30] Mao's China was divided into the revolutionary hierarchy of *hong wulei* (five red categories), *hei wulei* (five black categories), and *niu gui she shen* (monsters and demons). Why this particular form of alienation was bypassed by Wang Ruoshui and Zhou Yang hardly needs explanation. The concept of class struggle and the privileged position of the proletariat were givens of Maoism-Marxism that left no room for contestation in the early 1980s.

Yet class stigma, like many other devices of economical and political alienation enumerated by Wang and Zhou, are after all tools of oppression utilized by an outside agent. The alienation school's emphasis on the external origin of political and economic alienation under state socialism sounded to them convincing enough to conclude that de-alienation could be achieved simply by resorting to the *objective* emancipatory means implemented by a revitalized socialist system and an enlightened Party leadership, a historical turning point theoretically materialized at the Second Plenum of the Twelfth Central Committee. It followed that the Party alone held the keys to the removal of estrangement defined in political, economical, or class terms. This is precisely the eulogy that Zhou Yang paid to the Party for its full capacity to initiate and accomplish de-alienation, an article of faith that both the critics and spokespeople of the Party embraced wholeheartedly. But I argue that it is precisely because of the alienation school's failure to critique alienation from within—the subjective practice of the oppressed on the one hand and Marxist theory on the other—and, above all, its obliviousness to the entire issue of internalized oppression that Zhou Yang's proposal for securing external means of eliminating socialist alienation suffers such serious theoretical limitations.

INTERNALIZED OPPRESSION

Indeed, we find evaded the whole question of the subjective dimensions of domination and oppression, or in Iring Fetscher's terms, the issue of "structural guilt and sin which may be immanent in certain social orders," a particular constitution of national character that allows a Stalin or Mao Zedong to remain in power for so many decades.[31] If the critique of socialist alienation were to have had any practical value for future emancipatory praxes, Wang Ruoshui and his colleagues would have had to dwell less on Mao Zedong's tyrannical rule than on the recognition that struggles for de-alienation are "often eroded and defeated 'from within' by the effects of internalized oppression."[32] One might condone (although not forget) the complicity of the oppressor and the oppressed during the revolutionary years, for the entire country's deification of Mao Zedong as a cult figure, a phenomenon that Wang Ruoshui and Zhou Yang designated as the "alienation of thought," was an irreversible trend of revolutionary romanticism or even fanaticism. But has postrevolutionary China outgrown the semiautonomous mechanism of internalized oppression?

The events following the Party's call for the Anti–Spiritual Pollution Campaign in the winter of 1983 "prove beyond the shadow of a doubt" for Stuart Schram that, "despite the categorical statement, in early 1979, that 'campaigns' or 'movements' would no longer be launched in China, the Chinese people are still so deeply marked by the reflexes created previously that, as soon as a target is designated, they all feel that their loyalty and activism are being tested in a campaign, and respond very much as they did to the calls of the past."[33] Although directives issued from the headquarters of the Central Command quickly held in check the intensification of the campaign, it was the leftist repercussions at the grassroots level—local witch-hunting activities—that reinforced more than ever the haunting spectacle of the perpetuation of oppression by the oppressed themselves.

What the alienation school failed to theorize and bring to consciousness was the problematic of subjectivity as a means of emancipation. Theorists like Wang Ruoshui fell far short of demonstrating that de-alienation is not a quasi-automatic result of the end of the external conditions of oppression (the bankruptcy of the "fetishism of politics," for instance), nor does it necessarily follow the dissolution of alienated labor. De-alienation, in other words, does not inevitably and miraculously descend upon the earth with the coming of communism that promises the elimination of private property—the source of all alienations, according to Marx. The cases of both China and the former Soviet Union serve as compelling rebuttals of Marx's "production paradigm" with its derivative dialectics of alienation and de-alienation.[34] Oppression cannot be adjudicated simply by a monological search for resources available from the outside. As long as the Chinese fail to acknowledge that "the patterns of thought and action inculcated through the experience of oppression take on a substantiality and a life of their own," alienation will be reproduced from within at any suggestive call for the return of the repressed.[35]

Although the alienation school implicitly questioned the dogmatic presupposition that emancipation is an unproblematic outcome of revolution, they risked repeating the same dogmatic political practice by staking the entire program of de-alienation on means completely extraneous to the individual's subjective consciousness. What the alienation school failed to incorporate into their theoretical construct was a discourse of subjectivity, which should incorporate not only the inquiry about the process of socialization of the subject into the roles of the oppressor and the oppressed, but also an examination of the transformative potential of subjectivity. Because the alienation paradigm did not address the problematic of emancipatory subjectivity, it was not a genuine oppositional movement against a reified, ossified, deracinated Party Marxism.

Perhaps because of this conceptual constraint, the breakthrough in the discussions of socialist alienation never occurred. The issue of subjectivity did not emerge until the latter half of the 1980s. But even then, Chinese cultural theorists were too obsessed with the problematic of China's cultural subjectivity in the face of neocolonial discursive hegemony to pay much attention to the emancipatory possibilities of the subjective practice of the individual. These two issues, alienation and subjectivity, have remained disconnected to the present day. De-alienation continues to be conceptualized in terms of the malfunction of the public sphere, which a benevolent political order—specifically, the Party's Four Modernizations Program—is considered sufficient to redress. The awareness of de-alienation as a subjective practice that can only take place within the private space of each oppressed individual has yet to find its way into the crowded cultural agenda of the nation. Despite their urgent call for liberation, the Chinese are slow to recognize that their most intractable nemesis is neither Mao Zedong nor Marxism, but the faceless oppressor internalized within each individual.

To criticize the absence of the problematic of subjectivity in the alienation paradigm is not to underestimate the difficulties of addressing such a joint thesis at the turn of the 1980s. For one thing, it was humanity not subjectivity that captured the epochal imagination at that particular historical juncture. A few theorists did speak of the "initiating capacity of the subject" (ren de zhudong xing) and of human beings as the "subject of praxis" (shijian zhuti) and the "subject of history" (lishi zhuti) in conjunction with their discussion of alienation.[36] But the persistent repudiation of Mao's voluntarism that came from both the official and unofficial fronts continued to cast a shadow over any significant attempt to reinvent the issue of subjectivity. Both Wang Ruoshui and Zhou Yang criticized Mao's overemphasis on "the subjective and motivating force of human beings" (*zhuguan nengdong xing*).[37] The revalorization of subjective forces, if misunderstood, could easily conjure up memories of the Great Leap Forward and would almost guarantee attacks by the newly converted anti-leftist ideologues. This was exactly the scenario that confronted Wang Ruoshui when Yang Xianzhen accused him of being a voluntarist for advocating a modest proposal for Marxist humanism.

But perhaps the most formidable barrier that precluded the alienation school from probing into the issue of subjectivity was the difficulty that all Marxists in socialist countries encounter in their reassessment of the Party's vanguard position. It should surprise no one that the Chinese Communist Party (CCP) reacted with such vigilance against the proposition of the alienation school. Hu Qiaomu and Deng Xiaoping knew only too well that the subtext that loomed large in the debate over socialist alienation was none other than the burning issue of whether the Party can be made into the sole legitimate subject of history.

Chinese Marxists such as Hu Qiaomu were familiar with the perennial battle waged between revisionists and Leninists in their interpretation of the proletariat's role in the movement of liberation. Whereas the former viewed the proletariat as a repository of self-consciousness and a spontaneous vehicle of self-emancipation, the Leninists, to cite one of their typical spokespeople, E. M. Sitnikov, dismissed such a proposition as a mere reincarnation of the Hegelian thesis of the Absolute Spirit.[38] The progressive consciousness of the proletarian subject, they insisted, could not possibly arise without the guidance of the Party. If the proletariat, or more specifically, the oppressed as a whole, were capable of becoming conscious of their reified condition and could thus trigger a spontaneous process of de-alienation on their own initiative, then the raison d'être of the Leninist elite party would evaporate.

The subtext here challenged the legitimacy of the Party as the self-ordained subject of history and contained a hidden critique whose subversive force the CCP could not afford to ignore. Understandably, Wang Ruoshui and the alienation school made no attempt to rehearse the terms of debate between the Leninists and anti-Leninists. As a matter of fact, not only did they refrain from critiquing Lenin's doctrine of placing the entire political initiative on the Party, but Zhou Yang, as I mentioned earlier, attempted just the opposite tactic; to forestall the Party's reaction, he reaffirmed its vanguard role in leading the oppressed out of the dilemma of socialist alienation. The complete avoidance of the question—whether the Party should serve as a mere aid or as an authoritative leader of the people in the process toward de-alienation—led eventually to the eclipse of the issue of the subjectivity of the oppressed.

Inasmuch as the Marxist-Leninist Party had been conceived as the sole engineer of emancipation and the concept of liberation was reduced to being a historically determined collective movement, the oppressed once again emerged as an inert mass whose self-consciousness remained as oblique as their individuality. Under such a theoretical premise, the issue of the emancipatory potential of the human subject could only appear irrelevant, or superfluous at best. The Party question and the issue of self-consciousness of the oppressed are deeply interlocked—the cancellation of one issue automatically leads to the abolition of the other. It would be easy for us to exonerate Wang Ruoshui and his colleagues' disregard of the issue of subjectivity by simply attributing their theoretical oversight to their acute awareness of the familiar impasse: the stakes were too high for a plunge into either one of the twin issues. I am, however, dubious about their ability to comprehend fully how far the subtext of the Party question could have led them to the issue of the subjective domain of de-alienation. I doubt if they were ever aware that the Party question and the subjectivity question make up two sides of the same coin. That Wang Ruoshui was aware of the specter that the first question evoked hardly guaranteed his recognition of the issue of subjectivity. Ironically, it was perhaps Hu Qiaomu and the Party rather than Wang Ruoshui who correctly appraised the subversive potential that underlay the submerged question regarding the Party and the undeclared agenda of subjectivity.

COUNTERPROPOSALS

Most Western specialists commenting on the controversy over socialist alienation are generally critical of the Party's position and endorse Wang Ruoshui and Zhou Yang's theses without making significant qualifications.[39] Such an anti-Party stance seems a default position that is ultimately meaningless in the absence of a genuine engagement in the counterproposals of Hu Qiaomu's camp. First of all, some of Wang and Zhou's critics were opposed to the two theorists' adoption of the term *yihua* as a vague catchall for the inhuman "residue" that can still be found in the new society.[40] Although underlying the critics' opposition is the ideological position that the term "alienation" is meaningful only if it remains a conceptual category confined within the historical context

of capitalist society, seen from a different ideological standpoint, the notion of imposing a moratorium on the use of the term may not be totally
irrational. The ideological standpoint I am referring to comes very close
to Hu Qiaomu's famous critique of the circular logic of the alienation
paradigm. In emphasizing the dialectics of the negation of the negation
(unalienated human nature—alienated human nature—de-alienated human nature), the humanists, Hu argues, merely reiterate the worn-out
theological formula of "paradise—paradise lost—paradise regained."
The "succession of communism to capitalism," he continues, "signifies
the great progress humankind made on their productive forces and social relations, but not at all a return of some abstract and determinate
human nature."[41]

Ironically, this is a viewpoint to which many Western Marxists also
subscribe. Commenting on Habermas' critique of Marx's production
paradigm, Ludwig Nagl concludes that the "alienation/de-alienation
scheme" embedded in Marxian paradigm is "an expression of a 'monological philosophy of consciousness.'"[42] Habermas regards the Marxian
faith in the programmed "homecoming" of alienated human nature
as an embodiment of the "philosophy of reflection" that valorizes the
notions of autonomy and self-formative process (the autonomous completion of the dialectics of alienation) at the expense of "the philosophy
of praxis."[43] The structure of modern society, in other words, can
hardly be analyzed adequately in terms of the romantic concept of
"return to an origin" that "in Habermas's view infests all classical versions of the alienation/de-alienation theory."[44] As both Chinese and
Western critics of the alienation paradigm argue, human history is far
too complicated to be contained within the single metaphysical configuration of the downfall and return of a human nature originating in
primeval plenitude.

The dialectic structure of alienation that dictates that a loss must be
reconquered and a lack refilled also presupposes, as Lukács takes for
granted, that once a subject is reified into a commodity, the situation of
reification "would at once become primed for consciousness."[45] What
Lukács envisions is thus nothing short of an idealist myth that the oppressed, simply because of their entrenchment in oppression, are not
only automatically endowed with an emancipatory consciousness but
are also capable of concocting their own therapy and reversing the situation. The Hegelian overtone of dialectics—the self-propelling impetus
of the negation of the negation—thus turns the alienation paradigm
from its potential of being grounded in a social theory of praxis into a

pure "speculative philosophy" (*sibian zhexue*). Truly, as Huang Nansen challenges the alienation school, "Why cannot alienation lead to more alienation rather than a return to the origin?" The inquiry boils down to an even more specific question, "What is the driving force that motivates this process [of return]?"[46]

It is now obvious that attributing this driving force to the mere working of the dialectics of the negation of the negation is too simple to be of any explanatory value. It is also highly questionable whether human beings' return to the original nature is necessarily self-conscious, as both Marx and Lukács assume. And, furthermore, to presuppose that such a return can only be a complete return merely reveals the utopian mode of armchair thinking. Modern Chinese history—specifically, Mao's revolution—has shown us time and again that no emancipatory subjective practice can escape its own reification and its tragic complicity with domination. The belief, even on the most theoretical level, in the "completion" of a liberatory cycle and thus the existence of a hypothetical finale risks nourishing a self-deceptive mode of thought that Chinese revolutionaries have practiced diligently for more than a decade. The Revolution, they have learned in retrospect, is not the ultimate epiphany, but the biggest delusion of all. In a strange twist, the concept of Mao Zedong's permanent revolution looms large once more as a parable for human beings' continual struggle against reification.

This critique of the young Marx's alienation theory should serve to illustrate that the theoretical value of the semiautonomous process of dealienation has to be sought elsewhere than in its validity as a social theory. Brugger is incisive in his speculations on the potential contribution that the alienation school could have made to the emancipatory task confronting the Party at the turn of the 1980s, had the controversy not been terminated so abruptly: it could have contributed to the possible working out of "a socialist telos which takes unalienated human nature as its goal."[47] The beginning of any emancipatory practice should start with the setting up of the terms of emancipatory goals by which the objective technological possibilities (namely modernization) can then be evaluated. But Deng Xiaoping and the orthodox circle of Marxists adamantly believed that they could proceed in the task without such a goal. What they aspired to—turning the means into an end in itself—has indeed come to pass, at an escalating speed in the 1990s. Modernization for modernization's sake, rather than for humanity's sake, has given birth to a monster named Development that will in no time witness the reenactment of alienation in the Deng era in different ideological terms. The "brave new world" that seems to be emerging may yet turn out to be one in which even the authentic version of Marx's alienation à la capitalism may finally have a future in China.

Perhaps if Deng Xiaoping and his inner circle had foreseen the ideological disintegration of orthodox Marxism that followed the slowly winding down Anti–Spiritual Pollution Campaign in early 1984, the Party would have resisted less vigorously the idea of incorporating socialist alienation into the official interpretive compass of Marxism, thus opening up a space for the discussion of a genuine socialist humanism.

MARXIST HUMANISM AND THE QUESTION OF VOLUNTARISM

The official refutation of the thesis of socialist alienation could not but foreclose its twin thesis of humanism. Presented as a single ideological package, alienation and humanism go hand in hand. Inasmuch as the overcoming of alienation entails the return of humanity, the young Marx reemerged for the Chinese alienation theorists as a humanist at large. The battle between the alienation school and its opponents is too predictable to be worthy of thorough treatment here. The Party's stance was clear: the young Marx treated humans (*ren*) as an abstract and universal category—an idealist standpoint under the heavy influence of Kantian-Hegelian-humanist anthropology—whereas the mature Marx understood *ren* in the correct terms of social relations. The Party also insisted upon the total absence of any historical continuity between the two Marxes. As a result, the myth of two Marxisms, namely, Humanist Marxism and Materialist Marxism, is simply a theoretical fallacy to be dismissed.[48] To combat such an uncompromising perspective, the alienation school sought ideological backup from Soviet, Polish, and Yugoslav philosophers who argued in the same impassioned tone that the two Marxisms by no means form an antagonistic relationship.[49] Citing Lenin, Adam Schaff, and other socialist comrades, Chinese theorists proclaimed that there is no epistemological break between the young and mature Marx,[50] that the biological nature of human beings is fundamentally immutable and their social attributes are historically determined, that Marxism and humanism are complementary to each other,[51] and that even some Soviet philosophers propounded the existence of an abstract human nature that "never disappears regardless of any circumstances, and which just 'underwent transformation in different historical ages.'"[52]

It was Wang Ruoshui again who initiated the controversy over Marxist humanism by attempting to reintegrate the value of the individual into
Marxism. In two seminal essays—"Ren shi Makesi zhuyi de chufa dian"
(Human beings are the starting point of Marxism) (1981) and "Wei rendao zhuyi bianhu" (In defense of humanism) (1983)—he daringly declares that human nature is not equal to class nature, a statement that
challenged Maoist-Marxist-Leninist orthodoxy and anticipated severe
criticism from the ideology police. Wang reminds his readers of the historical contribution that humanism made to antibourgeois ideology in
Western societies, yet he cautiously insists that a theoretical emphasis on
the value of the individual by no means amounts to an endorsement of
individualism. On the contrary, such a view helps remedy the socialist
philosophy of class nature, which, according to Wang, reduces a human
being to a creature no less abstract than that to be found in bourgeois
ideology. The country made a mistake during the Cultural Revolution,
Wang Ruoshui proclaimed, in setting up an antithetical relationship between revolution and humanism, a mistake that led to antihumanism.[53]

In the end, those two essays do not address anything that the Chinese
people had not already experienced firsthand, and they certainly appear
cliché to most modern Western readers, no matter how violently they
might have electrified the entire circle of writers and intellectuals at the
turn of the 1980s. And yet even a retroactive reading of Wang's essays
today still evokes the historical memory of a resistance cast in powerful
rhetoric: "What humanism is opposed to are two things, one is 'god-ism'
[shendao zhuyi (the deification of the leader)], the other, 'animalism'
[shoudao zhuyi (the degradation of human beings into animals)]."[54]

Such earnest resistance was certainly not lost on Hu Qiaomu, whose
rebuttal against Wang Ruoshui incorporates his own partial concession
to the impassioned call for a humanism defined in staunchly Marxist
terms. In his critique, Hu affirms the general currency of Wang's two
core terms "socialist humanism" and "revolutionary humanism"—old
Maoist catchphrases.[55] But Hu insists that socialist humanism should
only function as an ethical principle, not as a worldview that could account for the evolution of human history and society, a mistaken perspective that Hu ascribes to Wang Ruoshui's idealist approach.[56]

By February 1984, in response to Hu Qiaomu's charge, Wang Ruoshui started formulating a counterargument, published as an internally
circulated essay titled "Wo dui rendao zhuyi wenti de kanfa" (My views
on the issue of humanism) (1986). In this rebuttal, Wang's defensive gesture forces him into the self-defeating position of having continually to

redraw the ideological boundaries of humanism. To cite one typical example of his hemming and hawing: "Humanism certainly needs an ideological foundation. But that foundation can either be idealism or materialism. It can either be a historical view based on the concept of abstract human nature, or a historical view based on materialism and science."[57] By highlighting the concept of "sublation" (*pipan de jicheng*), Wang argues that there existed between Marxism and various historical ideologies of bourgeois humanism a dialectical rather than an oppositional relationship. In addition to fundamental moral and ethical principles, he enumerates the content of such heritage from historical humanism as "human freedom," "human liberation," and the totalized evolution of "Homo universal" (250). But just as his rhetoric edges dangerously close to a proposition of bourgeois humanism, Wang Ruoshui steers clear of troubled waters by retreating into an equivocal "neither-nor" rhetorical strategy. In every twist and turn of his argument, he never forgets to remain uncommitted so that he avoids pinning himself down to a single position. It is no small wonder, then, that Wang Ruoshui's endorsement of the voluntarist aspect of humanism suffers continual qualifications as he maintains that "the fundamental principle of humanism does not have any binding relationship with idealism, nor does it necessarily enter into any conflict with materialism" (245). This is tantamount to advocating the eclectical position to which the theorists in defense of two Marxisms usually subscribed, namely, the potential reconciliation between voluntarism and determinism and between freedom and necessity. The propagation of this kind of dialectics appears to be more a sophist mode of persuasion than a genuine engagement in the issues. One cannot, however, blame those who got stuck in this aborted debate. Hu Qiaomu's insinuation of the ideological incorrectness of the humanists' views almost guaranteed their need to adopt such malleable terms.

Nothing more can be said about the predictable dialogues between the humanists and their rivals without reproducing ideological clichés that hardly deepen our understanding of the controversy in question. What I wish to pursue now is an issue I posed at the beginning of this chapter: the strategic position of Sartre's existentialist humanism within this entire brouhaha.

To speak of Sartre is to return to the issue of voluntarism. In their encounter with existentialism, Chinese theorists of humanism found themselves caught in a double bind: they were spellbound by the Sartrean appeal to free will, but in order to introduce existentialism into the Chinese intellectual dominion, they had to simultaneously defeat it with a Marxist determinist critique. It was difficult to tell, sometimes, whether such seemingly perfunctory critiques were merely ideological reflexes or disingenuous measures consciously adopted to desensitize the system of censorship. In any case, those treatises and books on Sartre that flowed into production did not mystify the savvy Chinese reading public, who knew well the formula of "introduction plus critique" and could follow it as a menu for helping themselves to the real meat while relegating the Marxist rhetoric to the scrap heap.

Such was the scenario that Chinese readers encountered when they were exposed to a critical introduction to Sartrean existentialism: they learned that Sartre had designated his existentialism "humanist philosophy" (*renxue*), that this science propagated self-transcendence and self-realization, that the starting point of Sartrean humanism is the individual, that human essence is self-determined rather than historically determined, and that this philosophy, because of its emphasis on subjectivity, provided the "missing link" in Marxism. Such explications of Sartre, usually saturated with ideological ambiguities, were almost always followed immediately by a counteractive critique that dwelled on the incompatibility of Marxism and existentialism.[58] Everything endorsed by Sartrean humanism was under fire and amended: human beings are always the product of the sum total of social relations, not of subjective will; the individual is never absolutely free to make his or her own choice since every choice is made under a historically specific circumstance; and so on. To complete this double-wrapped promotion package of existentialism, a dogmatic conclusion that Sartre was ideologically suspect had to be inserted—no matter how halfhearted and ambiguous this condemnation might sound. Included in the rhetorical castigation was the routine critique that Sartre mistakenly pits a naive voluntarism against mechanical determinism, that his humanist philosophy amounts to nothing other than a petty-bourgeoisie's resistance to domination, and that his optimism is eventually deprived of any concrete social reality.[59]

That Sartre would surface, however fleetingly, in the Chinese controversy over humanism raises the inevitable question: To whom was the citation of existentialism beneficial or detrimental? It goes without saying that in the realm of state ideology, it was the young Marx who emerged as the center of gravity for the debate. Sartre, however, enjoyed his own prestige in post-Mao China once existentialism began sweeping college campuses and converting many disillusioned young students. It was strategically suicidal for the alienation school to respond to the beckoning allure of existentialism; they were well aware that the core of Sartre's philosophy had always been petty-bourgeois subjectivity. Both Wang Ruoshui and Zhou Yang were cautious not to overstep the ideological boundary of Marxism whenever their discussion of humanism brought them close to an encounter with Sartre. In fact, in defining socialist humanism, Wang Ruoshui is careful not to conjure up the haunting presence of existentialist humanism even though he stresses "issues of human value, human dignity, human liberation, and human freedom" in conjunction with his discussion of proletarian revolution and communism.[60] Zhou Yang, a more seasoned politician well versed in making preemptive strikes, goes a step further by expressing concern over the negative impact on young Chinese students of "certain [humanist] schools of modern Western philosophy."[61] Undoubtedly, it is existentialism that he alludes to here. Zhou and Wang had withstood far too many hostile attacks in their defense of the young Marx to court more danger by soliciting any public flirtation with existentialist humanism. The best they could do was either evade the entire issue of existentialism or publicly reject any affiliation with Sartre.[62]

Yet, while the two leading theoreticians of the alienation school were thus theoretically constrained within the Marxist framework in their approach to the issue of humanism, some of their supporters displayed fewer scruples about playing the Sartrean card. The occasion of Sartre's death in April 1980 provided a convenient opportunity for the publication of many academic essays on Sartre. In the name of critiquing the philosopher, Chinese theorists did not hesitate to elaborate on the major tenets of existentialism and, more importantly, foreground those aspects of the philosophy that promised a cross-fertilization with a critically defined Marxism: the thrust of existentialism to unite philosophy and praxis, the identification of freedom with revolution, and no less significantly, the simultaneous anti-Stalinist and anticapitalist articulation of the philosopher. Speaking in Sartre's voice, such essays reiterated and succeeded in reinforcing a claim that the alienation school had already propagated time and again: Marxism has undergone an ossification and transformed itself into "antihumanism." Perhaps the most deadly ammunition that the explication of Sartre provided for Chinese alienation theorists was his pungent criticism of the Soviet Union and his forceful condemnation of the phenomenon of socialist alienation, which, in the philosopher's view, took the particular form of "expansionism, bureaucratism, authoritarianism, and doctrinarism."[63] No Chinese readers confronting those pages could mistake such innuendoes against the

CCP for an innocuous analysis of Sartrean philosophy. Oddly enough, however, the Chinese theorists' veiled criticism of socialist alienation attracted far less attention than did Sartre's endorsement of voluntarism.

In the end, the debate over socialist alienation and Marxist humanism failed to rescue itself from the moot issue of voluntarism versus determinism. No alternative paradigm—whether it be Sartre or the young Marx—could emerge in that kind of political climate without being compromised, or more precisely, being proved incorrect before it was reassimilated into the iron hold of historical determinism and cited as yet another statistical triumph of the perpetual logic of the dialectics of bipolarity. The legitimate comparison, or contrast, of Sartre and Marx, of voluntarism and determinism, and of the two Marxisms—opposite terms soon to be recast into mere variations of the same principle of dialectical opposition—only serves in the end to demonstrate nothing but "the structural differentiations of a single originally undifferentiated Marxism."[64] Hegelian dialectics has the last laugh. Marx succeeds in co-opting Sartre. And in the process of merging the latter into the former, Marxism brings the final closure to its potentially infinite contestation with its rival philosophy. In so doing, it ends up disarming the self-motivating potency of existentialism.

What was being taken for granted is the view that an emancipatory practice motivated "from without"—the Party's mandate to end Mao's era—would ensure the liberation of the subject. The real lessons of Sartrean philosophy—that genuine emancipation is contingent and can only be self-motivated and that the emancipatory character of subjectivity is not to be predetermined as the result of an inexorable progress guaranteed by Reason and History—continued to elude Wang Ruoshui and his fellow travelers. Although Wang spells out clearly in his preface to Wei rendao zhuyi bianhu (In defense of humanism) (1986) that the "purpose of raising the problematic of humanism and alienation is precisely to awaken the subjective consciousness of humankind," he remained an obstinate believer in the benevolent laws of historical development and mistook the mere awakening of the subject for the attainment of subjective consciousness. The assumption that such a consciousness, long mystified under domination, will emerge by itself with the dawning of the new era only confirms the vicious cycle of dogmatic determinism. Perhaps Wang Ruoshui and his comrades did not jump out of the ideological enclosure of materialist doctrine after all. For if he believed that the creation of an enlightened regime alone would lead to "the rupture with the continuum of domination,"[65] he proved to be deeply entrenched in the mode of thinking characteristic of historical determinism.

What the Chinese can no longer afford to evade is the issue of the transformation of subjectivity whose eventual appearance is not guaranteed by the transformation of society alone. In this context, it is more urgent than ever to redefine the problematic of voluntarism in terms beyond its conventional role as nothing more than an ideological foil for determinism. How to reinvent voluntarism to serve the cause of de-alienation has undoubtedly posed an unanswered challenge to the alienation school and Chinese humanist advocates. But unless one looks into the collusive relationship between subjectivity and the reproduction of domination, and until Chinese citizens are courageous enough to accept the moral responsibility for the failure of Mao's revolution, the nation will never outgrow its habit of scapegoating the lesser evil. Perhaps it is high time for us to ask whether it was the voluntarism of one single person or the voluntary collusion of the entire nation that paved the way for socialist alienation and antihumanism in China.

There is no better way of concluding this part of my discussion of subjective emancipatory consciousness than to cite Wei Jingsheng's most recent proclamation after his release from prison: "We cannot look to a savior or some 'righteous minister' to free us and save us, and we must not pin all our hopes in other places. Only when we are determined to rescue ourselves will others be willing or able to help us. There is a sense in which [the] cowardliness and vulnerability of a populace can be seen as a cause of a tyrant's violence."[66]

"WHO AM I?": THE PROBLEMATIC
SELF AND ALIENATION

Though prematurely foreclosed upon in the realm of ideology, the discussion of alienation was by no means over in post-Mao China. Just as Lukács argued that reification can only be overcome by the aesthetic subject that can recreate a unity of subject and object, theory and practice, Chinese writers at the turn of the early 1980s understood almost instinctively the liberatory function of their practice. Not surprisingly, it was literature and not the intellectuals' ideological critique of orthodox Marxism that undertook the mission of de-alienation and championed the cause of humanism for several years to come. For a short while, writers took upon the task of philosophers by concentrating on the theme of alienation and celebrated the return to unalienated human nature.[67]

Chinese authors were by no means more immune to censorship than the intellectuals who debated ideology. In fact, they were so familiar with the mechanism of the system of critique and countercritique that they felt compelled to make public statements of their positions (*biao tai*) whenever the occasion arose. What greeted writers at the apex of the controversy over socialist alienation was the usual theatrical spectacle of contradiction: they felt obligated to echo the official discourse in one symposium after another by going through the mechanistic charade of cautioning themselves rhetorically against the depiction of abstract human nature at the expense of class nature, and yet at the same time they condemned earnestly the theoretical practice of socialist realism in its emphasis on the delineation of "typical" rather than "individual" characters.[68]

Despite the expected infiltration of the official discourse into the realm of the arts and literature, many writers who had mastered the knack of dodging political criticism accomplished a historical breakthrough despite the strict surveillance of the Party. The ideological freeze long imposed on the issue of humanism, "human touch" (*renqing wei*), and a commonly defined aesthetic appeal—all ideological taboos in the bygone days—witnessed its own dramatic thaw, as veteran aesthetician Zhu Guangqian had fervently pleaded.[69] For almost half a decade, the celebration of the creative self newly emancipated from ideological enclosure had made its imprint on every literary product from Liu Xinwu's provocative statement "I am I, myself" to Dai Houying's epochal piece *Ren a ren.*[70] All of a sudden, the theoretical possibility of the autonomous and infinitely open self gripped the imagination of both writers and readers. Still the liberatory rhetoric did not end in an all-encompassing eulogy of the omnipotence of the creative self. Crisscrossing the discourse of creative subjectivity in these years was an awareness that the dissemination of the enclosed self made it necessarily problematic and paradoxical: Once set free to express itself, the self is bound to register the dramatic changes and contradictions that took place in cultural, economic, and sociopolitical sectors.[71] Although some eclectic critics insisted that the prevalent contradictions in socialist China were not necessarily identical to the phenomenon of alienation, a "Kafka tidal wave" (designated by one critic as nothing other than a "heat wave of alienation") swept over the field of literature well into the mid-1980s, apparently resonating with the emergence of the theme of the problematic self.[72]

It seems obvious that China's postrevolutionary writers would be most susceptible to Kafka and the literature of the absurd. Rampant political movements had not only alienated human beings from each other, they had also shattered the very foundation of self-identity, as the politics of survival and victimization turned every individual into an eyewitness of the psychic split between his or her own public (i.e., political) and private self. This spectacle of socialist alienation is vividly delineated by the philosopher Gao Ertai as the inevitable outcome of the "absolutization of class struggle," by which he meant the political process that transformed every individual into his or her own enemy by mandating "self-exposure" and self-critique.[73] Schizophrenia became the norm of existence. Kafka's dramatic parable of metamorphosis drove home for alienated Chinese intellectuals the insanity of revolutionary surreality. One could not frame the Revolution in better metaphoric terms than in the Kafkaesque plot of absurdity. The "children of revolution" felt like cornered beasts in their unexpected encounter with an anonymous alien power that subjugated them with their own cooperation. Not only were their daily lives marked by the contradiction between what they believed and what they professed to believe, they experienced yet another form of contradiction: their dual identity as victims and victimizers at the same time. Herein lies the real absurdity of the revolutionary subject.

This is a subject that ultimately failed to absorb its own negativity, and because of its belated awareness of its own fragmentary condition, it responded sluggishly to the issue of the problematic self in the postrevolutionary era. Gao Ertai's inconspicuous outcry against the revolutionary subject's self-dichotomy and self-alienation remained an abstract theory that failed to solicit meaningful responses from creative writers in the early 1980s. Genuine inquiry into alienated subjectivity did not come into being until the mid-1980s, when the "root-searching" (xungen) school and the young experimentalists heralded a much more sophisticated cultural (or in the latter case, an anticultural) and aesthetic agenda. But in the early eighties, as the literary world hailed the achievement of the various genres born in quick succession—the "wounded literature" (shangheng wenxue), "literature of self-reflection" (fansi wenxue), and mainstream humanist literature—what greeted readers remained a homogeneous configuration of the self that was no less formulaic than that portrayed earlier in socialist realism. Only the formula was different. Now the individual rather than the collective hero and heroine appeared on a pedestal. But because postrevolutionary writers in the early eighties immediately felt the moral compulsion to reinvent a fictional subjectivity that was diametrically opposed to the closed, passive, and apathetic persona of the revolutionary subject, no other alternative was prescribed except a complete categorical reversal of negative characteristics.

What was born on urgent demand at the beginning of the 1980s was a fictional persona "made of flesh and blood, love and hatred, a being full of emotions and desires with a capacity for contemplation"—in other words, an open, dynamic, compassionate, and upbeat self that is larger than life itself.[74] And yet the seamless consistency underlying such an optimistic portrait eventually afforded little opportunity for a more somber reflection on the rifts and contradictions lurking in this seemingly wholesome character whose naive belief in the redemptive power of human love is ultimately not qualitatively different from the faith of the revolutionary hero or heroine in the regenerative potency of class love.

There are exceptions, of course. Lu Yao's *Rensheng* (Life) (1982) and Li Ping's "Wanxia xiaoshi de shihou" (When the sunset clouds disappeared) (1981) touched, however superficially, the issue of the problematic self.[75] But the public's fetishization of the saintly figure Lu Wenting in Shen Rong's *Rendao zhongnian* (At middle age) (1980) merely reinforces the impression that China's postrevolutionary understanding of socialist humanism was still premised on an aesthetics of totality that could only once again deliver a transparently poised human subject.[76] Contradictions and psychic schism remained a territory untrodden by writers who joined the rush for the glorification of a *totally* liberated subjectivity at the turn of the 1980s.

It was in this context that Zong Pu's story "Wo shi shei?" ("Who am I?") (1979) brought to the fore an ambivalent epochal question as yet unarticulated and unaddressed. Whether the question was posed awkwardly or simply aborted in the end should not defer us from rescuing this tale from relative obscurity. It is not just another formulaic example of humanist literature in post-Mao China. Despite the author's lack of awareness of the potential danger in posing such a question, any study of the modern history of the Chinese problematic self should begin with this unostentatious story, because it captures in a nutshell precisely Gao Ertai's definition of what alienation is: self-estrangement, personality split, and self-negation.[77]

"Who Am I?" tells the story of the schizophrenic vision of a persecuted victim, Shu Mi, who loses her sanity after her lover commits suicide during the Cultural Revolution. Narrated in the first person through a deranged consciousness as rhetorically unreliable as that in Lu Xun's famous story "The Diary of a Mad Man," the tale contains a scathing commentary on the negative transformative power of the Revolution. In her hallucinatory fevers, Shu Mi witnesses her own transformation from a demon into a snow-white little flower, and then, in a moment of dramatic irony, into the horrible form of a huge worm. Here Kafka's parable of metamorphosis fits remarkably into the new Chinese context, for what better metaphor is there of a nightmarish vision of species alienation and self-fragmentation than the metamorphosis of human nature into beastly nature?

Each transformation triggers in Shu Mi a moment of self-recognition that coincides with the troubled moment of self-inquiry and culminates in her increasingly weakened rhetorical question, "Who am I?" Caught in an alternating spiral of self-bewilderment and self-detachment, she is ultimately unable to answer the question. "Am I therefore a poisonous worm? No! But who am I after all?"[78] In a bout of panic attacks, a delirious Shu Mi imagines herself melting into "particles of dust" and "thin air" and agonizes, "Oh this self of mine, this disappearing self of mine, who am I after all?" (40).

Absurdity, however, is not a trademark of Chinese writers who trace their descent through revolutionary romanticism. The allure of a dramatic "return to origin" proved too strong for Zong Pu to resist. Predictably, Shu Mi's quest for reintegrated humanity must end positively. That moment arrives when the heroine sees the ideogram *ren* (human being) etched into the sky in an inverted "V" by a line of wild geese as she jumps to her suicidal death in the cold waters of the lake. In this theatrical encounter of the two epochal themes, alienation and humanism, it is undoubtedly the latter that gains the symbolic upper hand. This is but one more instance that characterizes the optimistic spirit of the early 1980s, a zeitgeist that was to suffer a severe setback toward the latter half of the decade, which would witness, among other signs of depression, the powerful resurgence of the theme of alienation.

Zong Pu's story, like many other sentimental morality tales chronicled in the early 1980s, voices an extravagant faith in humanism's ability to resolve an open-ended series of alienations. De-alienation, like the aerial sign of *ren*, occurs instantaneously in the dramatic form of deus ex machina. Given the effortless recovery of Shu Mi's split self, the theme of the problematic self was launched in vain. The ironic vision of the protagonist, her self-image hovering ambivalently upon the sign of the demonic and the beastly, is dissolved in a hollow congratulatory homage to a figurative humanism.

"Who am I?"—am I a victim or a victimizer, a self totalized or problematic, a human being or a demon? Without engaging, beyond the mere
rhetorical level, with those post-Mao epochal questions, Wang Ruoshui
and Zhou Yang's project of emancipation via humanism eventually remained as nominal as Zong Pu's. Is an emancipatory theory and practice ever possible without the exploration of the self-motivating process
of de-alienation from within?

TWO

High Culture Fever

*The Cultural Discussion in the Mid-1980s
and the Politics of Methodologies*

If the Marxist intellectuals' theoretical inquiries into the issue of alienation in the early 1980s struck an ambivalent note toward the unfolding decade, then the mid-1980s witnessed a symphony of unmitigated optimism. As the state's modernization program steered the country into imagined prosperity, the intellectuals not only collaborated with the Party in its reconstruction of the socialist utopia, but busily proliferated their own discourse on thought enlightenment. All this seemed to point to the consummation of a utopian vision, which the 1989 crackdown suddenly aborted.

However, the reversal of the utopian vision dramatized in June 1989 did not take place overnight. As much as the mid-1980s were moving toward a visionary perfection of the twin projects of modernization and enlightenment, they also witnessed a continual sequence of sociocultural and economic spectacles that cast shadows over the social psychology of a people dreaming of an attainable utopian future. In 1987, signs of setback were already obvious. What was at stake was not only the elite's agenda of enlightenment, but also the vision of a yet to be consummated project of socialist modernization. Contrary to the public's great expectations, the Thirteenth Party Congress held in October delivered an official statement that China was still lingering at the "primary stage of socialism." Premier Zhao Ziyang's anticlimactic declaration at the Party Congress not only sharpened the sense of crisis that a failing urban reform had already engendered, but also demoralized the nation's utopian dreamers and plunged them into an inverse dystopian mood.

In the realm of cultural production, what accompanied the onslaught of various "fevers" in writers, artists, and intellectuals (the fever about *One Hundred Years of Solitude* in 1984, the fever for root-searching and new methodologies in 1985, Culture Fever in 1986)—in sum, post-revolutionary fevers about knowledge (*zhishi re*) and enlightenment—was the rise of new anticultural heroes such as the rock star Cui Jian and the post-Bei Dao generation of young poets who sneered at the myth of humanism and the politics of resistance that he once sang for.[1] The emergence in the mid-1980s of the new myth of *qigong* (the art of material energy) in the name of pseudoscientism further prompted critics' periodic denunciation of the 1980s as "a chaotic period." As one disillusioned intellectual put it, this was not a period in which heroes were given birth. This was, on the contrary, an era in which miracles and superstition triumphed over rational forces, an era in which "our nation is seeking inspiration from the symbols of ancient civilization, i.e., the Great Wall and the dragon. Individuals on the other hand are searching for formulas of longevity from *qigong*."[2] This seems, in short, an apocalypse, an eternal erosion of utopia.

Yet I argue that the dystopian mood toward the latter half of the 1980s should not be seen as diametrically opposed to the utopian ecstasy of a history on the verge of fulfilling its promises. The reverberation of such a tempered mood by no means deserves emotionally charged dismissal as "a chaotic period." On the contrary, the existence of such a mood enables us to accommodate the other possibility of interpretation: we may transcend a locked-in either-or binary perspective—utopianism or dystopianism—by situating the conflicting Chinese discourse of modern consciousness (*xiandai yishi*) at the intersection where conditions of possibility proliferated, which constituted, on the symbolic level at least, a locale as rapturous as unadulterated utopianism.

Indeed, contrary to conventional expectations, the hermeneutic circle of "modern consciousness" was not made up of overarching terms denoting rationality and optimism alone (see chapter four, this volume). The term's semantic boundary was continually overshadowed by emerging ambivalent categories such as "crisis consciousness" that conjured up specters of unreason and nihilism right at the threshold of the epoch's promising entrance into the age of reason. The fissures in the totalizing discourse of utopian rationality were conspicuous enough to cast into doubt the very metaphor of consummation. I want to suggest that a euphoria that seemed eternal at several memorable junctures of the mid-1980s experienced its own moment of uncertainty when it grew increasingly conscious of the potential splitting of social mores into conflicting critical responses to the making of the Chinese modern. It was exactly due to the diversity of such responses from the elite that the Cultural Discussion (*wenhua taolun*) came into being as a forum for open debates of what modernity meant to a postrevolutionary society in transition. In its heyday, the Discussion was a great intellectual fair that provoked little intervention from the Party. Ideas poured forth as the cultural elite searched for paradigms that would steer China into a tantalizing future. Needless to say, participants in the Cultural Discussion were self-conscious of their privileged position as the architects of Chinese modernity. Underlying their innocuous discussions about methodologies, the issue of cultural politics loomed large.

For a short span of approximately two years between 1984 and 1986, the panoramic display of "one hundred schools" was an eyeful. Each school had its own prescription for a polymorphous modernity that extended from the sociocultural to the aesthetic. In classifying the different trends of thought that emerged during the Cultural Discussion, most critics focus on debates over sociocultural modernity and treat aesthetic modernity as a separate issue. A single chapter, of course, hardly allows me to do justice to the twin foci of modernity. But the fact that I cannot map out aesthetic modernity thoroughly until chapter four and chapter five does not suggest that it is irrelevant to the focus of the present chapter, the Cultural Discussion. On the contrary, as I emphasized in the introduction, aesthetics and the sociocultural are so closely intertwined that it is inadequate to examine the Chinese definition of modernity solely from the perspectives of cultural philosophers. Inasmuch as the Cultural Discussion grew out of the intellectuals' acute consciousness of the cultural agenda of modernization, the writers affiliated with the root-searching (*xungen*) school played a role as important as that of the cultural philosophers in their reflection on the collision of the ideological horizon of modernity with that of tradition.

Thus whereas modernity meant the propagation of scientific rationality (*kexue lixing*) for Jin Guantao on the one hand, it meant something completely different for the root-searching school on the other: making and maintaining a productive liaison with cultural traditions and substantive reason.[3] Aesthetic modernity's multiple interactions with the Cultural Discussion did not simply give rise to different schools of creative writing. They also led to the emergence of language fever that in turn triggered a growing awareness among literary critics of the intimate relationship between language and the ideological formation of Maoism.[4] All of those literary events were actually part and parcel of the cultural critiques that flourished in the mid-1980s. Taken together with the various contesting expressions in the realm of social thought, they formed the ensemble of the Cultural Discussion.

Most Chinese critics such as Chen Kuide and Chen Lai identified the main orientations underlying the Cultural Discussion in categorical terms of scientism versus culturalism.[5] The group of "Marching toward the Future" headed by Jin Guantao bore the brunt of criticism because of its narrow and exclusive focus on the scientific approach to modernity. The technocratic vision posed a threat to the traditional elite in more than one way. Not the least intimidating was the message that modernization depends upon the establishment of a new power center built no longer on the soft culture of thought enlightenment but rather on the hegemony of scientific and technical knowledge. Many critics who questioned Jin Guantao's project thus welcomed the counterproposals advocated by cultural philosophers such as Li Zehou, Gan Yang, the *qimeng* (enlightenment) school, and the neo-Confucianists, all of whom went beyond scientism by returning to the issues of cultural politics induced by the confrontation between tradition and modernity. Gan Yang's hermeneutic critique (manifested in the editorial principle of *Culture: China and the World*),[6] the *qimeng* philosophers' search for the indigenous source of critical thinking, and the neo-Confucian focus of the Academy of Chinese Culture (*Zhongguo shuyuan*) all represented efforts to problematize and delegitimize instrumental reason.

Whether modernity signified the material substance (*ti*) of scientific methodologies or some ethereal substance waiting to be defined, all the preceding schools of thought subscribed to a utopian vision. The modern, in other words, was not confined within the here and now. Paradoxically, it evoked a future-oriented stance. What was undesirable for intellectuals of a different ideological bent—for example, Gan Yang and Chen Lai on the one hand, Bao Zunxin and Jin Guantao on the other—was surely a modernity that brought no promise of evolutionary progress.

It is this focus on the future, rather than on the present, that characterized the discourse of Chinese modernity of the 1980s as profoundly utopian. Although the discursive project of the cultural elite was instrumental to the state's programs of modernization in many cases (in particular, Jin Guantao's contribution to and involvement in Zhao Ziyang's reform think tank), theirs was a discourse that not only staked everything on the notion of a theoretical leap from the present to the future, but which took as its point of departure a top-down intellectual perspective that constrained a genuine dialogue with those forces that operate at the grassroots level in the shaping of "on-going and emerging [local] institutions."[7] The reform agenda conceptualized as such could not but privilege the discursive over the experiential, superstructure over infrastructure, the central over the local, theory over practice, product over process, and by implication, the elitist discourse of culture (which included theorizing about a single feasible economic paradigm) over the diversified quotidian experiments of China's rural and local economic sectors with alternative modes of production that could not be neatly categorized by either state socialism or free-market capitalism.

Many have speculated about the influence of Western futurology on post-Mao China's obsession with evolutionism. Listed as one of the thirty-three books that changed post-Mao China, Alvin Toffler's *The Third Wave*, whose Chinese translation appeared in 1983, told intellectuals both within and outside the Party apparatus a story of "tremendous hope and prospect."[8] It was Toffler's critique of the pessimism underlying *The Limits of Growth* that instilled in the Chinese intellectual leadership a renewed sense of "urgency and responsibility"—the urgency to start a new technological revolution depicted in *The Third Wave* and the responsibility to achieve "socialist modernization" and to march toward the "world and the future."[9] Eventually some even credited Toffler for the Party's Great Awakening to the importance of knowledge and intellectuals in the new era. Thus although Bill Brugger and David Kelly detect a "dystopian aspect" of the Chinese futurological research, the future that Chinese intellectuals faced in 1985 was nonetheless unambivalently bright and triumphant.[10]

The syndrome of leaping toward the future was so strong that modernization in the 1980s emerged as a utopian discourse rather than as a material practice. How this utopianism could claim its difference from Mao's is a pregnant question not raised by those who decried Mao's voluntarism with such vehemence. It is no small irony that although the epoch of the 1980s prided itself for discoursing against Maoism, its spokespeople continued to practice Mao Zedong's faith in changing China from the top, believing that the power of ideas determines and shapes socioeconomic reality. We can argue that the Maoist voluntarist principle, "the subjective can create the objective," was no less prevalent in the culturalist discourse of the mid-1980s than in Mao's promotion of the Marxist-Leninist theory of permanent revolution.[11] Underlying the Cultural Discussion is the proposition that correct methodology is the first and essential prerequisite for effective modernization. Modernization now replaced revolutionary action as the end result, and methodological retooling replaced ideological remolding as the means to determine the course of history. In the final analysis, the discourse of the 1980s was as heavily imbued with voluntarism as Mao's revolutionary discourse.

VARIATIONS OF THE AESTHETIC MODERN

Perhaps it was only in the realm of the arts and literature that the challenge of modernity to post-Mao China could trigger a radical process of demythologizing the rational, utilitarian imperatives and all the other trappings of human consciousness promoted by a hypertrophic sociocultural modernity. The relationship of aesthetic modernity with modernization was almost always a troubled one. In China, as everywhere else in the world, so-called modernism is not an aesthetic complement of social modernity, but rather a vehicle of intervention in the "progress" syndrome of modernization. Thus the aesthetic modernity of the 1980s neither necessarily reflected nor simply chimed in with the evolutionist ethos of China's social and cultural modernity. On the contrary, as the 1980s progressed into their second half, more and more writers and artists began to revel in fragmentary images of the irrational and the subliminal. Paradoxically, they created an aesthetic utopia out of the imaginary bankruptcy of social utopia: it was in dystopian imagery that utopianism of the highest order could be articulated. Even the root-searching school that engaged in the most intimate historical dialogue with the agenda of cultural modernity came to ground its utopian vision not in the realizable future, but in the past.

The aesthetic modernity of the 1980s generated inquiries no less unsettling than those raised by social modernity. The central problematic concerned the issues of authenticity and cultural subjectivity. How could one distinguish—a question addressed by critics and tacitly seconded by Party ideologues—art and literary texts that represented "genuine" epochal responses to modernity from those that simply exhibited a "spurious" aesthetic modernity as the latest in intellectual fashion? Given the clamor against a "pseudomodernism," any writings that celebrated the themes of schizophrenia, angst, the libido, and the absurd—themes that echoed Western influence—were suspect. This sporadic burgeoning of the irrational that emerged in the high culture during the 1980s was ominous enough to precipitate the forming of the united front of the diverse spokespeople for rationality, whether instrumental rationality (the Party) or substantive rationality (neo-Confucianists and realist writers). The exclamation made by one spectator at an avant-garde art exhibition—"This is sheer neurosis!"—was symptomatic of the indictment of Chinese "modern" art and literature in general.[12] Yet amid all the hustle and bustle to inauthenticate the irrational, the prosecutors of Chinese "modernism" and avant-garde art forgot to ask whether so-called Chinese rationality (in whose name their verdict on the "modernists" was voiced) could be exempted from the charge of emulating Occidental modernity. After all, there is no guarantee that the category "reason" existed in China prior to the arrival of the Enlightenment modernity in the twentieth century. Reason, especially the kind that is invested with such confidence in deconstructing mythologies, may not be more indigenous, and therefore may not be more "authentic," than its alleged opposite, unreason.

Regardless of the competition among the cultural and literary elite for the right to name the Chinese modern, its various interpreters were acutely aware that the norms that Chinese modernity had to create out of itself were traversed by contradictory motifs. These numerous "rational-izing" and "irrational" responses to the Chinese modern ran the gamut from the emulative measures of, to interventionary measures against, reproducing the Enlightenment formula of instrumental reason. Not surprisingly, and yet not without a twist of irony, the most enthusiastic endorsement of instrumental rationality came from the central organ of the CCP, which took upon itself the historical task of modernizing China. The Party's well-timed announcements of successive five-year plans and, in contrast, its ever changing commitment to legal, political, and thought reform demonstrated that modernity meant for the Party nothing more than the efficacious implementation of functional imperatives of economy and administration (which is usually known as "social modernity"). Modernity understood in those terms is based on the technocratic notion that the process of modernization is guided by material constraints that follow the dictates of instrumental rationality alone. Equally appreciative and emulative of the ideals of the Enlightenment, and yet critical of the Party's orthodox interpretation of reason, were those intellectuals (such as scientists Fang Lizhi and Jin Guantao) whose call for the reconstruction of the pure reason of science was undoubtedly a reaction against the domination of the irrational during the Cultural Revolution. For them a genuine endorsement of modern rationality must start with the veiled critique of the inherent irrationality of the instrumental reason on which orthodox Marxism was founded.

Such conflicting receptions of "reason" among its various initiates were indicative of the tortuous journey that the notion was to travel throughout the 1980s. In China's cultural sector, the initial fascination with the primacy of cognitive-instrumental rationalization declined fast toward the latter half of the 1980s as more and more writers and cultural theorists resisted the subjugation of the aesthetic-cognitive to technical rationality. In their ideological struggle against instrumental reason, aesthetic modernity's most radical practitioners sometimes empathized, oddly enough, with those who tried to revive neo-Confucianism.

Yet even aesthetic modernity, which served in its various ideological guises as a means of resistance to Maoist-Marxist ideology on some occasions and scientism on others, was less unified than what the debates over Chinese modernism (1984) and pseudomodernism (1988) might convey. Within the aesthetic, one can perceive scattered subcults, each singing a different tune of the ideology of resistance and each pulling ever deeper into their own unreason. One of these subcults was consumed by unrelieved self-mockery, another by exhausting ingenuousness. I refer here to the cohort of young Chinese "modernists" (*xiandai pai*) in the first case and the school of middle-aged root-searching writers in the second. Their respective inspiration from J. D. Salinger's Holden and Garcia Marquez's magic realism was symptomatic of an ever widening generation gap, as one side fiddled with sacrilegious sentiments and the other burned with passion for roots of all kinds.

The high-minded experiments of young *xiandai pai* such as Liu Suola and Xu Xing with the concept of ennui (whether Salingerian or post-revolutionary) predictably collapsed during the late 1980s into the secular version of a playful boredom in Wang Shuo's "hooligan" (*pizi*) literature, a new form of writing that dallied with the cult of *wanr* (play). Yet one should refrain from dismissing the "degeneration" of the high modernist culture of boredom into the fiction of mindless playfulness as a happening whose repercussions are confined within literary circles. The very notion of "play," the latest aesthetic fad, is no more and no less a byproduct of the modernity of commodity economy, which has given rise in urban centers of all sizes to roughnecks who cash in on the new socioeconomic order with a mirthful abandon. They make a livelihood by cheating, tricking, and accumulating money that comes and goes without much ado.[13] This newly emerged, resourceful underclass that dwells on the margin of law is portrayed in the literature of "play" and in current best-sellers, soap operas, and commercial films. Thanks to the speedy reproduction by the media of the "Wang Shuo phenomenon," the notion of play has been quickly assimilated into the facetious rhetoric of "gamesomeness" that the urban public has adopted to capture the post-Tian'anmen ethos that plays fast and loose with almost every conceivable facet of human life.

In contrast, the emergence of *xungen* literature in 1985—a timely response to Garcia Marquez's mythologizing impulse—foregrounded a utopian, albeit self-consuming, fever for the aestheticization of the cultural and the political. In chapter five I discuss the intricate relationship of the *xungen* aesthetics with the *zhiqing* (reeducated youth) phenomenon. I argue that the utopian discourse of the root-searching writers cannot be fully comprehended unless one keeps in mind their earlier Red Guard background. The confessional excess of the school will appear in a new light once we provide the missing link between its aesthetic vision and the particular process of individuation to which its writers were subjected in their formative years—a period that coincided with the Cultural Revolution and with its utopian politics of thought reform.

The simultaneous emergence of the concepts of "ennui" and "root-searching"—the individualistic turn coexisting with the collective return—is but one example of the many contradictions that marked the aesthetic experience of the mid-1980s. The splitting of aesthetic modernity into opposite directions—the cynic survivalism of *xiandai pai* and the evangelistic dream for a better future and culture of *xungen* literature—is more than part and parcel of a much touted stylistic revolution of Chinese postrevolutionary writers. The split is an example of how works of art came to respond formally, if not to correspond, to the changing forms of individuation and socialization.

The battles over style are battles over the social. The emergence of the "Wang Shuo phenomenon" drove home poignantly once more the message that in post-Mao China, the sensational impact (*hongdong xiaoying*) of the aesthetic on the social may have outlived the much deplored "literary depression" of 1987. If one goes by Max Weber's definition of modernization as a process constituted, among other things, by the differentiation of various value spheres (such as the aesthetic, the moral, the legal, the socioeconomic) in accord with their own logics, then the continual liaison between the aesthetic and the social in post-Mao China could be seen either as an intractable remnant of China's premodernity or as a telling sign of one of the specificities that came to define the Chinese modern.

The difficulties with initiating, feeding, and sustaining the differentiation in question—a particular experience of the Chinese modern—will emerge as an undercurrent throughout this chapter. They serve as the reminders of the futility of mapping Chinese aesthetic modernity as a unified landscape internally, or as an autonomous regime externally. Thus the discourse of "Chinese modernism" further multiplied itself as the continual complicity of the aesthetic with social modernity spelled out the impossibility of treating the former in its own terms. Any investigation of aesthetic modernity during the 1980s, to which chapter four is devoted, will inevitably cross-reference the practices and discourses of sociocultural modernity.

I cannot emphasize strongly enough the seamless intertwining of aesthetic modernity with the cultural discourse. All the problematics that emerged from Chinese aesthetic modernity—the ideological content of the so-called modern consciousness, the applicability of the system and control theory to literary criticism, the social efficacy of aesthetic intervention, the debates over Chinese modernism and postmodernism—helped multiply both the infinite possibilities and the risks of the Chinese modern to overtake its own epochal logic.

Both the possibilities and risks in question rested on one dilemma: the aesthetic modern's instinct of coming to terms with modernity's raison d'être was continually distracted by its equally powerful capacity to generate contradictory discourses that could not be contained within the prescribed project of global modernity. How are we to define the characteristics of the Chinese aesthetic modern? Did the so-called Yuppie *xiandai pai* earn the right to name those characteristics? Or was it the root-searching school that could make claims to the title of Chinese modernist? What about disparate elements like Mo Yan and Wang Meng whose voices were part of the chorus of the modern? And finally, was experimental fiction "residual modern" or the precursor of "Chinese postmodernism"?[14]

The Chinese anxieties about naming the Chinese modern (both in social and aesthetic terms) persisted throughout the decade of the eighties. Perhaps we can ask instead: why should anyone (anyone but the elite) care if Chinese social modernity is designated capitalist or socialist, or if Chinese art and literature are labeled modernist, pseudomodernist, or even postmodernist? What is truly at stake, I ask, if the ritual of naming loses its significance in an age of as-yet unfulfilled possibilities?

The very awareness of the ambiguity of the unnamable—a Chinese modernity on the threshold—prompted Gan Yang to posit the risky proposal of "the alternative modern" as uniquely Chinese.[15] This strategy, which highlighted the primacy of the indigenous condition, formed a sharp contrast to an opposite and perhaps even more perilous position held by avant-garde critics who urged China into the globalization of culture. Pandering to the West's latest cultural logic, that small group of postmodernist critics turned Gan's threshold proposition into the hazardous venture of collapsing the epochal marker of modernity into that of postmodernity.

But this is after all what adventures are all about: a journey fraught with promising possibilities and hidden risks. Such was the winding course of China's cultural modernity in the mid-1980s, whose epochal cause célèbre was undoubtedly the Cultural Discussion.

As a series of gradually unfolding responses to the reform fever that seized the first half of the 1980s, the Discussion should not be seen as a cataclysmic event, because there was no beginning or end to speak of. It can only be understood as an increasingly self-conscious epochal sentience. This was a zeitgeist that expressed its own anxiety over two conflicting historical burdens: a modernity short of models and a modernity saturated with models. The shifts in discursive practices during the Discussion characterized the radical notion of a zeitgeist that imagined that it could have it all. It was an epochal sensibility that wanted to look forward to the future, remember the past, and seize the authentic moment of an innovative present. In the end, it was the historical consciousness of Chinese modernity's dual dependence upon the past and future that endowed the Cultural Discussion with an encyclopedic plenitude beyond the reach of any local determination provided by the early twentieth-century debates known as the May Fourth Movement.

Thus although each of the major themes of the Cultural Discussion—the dominant voice of instrumental rationality and scientism, the revival of Confucianism and the *qimeng* school, and the marginal practice of hermeneutics—might conjure up shadow images of the May Fourth debates, the Discussion did not recycle old historical imagination in the simplistic sense. Conflicting as they were, those themes have to be examined in an ensemble fashion so that the complexity of the polymorphous modern can manifest itself. Furthermore, each theme (with its temporal anchor cast in the future, past, and the present respectively) can only derive its ultimate meaning from the context of a zeitgeist that was not merely conscious of, but also increasingly confident in its own capability to go beyond the present. It was no longer the terms of crisis (which confined the May Fourth discourse to the perpetual present), but those of thought emancipation (a post-Maoist imaginary into which all three temporal orders were merged) that determined the spirit of Chinese modernity in the

1980s and distinguished the new era from the May Fourth period. For the same reason, whereas May Fourth intellectuals could only conceive of and emulate the single model of Eurocentric modernity, postcolonial global geopolitics has turned the notion of pluralism into a reality.[16] Today, the Chinese intelligentsia at home and abroad has no difficulty imagining and sometimes even vaunting an alternative modern—whether it is identified as the East Asian model of neo-Confucianism or the hybrid Chinese socialist paradigm still in the making.

It is in the context of the well-assorted modern that I shall address the central concern of this chapter: the intellectuals' discourse on cultural modernity. The Culture Fever and the accompanying Discussion will eventually find its way into the textbook of contemporary Chinese history. Meanwhile, its participants will slide further and further into irrelevance as the future brings them in the 1990s not the ever faster accumulation of intellectual capital, but a consumer culture that seems to have reserved no niche for them.

CULTURE FEVER

The elite's reversal of fortune in the 1990s must have come as a surprise to those who were historical witnesses of the Cultural Discussion in the mid-1980s. In the eighties it was undoubtedly the knowing subject that seemed to gain the upper hand over the consuming and producing subject. In short, intellectuals rather than average citizens appeared to be the unequivocal spokespeople for the Chinese modern.

Academy and research institutes naturally emerged as the locales where the Cultural Discussion took place. It is important to note that although the media attention to Culture Fever peaked in 1985, a few occasional feverish hot spots were already manifest in the early 1980s. In order to trace the career of each cultural agenda that the Discussion addressed throughout the first half of the 1980s, I enumerate in brief the sequence of events that fed the heat into flame.

• In October and November of 1981, the Editorial Division on China's Problems at the United Nations participated in a global project titled "The History of Science and Culture of Humankind" under the jurisdiction of the UN's Education/Science/Culture Commission. The division's contribution to the project consisted of a study of the conflicts of cultural trends between China and the West and between tradition and modernity. The focal point of discussion was how contemporary China could modernize ancient Chinese civilization.

• In June and December of 1982, two symposia on "The Study of Cultural History" were held in Shanghai. The main participants included history faculty from Fudan University, fellows from the research institutes of history and modern history at the Beijing Chinese Academy of the Social Sciences, and Chinese editors and specialists involved in the UN project such as Zhou Gucheng, Tan Qixiang, and Cai Shangsi. The symposia produced a journal *Zhongguo wenhua* (Chinese culture) and the "Chinese Culture Series." In October of the same year, Jin Guantao and those associated with *Ziran bianzheng fa tongxun* (Newsletter of the dialectics of nature) held a workshop in Chengdu of Sichuan Province on "Why Modern Chinese Science Lagged Behind." The conference volume *Kexue chuantong yu wenhua* (Scientific tradition and culture) was published subsequently by the Science and Technology Publishers of Shannxi Province.

• In March and November of 1983, two conferences were convened by Hong Kong University on the theme of "Modernization and Chinese Culture." Among the attendants were renowned scholars Fei Xiaotong and Zhao Fusan and established social scientists and anthropologists from mainland China, Taiwan, Hong Kong, Japan, the United States, and Singapore. The conference introduced several topics: the influence of modernization on Chinese society, the continuity of traditional culture, and the sinification of the social sciences.

• In fall 1984, a symposium sponsored by Zhonghua Bookstore and the history department of Beijing Normal University was held in Zhengzhou of Henan Province. As a result of the symposium, Zhonghua Bookstore was commissioned to publish a series of studies on modern Chinese cultural history.

• In the latter half of 1984, the first symposium on the "Comparative Studies of Chinese and Western Culture" was held in Shanghai. In its wake, a research center for the "Comparative Studies of Chinese and Western Culture was formally established in Shanghai.

• In 1985, the major players of the Cultural Discussion entered the arena officially. The Planning Committee of the Academy of Chinese Culture obtained blessings from the Central Party Secretary and was formed under the aegis of the Party. The committee could challenge with confidence any competitor to outdo its team, which included

Confucian celebrities such as Feng Youlan, Liang Shuming, and Ji Xi-
anlin. In March 1985 and June 1986, the committee held large lecture
sessions in Beijing on Chinese culture and comparative culture studies
of China and the West. The content of those sessions varied. Although
specific topics on culture such as Confucianism and modernization, the
characteristics of Chinese philosophy, and the values and future of traditional Chinese culture formed the central foci of those lecture sessions, the Academy of Chinese Culture by no means pursued a monolithic path of inquiry. Occasionally, topics on science and futurology
were also addressed. The comprehensive scientist and culturalist approach should surprise no one if we remind ourselves that a great majority of the members affiliated with the academy were well-trained
Marxists. Those invited to deliver the lecture series were all renowned
culture specialists: Liang and Feng, Ren Jiyu, Li Zehou, Chen Guying,
and scholars from Australia, Hong Kong, France, and America (such as
Tu Weiming and Cheng Chung-ying).

• Several other significant events took place during 1985. The Chinese
Research Institute on Confucius was established in Beijing. (This institute and the Chinese Foundation of Confucius established in Qufu in
1984 formed the two major centers of Confucian studies in China.) The
"Salon on Culture Studies" was established in Wuhan. And various
organizations of culture studies mushroomed in Shanghai, Xi'an, and
Guangzhou.

• Echoing the efforts made by the Academy of Chinese Culture, Wuhan
University held a workshop in December of 1985 on "Modernization and
Traditional Chinese Culture." Lecturers included Xiao Jiefu, Tang Yijie, and
overseas Chinese scholars such as Cheng Chung-ying and Tu Weiming.

• Between January 1985 and June 1986, newspapers across the nation
published approximately two hundred essays on the subject of Chinese
culture. Special columns were created in major papers to facilitate the
voicing of views on such issues as whether China was experiencing a
genuine cultural renaissance.

• In 1986, Gan Yang's *Culture: China and the World* Editorial Committee was established in Beijing. The committee was made up of young
and middle-aged cultural elite whose mission was to introduce, through
massive translation projects, Western masterworks of the humanities and
the social sciences. The two translation series that the committee edited
and published exercised considerable influence on university students
and reform-minded elite.

• It is worth noting that throughout 1986, semiofficial symposia on "Strategies of Cultural Development" took place one after another in Shanghai, Guangzhou, and other big cities under the aegis of Party reformers. Topics for discussion predictably focused on ideological issues such as the relationship between Marxist and non-Marxist theories, the link between economic reform and cultural reform, the development of Marxism, and the reform of socialist systems in other parts of the world.

• In January 1986, an international conference on Chinese culture was convened at Fudan University in Shanghai. The major themes of the conference were the reevaluation of traditional Chinese culture and the relationship between Chinese and Western culture. In March 1986, a conference on "Traditional Culture and Modernization" was sponsored by the Propaganda Department of the CCP's Municipal District of Shanghai, *Wenhui bao* (*Wenhui news*), and *Jiefang riba* (Liberation daily). In April, the Chinese Foundation of Confucius and the journal *Kongzi yanjiu* (Studies of Confucius) held a joint meeting in Qufu, Confucius' birthplace, to examine the relationship between socialism and Confucian traditionalism. Also in April, graduate students of Central Party Academy, Beijing University, People's University, Beijing Normal University, and the Chinese Academy of the Social Sciences gathered to discuss problems of Marxism and the cultural conflicts between China and the West. Research centers were founded at various academic institutions: the Center of East-West Comparative Cultural Studies at the Shanghai Academy of the Social Sciences and at Beijing Normal University; the Center of Philosophy and Culture at Qinghua University; and the Center of Chinese Classical Studies and the Center of Comparative Literature at Shenzhen University.

It only seemed natural that the discussion of traditional and modern culture should precipitate a small handful of workshops on the comparative methodology of culture studies. In April 1985, the first coordination session on the "Research Planning for Chinese and Comparative Culture Studies" was held in Shenzhen, China's showcase economic zone. During the session, a detailed blueprint was mapped out to guide scholars of each participating city in developing their own research plans. Special attention was paid to the history and geographical significance of each city so that the research agenda assigned to each local cluster was geopolitically and culturally specific. For instance, scholars from Xian, the old capital of Han and Tang, were to focus on the study of Han-Tang culture; those from Guangzhou would emphasize the study of contemporary Lingnan (the area south of the Five Ridges) mercantile culture; and academics based in Shanghai and Beijing, the two cradles of modern and contemporary cultural and literary revolutions, were expected to emphasize theoretical and methodological issues—comparative studies of Chinese and Western culture on the one hand, and the problematics of tradition and modernity on the other.

Toward 1986, the increasingly deepening consciousness of culture studies as a new discipline unmistakably defined the later phase of the Cultural Discussion in terms of an intensified methodology fever. The Hangzhou conference held in May 1986, a sequel to the Shenzhen planning session, was much more articulate in this regard. It foregrounded the macroperspective (*hongguan*) of culture studies in its search for analytical models. Theoretical questions about cultural typology, structure, and function were raised. The abstraction of the vocabulary deployed during the discussion at the conference could be seen as a sign that Culture Fever was taking an introverted turn. Certainly, the other items that appeared on the conference agenda (for instance, the problematic lessons taught by the sinification syndrome) reinforced the impression that a more thoughtful review of the Cultural Discussion had finally begun. No less importantly, the conference was self-conscious of the current Culture Fever as a historically specific happening. Given this awareness, the conference participants had to confront the embarrassing question: how different was the Cultural Discussion from that which took place seventy years ago? The raising of the question itself was significant because it brought to the fore a hitherto neglected topic, the haunting relationship between contemporary Chinese "cultural renaissance" and the May Fourth Movement in 1919.

Gan Yang and other Chinese intellectuals at home would fain believe that their revisiting of certain familiar May Fourth themes (antitraditionalism, modernity, China versus the West, scientism, the reformist trilogy of technology, politics, and culture) did not simply reproduce the earlier intellectual and cultural platform. Some proclaimed that the contemporary Cultural Discussion illustrated "a return" to May Fourth problematics on "a higher [theoretical] level."[17] Others such as Su Xiaokang and Chen Kuide emphasized that the Culture Fever of the 1980s was distinctly different from the May Fourth Movement because the former grew out of "internal cultural conflicts" and the latter was triggered by external crises of national survival.[18]

Those were arguments made by the actual participants in the Cultural Discussion, whose partiality for the movement of their own making was more or less predictable. Precisely because they had invested such a high stake in the historical evaluation of the Culture Fever, their own word on the issue could by no means be taken as final. Some China specialists in the West were hardly convinced that the question about the relationship between the culture movement of the 1980s and that of the 1920s could be so easily settled. The image that came to them of the Cultural Discussion of post-Mao China is certainly not the imaginary spiral movement that allegedly characterized the new epoch's qualitative break from 1919, but rather the dubious spectacle of Chinese intellectuals going through the revolving door of history without ever making a new entry.

The speculations about the historical continuity or discontinuity between the May Fourth period and post-Mao China surfaced at a time when the Cultural Discussion had evolved beyond the stage of initial frenzy. But right at the moment when a critical space was opened for rigorous self-reflection, there seemed little time left for genuine introspection. Once again, political intervention halted the burgeoning self-critical momentum that the Cultural Discussion had finally gathered toward the latter half of 1986. What ensued foreshadowed the abortive ending of the once promising decade of the 1980s.

In late 1986, with Hu Yaobang's ouster, Culture Fever suffered a dramatic setback. The subsequent campaign against bourgeois liberalism succeeded in all but arresting the blooming of one hundred schools that the Cultural Discussion stood for. The long list of censored works not only included newspapers such as *Shehui bao* (Society newspaper) in Shanghai, literary journals such as *Nanfeng chuang* (Window to southern winds) in Guangzhou, and books such as Yan Jiaqi and Gao Gao's *Wenge shinian shi* (Ten years' history of the Cultural Revolution), but also film productions such as *Furong zhen* (Hibiscus town), *Huang tudi* (Yellow earth), *Yeshan* (Wild mountain), *Heipao shijian* (The incident of black canon), and *Yige he bage* (One and eight).[19] In February 1986, the Party initiated the twenty-fourth anniversary memorial of "Learning from Lei Feng the Revolutionary Model." Another thought reform campaign loomed on the horizon. It was not until summer 1988 that the Culture Fever would be kindled anew with the outbreak of controversy over the popular TV documentary series *Heshang* (Yellow river elegy) (1988)—the subject of my next chapter.

Heshang asks many hard questions about modern as well as imperial Chinese history. The documentary raises the May Fourth question

as an intriguing metaphor for the unfulfilled radical moment of historical discontinuity that could, but failed to, deliver Chinese society from
the tyrannical cycle of "ultrastability"—a theory propagated by Jin Guantao and the production team of *Heshang*. Su Xiaokang, the chief
scriptwriter of the series, was planning a sequel named "The May
Fourth" when the political tempest of June Fourth finally brought down
the curtain on the Cultural Discussion together with all its attendant
happenings and epiphanies.

In retrospect, the second coming of the Culture Fever in 1988 had a
far greater sensational impact on the national psyche than that created
by its tortuous earlier career. The accessibility of television brought home
the tangible imagery of various cultural issues raised in the TV series.
Such a wide popular appeal, however, only helped revive the Cultural
Discussion for a fleeting moment. I doubt if the Discussion could have
regained its earlier momentum even without the intervention of the
Tian'anmen Square crackdown. *Heshang*, and the fervent cultural debate that it triggered, was doomed to defeat its own purpose because the
reformist agenda that the series' production team promoted was deeply
implicated in Zhao Ziyang's reform program and in his struggle against
the old-timers. Once its complicity with Party politics took its own
course, the Cultural Discussion could not but compromise its original
enlightenment agenda. The discourse that the cultural elite constructed
laboriously between 1985 and 1986 lost much of its critical edge and
fell into the hands of interested parties as an ideological instrument for
power struggle. The unfortunate political liaison unsurprisingly paved
the way for the later official condemnation of *Heshang* as the most pernicious "poisonous weed" that fed the "innocent minds" of young students who swarmed the Tian'anmen Square in the long portentous summer of 1989. And yet even before its eventful closure, the Culture Fever
and its accompanying utopian optimism were already expiring. "Cultural depression" and "crisis consciousness" circulated in 1987 among
cultural and political circles to offset slogans like "renaissance" and
"looking toward the future." Although Chinese intellectuals still believed that they alone could dictate the agenda and determine the success or failure of China's modernization, after 1988, the participants in
the Great Cultural Discussion cherished far less confidence in their vanguard role and encountered greater difficulties in posing as disinterested
intellectuals than they did at the height of Culture Fever.

The preceding account of the facts and dates about the Cultural Discussion, dull as they may sound, should convey the picture of a simul-

taneously agitating and aspiring decade that staked everything on the immediate completion of the project of modernity—on the discursive level at least. Although Culture Fever could certainly speak of its own evolution as a culturally motivated phenomenon monitored and fed by academics at large, it was hardly innocent of the making of a well calculated, albeit camouflaged, political discourse that ascribed the country's pressing socioeconomic problems to an aging traditional culture at bay—an imaginary antagonist—rather than to Chinese socialism itself. It is worth noting that the Fever did not gather momentum until 1985, when economic reform began to encounter major barriers as it made its perilous journey from the countryside to urban centers. First and foremost, I therefore interpret the intensification of the Fever as a critical response that the entire cultural arena made to two major external catalysts: a modernization that fell short of realizing its economic promises, and the political censorship that banned any discourse that placed the burden of a thwarted reform on Deng Xiaoping's "Four Basic Principles." If the relentless critique of the socialist system was considered taboo, then the incrimination of culture was conceivably an alternative outlet. The pan-culturalism that the Discussion promoted therefore had a hidden agenda, which, as the TV series *Heshang* illustrates so poignantly with its blanket condemnation of traditional Chinese culture, renders any genuine cultural introspection everlastingly elusive.[20]

Herein lies the major paradox of the Cultural Discussion: on the one hand, its impetus was derived from real socioeconomic forces, and yet on the other hand, it gradually and inevitably evolved into a metaphysical discourse that failed to represent, but which grew to resist instead, the ongoing material process of modernization that eclipsed all the abstract cultural formulations that the Discussion generated. The modernity that the Cultural Discussion prescribed was in the end a modernity on paper, not in reality. Throughout the Discussion, intellectuals (most of whom considered themselves the think tank of the new era) took for granted that their interpretation of the modern—various utopian prescriptions to revitalize Chinese culture—did a tremendous service to the program of modernization. Little did they realize that this kind of "cultural commotions of utopian style" had unconsciously "withstood the actual unfolding of the [necessary] un-utopian process of modernization."[21] Nor could they ever imagine that the winding and complex course of modernization, involving experimentation with an uneven mode of production that is neither market dominated nor collectivized, could not be corrected or sped up by the mere concoction of an idealistic movement from above like the May Fourth enlightenment or the Great Cultural Discussion. Modern and contemporary Chinese history revealed time and again that it was the intellectuals themselves, their utopian faith, and their rushing of an unrealistic agenda of revolutionizing the nation overnight that invited intervention from above and jeopardized the radical space that they themselves helped create.

Although the autocracy of the regime can never shoulder enough blame, neither can those intellectuals directly involved in the sequence of events that led to the June Fourth crackdown. They cannot be acquitted of the responsibility of forcing a bootless revolution while a peaceful transformation of the system was already well under way. In this context, I applaud the appearance of the slogan "let go of utopia" that Chinese intellectuals such as Yan Bofei began to advocate. Let us keep this slogan in mind as I undertake the following analysis of the various utopian strategies adopted by different groups of participants in the Cultural Discussion.

MODERNITY AND SCIENTIFIC RATIONALITY: JIN GUANTAO, SYSTEM THEORY, AND THE PREMODERN MYTH OF TOTALITY

Jin Guantao, the Director of the Philosophy of Science in the Research Institute of the Academy of Natural Sciences, would agree with Max Weber that the transition to modernity could only be achieved through increasing rationalization. For Jin, the typical modern is incarnated in its desire for unity and system, in other words, for the pure form. Where can this formal rationality be sought? It certainly cannot be found in substantive rationality manifested in the traditional mode of *zhiguan* thinking (intuitive thinking)—for instance, in the theory of *tianren ganying*, the sympathetic unity of Heaven and (hu)man. Nor can formal rationality be derived from the modern Hegelian-Marxist dialectics, which stipulates the law of dialectic inversion as immutable and predictable and thus, according to Jin, fell into the trap of metaphysics that it claims to subvert from the very start.

Jin Guantao's struggle with dialectics is a subject that should be treated elsewhere. It suffices to say that in 1968, he underwent a methodological crisis at the discovery that the law of change that Hegelian dialectics wrote into itself is prescriptive at large.[22] A dialectics that foretells the negation of the negation reenacts nothing but the determinate mode of thinking that it critiques and condemns. Even as early as the late 1960s, the paradox of the determinacy of the indeterminate—a motif that would later mature into his controversial theory of ultra-stability—plagued the young scientist who reveled in the odyssey into the mind, oblivious to the violence that the Cultural Revolution incurred.

Jin's rejection of both traditional and Marxist modes of rationality led him on a long pilgrimage into the natural sciences. He emerged at the end of his journey an evangelist of scientific rationality (*kexue lixing*). But what distinguished him from other advocates of crude scientism (the renowned physicist Fang Lizhi comes to mind) is his ideal of constructing a dialogue between science and ethics, between natural sciences and social sciences, and between instrumental and substantive reason. Eventually, even his critics have to respect his genuine belief that the challenge of natural sciences to philosophy and the social sciences could revolutionize all three fields simultaneously. Hence the establishment of *lixing zhexue* (the philosophy of reason), a new system of values and methodologies, became his primary concern. Inasmuch as Jin Guantao aimed to redress the separation of formal process from content, albeit on the theoretical level, we have to give him credit for being well aware that the balance must be maintained between cognitive-instrumental and moral-practical-expressive rationality.

For Jin Guantao's generation, who experienced the traumatic disruption and destruction that the Revolution brought to China, the call for the reconstruction of rationality transcends mere academic interest. His preoccupation with "systematic totality," one of Jin's favorite critical categories, neutral as it may sound, signals an ideological as well as scientific activism because it serves as a reminder and critique of the catastrophic disorder during the revolutionary years. His aversion to the rise of the irrational toward the latter half of the 1980s can thus be put in perspective.[23] It is totality and order, not rupture and anarchy, that make up the analytic vocabulary of Jin Guantao's refurbished system theory. What can better tame the phenomenon of disorder than undertaking a rigorous examination of its birth as a predictable and recurrent anomaly that never fails to be reappropriated into an ultrastable system? The triumph of totality is complete. Yet how different is this closure—the indeterminate always risks the co-optation by the determinate—from the one engendered by Hegelian dialectics, which Jin Guantao claims to have discarded or transcended?

It appears that although Jin Guantao speaks of the developmental logic of indeterminacy that actually forms the first part of his "philosophy of reason," his fascination with systems, control, and information theory leads him eventually to the making of a so-called audacious premise characteristic of Hegelian dialectics at large: "Within each system of a given organization (including any given social structure), the growth of disorganizational elements is a regular rule."[24] To the extent that Jin Guantao did not (or would not) kiss a complete farewell to the master narrative of Hegelian dialectics, both Marxist and anti-Marxist scholars were justified to designate him, despite his futile protest, as a Marxist, Hegelian Marxist, of some sort.[25]

Although remaining mired in Marxian dialectics, Jin Guantao is unsuccessful in "preserving the Marxist concept of praxis," which presupposes a human agency that can break loose from a closed system of formulaic feedback and control mechanisms.[26] What then is his specific mode of analysis that pledges alliance with a totalizing scientific rationality, a rationality that allegedly enables and liberates the mind but at the same time encloses real human beings and human history within a superstable macrostructure? This brings us to Jin's theory of ultrastability, the development of a model of Chinese feudal society as a cybernetic system.

Drawing on organization theory, Jin postulates the existence of a regulating mechanism that enables different parts of a given system to achieve a functional equilibrium, which in turn guarantees the stability, hence the survival, of the system in any chaotic environment. He eschews the mechanistic division of the base from superstructure and abandons not only economic determinism, the central organizing category of Marxism, but also the logic of mechanical causality that has been outmoded by the indeterminacy principle of modern physics. What he proposes instead is a restructuring of the traditional Marxist concept of levels similar to that Althusser proposed for his model of "structural causality." An ultrastable structure is made up of successfully regulated relationships and circulations of functional input and output among three interacting subsystems ($zi\ xitong$): the economic, political, and cultural. Whenever antagonistic or "disorganizational" elements emerge to threaten the stability of a given system, four patterns of structural change may occur: total stasis, structural replacement, ultrastable structure resulting from periodic purgation, and total extinction of civilization.[27] The persistent capacity of Chinese society to dissolve subversive forces gives rise to the proposition of ultrastability.

The political radicalism of such a theory has evaded many of Jin Guantao's critics, and perhaps even the author himself. For if Chinese society is locked into this cyclical pattern of perpetual renewal, nothing short of a total revolution can break the cycle and bail China out of the stagnation of ultrastability. Here Jin has to disconnect the dialectics of progress from the perspective of a peaceful transformation of society. The liberated society can no longer be conceived of as the natural or logical result of the gradual unfolding of each subsystem toward reason; its realization has rather to be thought of as a catastrophic break from the bad continuum of stability.

The ideological implications of Jin's theory led to a stance that amounts to a total negation of cultural traditions he himself is not prepared to confront. According to his model, it is the Confucian *zongfa* (clan-centered) system that consolidates the integrative capacity (*yitihua*) of the empire-state.[28] Thus it is the complicity of the subsystems of the cultural with the political that prevents China from struggling free of the backward ideology characteristic of the small peasants' mode of production. Jin Guantao's veiled attack on Confucian ethics probably explains why anticommunist cultural conservatives in Taiwan such as Yan Yuanshu could join without qualms the CCP's condemnation of the *Heshang* series, which introduced Jin's theory of ultrastability to the national television screen in 1987.

Jin Guantao himself, however, seems ambivalent about the underlying agenda of his philosophy of reason. Does he merely want to provide a scientific analysis of history? Or should scientific rationality be seen as a means of ideological critique rather than as an end in itself? I propose that it is impossible to leave aside the issue of ideology and deal with the problems of his analytical approach on its own terms.

Much can be said about the fissures in Jin Guantao's theoretical framework. Although I am less concerned with the validity of his theory in its own right than with how it can be positioned ideologically in the larger discourse of Chinese modernity, a closer look at the gaps of Jin's theories often brings us closer to the latter inquiry. These gaps foreground the issue of ideology in their manifestation of Jin Guantao's peculiar interpretation of modernity, which is unconsciously split into three conflicting discourses—Weberian modernist, Marxist, and Confucianist—all at the same time.

I have already shown how Jin Guantao's methodological discourse is situated on the border of Marxist dialectics. The Confucian affiliation that I find Jin guilty of should surprise his readers even more, for he was identified during the years of Culture Fever as an indomitable warrior fighting for the cause of science against everything that the Confucian school stood for. How can we map out the ideological field of a man who seems to be everywhere and everyone's collaborator?

First of all, the three-tier diagram of subsystems, each of which seems to enjoy its own semiautonomy, is indicative of Weber's theory that the process of modernization is inevitably accompanied by the differentiation of value spheres. Yet Jin's insistence on the functional integration (*gongneng ouhe*) arising spontaneously among those subsystems also points to the presence of a holistic impulse that conjures up characteristically intuitive and premodern Chinese logic. This logic presupposes and privileges the concept of undifferentiated continuum, whose ultimate crystallization can be found in the theory of the unity of Heaven and (hu)man (*tianren heyi*)—a mode of thinking he took such pains to refute.

To note such discrepancies is to raise the question: Did Jin Guantao clarify the contradictory relationship between his Weberian modernist vision of a mediated relation among the subsystems and his unconscious recourse to the largely discredited Confucian idealism that prescribes the perfectly harmonious and substantive rationality? That he has not reached a heightened awareness of this problem is demonstrated by the fact that whereas thinkers like Tu Weiming congratulated him for still dreaming the Confucian dream (Tu considers Jin a Confucianized Marxist), others attacked him precisely for having abandoned it.[29] To complicate the picture, there were still others, anti-Confucianists and various brands of iconoclasts, who faulted him for not abandoning it thoroughly enough.

Because of such shifting ideological vocabulary, the efficacy of Jin Guantao's theories as an ideological critique is weakened to a great extent. His subtext for raising the banner of scientific rationality is the critique of the inadequacy of Confucian culture to meet the challenge of modernity. He attempts, therefore, to construct a modern system of epistemology in which the privileged position of Confucianism will be dissolved into nothing more than one of the many competing elements of that system. Implicit in Jin's theory of ultrastability is a deep-seated pessimism about the capacity of the old system to rejuvenate itself. All the scientific analyses of China's feudal structure seem to lead to a single question: How can self-critique and enlightenment arise from such a self-enclosed system? The proposal for a thorough reconstruction (*chedi chongjian*) of Chinese culture should thus emerge as the only logical and viable alternative.

But which part of traditional culture can best answer the epochal call for modernization? Can one map a reconstructed relationship between Confucianism and the new system sanctified by the culture of modern science and technology? Jin's answer to this question seems twice veiled. In numerous articles published jointly with Liu Qingfeng, his intellectual partner and spouse, on the project "Why Did China Fail to Give Rise to Modern Science?" he identifies the archculprit unambiguously as the "ethical centeredness" (lunli zhongxin) of Confucianism.[30] This traditional ideology of ethical centeredness "inevitably ascribed the judgment of ethical values to the explanation of natural phenomena. Once ethical norms were imposed upon natural phenomena, it was expected that one would sink into the quagmire of mysticism and superstition."[31] As for those scientific discoveries into which premodern China stumbled by pure chance, Jin Guantao proclaimed that they were made not for the sake of cognitive interests and curiosity, but predominantly for utilitarian purposes. The pragmatic mentality that Confucian ethics promoted was thus held responsible, in his view, for the deterioration of creative scientific reason into stagnant technological reason in traditional China.

Given Jin Guantao's account of the pernicious influence of Confucianism on the development of science in premodern China, one might conclude that it is the other schools of philosophy (religious Daoism, Moism, and the Yin-Yang Naturalist school, to name a few) rather than Confucianism whose relationship with scientific rationality needs to be reconstructed and remapped. But such is not the case. It is Confucianism, and Confucianism alone, that occupies a central place in Jin Guantao's system of thought. In fact, Jin's ideological stance could be much more easily configured if he had stopped at the simple condemnation of Confucian ethics. But he goes on to caution those to whom he has preached the virtue of scientism to be aware of its pitfalls. It is, I should add, certainly impressive that a fervent scientist like Jin Guantao could conceive of such a preemptive critique of instrumental reason, applying the notion of the Enlightenment becoming totalitarian with its own tools—a dilemma of Western modernity—to an as-yet unachieved, theoretically postulated Chinese enlightenment. However, although Jin Guantao's resistance to the blind faith in scientific rationality is highly admirable, his conclusion unveils an irony: The modernist's lingering faith in traditionalism dies hard.

> Humankind needs a wisdom that can *reign over* science and technology on a deeper level. . . . At this moment, our *look back* at Chinese culture is highly significant. [As early as] two thousand years ago, Chinese philosophers had struggled free from the bondage of theology. They took as the basis of

their thinking the behavioral norm and ethical foundation of human beings themselves and had thus developed their unique culture. Regardless of why this ideology of ethical centeredness stood in the way of the progress of modern Chinese science and technology, the remarkable thing is the undaunted and tenacious spirit that the Chinese race exhibited in the creation of its own culture. We can imagine, once the Chinese race recognizes the cultural value of modern science, and once they incorporate this scientific spirit into her *cultural quest for unity and harmony*, then undoubtedly, a new culture that will *represent the future of humankind* will dawn on the horizon.[32]

The specter of Liang Qichao has risen anew from the ashes of history. What else but the harmonious spiritual culture of traditional China returns to greet us in a hypothetical new triumph? What Jin Guantao alludes to in these concluding remarks about the global prospect of scientific culture sounds akin to Liang Qichao's fin-de-siècle sermon that it was Chinese civilization that would bring ultimate salvation to a reified materialist culture of the West. The allure of return seems as tantalizing as ever for Chinese intellectuals—whether they label themselves as Marxists, neo-Confucianists, modern scientists, or all of the above. Is it possible that not even a scientist is immune to the compensatory logic of spiritual victory (*jingshen shengli*)? The lesson that Jin Guantao can learn from his own words is this: He should continue to cultivate the critical power of scientific reason and leave the messianic mission of "salvaging" the West from scientism to humanist academics in the Western ivory tower. It is the pursuit of the critical power of rationality alone that can bail Jin's project out of mere methodological utilitarianism. The philosopher has yet to discover the "specific theoretical dynamic" of reason that "continually pushes the sciences, and even the self-reflection of the sciences, beyond merely engendering technically useful knowledge" or beyond merely providing a scientific analysis of historical data.[33]

Given Jin Guantao's overriding interest in the methodological rather than the critical content of instrumental reason, it seems predictable that the term "enlightenment" is not a privileged one in his theories. However, he is still in many ways an heir of the Enlightenment tradition for which history appears as a progress toward reason. And because Jin seems to imply that China's ethically centered ideology can protect the Chinese enlightenment from ravages of reification, the rationalization of Chinese society, in Jin's view, could succeed in yielding the harvest of a utopianism unaccompanied by shadows of objectification. In this, ironically but not surprisingly, Jin Guantao's ideal of utopia echoes in spirit the one carved by reformists within the CCP. The Party reformers' promotion of the socialist "spiritual civilization" (*jingshen wenming*) is partly meant to remedy their earlier excessive emphasis on the material progress that the Four Modernizations Program calls for.[34] Both the Party and Jin Guantao have recognized, at one peculiar moment of ideological collusion, that social modernity goes hand in hand with a cultural modernity that stresses the modernization of humanity defined in terms of the collective and the regulated—whether such project is designated a socialist or Confucianist one.

Thus paradoxically Jin Guantao's interest to find a place for humanity in his scientific project—an effort materialized in *Rende zhexue* (The philosophy of human beings) (1988), the culminating volume of his trilogy for the philosophy of reason—leads him to a blatantly traditionalist perspective that his scientism is supposed to resist.[35] For Jin Guantao the humanist, the development of evolutionary dynamism of social modernity apart from a viable cultural modernity is undesirable. He, as well as many Party loyalists and neo-Confucianists, could well appreciate the braking effect of tradition (whether socialist or Confucianist), without which, contemporary beings would be delivered over without any protection to the functional imperatives of economy and administration. Jin Guantao's deep-seated faith in the compensatory role of tradition to a social modernity gone astray renders any clear-cut classification of his ideology almost impossible. His unintentionally complicitous bonding with the Party and neo-Confucianists is further strengthened in that he is no less vehement in his attack on the emergence of the irrational than his alleged Confucian and Marxist rivals. Li Zehou's insightful comment applies to the deep structural correspondence between Jin Guantao's scientific rationality and the Chinese rationality of which Confucianism is characteristic: "The pragmatic rationality of Chinese tradition not only does not contradict it [the vigorous Western logical analysis and its seamless mode of reasoning and thinking], but it can help promulgate it."[36]

Is Li Zehou asserting another instance of the powerful mechanism of the sinification syndrome? Or is there really such a thing as a sinicized form of scientific rationality? Jin Guantao himself has taken pains to remove the stigma of Eurocentrism that is attached to scientific reason and reached the conclusion that the national, Western hegemony of scientific culture is an outmoded idea in today's situation of multinationals. He claims that scientific reason is not Occidental. It is quite possible that China could reinvent its own indigenous version of scientific rationality that may yet supplement, or even replace, Western scientism and serve as the global paradigm to come. The ideology of the alternative modern resurfaces. Amid the presence of a resuscitated sinocentrism in defiance of a rampant Eurocentrism, the question as to whether Jin Guantao is a traditionalist or antitraditionalist, Marxian scientist or Confucian humanist may be ultimately meaningless.

CONFUCIAN REVIVALISM

Jin Guantao's agenda of scientism forms but one of many responses that Chinese intellectuals made to the quest of the new era for a modern ideology that can replace the defunct unifying power that Maoism-Marxism once provided. But in post-Mao China, the advocacy of scientific rationality always risks the danger of being compromised by its opposite—substantive reason embedded in traditional ethics and *xuanxue* (metaphysics). I have shown how Jin Guantao's future-oriented time-consciousness paradoxically provided him privileged access to the premodern myth of totality and harmony. At the same moment that he propagated instrumental reason with the deepest conviction, his future-oriented gaze became ambiguously, albeit involuntarily, entangled in the imaginative reconstruction of an ethical totality borrowed from the idealized past of communal canons. The *qigong* phenomenon exemplifies the same paradox at work. Although its supreme masters such as Yan Xin never ceased to emphasize the scientific foundation for the art on lecture tours in the West, the quick spread of the "art of material energy" among every social stratum throughout the 1980s was hardly the result of the blossoming of a nationwide interest in scientific knowledge. On the contrary, the Yan Xin cult owed its popular appeal to the superstitious belief that common folk invested in the magic healing potency of *qigong* and to their remembrance of a past populated by legends of Haideng the High Priest, ancient swordsmen and boxers, and various other miracle workers and Daoist shamans.[37]

The danger of a relapse into the backward gaze reflects the epochal (un)consciousness of the historical bondage of tradition within which even the most revolutionary feats of modernity are embedded. It also serves to indicate that it is probably cultural ideology, rather than modern science, that stands a better chance of filling in the ideological gaps left by Maoism-Marxism. Surely toward the end of 1986, the term "culture" replaced that of "science" as the password for the Cultural Discussion. The revival of neo-Confucianism (*ruxue fuxing*) can thus be taken as a response that the CCP and cultural conservatives made to the epochal demands of Deng's China for a substitute utopian vision in the face of Marxist ideological disintegration. Proudly presented in competition with the technocratic notion of rationality was this historicist view of substantive reason incarnated in traditional ethics.

Although Jin Guantao and the neo-Confucianists never carried on a nominal debate over the efficacy of scientific rationality versus substantive reason in their respective confrontation of the challenge posed by Chinese modernity, the oppositional agenda between the two parties evokes the ghost of the May Fourth debate of "science versus metaphysics" (*kexue yu xuanxue*) in 1923.[38] Nonetheless, most intellectuals such as Gan Yang and Su Xiaokang insisted that the major themes of the Cultural Discussion revealed a qualitative departure from, rather than a simple rehash of, the old May Fourth problematics.[39] One such qualitative difference can be detected in the neo-Confucianists' heightened awareness that the new cultural renaissance that they called for should not be defined as a simplistic revivalism, but rather as a dual, simultaneous movement of modernity's critique of tradition and tradition's critique of modernity.

However, the theoretical proposal about modernity's critique of tradition—which amounts to a self-critique of tradition—should not be taken at face value. Advocates of the "neo-Confucianism of the third stage" were obviously more concerned with the capacity of tradition to withstand the furious pace of modernity and all the problems that would accompany it.[40] Although Tu Weiming insisted that a neo-Confucian renaissance is based on the concept of "creative transformation" rather than equated with a conservative return to the Great Learning, the neo-Confucianists did not adequately address the intriguing theoretical question of how one can critique but at the same time inherit tradition.[41] On the other hand, tradition's critique of modernity cannot be genuinely executed either. With the rise of the myth of "Four Asian Dragons," the 1980s saw the possibility of collaboration rather than confrontation between the two seemingly antithetical terms of tradition and modernity. Overseas neo-Confucian scholars like Tu Weiming and Yu Yingshi played an important role in driving home the dramatic message. Their ideological interventions from abroad strengthened the belief that Confucian tradition not only does not jeopardize, but on the contrary, facilitates the modernization process. Tu cited examples of Taiwan, Singapore, and other prosperous East Asian countries, and Yu traced the positive influence of Confucian culture on mercantilism back to the Ming and Qing period.[42] The timely entry into the Cultural Discussion of

overseas discourses on neo-Confucianism helped shape the central thesis of the Chinese debate over traditional culture and modernization. The
thesis that both Tu and Yu foregrounded derived its ultimate reference
from Max Weber's theoretical framework laid out in *The Protestant
Ethic and the Spirit of Capitalism:* Can Confucianism be creatively transformed into a new ethos and ethics that could serve as the ideological
foundation for Chinese modernization?

The implicit reference to Weber was well taken in China because it
corresponded to the series of Weberian inquiries that Chinese intellectuals themselves had undertaken even before the "Weber fever" reached
its peak toward the second half of 1986 with the appearance of the Chinese translation of *The Protestant Ethic.* If, as Weber implied, modern
Western capitalism is supported by the spiritual culture of Protestantism
(characterized as a model of rationality based on a synthetic vision of
"other-worldly" quest and "inner-worldly asceticism"), then did not the
successful experiment of East Asian countries with capitalism indicate
that neo-Confucianism can serve East Asia as Protestantism served the
modern West? The Tu-Yu proposition about the compatibility of Confucian culture with an East Asian modernity provided neo-Confucian
advocates at home enough ammunition to combat the school of total
westernization (*quanpan xihua*), whose message was powerfully delivered in the iconoclastic voice of *Heshang.*

Mainland Chinese cultural critics were indeed fascinated with the
prospect of cultural self-positioning that neo-Confucianism promised.
It is exactly this "articulation of native culture into a capitalist narrative," as Arif Dirlik argues, that made the East-Asian Confucian revival
at home possible in the first place.[43] Such a pan-East-Asianism ("Confucian thought is the symbol of Eastern culture") gave rise to speculations that "Confucius not only belongs to China, he also belongs to
the entire world."[44] The possibility that Confucian thinking may transcend temporal, spatial, ethnic, and geographical boundaries invigo-
rated many Chinese Marxists who were willing to talk about the "complementality" as well as contradiction between socialist modernization
and Confucian ideology.[45]

Although Chinese Marxists talked much about how the positive elements of Confucian ethics—especially its emphasis on patriotic values
and intellectuals' *youhuan yishi* (anxiety and crisis consciousness)—can
benefit the socialist campaign of the reconstruction of spiritual civilization, they were much more engrossed in exploring the collaborative, or
complicitous, relationship between the Master's philosophy and the

mode of production, capitalist or socialist. It is the vision marked by the profitable co-optation of tradition by modernity—Confucianism serving the interests of socialism and capitalism—that characterized the contemporary Confucian renaissance first and foremost as a movement traversed by materialist motifs that placed high stakes on the solidarity between tradition and modernity. The constellation of the past in relation to the present during the 1980s has thus undergone a specific change from the May Fourth period, whose historical experience was confined within the antagonistic configuration between these two terms.

The task of mapping out the strategic position of Confucianism in the discourse of Chinese modernity subverts the bipolar oppositional formulae prevalent during the May Fourth period: *zhongxi zhi zheng* (China versus the West) and tradition versus modernity. On the one hand, arguing against what Weber proclaimed in *The Religion of China: Confucianism and Taoism,* Chinese Confucianists were eager to demonstrate that just like Western Protestantism, "neo-Confucianism could not only adapt but also pander to the spirit of capitalism."[46] From this view, Confucianism is no less susceptible to instrumental reason and materialistic motivation on which capitalism is based than capitalism itself. And yet on the other hand, Confucian tradition was originally evoked as an antidote to the Western model of modernity. Whether Confucianism liberates or colludes with modernity is an issue that none of its advocates or even its opponents are ready to confront. Liang Qichao, Zhang Taiyan, and all those genuine defenders of Confucianism in the early twentieth century would certainly toss and turn in their graves if they suspected that the so-called modernization of Confucianism (*ruxue xiandai hua*) might lead to its ideological alliance with materialism and a modernity that gains ascendancy over the utopian past appropriated for the pure interests of the present.

Although the validity of the East Asian model remains to be seen, the theoretical possibility for the alliance between Confucianism and capitalism, or in Weberian terms, the potential collapse of substantive reason into instrumental reason, emerged as a phenomenon no less scandalous than the (reverse) co-optation of science by Confucian ethics in Jin Guantao's system of thought.

The internal drive for self-negation within the ideological realms of scientism and neo-Confucianism does not simply tell us about the contradiction of the zeitgeist of the 1980s. It also indicates that those who made claims to the purity of either position failed to capture the essentially ambiguous makeup of contemporary Chinese culture and society.

The internal development of science and morality, of efficacy and truth value, bears effects of domination as well as of emancipation. It is precisely the recognition of the ambiguity of the modernization process—progressive and atavistic at the same time—rather than the identification of a single unambiguous model, that needs to be foregrounded in our discussion of the agenda of Chinese modernity.

If such ambiguity escaped the advocates of neo-Confucian revivalism, the CCP was even less equipped to deal with it. This is not to suggest that the Party was short of ambivalence in its reevaluation of Confucianism. The long process of the rehabilitation of Confucius in post-Mao China could be traced back to 1978 when the first symposium on the studies of Confucianism was held at Shandong University. A consensus was reached among Marxist ideologues in the succeeding years that the era of Confucius-bashing (*fan Kong*) was as passé as the eras that turned Confucianism into a cult (*zun Kong*).[47] During the first half of the 1980s, it indeed looked as if the Party was interested in nothing but a serious academic reappraisal of Confucianism, for whom the issue of critique was as crucial as that of heritage. However, the ambiguous tone of the reappraisal underwent a subtle change as the indigenous project slowly evolved into an international one from 1987 onward.[48] All of a sudden, China's participation in the multinational agenda of the "Greater East Asia" overtook the simple local program of the cultural critique of traditionalism. The Party's agenda to endorse and to a certain extent initiate the reevaluations of neo-Confucianism during the Cultural Discussion was undoubtedly in part accounted for by its unambivalent sinocentric position, which showed little reluctance to sanctify an indigenous ideology as the single most efficacious model against the infiltration of foreign symbols (the list of which includes science, materialism, irrationality, and individualism à la mode).

What I wish to problematize, however, is not the Janus face of the postcolonial formula of East Asian Confucianized capitalism—its underlying impulse for self-empowerment and domination coexisting with an emancipatory capacity that frees the local from the hegemony of Western modernity. What I wish to lay bare is China's internal cultural politics that accompanied neo-Confucian revivalism, a politics that, unlike what the pan-East-Asian collaborative project implies, is unambiguously domineering without much liberatory potential. From beneath the camouflage of a seemingly innocuous cultural program (indigenous versus Western values) emerged a powerful hidden agenda only a politically disenfranchised Party apparatus would embrace with enthusiasm. What the

Confucian revival reinscribed was the hierarchy of social structure consolidated first by the absolute subjugation of the subjects to the Emperor, which reinforced the Party's mandate. The reinvention of the truth value of the collective (this time not a politically defined collective, but an ethical one) served as the regime's preemptive attack on the "poisonous blossoms" unfolded in the name of the individual.

The official support for neo-Confucianism should surprise no one. In October 1986, a national meeting on the future development of Chinese philosophy was convened by the official organ that laid out China's Seven Five-Year Plans for the disciplinary promotion of philosophy and the social sciences. Resolutions passed during the seven-day conference focused on the launching of a national project on the "Studies on Modern Neo-Confucian Thoughts." The two principal investigators of the project, Fang Keli, a professor in the philosophy department of Nankai University, and Li Jinquan, a professor at Zhongshan University, announced that the project would involve the collaboration of forty-seven specialists from sixteen research institutes over a period of ten years. In a follow-up meeting held at Xuanzhou of Anhui Province in September 1987, the research team decided to focus their studies on ten neo-Confucian masters: Xiong Shili, Liang Shuming, Feng Zhiyou, He Lin, Zhang Junli (the first generation); and Qian Mu, Fang Dongmei, Tang Junyi, Xu Fuguan, and Mou Zongsan (the second generation).[49] Although it is still too early to predict whether the mega-project will succeed in building a theoretical bridge between Marxism and neo-Confucianism, the official search for the dialogue between these two rival ideologies is certainly much more ominous than Tu Weiming is willing to admit. That the CCP "could better cherish the challenge posed by neo-Confucianism than by the advocates of Westernization" was not merely due, as Tu claims, to the fact that orthodox Marxist-Leninists were more sensitive to issues of ideology and moral values.[50] What was truly at stake was the self-interest of the Party in the face of the challenge of bourgeois liberalism. The complex issue of the legitimation crisis of Maoism-Marxism-Leninism that Tu mentioned but bypassed immediately should be subject to more rigorous examination if one is to fully comprehend the CCP's political motivation for endorsing the neo-Confucian revival.

Such an inquiry may in fact require more than mere critical insight, with which Tu Weiming is equipped aplenty. Perhaps it was mainland intellectuals' personal experiences during the Cultural Revolution that enabled them to suspect what Tu could not: The historical continuity of

Confucianism to Chinese Marxism. It was none other than memories of the ideological collusion between the two that prompted mainland critic Yang Binzhang to retort both to overseas Chinese scholars' complacent promotion of neo-Confucianism in mainland China and to the Party's suspicious involvement in Confucian revivalism.[51]

As outlined earlier in this chapter, the Party's collaboration with traditionalists took various guises. It endorsed the establishment of the Academy of Chinese Culture—the bulwark of neo-Confucianists—and supported the series of workshops that the academy sponsored. The presidency of the Association of Confucian Studies was given to Gu Mu, the vice-premier of the State Department. And the various discussion sessions entitled "Strategies of Cultural Development" held in Shanghai and Guangzhou throughout 1986 were all activities administered by the reformers' quarter within the Party.

The CCP's alliance with neo-Confucianism appears even more problematic if one recalls that the CCP was the main organ that stipulated and carried out various modernization programs. The contradictory strategies that the Party adopted—that it could declare allegiance with tradition (the site for substantive reason) and modernity (the site for instrumental reason) simultaneously—reveal not only the nature of the expedient measures required for its political survival, but more importantly, suggest that tradition is by no means immune to the regimen of instrumental reason whenever it plays into the hands of political authorities. That is to say, if Confucianism itself is susceptible to instrumental rationality, the Party should experience little ideological inconsistency in courting its partnership.

As the other party of this pragmatic union, neo-Confucianists had less to gain. The potential and actual co-optation of Confucianism by Marxism only accelerated the process of the delegitimization of the former. Those who vowed against Marxism inevitably found Confucianism guilty as well. The intense aversion to tradition voiced in *Heshang* should not simply be seen as a scapegoating attempt by its scriptwriters to deflect attention from the real target, the communist system. On the contrary, tradition was condemned precisely because Su Xiaokang unconsciously recognized its collusion with the system itself, despite the fact that his later self-critique told us a different story.

On the whole, Chinese Marxist critics made no secret that they undertook the reevaluation of neo-Confucianism not on its own terms but from the Marxian perspective. Whereas they had no qualms in discussing the interrelationship between Confucian ethics and modernization, they rejected the notion of Confucianized capitalism as a typical idealist mode of thinking. All good orthodox Marxists would insist that it is base structure rather than superstructure that should be taken as the last instance of determination. Furthermore, as their own project of co-opting Confucianism is well under way, Chinese Marxist scholars are not oblivious to the hidden agenda of neo-Confucianism (especially its overseas advocates), whose primary goal, they proclaim, is to "assimilate and dissolve" Marxism.[52] The optimistic talk between Marxists and neo-Confucianists about the search for common ground can therefore only deceive those who imagine that idealism can wed materialism and live happily ever after.

The complex relationship between Marxism and Confucianism in the 1980s taught us that the unpopularity of Confucianism among the younger generation of mainland intellectual circles was a phenomenon that did not always have anything to do with the vice and virtue of Confucian culture. Unless we examine the shifting relationships between tradition, modernization, and Chinese Marxism—their immanent antagonisms, compromising impulses, mutual attractions, and contingent accommodations—we will be unable to glimpse the complicity of power with knowledge in the seemingly antihegemonic discourse of the Cultural Discussion. Although 1985 was consecrated as the "methodology year," it was after all not a decade cleansed of ideology. The ebb and flow of methodological fever was hardly politically innocent. Nor could one assume that all the discourses produced during the Discussion were "unofficial" or even "antiofficial." The Party might not be the most eye-catching player in Culture Fever. And yet it certainly participated actively in unleashing certain discourses (such as the discourse of modern consciousness that I discuss in chapter four) while co-authoring others (such as neo-Confucianism).

In calling for a more honest reassessment of the role that the Party played in the Cultural Discussion, I wish to caution those (post-June Fourth exiles in particular) who blew out of proportion the antiestablishment mentality and the utopian character of the Discussion. In their view, the mid-1980s witnessed the confrontation and struggle between two diametrically opposed discourses: The "new civilian culture [minjian wenhua] oriented toward human rights, democracy, pluralism, and open-mindedness" and the "old official culture [guanfang wenhua] oriented toward authoritarianism, closed-mindedness, conservatism, and inhumanness."[53] In this imaginary map of bipolar opposition, Culture Fever emerged as the contemporary counterpart of the May Fourth

Movement. It was seen as a dramatic trigger that opened up an iconoclastic space for anti-Marxist critics to generate discourses *outside* the
power structure of the Party.[54] The thought that the Party could have
taken part in a movement that prized itself for emancipating the mind
was probably too sacrilegious for an elite who had always envisioned
themselves as an uncompromising oppositional force in modern and contemporary China.

Confucianism and Rationality   Having configured the intricate relationship between power and knowledge to which Confucian revivalism
inevitably gave rise, I now turn to the content issue: which aspects
of neo-Confucianism are considered dregs (*zaopo*) that obstruct the
project of modernity, and which aspect is identified as its quintessence
(*jinghua*) that comes to modernity's rescue?[55]

It is important to note, first of all, that both the advocates and critics
of the neo-Confucian school welcomed, and sometimes even solicited,
the constructive criticism that exposed the retrogressive elements inherent in neo-Confucianism. The primary target of such relentless critiques
is the philosophy's infamous liaison with an instrumental rationality that
consolidated authoritarian regimes throughout imperial Chinese history.
Given that an ultrastable political culture in premodern China was a
casualty of the domination of Confucian statecraft, many scholars claimed
that the repercussions of such a cultural heritage led to the malfunc-
tioning of modern society as well. Nobody, especially the Party reformers, failed to notice—in the fine print at least—how the seamless
structure of feudal bureaucracy obstructed the progress of China's
modernization. The extension of the hierarchical familial and social
structure to the workplace resulted in low efficiency and the continuation of the relations of production based on clan-centered consciousness—two nemeses holding in check the utilitarian functionalism on
which the Western definition of social modernity is based.

Any vigorous critique of Confucian hierarchy invites irrevocably a
reevaluation of the servile role accorded to the individual in the Confucian worldview. But once the subjugation of individual will and desire to the imperial and familial patriarch was identified as the real
site of contestation, the criticism of the functional inefficiency of neo-
Confucianism ran the risk of being turned into a defiant challenge to the
current regime, and indeed to any regime that gained its legitimacy from
the alleged mandate of the collective. The intimation of the tyranny

of the collective was a political land mine on which mainland anti-Confucianists had to dance with extreme trepidation.

Of course, whether neo-Confucian ethics obstructs or facilitates the East Asian narrative of capitalism is an intricate issue not easily resolved by either a wholesale condemnation of Confucianism or the theoretical hypothesis of Confucianized capitalism. A more levelheaded critic of neo-Confucianism in Deng's China aspires to a position between the extremes, recognizing the rational elements of Confucianism but critiquing its proponents' attempt to inflate the role that Confucian cultural philosophy played in modernizing East Asia.[56]

But whenever the issue of cultural subjectivity is foregrounded, those who hold the middle ground are tempted to give in to the proposition of the alternative modern. Much of my discussion in the previous section illustrates that the postcolonial politics of localism versus Eurocentrism has led prosperous East Asian countries (and their elite representatives) to the making of a contestatatory narrative of modernity. This East Asian discourse on modernity is based on the notion of a collectively oriented entrepreneurship and clan-centered ethics, which, according to its narrators, benefits instead of cripples productive relations in modern society.

Neo-Confucian advocates have repeatedly claimed that their philosophy provides sources of substantive rationality that can combat the adverse effects of a social modernity caught in extreme functionalism and antihumanist efficacy. Advocates of neo-Confucian revival share the Weberian conviction that moral and spiritual values play a constructive role in rectifying the fetishization of Western material culture.

At first sight, the fundamental recipe for the promotion of Confucian substantive rationality seemed to comprise a simple concoction of a plain and wholesome Confucian spiritual diet that was meant to neutralize the pungent flavors that modern Western values left on the palate of a modernizing China. A binary paradigm between two sets of opposing terms—Confucian and Western values—were thus set up. And there was no doubt that the first set of terms was privileged over the second. Thus collective wisdom was pitted against idiosyncratic genius, a harmonious coexistence with Nature against domination over Nature, a mechanism of well-regulated interpersonal relations against egocentric mores, communal rapprochement against alienation, human-centered worldview (*renben zhuyi*) against materialism, idealism against functionalism, reason against desire, and middle-of-the-road (*zhongyong*) mentality against extremist positioning. The simplistic structuralist principle at work here needs little explanation or elaborate criticism. Anyone who has overcome the human anxiety of classification and the structuralist impulse of polarization will perceive that those generalizing formulae hardly characterize fully or exhaust either Confucian or Western values.

The picture was further complicated by the potential reversibility of certain terms of substantive rationality into its opposite, instrumental reason. For instance, "collective wisdom" could undergo the process of instrumentalization and be turned into a tool serving an ultrastable sociopolitical and cultural structure. The collective almost always dictates homogeneity, marginalizes the particular, smothers difference, and views creativity with suspicion. The "mechanism of regulated human relationships" never fails to conjure up the image of a traditional extended family preying on its individual members and the modern caricature of Maoist street committees prying into and controlling private lives in the name of harmonizing human relationships. "Human-centeredness" sounds especially suspicious since the term "humanity" is not only historically but also culturally specific. In the West it may mean celebration of individuality, rebellion against anything normative, or a leap to the primordial. In China, however, this breathtaking act of self-delimiting contradicts the true spirit of *renben*. Confucian human-centered epistemology rarely positions the self as a term in its own right. In fact, it may not be an exaggeration to say that the self is hardly aware of its own boundary because it is never differentiated from the whole in the first place. Furthermore, in its emphasis on moral principles, this kind of epistemology collapses into ethics. And when one considers how such ethical constraints contributed to the maintenance of the functional coherence of power both in imperial and modern times, one wonders how it can claim its unequivocal superiority over Western materialism. After all, both *renben* ethics and materialism can yield deformed human beings, since the former may nurture totalitarian instinct, and the latter, reification. How could one cure the other, or to speak in the diction of instrumental reason, how can the instrument of the Sovereign Patriarch bring salvation to that of Mammon? This seems to be an issue that deserves serious scrutiny.

Finally, the notion of "golden mean" yields an excess of eclecticism that often guarantees the continuation of the status quo at the cost of daring conceptual revolutions. Eclecticism, in fact, predictably summarizes the gist of the main staple of modern and contemporary neo-Confucian revival, that is, the manifesto of *fanben kaixin* (returning to the source [Confucian ethics] and opening a new path [science and democracy]). The 1980s were a different time than 1958, when this manifesto was first launched by Mou Zongsan, Zhang Junli, Tang Junyi, and Xu Fuguan.[57] What appeared in 1958 as a revolutionary proposal of modernizing Confucianism looked in the eighties like just another variation of the clichéd formula of "Chinese substance and Western means" (*Zhongti xiyong*). There was no shortage of critiques of the cultural logic of blending from mainland Chinese Marxist critics, to whom the neo-Confucian Way that is "sagely within and kingly without" (*neisheng waiwang*)—the scenario of a Confucian moral culture wedded to Western pragmatism—is paradoxical at best. Many questioned the inner incentive and capacity of neo-Confucianism to invent a new modern democratic and scientific culture. The *minben* (for the people) orientation of the Confucian art of governance was demystified by many as characteristically Machiavellian, and the neo-Confucianists' effort to extract cognitive subjectivity from the ethical-moral subject (*liangzhi*) proved to be merely self-deceptive from the very beginning.[58] Bao Zunxin was most articulate in summarizing the representative position of Chinese anti-Confucian critique: "If the value system of tradition is not shattered, then [it] does not signify progress but eclecticism instead; it does not mean the expansion of new frontiers but conservatism, not physics but ethics."[59] All the criticisms exemplify once more the inner contradiction between the orthodox Marxian scientific worldview and a fundamentally idealist philosophy such as the "Learning of the Principle of Reason" (*lixue*)—the dominant trend of Song and Ming neo-Confucianism—upon which the contemporary neo-Confucian revival is based.[60]

Neo-Confucianism and Western Marxism   Disagreement between Marxism and neo-Confucianism may indeed lead us to renounce the hypothesis that the materialist and idealist standpoint can reach a common understanding about how to best define modernity. But the fantasy about the possible union of those two rival ideologies has just begun. In fact, the neo-Confucianists' critique of Western instrumental rationality raises the theoretical possibility of a neo-Confucian revisionism that is no less scandalous than the so-called Confucianized capitalism. If contemporary Confucian proponents had no qualms in forging a liaison with capitalism, one may argue that a diametrically different ideological collusion with Western Marxism is equally a plausible supposition that is worth exploring.

Although mainland scholars like Tang Yijie, Fang Keli, and their Marxist peers are interested in mapping out the conflux between dogmatic Marxism and Confucianism, the possibilities that Western Marxism has a lesson or two to teach both Chinese Confucianists and Chinese Marxists seems to have eclipsed their imagination. When asked why Chinese intellectuals did not seek any inspiration from Western Marxists, the formulaic response is the simple dismissal that "it is not very useful to us."[61]

Indeed, Herbert Marcuse's critique of the one-dimensional society of capitalism and Theodor Adorno and Max Horkheimer's denunciation of the paradox of the European Enlightenment have nearly canceled out every potential influence they could exercise on Chinese intellectuals, whether neo-Confucianists or Marxists. It is understandable that any critique of capitalism, and indeed, of modernity itself, should be unpalatable to a nation in a craze for modernization. In a similar manner, Adorno and Horkheimer's negative appraisal of the Enlightenment fails to appeal to an elite whose lament for the May Fourth Movement as an unfinished project of enlightenment seems to perpetuate itself indefinitely. Interestingly, yet not surprisingly, it was only through Erich Fromm—via Freud—and through the subject of psychoanalysis that the Frankfurt School left its feeble imprints on the psyche of Chinese intellectuals during the 1980s.[62]

Predictably, research on the Frankfurt School and Critical Theory in post-Mao China remained academically oriented.[63] Few studies were undertaken on the ideological implications of Adorno and Horkheimer's *Dialectic of Enlightenment* for the discussions of Chinese modernity. What escaped Chinese intellectuals' attention is not only the authors' critique of Occidental rationalism but also their totalizing criticism of the bondage of instrumental reason and domination, themes that nearly all of China's neo-Confucianists had touched upon in their efforts to promote the ultimate antidote—spiritual culture of the East.

The kindred spirit between Adorno, Horkheimer, and the contemporary neo-Confucian revivalists makes one wonder if the latter—especially neo-Confucianists on mainland China—could benefit from the former's critique of capitalism or learn from the Critical Theory's core arguments against instrumental reason something about their own critique of Western scientism and the Occidental mode of modernity. What strengthens the theoretical possibility of such a cross-fertilization between neo-Confucianism and Western Marxism is the close resemblance of the antidote that each party prescribes in its treatment of the alienating function of instrumental reason.

Horkheimer criticizes the rigid dualisms of spirit and nature, the ideal and the real, and speaks of the "critical spirit" as one that "prepare[s] in the intellectual realm the reconciliation of the two [namely, subjective and objective reason] in reality."[64] Both Adorno and Horkheimer are aware that substantive reason, although part of bourgeois enlightenment ideology, is nevertheless a humanizing factor. Inasmuch as they depict late capitalist culture as narcissistic—the subjective and the private leaving little space for the objective and the public—both Marxists sound like neo-Confucianists who complain about the banishment of the questions of communal values from the domain of rational thought. And to the extent that they condemn Western history as a process that starts from the self's renunciation of nature and community (everything that is antithetical to it) and concludes with the self's self-renunciation, they seem to yearn for the curative magic of all those good old Confucian dictums such as *tianren heyi* (the unity of Heaven and [hu]man), *liyong housheng* (utilizing resources and enriching the lives of the people), and *wanwu yiti* (myriads of phenomena in One Being).

Speculations about such ideological affinities notwithstanding, a radical critique of reason in Adorno and Horkheimer's fashion risks alienating the neo-Confucianists for one good reason. We only need to follow the history of counter-Enlightenment in the West—from Nietzsche to Derrida via Heidegger and from Nietzsche to Foucault via Bataille—to understand that a radical critique of reason inevitably leads to the critique of the sovereign rational subject and, by extension, to a frontal attack on the whole tradition of humanism itself. What is at stake is the entire value system of the conscious (as opposed to the unconscious), the conceptual (as opposed to the preconceptual or nonconceptual), the rational (as opposed to the irrational), the moral subject (as opposed to the decentered body of desire), and fusion (as opposed to diremption). It is easy to comprehend why Chinese neo-Confucianists and virtually all the Chinese advocates of modernity were not prepared to join forces with the progenitors of Western post- or anti-Enlightenment philosophy.

What this entails is that the Chinese ad-lib response to the Frankfurt School, "it is not useful," tells only half of the story. It tells us what Chinese neo-Confucianists chose to negate in Western Marxism: the whole package of antihumanist and anti-enlightenment ideology. By perpetuating the habit of instinctually evaluating the intellectual goods delivered to their door, Chinese cultural elite neither fully grasp the risks if they purchase the goods nor understand in advance what is at stake if they reject them. Decisions always have to be made in a haste. And the turnovers of ideas are so speedy that the intellectual market of Deng's China in the late 1980s was already buying the fantasies about the "late-capitalist" cultural logic of Chinese postmodernism.

My purpose in undertaking this brief analysis of the possible dialogues between neo-Confucianists and the two representative figures of the Frankfurt School is to pose the question, What is at stake if the former renounces the latter as an unusable commodity? Although in the course of formulating this question, I have already speculated about possible answers, I wish to recapitulate the crux of the problematic: What is at stake is the eventual failure of the neo-Confucianists and their official patron, the CCP, to truly understand the ambiguities of the rationalization and modernization process that China is going through at this historical moment. Their alliance, pronounced in the first case, and unpronounced in the second, with capitalism further deepens the conceptual fallacy that they can pay any price demanded by the economic progress that comes with modernization. The June Fourth tragedy is one dramatic ransom paid in one installment. There are other smaller dues to be collected. Ecological imbalance and environmental problems are certainly on the list, as are a few classic capitalist evils such as sharpened class conflicts, the return of prostitution, and alienation not of the socialist kind, but of a brand that *Harper's* deemed marketable. Appearing in the magazine were translations of slogans on the "cultural T-shirts" that Chinese urban youths loved to wear before they were banned in June 1991: "Depleted," "There is no tomorrow—get drunk today," "I'm terribly depressed! Keep away from me!" "Life is meaningless," and the climactic narrative, "I don't have the guts to be a smuggler, I don't have the capital to be an entrepreneur, I don't have the cunning to be an official. I mess around, I break my rice bowl, I am nothing."[65] How neo-Confucianism can bring relief to such social dislocations while planning for a merger with capitalism is both a paradox and an impasse that the neo-Confucianists should examine in their own critical discourse.

AT THE MARGIN: THE ENLIGHTENMENT SCHOOL
AND THE HERMENEUTIC EXPERIMENT

The neo-Confucian revival ushered onto the central stage of the Cultural Discussion a time-consciousness in which the present can no longer define itself by posing against the past. The neo-Confucianists have reiterated that only through the remembrance of tradition can Chinese modernity be rescued from colonization by the Western model. This is a culturalist position grounded in the perspective of historical continuity rather than in the fantasy of making a leap into the future from a zero-degree present, a position held by radicals like Liu Xiaobo.[66] Neo-Confucianists were not the only participants in the Cultural Discussion who stressed the inner drive within tradition to perpetuate itself in continuous self-rejuvenation. In this section, we shall take a look at two of the marginal, albeit infinitely suggestive, discourses that explore the theme of the diachronic relationship of tradition to modernity from epistemological standpoints markedly different from neo-Confucianism: the *qimeng* (enlightenment) philosophy and the hermeneutic school of thought.[67]

The Qimeng *School*   The *qimeng* school, whose advocates included Xiao Shafu, Feng Tianyu, and Shen Shanhong, did not simply present a retrospective show of tradition like the neo-Confucianists. Tradition, in their view, had a serpentine course of its own, untamed and collusive. The *qimeng* philosophies revisited those historical crossroads where tradition encountered modernity. One such crossroad—the late Ming and early Qing dynasty, from the reign of Shenzong Emperor (1573–1620) of Ming dynasty to Kanxi Emperor (1662–1723) of Qing—was highlighted by Xiao Shafu, Feng Tianyu, and Shen Shanhong as the beginning of the Chinese enlightenment tradition from which they claimed that the May Fourth iconoclastic thinking originated.

Under the heavy influence of the Western paradigm that attributed the birth of critical reason (the Age of the Enlightenment was known as the Age of Reason) to advanced materialist culture, the *qimeng* school advocates were eager to demonstrate that the material condition of China in the late sixteenth century was already ripe for the rational critique of superstition, transcendental thought, and the ancien régime in whose terms tradition was usually defined. What they presented was a bustling picture of Southeast China under the sway of a burgeoning capitalist mode of production at the turn of the seventeenth century, a picture still contested among social and intellectual historians.[68] This was the period, Feng Tianyu and Xiao Shafu proclaimed, that Chinese intellectuals first practiced the rationalist critique of the idealism of the Song-Ming neo-Confucianism.[69] And, thanks to the quick development of printing techniques and other means of disseminating knowledge,

these intellectuals founded the "learning of practice" (*shixue*) that
stressed "objective investigation over subjective speculation" and "concrete evidence over empty talks."[70] The origin of Chinese enlightenment
and cultural modernity, Feng and Xiao contended, should therefore be
pushed back from the May Fourth period (a period intimately connected in the popular memory with foreign imperialism) to the late sixteenth and early seventeenth century. Accompanying this revisionist attempt to relocate the genesis of Chinese modernity, a long list of China's
earliest "enlightenment philosophers" was introduced and scrutinized
rigorously: Gu Yanwu, Huang Zongxi, Wang Fuzhi, Fang Yizhi, Xu
Guangqi, Mei Wending, and Tang Zhen.

The enlightenment school derived its nomenclature from the revalorization of the notion of *qimeng*. However, in contrast to those who
defined the May Fourth Movement as first and foremost an aborted enlightenment movement engendered by the confrontation between Chinese and Western culture, the school formulated a hypothesis that the
seeds of enlightenment were already sown *within* the Chinese virgin soil
long before the imperialists' forced entry and that they could trace the
historical continuity of the *qimeng* motif throughout the late imperial
history all the way to May Fourth. Modernity was understood as a self-
generated, albeit crisis-ridden process already incorporated within a premodern Chinese history that was marked by sudden critical branchings
from tradition into unpredictable destinations. For cultural critics, locating such branchings amounts to the sharpening of their consciousness
of the moments of "missed decisions and neglected interventions."[71] A
look backward to the treacherous paths of China's past where perilous
conditions of possibilities converged and then dissolved by chance presented an alluring invitation to those who were eager to prove that
China can make its own modernity on its own terms.

To understand why Xiao Shafu, Feng Tianyu, and their colleagues felt
compelled to recover an indigenous discourse of enlightenment, we need
to look into the enlightenment complex from which Chinese elite have
suffered since the May Fourth period. Underlying this complex is their
unquestioned premise that enlightenment serves as the primary catalyst
for the making of the modern and their uncomfortable recognition that
the *qimeng* model prevalent during the 1920s was fundamentally an imported conceptual category. That a Western model of enlightenment
could yield only a colonial modernity in China was a theoretical predica-
ment from which nationalistic Chinese intellectuals would fain extricate
themselves. The long quest into China's historical past for seeds of en-

lightenment was therefore an indispensable task for those whose hidden agenda was to tame the hegemonic Western discourse of enlightenment. Anyone familiar with the cultural politics of localism could predict the ultimate conclusion reached by the *qimeng* school: Modern China's search for sociocultural modernity was internally motivated and had a history and model of its own.

Paradoxically, the advocates of the *qimeng* school could only take leave of the Western masters in theory. In practice, it was science and democracy—the two familiar markers of Western Enlightenment—that guided their search for those early landmarks of modernity in premodern Chinese discourse. Thus they claimed to have rediscovered an embryonic democratic consciousness (*minzhu zhuyi yishi*) in late Ming and early Qing thinkers as well as a burgeoning scientific spirit illustrated in the two epochal dictums *hewu jiuli* (investigating materials to look into their principles) and Gu Yanwu's *jingshi zhiyong* (governing the world for practical purposes).

To compound this dilemma of reinventing Chinese history in Western epistemological terms, the school confronted an even more daunting technical problem in that they tried to regain access to the subversive voices within a history dominated by Confucian orthodoxy. Contemporary *qimeng* advocates were of course no poststructuralists trained to track down gaps, absences, lapses, and ellipses in a given text. They were unaware of the problem that no matter how hard one tries to extricate the seditious moments from a predominantly hegemonic discourse, the two remain overlapping and curiously interdependent territories. The treasure hunt for moments of enlightenment in the late Ming and early Qing texts ended up privileging certain fleeting phases of modernity spotted in both personal and historical contexts. What was retrieved was a long list of discrete points of connection and correspondence—ranging from Gu Yanwu to Liang Qichao and Zhang Taiyan—that told us little about the paradoxical landscape of local resistance where nascent antitraditional forces emerged and then receded in cases such as Liang Qichao (1873–1929) or where they coexisted with old cultural canons in cases such as Fang Yizhi (1611–1671), whose half-scientist profile merged into his Confucian, Daoist, and Buddhist triple personae.[72]

Nor did such a list succeed in answering questions about the larger historical processes that assimilated or rationalized subversive discourses. The fact that modern historians had access to those texts suggests that the texts had been co-opted by and incorporated into the canonical tradition at large. Should one not ask whether such discourses underwent a process of domestication? And to what extent? What was written off and rearticulated during such a process? Was there a built-in mechanism within each discourse that promised its survival and kept it from being outlawed from the historical archive? And what desensitizing measures need to be applied to them so that they serve as models of inspiration for the present-day enlightenment devotees? By the same token, the study of the texts' complicitous relations with that part of tradition that defeated the spirit of modernity would enable us to trace patterns of the historical vicious cycle that delivered visions of liberation only to dissipate them into the abyss.

If the *qimeng* advocates truly wished to learn from China's own history, they would be more interested in the collaborationist than the antagonist aspect of the early *qimeng* masters' relationship with tradition. Only then could they begin to understand that it was oftentimes the "enlightenment philosophers" (whether the early Qing or the May Fourth thinkers) who defeated themselves in the end. All were torn between two cultural personalities: one pushing them toward modernity, and the other pulling them right back into the recalcitrant hold of tradition. The dilemma of "fighting against tradition from the standpoint of tradition" characterized all Chinese enlightenment discourses.[73] The late Ming and early Qing masters were by no means immune. Seen in this context, China's premodern discourse of enlightenment calls for critical appraisal rather than premature applause.

My reservations about the *qimeng* school's idealization of those early thinkers notwithstanding, certain themes sketched out in the latter's writings are so strikingly innovative that they outstrip their own epochal consciousness and echo contemporary critical impulses. For instance, Wang Fuzhi (1619–1692) refuted the puritanical doctrine of Song-Ming neo-Confucianism—"Depositing the Way of Heaven [by] exterminating human desire"—by proclaiming the opposite: "The Way of Heaven and the desire of human beings share the same substance in form, but are [only] different in their content transformation" (*tianli renyu tongxing yiqing*).[74] In 1662, Wang's contemporary Huang Zongxi (1610–1695) published *Mingyi daifang lu* (Waiting for the dawn: A plan for the prince), a radical text made up of the critiques of authoritarianism and half-baked theories about civil rights.[75] Huang was also credited for spelling out that both industry (*gong*) and commerce (*shang*) were fundamental to the governing of the state.[76] Tang Zhen (1630–1704) went a step further than Huang Zongxi by preaching egalitarianism ("If myriads of things were made equal, then each would be able to find its own place") and calling all emperors since the Qin dynasty (221–207 B.C.) "bandits."[77] And then there were the earliest pioneers of Chinese science—Fang Yizhi, Xu Guangqi (d. 1633), and Mei Wending (d. 1721) whose relationship with *xixue* (Western learning) was sometimes characterized by total compliance and sometimes by critical selection.[78]

An indulgent look at this impressive catalogue may convince us that a budding empiricism paired with a slowly evolving civil rights (*minquan*) movement steered seventeenth-century China to the threshold of enlightenment. Didn't Liang Qichao compare Huang Zongxi's *Waiting for the Dawn* to Rousseau's *Du Contrat social* (1762) and congratulate Huang for anticipating the latter by a hundred years?[79]

Yet it remains uncertain how contemporary *qimeng* scholars might make best use of this catalogue to promote their own cause. Was the list construed by them as a discourse of modernity only after they subjugated it to a laborious process that filtered the moments of enlightenment from the premodern and darker moments of history? Or was nothing more than a neo-Confucian discourse disguised by a pseudonym? The first perspective suggests the school's dubious affiliation with the modernists' camp, whereas the latter perspective conjures up the possibility of the *qimeng* proponents' fruitful collaboration with the neo-Confucian revivalists: the catalogue of the rational minds of the Ming-Qing dynasty might be presented as the testimonials not of modernity, but rather, of neo-Confucian tradition that gave credence to its own capacity to produce progressive and enlightening elements within itself.

Most critics have adopted Guo Qiyong's position by distinguishing the *qimeng* school from their neo-Confucianist contemporaries. Tu Weiming, on the other hand, had the right instinct in proposing, however subtly, the potential fellowship between the Confucianism of the third stage and the followers of the school. He disagreed with Feng Tianyu and Xiao Shafu's argument that the Ming-Qing philosophers were critical of the negative capacity inherent in the Song-Ming neo-Confucianism in constricting the growth of elements of enlightenment. Instead, Tu insisted that the so-called enlightenment movement that unfolded in the late sixteenth century belonged to the Confucian tradition itself. It was a "categorical error," therefore, to crown the advocates of "the learning of practice" such as Huang Zongxi, Gu Yanwu, and Yan Yuan as anti-Confucian and stand them in an antagonistic relationship to the neo-Confucianists of the Song and Ming dynasty.[80]

Theoretically, both positions—whether we designate the *qimeng* school fellow travelers with modernists or neo-Confucianists—lead to problematical hypotheses. I have suggested how the school's attempt to discover what is modern about premodern China risks overglorifying the "enlightened" blossom without recognizing its deep entanglement in dense, poisonous weeds. The coexistence of these two domains (possibilities of enlightenment and lethargic forces within tradition) makes the proposition of separating the one from the other almost impossible. Tu Weiming was right to assert the collaborative aspect of the Ming-Qing philosophers and the Song-Ming neo-Confucianists, although a counterargument can be made that such collaboration should elicit suspicious frowns rather than applause, contrary to Tu's convictions. Thus the deadlock: To promote a model that is inseparable from the counterforces that compromised its efficacy can only deepen the syndrome of schizophrenia that disarmed the May Fourth modern intellectuals. Wasn't the seventeenth century model in this sense a precedent for, rather than a potential relief to, the aborted May Fourth enlightenment? As a result, any effort to retrieve the modernist raison d'être from the *qimeng* school cannot but sound problematic.

The collaborationist project between neo-Confucianism and the *qimeng* school invites its participants on a mind journey that is no less crisis-ridden than the separationist-modernist path discussed above. The danger this time is the ideological co-optation already at work in some of the *qimeng* discourses. Although the anti-imperialist discourse and the propagation of people's rights prevalent in Huang Zongxi's *Waiting for the Dawn* seems to deliver an image of the champion of modern democracy, the primary principle on which the work is based is derived from Mencius' view of *guimin* (valuing the people), a view deeply constrained within the overarching terms of monarchism.[81] This is not a people-centered political philosophy but rather a strategy aimed at ameliorating the contradictions between the ruler and ruled and, eventually, a utilitarian means of improving the efficacy of sovereign power. Huang's other proposals for the reform of the imperial system point to further conceptual limitations as he fails to extricate them from the traditionalist discourse of absolute monarchy. Tang Zhen's theory about *yangmin* (nurturing the people), a parallel concept to *guiming*, can also be traced to the influence of Mencius. In voicing his radical critique of dictatorship, he produces a major work on the art of learning and governance, *Qianshu* (Hidden writings), that includes chapters like "Zun Meng" (Paying homage to Mencius) and "Zong Meng" (Enshrining Mencius) that clearly reveal the Mencian heritage in which the making of a statesmanship *for* the people means the same as the polity *by* the people.

It is interesting to note that whereas some intellectual historians point to this ideological bonding between the early Qing masters and neo-Confucianism as an undesirable sign of constrained historical imagination, others such as Yu Yingshi foreground the bonding unapologetically.[82] A typical neo-Confucianist would argue that any contemporary school's lingering ideological affiliation with the neo-Confucian heritage is in fact an asset rather than a bond to be dissolved. Thus Yu took pains to demonstrate that Huang Zongxi's putative political radicalism reveals the reformist spirit that has always been part and parcel of the politico-pragmatic tradition within neo-Confucianism. The scholar-official's concern with the welfare of the people and with the art of governance is not something outside the Confucian discourse. The Marxist praxis is to revolutionize the world; the Confucian one, Yu reminded us, is to realign an imperfect world order. Following this line of argument, we have to reassess carefully the historical position of the Ming-Qing enlightenment philosophy: what does it mean that Huang Zongxi and his fellow travelers did not deliver a radical perspective of democratic revolution? Did they fail to follow through the enlightenment agenda? Or was their agenda from the very start a neo-Confucianist one—an agenda that never meant to reach beyond the mere task of readjustment and ritualistic censure of the regime? In other words, is their critical impulse a radical one that fell short of realizing itself, or a conventional one that delivers an exquisite performance of the "mainstream Chinese thinking"?[83]

The preference of the contemporary *qimeng* school is quite obvious. The catchword for the 1980s is certainly not "mainstream." They would rather accept the limitations that come with the first alternative than be stuck with a label that conveys the sense of a stagnant continuity rather than a turning point for change. In other words, they would like to present the early enlightenment discourses as overlooked interventions rather than as formulaic expressions of the status quo. The difficulty of taking this position, however, resides in the fact that as Xiao and Feng (each with his own ideological agenda) demonstrated, the Ming-Qing thinkers were deeply implicated in the traditionalist discourse. The crux of the matter is not whether one can ignore or rationalize the existence of such an ideological collusion, but how to expose it, and in the course of doing so, how to turn the liability of collusion into a critical instrument with which contemporary descendants of the *qimeng* philosophy can accomplish the following tasks in sequence: penetrating the paradox of Chinese enlightenment to its core, dissolving the twin poetics of *qimeng* and utopia, and in their place proposing a new kind of post-topian critical writing.[84]

The Hermeneutic Experiment: An Epistemological Turn toward Self-Positioning?   Perhaps no one is more persuasive than Gan Yang in demonstrating that the current program of neo-Confucian revival is a "pseudoproposition" and a humiliating gesture of traditionalists' "capitulation" to the demands of modernization.[85] Although he still has faith in the neo-Confucianists' efforts to recover substantive reason to rescue modernity from self-alienation, he believes it is "off the track" to relocate (or reinvent) instrumental rationality in neo-Confucianism (i.e., seeds of science and democracy) for the purpose of serving modernity.[86] He shares the Weberian conviction that modern society dictates the differentiation of value spheres. Hence the splitting off of both rationalities in opposite directions is a natural reality that neo-Confucianists simply failed to comprehend. The creative reappropriation of substantive rationality into an instrumentally rationalized society is a utopian perspective, which in his view does not work in modern Chinese society. His proposition is neither sentimental nor cynical: exterminate the link between the Hegelian dialectics of totality and neo-Confucianism, facilitate the bankruptcy of the Hegelian myth of totality (the happy historical fusion of instrumental and substantive reason), and allow the separate realms—the cultural, social, cognitive-instrumental, and aesthetic-moral—to coexist and prosper in their own terms.[87]

The question still remains: How should neo-Confucianism justify its raison d'être and reposition itself in a modern society? Gan Yang proclaims that the proper niche for neo-Confucianists is in the temple of academy, a pure elitist and idealist domain where they can make a total commitment to *Geisteswissenschaften* (the human sciences) rather than to sociopolitical reform. The reappointment of neo-Confucianists to the guardianship of the humanist tradition is an ideological strategy that Gan Yang designates as *wenhua baoshou zhuyi*, "the conservationism of culture."[88] Needless to say, although Gan Yang spells out quite clearly that the "culture" to be "safekept" and "guarded" by neo-Confucianists is *renwen chuantong* (the heritage of humane studies) as a whole rather than some mainstream Chinese, or more specifically, Confucian culture, his proposition about the "conservationism of culture" suffers various misinterpretations in the hands of both pro- and antitraditionalists. Ironically, a typical critique is to relegate him to the camp of cultural conservatives like the neo-Confucianists he himself has criticized rigorously.[89] Without investigating its meaning carefully, some of Gan's critics, including Tu Weiming, collapse the term "conservationism" easily into the modern concoction of *baoshou*, "conservatism."

What confounded Gan Yang's critics was the seeming contradiction between his radicalism (consider his well-known 1985 manifesto "breaking away from tradition is the best way of inheriting tradition") and his 1988 proposition about conservationism.[90] Very little has been said about Gan Yang's significant modification of Gadamer's hermeneutic vision in his earlier relentless critique of Confucian traditionalism.[91] One can well imagine that given his background in hermeneutic philosophy, Gan would be a natural advocate of conservationism from the very start. But in 1985, the persona he projected was characterized by an articulate defiance toward tradition. It was hardly surprising that for the first few years during the Cultural Discussion, those associated with the Committee of *Culture: China and the World,* of which he was the spiritual leader, were often mistakenly relegated to the school of "total westernization," a label they shared with unredeemed radicals like Liu Xiaobo for quite some time. Did Gan Yang go through an intellectual transfiguration between 1985 and 1988 in his approach to the notion of tradition? Or did his two agendas—radical discontinuity between tradition and modernity on the one hand, and conservationism on the other—merely coexist as two sides of the same coin?

Putting aside the thorny issue of Gan Yang's subtle transformation from an uncompromising radical to a radical conservationist, let us focus on the methodological position of his latter persona. First of all, the hermeneutic roots of Gan's conservationism seem obvious. His position privileges the notion of the fusion of horizons, an unmistakable proposition of hermeneutic epistemology. How to reinvent tradition from the standpoint of contemporaneity—a hermeneutic rewriting of "historical continuity"—carries the main burden of Gan Yang's cultural criticism. At the same time, we should recognize that Gan Yang was increasingly skeptical about the privileged vantage point of modernity. He raised the new strategy of fighting at both battle fronts (*liangmian zuozhan*), which dictated the double critique of modernity and tradition as central to the mission of cultural introspection undertaken by contemporary Chinese intellectuals.[92]

The major contribution Gan Yang made to the Cultural Discussion can be recapitulated as the substitution of a diachronic paradigm for a synchronic one. In discrediting the older terms of debate—*zhongxi zhi zheng* (China versus the West), a spatial configuration that dominated thought since the late Qing dynasty and drew the current Cultural Discussion deeper and deeper into a deadlock—Gan Yang foregrounded the antagonism between tradition and modernity and redefined the history of modern China since the late nineteenth century in terms of the battle between substantive and instrumental reason.[93]

The paradigm *gujin zhi zheng* (tradition versus modernity) entered the Cultural Discussion as an epistemologically revalorized binary.[94] To those who cast a suspicious look at the so-called new paradigm and wondered how one could differentiate it from its May Fourth precedent, Gan Yang made no better reply than a vague rejoinder that its contemporary form had collected more depth.[95] To give Gan Yang the benefit of the doubt, I will demonstrate, in Gan's spirit, the challenge that he posed to the various interpreters of Chinese modernity.

Gan's fundamental strategy is again metonymical. It is not "modern consciousness," he claims, but rather the concept of "tradition," that needs to be subject to a creative reappraisal. An invitation to reinterpret tradition predictably leads to its revalorization. During this adventure into the epistemological field opened up by hermeneutics, Gan Yang accidentally ends up pleasing traditionalists and orthodox Marxists, both of whom have a huge stake in enshrining the past—whether it is seen as a Confucianist or socialist past. His ultra-leftist critics and those traditionalists who claim to have found an ideological ally in him seem not to have noticed that the very notion of reinventing the past—opening a hermeneutical circle—is itself a modern ideology (and more specifically, a modern school of philosophy and literary criticism).

The ideas of Western hermeneutic phenomenology were first introduced to China through academia. In summer 1983, the Institute of Foreign Philosophy of Beijing University sponsored a series of lectures on "Post-Analytic Philosophy," which covered a long list of modern Western philosophers: Heidegger, Wittgenstein, Gadamer, Ricoeur, Derrida, and Richard Rorty. A conference on "Philosophy and Hermeneutics" was held in Shenzhen in 1987.[96] Gan Yang himself translated Ricoeur's *The Conflict of Interpretation*. Even without his formal acknowledgment of the influence of hermeneutic theory, his writings deliver more than a handful of its imprints:

> Tradition is something "that has not yet been prescribed." It is always in the process of making and creating. It forever unfolds to the "future" infinite possibilities or a "world of possibilities." Exactly because of this [nature], "tradition" can never be equated with things that "already existed in the past."[97]

> Facing "tradition," [every generation of us Chinese] should undertake a mission whose burden cannot be carried by the "past." This mission is to create that which was absent in the "past." (57)

> Specifically, the "tradition" that we understood is the sum total of the possibilities engendered by the endless encounters, confrontations, conflicts, and appropriations (the new homogenizes the old) that took place between the "past" and the "present." (60)

The hermeneutic dialogue of the present with the past delivers a holistic experience of temporality that does not single out serviceable inheritance and relegate the rest to historical amnesia. Gan Yang would agree with the *qimeng* school that the past is connected to the present by a chain of continual destiny from the Ming-Qing Confucian gentry all the way to the May Fourth iconoclasts. However, in contrast to the school's selective memory that recognizes only those so-called enlightened moments (the exemplary past) in history, Gan's hermeneutic remembrance of the past takes stock of its entire holdings, unsightly as well as exemplary. This epistemological reorientation is especially significant to the Chinese people whose nostalgia for the golden past coexists with their habit of blocking the bad memories that testify to the guilt and shame of their own history. Nostalgia is only a sham copy of genuine historical consciousness. The solidarity of the present with the past takes the form of onerous introspections rather than nostalgic celebration of the moments of fleeting glories.

The beneficial service of hermeneutics to the Cultural Discussion extends to the neo-Confucianists as well. The paradox of hermeneutic understanding should drive home a message that even the most savvy representatives of neo-Confucianism at present only vaguely perceive. Nearly all neo-Confucianists admit that modernity poses such a challenge to tradition that the latter has to be reinterpreted in order to serve the former better. What they are not prepared to accept is this paradox: The hermeneutic call of reinventing the past leads inevitably to the demythologizing of the past. The "objective" meaning in history can no longer be spoken of, for history cannot be known except through the subjectivity of the historian. Who is to "create that which was absent in the 'past'" but the interpreter who stands on the shifting ground of the here and now?

It is this issue of the subjectivity of the perceiving and interpreting subject that serves as the focal point of reference in the ideological agenda underlying Gan Yang's hermeneutic exercise. I want to emphasize that no intellectual game and no methodological fever in modern and contemporary China can ever claim ideological innocence. In Gan Yang's case, he is immune neither to the trap of the historical "anxiety consciousness" he himself has ridiculed nor to Chinese intellectuals' peren-

nial project of reconstructing the cultural China.[98] The issue at hand—
the cultural subjectivity of China—is unnamed in his critical exercises.
His surface text seems clear and simple: an interpretive reorientation that
attempts to bail the Chinese discourse out of the old spatial paradigm of
the local (*zhong*) versus the global (*xi*) and replace it with the temporal
paradigm of tradition versus modernity. Hermeneutics thus rescues Chinese critics who have been stuck for decades in the pseudo-binary of sinification versus westernization. And with that binary goes the conceptual
barrier that China is modernizing itself at the bidding of external ag-
gressors. Once this barrier is passed, the suggestion that China can revolutionize itself from within looms large. What else but the "confronta-
tions and conflicts" between tradition and modernity could trigger the
radical change that swept modern China? At this point, Gan Yang only
needs to valorize the paradigm of tradition versus modernity as part of
his overall hermeneutic project that grew out of the politics of resistance—a project that empowers an indigenous subject to write against
the colonial discourse that deprives the colonized of its agency to make
its own history. Yet Gan Yang does only half of the job. He foregrounds
the temporal paradigm without accompanying it with a parallel discourse that would lay bare his hidden twin agenda of resistance and subject formation.

I shall make an attempt to pick up where Gan Yang left off. To do so,
I propose to retrieve the ideological agenda underlying his hermeneutic
project in the following terms: Hermeneutics provides a timely epistemological revolution and serves as a methodological tool that could help
Chinese theorists rediscover the agency of change from within and redefine the terms of resistance as modernity versus tradition, thus de-
priving the West of its power to dictate the pace and agenda of China's
modernization and moving the entire arena from the global back to the
local subject again.

Gan Yang's unarticulated concern about cultural subjectivity finds its
various manifestations in several of his later projects, all of which are
characterized by his fervent search for an alternative modern, which in
the wake of the Tian'anmen crackdown is defined more and more in economic (reformative) rather than in cultural (revolutionary) terms.[99] Yet
whatever topics of inquiry Gan chooses, whether they are possibilities
of a "gradualist reform" or the model of "development without privatization,"[100] he reveals more poignantly than ever one of the unnamed
anxieties that plagued the participants of the Cultural Discussion: Does

China still remain a cultural subject of its own integrity after unlatching nearly all of its floodgates to Western methodologies? The issue of cultural subjectivity is an important one that deserves a chapter of its own. For the moment, I shall pursue the significance of the hermeneutic project only a bit further. The major task of tracing the mutation of the subject throughout the 1980s will be taken up in chapter five, "Romancing the Subject."

What needs to be examined in conjunction with the ideological agenda underlying Gan Yang's temporal paradigm of tradition versus modernity is the thorny issue of subject formation. Although Gan Yang's influence was mainly confined within academia, and more specifically within the Editorial Committee of *Culture: China and the World* (a group of young scholars from the Chinese Academy of the Social Sciences and students from Beijing University), his thoughts often reverberated in theoretical discourses that seem to move, however imperceptibly, toward a revitalized sinocentrism that is both antihegemonic and hegemonic at the same time.

One such reverberation occurs in Zhang Xudong's intriguing comment that "it is the natural-historical *langue* of Chinese society that is determining the cultural *parole* of any invading discourses [from the West]."[101] Utilizing the Saussurean paradigm of langue versus parole, Zhang turned the Western langue into the subordinate position of parole—an ingenious reversal of Joseph Levenson's earlier formula that privileges the West in its discursive power relationship with China. According to Zhang, the Chinese intellectuals are simply experimenting with various Western speech acts to articulate the Chinese grammar. China, instead of the West, reemerges as the crowning subject and the host of the linguistic game. We are, in other words, brought back to the supreme logic of the "Chinese experience." And what comes to mind but Mao Zedong's Chinese Marxism and the saga of the Taiping Heavenly (Christian) Kingdom (1850–1864)—two supreme examples of how China borrowed Western vocabulary merely to serve its own agenda and interests?

The emergence of the politics of subject formation is compelling in an era in which global capitalism homogenizes local space with both its material and discursive goods. It is imperative that the crisis of Chinese cultural identity should lead to resistance, and resistance to subject formation. What looks ominous, however, is not the discourse of autonomy that every project of self-formation is bound to emphasize. The moment of danger begins when such a project theorizes and wills its ultimate subjugation of the Other—the reversion of the once-dominant Western discourse into the subaltern position of mere parole. What this seemingly antihegemonic project manifests is the mere inversion of the Hegelian dialectic: that the slave can be empowered and turned into the image of the master. This is a dilemma that can best be captured in the imagery of a cycle. The politics of resistance dictates the construction of an empowered national and cultural subject, and the subject, once empowered, cannot but initate another project of hegemony. A new problematic emerges when we simply substitute the imperialist project with an ethnocentric project. Solving the double bind of the discourse of subject formation is a herculean task. And yet, cultivating a sharpened consciousness of this dilemma should be the most important responsibility of every enlightened Chinese critic who writes against Eurocentric hegemony with missionary passion. To identify—and to critique in turn—nostalgia for sinocentrism in one's own discourse is still a viable alternative to a simple reversal of Levenson's Eurocentric logic.

The subscription to nativist romanticization that Zhang Xudong's comment seems to constitute is something that the Chinese hermeneutic school has yet to reckon with. But for a long time, Gan Yan's influence was felt in a quite different realm via the Committee of *Culture: China and the World*. For many young scholars and students on university campuses, Gan's mentorship was delivered through his editorship of the two major translation series entitled "The Library of Modern Western Academic Learning" and "The Library of New Knowledge" that the committee put forth in quick succession in the mid-1980s. Both series introduce the Occidental tradition in a systematic way. The first series focuses on twentieth-century Western scholarship in philosophy, the social sciences, and the humanities, including Husserl, Heidegger, Sartre, Merleau-Ponty, Marcuse, Adorno, Habermas, Gadamar, Ricoeur, Foucault, Derrida, Rorty, Nietzsche, Cassier, Jung, Shaklosky, Eco, Todorov, Freud, Benedict, Weber, Mills, de Beauvoir, and Levenson. All contributed to the boom of ideas that led to the crowning of the mid-1980s as the years of methodology fever. To complement the first heavily theoretical series, the second series is made up of lighter fare in three different categories: biographies of masters in Western culture (Freud, Weber, and so on), influential "minor works" by Western writers such as Camus' *Le Mythe de Sisyphe* and M. Buber's *Ich und Du*, and foundation series in any branch of knowledge such as the Prentice-Hall Foundations of Philosophy Series.

Such an inventory seems to contradict the very principle that Gan Yang articulates in his hermeneutic project. The Chinese Hermes is preoccupied with Western, rather than indigenous or even East Asian tradition. One wonders how this overemphasis on Western academic learning qualifies, if not undercuts, his own project of subverting the old ideological configuration that privileges the "West" over the "East."

Perhaps Gan's tradition versus modernity paradigm is meant to be nothing more than an academic discourse (such was the fate that he prescribed later to the neo-Confucian discourse) that marginalizes itself knowingly.[102] Although the epistemological turn that hermeneutics introduced during the Cultural Discussion carries immense possibilities of revolutionizing a Chinese historical consciousness rooted firmly in the temporal past, it seems too much an elitist concoction to compete with other discourses that gained easier access to the public thanks to their idiomatic expression articulated in the common vocabulary of science (Jin Guantao) and ethics (neo-Confucianism). The notion of enlightenment (*qimeng*), an indigenous term that underwent a semantic transformation in the late Qing, had just acquired an aura of familiarity and made its way finally into the national psyche.[103] In this regard, the *qimeng* school stood a better chance of joining the mainstream culturalist platform than Gan Yang and his colleagues. *Jieshixue,* the newly coined Chinese equivalent for "hermeneutics," will have to wait longer to find its niche in the heartland of China.

But doesn't this expectation run counter to Gan Yang's own prescription for modern society? He has argued all along for the differentiation of the cultural from the social sphere. Perhaps, then, the most appropriate place for *jieshixue* is where it belongs now—the ivory tower at the margin of social discourse. Intriguingly, a passionate critic of elitism himself, Gan Yang has actively promoted the making of elitist discourse through his fervent involvement and investment in the Committee of *Culture: China and the World.* His contributions to the systematic introduction of Western thinking to post-Mao China are invaluable. One cannot help wondering whether the brilliant philosopher will be remembered primarily as a distributor of Western thought or as a practitioner of indigenous cultural politics in the era of "postcoloniality."

LI ZEHOU AND THE MARXIST RECONSTRUCTION OF CONFUCIANISM

Although no other critic in post-Mao China could compete with Li Zehou's influence on China's elite culture throughout the 1980s, Li's place in the Cultural Discussion was an ambiguous one. Pledging no

public allegiance to any of the schools mentioned above, he scandalized
neo-Confucianists with his famous proposition of *xiti zhongyong* (Western substance, Chinese application) and incensed young radicals with his
repudiation of their total rejection of Confucianism. In fact, at the 1993
American convention of the Association for Asian Studies, Li spoke critically of the modern neo-Confucianists' attempt to inherit the Song-Ming
tradition of moral metaphysics.[104] And yet his consistent espousal of such
Confucian principles as "practical rationality" (*shiyong lixing*) and the
unity of Heaven and (hu)man helps restore, in a self-contradictory fashion, the image of a Confucianist with whom Tu Weiming can claim alliance, and at whom an advocate of total westernization like Liu Xiaobo
lashes out in righteous anger.

    To further complicate his ideological makeup, Li Zehou presents him-
self as an orthodox Marxist who approaches Kant on two conflicting
epistemological grounds. On the one hand, he recognizes that Kant is
the true philosophical predecessor of Marx, for Kantianism prefigures
the materialist thesis of the irreducibility of being to thought; and yet on
the other hand, Li Zehou is eager to foreground the idealist framework
of Kantian epistemology (to examine the "subjective psychological structure of human subjectivity" in terms of the Kantian triple inquiry into
epistemology, ethics, and aesthetics) as a priori for the rejuvenation of
Chinese Marxism.[105]

    Li Zehou's double call for "constructing two civilizations" (the ma-
terial and spiritual civilization) is symptomatic of his accommodative
streak that always seeks to merge materialism and idealism in a continuum reminiscent of middle-of-the-road Confucian eclecticism.[106] Therefore, instead of valorizing Li Zehou's philosophy as a site of contestation, I suggest that we examine it as a site of conciliation where an
ongoing process of ideological negotiation among historical materialism, idealism, and Confucian rationalism takes shape. Bearing in mind
his penchant for the philosophy of the unity of Heaven and (hu)man, we
should anticipate that Li Zehou's theoretical practice faithfully enacts
the Confucianist instinct for reconciliation. The meeting of classical
Marxist with reformist Confucian ideology thus sets the moral tenor of
his philosophy of modernity.

    The ideological double identity underlying Li Zehou's vision for Chi-
nese modernity betrays moments of awkwardness and uncertainty whenever he fails to articulate which of the two ideologies, Confucianism or
Marxism, orchestrates the process of appropriation and prescribes its
final results. The making of such an ideological choice is bound to be

difficult for those who subscribe to the double identity in question. Li Zehou's agenda, however, is always marked by his concern to enlist neo-Confucianism's service to modernization without compromising his deep commitment to Marxism.

It is the pursuit of this agenda that leads Li Zehou to propagate many radical propositions central to the classical heritage of historical materialism. My use of "radical" here calls for explanation, since Li Zehou's subscription to Marxism has earned him the diametrically opposite title of "conservative" among the circle of young iconoclasts. In the anti-Marxist climate of post-Mao China, anyone bold enough to keep talking about how toolmaking, and by implication, how the mode of production rather than an abstract human nature, determines the course of history, inevitably invites the stigmatic label of conservatism. Little do Li's critics comprehend that because unreconstructed humanism now prevails in Deng's China as the new religion, it is those who dare to swim against the sentimental tide of humanism who truly deserve to be called radical. Whatever eulogies or criticisms should accompany our reading of Li Zehou, it is quite refreshing to see one human being challenge the humanist dogma of entitlements. It is a profound irony, especially for those of us who study China from a distance, to witness how Chinese intellectuals who suffered under the tyranny of the majority during the long revolutionary years fail to appreciate the ritualistic meaning of Li Zehou's defying the norm of the day.

A thorough review of Li Zehou's philosophy falls outside the main configuration of this chapter. What interests me here is how Li Zehou appropriates Confucianism as a Marxist and how ideological cooptation takes place in both directions. More often than not, tracing the ambivalent career of Li Zehou's Marxian Confucianism (or should I say, Confucian Marxism?) leads to the unraveling of the inner contradictions of such a project. For orthodox Confucianists, Li's revisit of their favorite conceptual categories such as Chinese substance and Western means, the unity of Heaven and (hu)man, and practical rationality signifies nothing less than an act of irreverence, inasmuch as he reactivates those categories for the purpose of serving the agenda of modernity rather than the declining indigenous tradition.

On the surface, Li Zehou's mission is no different from that of Chinese neo-Confucianists, since both parties are engaged in the task of reviving Confucian tradition for modernity's sake. The difference, however, lies in the mode of ideological retooling that takes place concomitantly with the act of reinterpreting the Confucian canon. Whereas neo-Confucianists revert to the Song-Ming *lixue* with its emphasis on moral cultivation as the locus of salvation to combat modernity's excess of instrumental reason, Li Zehou departs from such idealist babble about "sagehood" and "inner nature" by revalorizing the materialistic principle of the economic laws of historical development. It is his focus on dialectics, not metaphysics, on base structure, not superstructure, and on Engels' historical materialism, not the Frankfurt School Marxism, that distinctly differentiates his system of thought from any idealist school—neo-Confucianism included. It is hardly surprising that Li's materialist reinvention of Chinese categories should incorporate a trajectory of Marxian principles: the final instance of economic determination in *xiti zhongyong*, humanized nature in *renhua ziran*, and the concept of practice in *shiyong lixing*.

Xiti zhongyong: *Western Learning as Substance, Chinese Learning as Means*

> Today, we have to come up with a clear definition when we use the two categories *ti* (substance) and *yong* (application). I used the term "substance" differently from other people. It includes material and spiritual production. I emphasize time and again that the ontology of society is one and the same as the [material] being of society. If we interpret "substance" in terms of the [material] being of society, then it includes not only ideology, not simply some "isms," but also the mode of production of a society and the daily life [of its people]. Seen from the viewpoint of historical materialism, this is the real substance—the [concrete] mode of existence of human beings. What we meant by modernization is first and foremost the transformation of this "substance." In the process of this transformation, science and technology play a very important role. Science and technology are the cornerstones of the being of society because the development of the force of production that they trigger serves to motivate the changes of social reality and people's daily life.[107]

The quote illustrates how Li Zehou arrives at the radical conclusion that *ti* is the mode of production of society and the material condition of human life rather than a purely conceptual mode, political system, or the Confucian ethical hierarchy of three bonds and five relationships (*san'gang wulun*), interpretations derived from the idealist logic embedded in Zhang Zhidong's original concoction of *zhongti xiyong* (Chinese substance and Western means). Modernization understood in this new context means revolutionizing the premodern, feudal mode of production, characterized by Li as land-centered small peasants' economy, and replacing it with commodity-oriented economic production. Based on the assumption that scientific and technological revolution originated in the West, Li Zehou comes unexpectedly to the same conclusion espoused by advocates of total westernization: "Modernization means nothing other than westernization."[108] The radical implications of Li Zehou's reiteration of such an overquoted formula can hardly be appreciated if we identify his agenda for "westernization" as the same as that trumpeted by proponents of total westernization who embrace the liberalist vision. It is not the ideas of democracy and individualism, but the production of large modern industries that defines Li Zehou's conception of what the West stands for. By emphasizing the importance of modernizing China from the bottom up, Li reiterates the theoretical premise of orthodox Marxism—namely, the "ultimately determining instance" of base structure.

Li Zehou's materialist conception of history rang particularly true in the post-1989 era. The aborted utopianism at Tian'anmen Square taught one relentless lesson: that the course of history could not be changed by ideas alone. In the 1990s, it becomes more and more obvious that it is the economic rather than the ideological, political, or cultural that delimits the Chinese social imaginary. With the cultural elite pushed into the background and their project of enlightenment once more revoked by the Party hardliners, China has finally come down to earth in its pursuit of real, not symbolic capital. The decade of the 1980s that celebrated the conventional wisdom that "knowledge is wealth" is gone forever. The agenda of getting rich does not distinguish commoners from the elite but, on the contrary, privileges the former over the latter in the jungle where only the fittest survive. Thus since the late 1980s, even before the new decade dawned on the desecrated Tian'anmen Square, the search for alternative socioeconomic models in rural China has replaced the intangible cause of cultural renaissance as the problematic central to any discussion of Chinese modernity. Both at home and abroad, it is the emerging local socioeconomic roots rather than a uniform national policy, concrete models of rural enterprise rather than abstract economic paradigms, that form the central locus of any serious inquiry about the future of China's modernization. Now that economists and sociologists have reoriented their research and sought new models for rural and township economy by undertaking one case study after another (the Daqiuzhuang in Hebei, Fuyang in Anhui, and the Jinhua in Zhejiang model), it becomes clear that Gan Yang's formulation of *xiangtu Zhongguo* (Rural China) emerges as a more viable platform for Chinese social modernity than Tu Weiming's *wenhua Zhongguo* (Cultural China).[109] In the mid-1990s, Li Zehou's proposal of revolutionizing China's premodern mode of production sounds more timely, wholesome, and realizable than ever.

And yet as I mentioned earlier, Li Zehou is too much an advocate of fusion to be locked in a strictly materialist position for long. Although he subscribes to the vulgar Marxist theory of levels and gives more weight to the infrastructure in his proposition of Western substance and Chinese means, he cannot resist making sporadic references to Western "superstructure" (identified as "self-consciousness" or "ontological consciousness") and specifying it as an indispensable part of the "Western substance" that needs to be transplanted to China simultaneously with means of technological and material production.[110] The integration of such an idealist perspective into an otherwise materialist framework reveals apparent imprints of eclecticism. At times, it is difficult to tell if one doctrine really gains the upper hand over the other in this seemingly harmonious picture of ideological conjugation. A close examination of Li Zehou's works reveals, however, that he foregrounds the fundamental Marxist tenet of mechanistic causality even while he attempts to introduce the idealist problematics of human consciousness into the picture. Such a causal logic dictates that superstructure corresponds and responds to base structure and that the formal transformation of the latter would inevitably trigger a concurrent or subsequent transfiguration of the former.

Li Zehou's subscription to the fundamentally materialist law of cause and effect manifests itself in many ways. It is revealed in his definition of *xiti* as the sum total of both spiritual (ontological consciousness) and material (science and technology) production, with the former understood as a superstructural system that mirrors and reproduces the latter. It is still social being that determines consciousness rather than the other way around. The same mechanical causality is at work when Li concludes that "only after commodity economy has prospered, [can we] then gain the consciousness of liberalism and secure the foundation within which 'Western learning' could truly take root and develop."[111] Finally, it is this naive orthodox Marxist faith in the one-to-one correspondence between base and superstructure that enables Li Zehou to envision the potential change of the "cultural-psychological formation" of historical Chinese culture.

Relying upon the logic of mechanical causality, Li Zehou coined the term "cultural-psychological formation" (*wenhua xinli jiegou*) to account for the superstructural stability that seemed to survive each dynastic and revolutionary change that took place throughout imperial and modern Chinese history. Such a superstructural stability, Li argues, is built upon the relative infrastructural stability perpetuated by the economic system based on the agricultural mode of production. As long as such an economic system remains intact, the corresponding cultural-psychological formation—specified by Li Zehou in one instance as the clan-centered familial and social order and in another instance as the particular Chinese dialectics of bipolar complementarity—will recycle itself in the continual reproduction of a cultural logic that emphasizes ethics at the expense of ontology and epistemology and privileges functional harmony over resistance and agency.[112] One can almost conclude, following Li Zehou's argument, that it is the "sedimentation" (*jidian*) of the cultural unconscious that constitutes the bottleneck of Chinese modernity.

But Li Zehou's attitude toward the ultrastable superstructure of Chinese society is by no means as unambiguous as Jin Guantao's. Adopting Li's premise about the potential stagnation embedded in China's cultural-psychological formation, Jin Guantao forges a theory of ultrastability that condemns unambiguously the immutability of such a historical formation. A closer look at Li Zehou's treatise on the concept betrays no such blanket condemnation. As a matter of fact, Li always leaves room for further concessions in theorizing the notion of cultural-psychological formation. And in so doing, he allows himself to return later to revalorize the concept whenever the occasion for such a compromise may arise.

Unfortunately, such occasions abound. Li Zehou frustrates any reader who has little appetite for the Confucian art of expediency. Contradictory descriptions of cultural-psychological formation pepper the pages in various guises. What Li Zehou often resorts to is a double-headed argument. On the one hand, he conceptualizes cultural-psychological formation in ahistorical terms of "relative autonomy" and "self-regulation"; in so doing, he leaves room for the emergence of unpredictable elements that may yet destabilize the structural continuity of the firmly anchored cultural unconscious. On the other hand, his good materialist persona cannot help arguing for the opposite: that the ultimate material base of Chinese "small land-owners' economy" determines the predictability and immobility of superstructure. The word "autonomy" is thus counteracted in the text by "economical constraint," and yet the negative imagery of inertia that "cultural-psychological formation" unmistakably conjures up is at the same time offset by such aggressive qualifiers as "*active* equilibrium."[113]

Li Zehou's vacillating rhetoric about cultural sedimentation—that it is a completed circle at one moment and a kinetic motion at the next—indicates that he cannot decide whether superstructure is a mere epiphenomenon of economy or a semiautonomous force that interacts with and sometimes even overpowers economic constraints. The sight of an orthodox Marxist struggling to break out of his own methodological limitations is always intriguing. The breakthrough, however, never really occurs. And Li Zehou's mechanical application of the Marxist causal logic reinforces the paradox: China's premodern cultural-psychological formation is both static and dynamic. It is static to the extent that the land-centered agricultural mode of production in premodern China produces a superstructure rooted in fixed cultural and social practices. It is dynamic to the extent that the infrastructural change in forces of production prescribed by Li Zehou inevitably presupposes the potential (per)mutability of such a cultural-psychological formation: "[We] have to use the modernized 'Western substance' . . . to reconstruct 'Chinese learning' industriously, to change traditional Chinese cultural-psychological formation, and to transform its sedimentation consciously."[114]

The necessity of destabilizing the concept of a sedimented cultural-psychological formation is undoubtedly tremendous. What is at stake is the Marxist faith in praxis and change. In his 1993 appearance at the convention of the Asian Studies Association in Los Angeles, Li Zehou made a public effort to emphasize the living processes of the formation in question. He proposes that we change the English term "formation" into "forming," and "sedimentation" into "sedimentating," and thus succeeds in downplaying the ultrastable essence that he ascribed to the concept of "cultural-psychological formation" earlier.[115]

Tianren heyi: *Retrograde Cultural Unconscious or an Antidote for Modernity in Excess?*   Li Zehou's presentation of the Confucian concept of *tianren heyi*—the unity of Heaven and (hu)man—part and parcel of the cultural-psychological formation of premodern China, reveals the contradictory pull that he always feels whenever he is called upon to reevaluate Chinese tradition from the Marxist vantage point. The perfect equilibrium between human beings and their environment, between internal and external human nature, and between the individual and the collective is endorsed on the one hand as the "active adaptation" of human beings to the "rhythms of nature," but problematized on the other hand as a form of the "passive" human "obedience and worship" of a Heaven that predetermines and dictates the terms of human destiny.[116]

Li Zehou's critical interpretation of *tianren heyi* as a quietistic "mental landscape,"[117] both moralistically and metaphysically defined, contains within itself an implicit critique of the Song-Ming neo-Confucianism that took root in a highly introverted worldview with its emphasis on the doctrine of *neisheng* (sageliness within), the rigorous self-cultivation and disciplining of worldly desires. Li Zehou is at his best when he traces and articulates the historical tension between the Confucian twin doctrines of *neisheng* and *waiwang* (kingliness without). It seems predictable that a Marxist like Li Zehou should unambiguously endorse the latter strategy—the salvation of society—as a higher form of practical rationality than the salvation of the soul that the former doctrine embodies.

Yet if we interpret Li Zehou's emphasis on the doctrine of "kingliness without" only in terms of his ideological commitment to Marxian praxis, we risk simplifying the ideological subtexts underlying his philosophy of modernity. Li Zehou's effort of accentuating the politics of governing (that is what kingliness is all about) also grows out of the orthodox Confucianist calling to serve. He comes closest to embracing the ideas of the *qimeng* school when he cites Gu Yanwu, Huang Zongxi, and Tang Zhen, the Confucian masters of early Qing dynasty, as the genuine spokesmen for the doctrine of kingliness.[118] The Qing masters' critique of sovereign rights and their simultaneous advocation of certain embryonic concepts of constitutional equality and democratic representation embody for Li Zehou the spirit of modern enlightenment thought.

Gu Yanwu and the cohort of enlightenment scholars offered Li Zehou a viable alternative to modernize Confucian tradition, namely, the separation of the demands of sageliness from those of kingliness, and to put it without metaphorical flourishes, the potential disengagement of statecraft from ethics and politics from morality. Underlying this separatist logic is a modernist assumption that the old Confucian insistence on *zhengjiao heyi* (the unity of politics and ethics) was responsible for all the evils that plagued premodern China—the lack of a well-grounded epistemological, liberal democratic, and independent scientific tradition—in theoretical terms, the undifferentiatedness of substantive from instrumental reason.

Here Li Zehou stumbles into another paradox, for his questioning of the unity of politics and ethics contradicts his enthusiastic endorsement of the unity of Heaven and humans. What does *tianren heyi* symbolize but the interpenetration of the natural and the social, sensibility and rationality, and on a higher theoretical level, the continuum of substantive and instrumental rationality? Such a prescribed continuum may indeed perpetuate itself: It includes the private and the public, sageliness and kingliness, and in quotidian terms, ethics and politics. The contradiction of Li Zehou's position on the question of continuum seems inexplicable. It illustrates once more the ideological intervention of the utilitarian agenda of modernization. As long as Li is attracted to the practical strategy of enthroning instrumental reason to accelerate China's modernization program, substantive rationality and its various manifestations (sagely virtues among them) have to be disengaged from the former. In extrapolation, ethics and the realm of the private (*jiao*) have to be extricated from the political and the public (*zheng*). Obviously, Li Zehou's total commitment to the cause of modernization compromises his project of revamping the doctrine of *tianren heyi* and renders his theoretical reconstruction of continuum inherently paradoxical.

My purpose in pinpointing this contradiction in Li's epistemic system is not to resolve it but rather to highlight the shifting ideological grounds on which Li Zehou's philosophy stands. Such inconsistency emerges at the most unlikely moments. No sooner have we arrived at our conclusion about the pragmatist and modernist persona of the philosopher who practices Weberian separatist reasoning, than we confront another ideological somersault: A now equanimous Li Zehou extolls the philosophy of totalitarian harmony by reconstruing the utopia of *tianren heyi*.

The supple content of *tianren heyi*—the unity of bipolar opposites— invites open-ended inquiries for it is impregnated with all kinds of semantic possibilities and ideological visions. Li Zehou's reinterpretation of the concept was by all means a timely move. The old Confucianist hermeneutics that presupposes the existence of a benevolent Heaven that predicts and observes the passive fusion of bipolar pairs has definitely lost its appeal in the modern age that stakes everything on the agency of human beings and privileges conflicts and difference rather than premeditated harmony and homogeneity. To modernize the concept of *tianren heyi*, Li unmistakably speaks in the Marxist lingo: "[The transformation of] *tianren heyi*—how to evolve it from quiet observation to action, how to absorb the sublime and tragic spirit of the West, and how to bestow upon it an inner motivating force that will enable it to break out of silence and to chase [after desires] vigorously—only when [we] build the concept upon the Marxist theoretical basis of 'humanized nature' can we arrive at a fundamental solution [of its transformation]."[119]

The ideological reinvestment underlying the revamped concept calls for further explanation. Li Zehou starts the process by suggesting the impossible: that we divest the concept of its material underpinning. To achieve this goal, he delivers a working hypothesis that seriously compromises his avowed materialist position: Once we "extricate" from *tianren heyi* "those passive elements characteristic of the small-scale agricultural mode of production," the concept will reemerge as a useful category for contemporary philosophy.[120] Insofar as all true believers of orthodox Marxism take as its most sacred decree the indivisibility of base and superstructure, this is certainly a sacrilegious statement. The unabashed call for the abstraction of the material base from the content of cultural production gives rise to the most flagrant blunder that the Chinese Marxist committed. This is clearly one of the most poignant moments that reveals, without the theorist's own awareness, the co-optation of Marxism by his hidden Confucianist agenda.

This unspoken agenda has been shared by many of Li Zehou's Confucian forebears and his contemporaries who are single-mindedly devoted to the cause of delivering the golden mean from modernity's excessive impulse at all costs. Li Zehou's second step to modernize the concept of *tianren heyi* is precisely to ensure that the Confucian aesthetics of harmony serve as the most efficacious antidote for the emotional, sensual, and material surplus identified as the notorious second nature of capitalist modernity. It is Li Zehou's recognition of the rupture of culture with nature, a price paid by modern society as it marches through history from primitive communities to capitalism, that prompts him to turn to Marxian metaphors in search of an interpretive framework that would help rehabilitate the unity of Heaven and (hu)mans.

Li Zehou's Marxist rewriting of *tianren heyi* did not bring redemption to a world torn asunder by the extravagance of human imagination. In fact, the new version exacerbates the anthropocentric view that runs counter to the original spirit of *tianren heyi*. The marriage of the Marxist view of a tempered nature with the Confucian aesthetics of the happy continuum of the noumenal and the phenomenal promises a rocky relationship from the very start. First of all, the classical Marxist view of "humanized nature" emphasizes the increasing domination of human beings over nature as an indispensable process of the progressive emancipation of human society from the tyranny of natural necessity. The development of the forces of production goes hand in hand with the gradual conquest of nature.

Li Zehou's reinscription of *tianren heyi* in the Marxian conceptual framework inevitably follows the same humanistic logic of the taming of the wild. The "wilderness" in question not only serves as a metaphor for Nature with a capital "N" but also for the unruly forces residing within human nature itself. Li believes that this double focus on the metaphor of humanization (*renhua*)—the humanization of Nature and the arduous "permeation and sedimentation of rationality" into the "inner nature" of human beings—promises the harmonious fusion of reason and sensibility.[121] Yet it is difficult to take this metaphor of fusion at face value. The picture he provides of the meeting of the senses and reason actually involves the process of the domestication of the one by the other. Regardless of the occasional adjustment he makes to redress the tilted scale (he resorts to terms such as "interpenetration" and "mutual internalization," "the deposits of sensibility in rationality," and "the deposits of Nature in society"), Li Zehou is more susceptible to the reverse logic: "Sexual desire is turned into love, natural relations into human relations, natural organs into aesthetic organs, and the libido into passions for the beautiful."[122] As the philosopher proudly declares, what emerges from this process of sublimation and humanization is the "ultimate manifestation of subjectivity," an entity that can hardly be associated with any sense of autonomy, since it is conceived first and foremost as an end product of socialization. In Li Zehou's epistemological configuration, the subject (zhuti) is not a lone signifier freed of prescribed content. It is not defined in terms of "subjective consciousness, emotions, and desires of the individual," but rather in collective terms of "social consciousness" and "cultural-psychological formation."[123] Eventually, it is the subjugation of the senses to reason, the natural to the sociocultural, the individual to the community, rather than the harmonious coexistence of the two, that constitutes Li Zehou's contemporary recoding of tianren heyi. This is, of course, a far cry from the aesthetic imaginary that the concept originally delimited.

Li Zehou is certainly not oblivious to human beings' changing attitude toward nature in modern, premodern, and postmodern societies. He specifies the potential allegiance between premodernity and postmodernity: Our ancestors lived in the "arms of Nature," whereas contemporary ecological correctness has driven alienated postmoderns to an increasingly urgent call for the return to nature.[124] What he places in question here is the anthropomorphic view that privileges humanity at all costs. Li's acknowledgment of the pitfalls of modernity's exploitation of nature for the advancement of human welfare makes it even more difficult for us to comprehend why his rewritten version of tianren heyi is firmly grounded in human-centered consciousness. It appears that the classical Marxist heritage of humanized nature is the wrong paradigm to appropriate. Perhaps the ideological alliance the philosopher should forge is one with a Marxism of a different brand.

This speculation returns us once more to Adorno, Horkheimer, and the *Dialectic of Enlightenment*, which takes as its point of departure the reconstruction of the harmonious relationship between nature and human beings. What Adorno and Horkheimer subvert is nothing short of the classical Marxist view of humanized nature, instrumental reason, and the Enlightenment notion of progress. This is a Janus-faced view of modern Western history that exposes the dialectics of Enlightenment as none other than the negation of its own inflated agenda. The price of domination over nature, of which human beings themselves are inseparably a part, signifies the enslavement of the psychic by the social, id by ego, substantive by instrumental reason, spontaneous impulses by rationality—all oppressions committed in the name of emancipation. To redeem the fall of nature, Adorno and Horkheimer made a proposal that comes close to the Chinese aesthetics of *tianren heyi* but which also departs from it in emphasizing the ultimate nonidentity between nature and humanity. Perry Anderson's interpretation of this renewed Marxist vision illuminates the subtle difference between the Western Marxists' vantage point and the Chinese one: "A liberated society . . . its historical goal would be, not domination of nature, but *reconciliation* with it. This would mean abandonment of the cruel and hopeless attempt to dictate an identity of man and nature, by the subjugation of the latter to the former, for an acknowledgment of both the distinction and relation between them—in other words, their vulnerable *affinity*." [125]

The recognition of the "vulnerable" basis of this "affinity" between "man and nature" would certainly sound heretical to a Chinese Confucianist, for whom a harmony fraught with the seeds of contradiction, or in Anderson's view, with the nonidentity of bipolar opposites, is an uneasy harmony at best. And yet how can we save the aesthetic nirvana of *tianren heyi* from its complete saturation with inertia but emphasize, instead, the possibilities of change within seamless totality and continual growth after the "reconciliation" in question has come to fruition?

A passing comment made by Li Zehou surprisingly coincides with the spirit of "vulnerable affinity." "[Our recognition of] the importance of individual entity and its unique development . . . has rendered the original doctrines of 'sageliness within and kingliness without' and the 'complementality of Confucianism and Daoism' into a kind of impoverished and degraded 'primitive perfection.'" [126] In acknowledging the potential of "individual entity" to reinvigorate old doctrines of synthesis, Li Zehou comes close to suggesting the concept of nonidentity. Although he does not pursue the satiric implications that the metaphor of primitive perfection is capable of generating, the Chinese Marxist would agree with Adorno and Horkheimer's view that nonidentity between individual entities precludes "any harmony free of contradiction."[127] Only genuine discrimination promised by the principle of nonidentity can deliver the philosophy of *tianren heyi* from its incestuous self-reproduction of perfection. To break out of the autochthonous circle of predetermined harmony, Li Zehou can indeed learn a few lessons from the dialectics of Western Marxism, which, among other things, can instill into the utopian content of *tianren heyi* an overdue regard for the integrity of individual entities that Li Zehou himself speaks of with such sharpened postmodern epochal consciousness.

But the fruitful exchange between Li Zehou and Western Marxists would probably end right here. The former's condemnation of Western Marxism, and of the Frankfurt School in particular, forecloses at least for the time being any ideological alliance with its practitioners. Perhaps it is Li Zehou's deep revulsion to certain preconceived notions about Western Marxism that in part accounts for his turning away from Adorno and Horkheimer to the orthodox Marxist tradition for inspiration in his rewriting of *tianren heyi*.

I have little intention to vindicate Western Marxists here, although Li Zehou's understanding of the Critical Theory is problematic. Suffice it to say, his critique of Western Marxism tells more of the historical vision that post-Mao China is experiencing at this particular historical juncture: This is a China that negates the sum total of its Maoist phase; this is also a China that envisions itself entering the threshold of capitalist modernity and whose only agenda is to clear the barriers to implementing the capitalist mode of production. Under these terms, it is almost impossible not to pit Maoism against capitalism. The renunciation of Maoism, for the majority of China's elite, goes hand in hand with the unconditioned acceptance of capitalism. Li Zehou's hostility to Western Marxism thus completes its full cycle as he lashes out at the Critical Theory's "totalizing critique and negation of capitalism."[128] It is predictable that the conflation of Western Marxism with anticapitalism and anticapitalism with Maoism may pave the way for the final breakdown of discrimination between Western Marxism and Maoism—an ideological undercurrent that Li Zehou's thinking reveals periodically.[129]

"Practice" and Practical Rationality   Li Zehou's critique of Western Marxism is consistent with his distrust of a priori or nonempirical cate-

gories. Historical materialism, however, cannot claim to be the single source of inspiration for Li's concoction of *shiyong lixing* (practical rationality) and for the privileging of practice over praxis in his critique of Marcuse and his fellow travelers. In this dispute with the Frankfurt School over the primacy of praxis, it is Kantianism with its insistence on the need for an empirical component in knowledge and its antipathy to speculative metaphysics that comes to reinforce Li Zehou's materialist position.

Li Zehou's objection to the concept of praxis is based on the same logic that leads him to condemn the epistemological turn of the Frankfurt School toward the cultural study of superstructure from that of "labor, material production, and the economic life" of human beings, activities that he perceives as firmly grounded in base structure.[130] He complains that the term "praxis" in Western Marxism incorporates those human activities (patterns of quotidian life, theoretical inquiries, cultural activities) that have nothing to do with the fundamental core of social existence, namely, material production. In his view, social practice is the sum total of the activities of the actual human engagement in material production, which he defines in specific terms throughout his *Pipan zhexue de pipan* (Critiquing the critique of philosophy) (1979), a critique on Kant, as "using tools and making tools." In short, Li Zehou insists that because praxis is informed by, and sometimes even subjugated to, theoretical considerations, it cannot be considered as a pure category of practice. Quoting Marx and Kant at the same time, he trumpets with passion such truisms as "liberation is a historical activity, not an activity of the mind" and "it is not the 'a priori subjectivity' of human consciousness, but the historical human practice (rooted in material reality) that constitutes the truly great 'selfhood' of human subjectivity" (200). "Practical" in the Kantian framework points to what is experimental, which is not quite the same as Western Marxists' use of "praxis" as the "identity of theory and practice." Li Zehou, like those American pragmatists who prefer the Kantian experimental meaning without the dialectics, consecrates practice rather than praxis as the fundamental category of Marxist philosophy (363).

There is little space here for me to elaborate the philosophy of praxis in the history of Western Marxism. However, I should pinpoint the voluntarist implications in this concept. Although Marcuse, Horkheimer, and their colleagues understood true praxis as a collective endeavor, they acknowledged the necessity of voluntarism and were fascinated with the built-in orientation of "anthropogenesis," in other words, with the self-determined and self-generating nature of action and activity in whose terms the concept was originally conceived and articulated in the early writings of the Frankfurt School.[131] One can well imagine why Marcuse's well-known proclamation—"Theory will preserve the truth even if revolutionary practice deviates from its proper path. Practice follows the truth, not vice versa"—agitates the generation of Chinese intellectuals, Li Zehou among them, who suffered for nearly a decade from the theoretical experiment of the Great Cultural Revolution undertaken in the name of praxis.[132] Li's passing reference to 1958, the year that marked the inception of the Great Leap Forward, reflects an orthodox Marxist's condemnation of a revolution waged in the name of "subjectivist voluntarist belief" that "runs counter to the laws of history."[133] "Laws" in this context specify the motions of the forces and modes of material production. Such sporadic and carefully guarded critiques of Mao's legacy of permanent revolution and of the theoretical miscarriages that the Chairman orchestrated in his late revolutionary career serve as a telling sign of how the controversy over practice versus praxis that Li Zehou lays out in his philosophy is, to a great extent, politically motivated and grounded. We should not be surprised if the thinking promoted by the Frankfurt School—that theory serves as a guide to action, or in more radical terms, that theory is "the only form of *praxis* still open to honest man"—reminds Li Zehou chillingly of the historical lesson that Mao's China learned belatedly: Deviation from historical materialists' emphasis on practice often leads to subjective voluntarism.[134]

This short excursion illustrates the significant role that Maoism plays in Li Zehou's strategy of highlighting the agonistic relationship between practice and praxis. Once this particular subtext for the contestation of the one against the other is brought to light, we can better understand how the family feud (both practice and praxis are Marxist categories after all) took shape in the first place.

Li Zehou's separation of practice from theory, which owes its theoretical underpinning to historical materialism, follows yet another unlikely model—Kantianism. The separation in question finds its mirror image in Kant's distinction between ethical and pragmatic rules. Ethical rule is seen as following a categorical imperative based on the individual's "inner pure" reason, an a priori and universal consciousness that acknowledges and wills humankind as an end in itself. In contrast, pragmatic rule traces the track of common prudence and subscribes to the technical imperatives or means required to achieve desired ends. Following Kant's example of downgrading the capacity of pure reason to gain insight in the "things in themselves," Li Zehou privileges the principle of pragmatic rule and all the categories housed under its umbrella: objective (as opposed to subjective) considerations, means (as opposed to ends), and social practice (as opposed to pure reason). It is on the Kantian empiricist model that the theoretical construction of *shiyong lixing* is primarily established.

> The so-called practical rationality first and foremost points to a rational spirit or a rational attitude. . . . [For instance], Confucius provided the hermeneutics of "humaneness" to account for "rites." This [tendency] accorded with the general drift of "practical rationality." It is not by having recourse to some mysterious fervor, but by utilizing dispassionate, realistic, and rationalistic attitudes, that one can decode and deal with matters and tradition; it is by means of rationality that one can guide, satisfy, and mitigate desires, not by resorting to asceticism or hedonism to smother or to release them; it is neither through outbound nihilism nor self-bound egocentrism but through one's quest for humanity and for personal integrity that one can achieve equilibrium.[135]

The Kantian overtones of pragmatic rule are manifest in Li Zehou's insistence that the mind imposes its forms and categories on the sensory manifold. The categorical structure in which the mind decodes and organizes sensory experiences is identified by Li specifically as "practical rationality," a principle that dictates that "reason penetrate feeling, reason intermingle with feeling, and feeling serve reason."[136] The Kantian influence is palpable in this definition as Li Zehou bestows upon reason an a priori synthesizing capability to order and constrain phenomena.

It is worth noting, however, that it is precisely at this theoretical juncture that Li Zehou departs from Kant significantly. That is, he materializes the formal and formative principle of practical reason in terms of the Confucian rules of equilibrium to be arrived at through the taming of the natural and the sensual. One should ask how Li Zehou can justify the emergence of any equilibrium when the process of merging quoted above represents a colonizing process that subjugates feeling to reason, sensual nature to the human mind. The question that plagues Li's mind is certainly not the same that plagued Kant's: How is knowledge possible? Whereas Kant is concerned about the nature of the *restriction* of human knowledge, hence the ultimate inadequacy of the human mind to grasp the "things in themselves," Li is preoccupied with the *application* of human knowledge. A different question is raised: How can we produce knowledge for practical utilization?

To ensure the applicability of human knowledge, the mind has to emerge as the enabling monitor that processes the enormous corpus of sensory data and carefully sorts out the unserviceable from the useful. To arrive at this end, Li Zehou has to tone down the skepticism that characterizes the Kantian epistemology and rescue subjectivism from the Kantian transcendentalism that, by its intrinsic logic, denies human beings access to the external world. The subjectivism thus redeemed reaffirms human beings as the reasoning and thinking subject that owns the exclusive right to shape the phenomenal world in order to serve the anthropocentric project of "saving the world (humanism) and of self-completion."[137] Although Li Zehou constantly reiterates that the significance of the contemporary revisit of Kant resides in the latter's inquiry into the human "subjective-psychological structure (epistemology, ethics, and aesthetics),"[138] Li's inheritance of the notion of practical rationality from Kantianism is less articulate on the epistemological front than on that of pragmatics and teleology. In the same pragmatic spirit, he concludes that practical rationality and its ideological cradle, Confucianism, "are not obstacles to modernization."[139]

Li Zehou's direct linking of practical rationality with Confucianism requires little explanation, since the operating intelligence of the former is already couched in suggestive terms of equilibrium—the cardinal imagery of the Confucian golden mean. What needs to be emphasized is that practical rationality serves as the focal point of convergence where Li's Confucianist and Marxist dual personalities live out their contentious dialogues with each other. The concept of *shiyong lixing* can be turned into an enabling machine because it presupposes the telos of history as the utopian evolution of human society and insists that to achieve this end, the exercise of practical rationality should be defined in terms of *shehui shijian* (social practice)—the doctrine of "kingliness without" rings loud here—rather than in those of individual self-discipline (the doctrine of "sageliness within").[140]

Such a teleological view of history and pious appeal to the metaphor of the collective may have grown out of Li Zehou's deeply ingrained Confucian heritage. But the Marxist influence should by no means be understated here. In fact, the philosopher's Marxist commitment is more evident than ever when he insists that Kant's contribution to classical German idealism consists of his replacement of "individual sensibility" by a kind of "collective rationality," which, according to Li Zehou, should be clearly specified as an abstract version of the "social nature of human beings" that transcends their individual, biological, and ethnic characteristics. By the same token, the subject that exercises practical rationality is designated "not [as] the thinking 'I,' but the practising 'I,' not [as] any mental and metaphysical 'I,' but the collective 'I' made up of the masses and the social 'I.'[141] This heavy-handed plebian makeup of practical rationality cannot but subvert the elitist emphasis of Confucian ideology.

The continual wrestling between Li's Confucianist and Marxist personae informs most of his major works, whether he is engaged in reinterpreting Kant, reassessing the cultural psychology of premodern China, or reconstructing such categories as *xiti zhongyong, tianren heyi,* or *shiyong lixing* for modernity's sake. Each category conjures up the old familiar binary of tradition versus modernity. Yet Li Zehou's purpose in concocting the three formulae is to exorcise the binary paradigm of its antithetical urge that has precluded each term from forming a continuum with the other. Thus, for a brief moment, we witness the reconstructed doctrine of *tianren heyi* enact its own mediating principle in bringing together, first of all, the idealist order of the doctrine as the ultimate metaphor for the cultural unconscious, and secondly, the materialist reinterpretation of the doctrine that stresses the continuum between *tian* and *ren* as a result of human beings' conscious implementation of the Marxist program of humanized nature. It is this same knack in balancing excesses that accounts for Li Zehou's attentiveness to both the vice and virtue of Confucian concepts whether he is examining *tianren heyi* or *shiyong lixing.* Just as he acknowledges that the unity of Heaven and (hu)man, a concrete embodiment of the Chinese cultural-psychological formation, is dynamic and static in turn, so does he emphasize that practical rationality can both rescue China from modernity's superfluity and "stand in the way of the development of science and art."[142] Harmony and repression go hand in hand. The salvation, Li Zehou seems to suggest, lies in the simultaneous resuscitation of harmony and the release of the repressed. Both tradition and modernity need each other, inasmuch as the former will change and develop in response to the epochal demands of the latter.

The diffusion of hostile impetus between bipolar opposites remains a deeply Confucianist strategy. It can hardly account for the unique place that Li Zehou occupies in China's contemporary cultural scene. What distinguishes him from those neo-Confucianists who are consistently eclectic is the fact that Li's penchant for the concept of continuum suffers recurrent setbacks in the tug of war between his Marxian and Confucian twin ideologies. It seems always the former that emerges at the right moment to upset the perfect symmetry and frustrate his Confucian persona's compulsion to dissolve every binary.

In his own Marxist incarnation, Li Zehou continues to subscribe to the oppositional logic of materialism versus idealism, objective laws of history versus voluntarism. "Western substance" in *xiti zhongyong* is clearly defined in terms of the mode of production as opposed to the liberal idealist tradition that ascribes democracy and other superstructural fineries to the semantic core of westernization. In a similar vein, Li Zehou defines the concept of practice as human ventures grounded in and restricted to infrastructural activities. In contrast to praxis, practice is not to be viewed as those occurrences taking place on the political and ideological front (he cites as examples the Chinese Cultural Revolution and the May 1968 student uprisings in Europe) that privilege human consciousness as the dominant motivating force in history. Li's examples indicate that Marxism, and specifically historical materialism, serves as the base structure of his various philosophical inquiries into premodern and modern China.

In this continual struggle between materialism and idealism, between Marxism and Confucianism, Li Zehou's attempt to appropriate tradition and Confucianism into his Marxist materialist framework is a perilous journey in itself. Sometimes, it is Confucianism that gains the upper hand over its rival ideology. When such a moment of danger flashes through the textual space heavily armed with Marxist credos, we learn that cultural constraints—the "cultural-psychological formation," in Li Zehou's own words—supercedes conscious ideological subversion after all.

Li Zehou's case exemplifies once more the symptom of a modern cultural psychology that is by no means unique to the Chinese people: a profound utilitarian principle compels them to reinvent tradition at every turn of their encounter with an intimidating modernity. Of course, no reinterpretation of tradition is ever disinterested, Li Zehou's included. The question I raise is not whether Chinese intellectuals should, or should not, serve the interest of modernity (they do not yet have the luxury of Western Marxists to denounce such an interest and flay capitalism). Instead, I ask whether they are aware of the conflict that exists between the capitalist ideology of modernity and their own avowed cultural politics (whether it is Jin Guantao's scientism, neo-Confucianism, or Li Zehou's Marxism), and no less important, whether they are capable of scrutinizing their own ideological compromises that such a conflict inevitably incurs.

Li Zehou, like the majority of the participants in the Cultural Discussion, took the subtext of modernization for granted. One wonders if he ever recognized that the infrastructural change of China's mode of production for which he argues in his proposal of *xiti zhongyong* will necessarily unleash forces from the sociocultural, ideological, and political spheres that will dismantle utopianism of all kinds, Confucianist or socialist. Is he ready to reckon with the cultural logic of capitalism after endorsing the capitalist mode of production wholeheartedly? Does he really believe that the doctrines of continuum propagated in *tianren heyi* and *shiyong lixing* can survive the fluctuations of the stock market and the crude awakening of subjectivity and sensuality?

The square at Kaifeng's Temple of the Minister of the State (*Xiangguo si*) where the Song emperors used to perform state rituals is turned into a discotheque at nightfall.[143] The day may not be too far off when the revolutionary holy base Yan'an will sponsor a Mao Zedong impersonators' extravaganza. Could Marxist Li Zehou foresee all this and still celebrate it—the coming of capitalist modernity to China accompanied by all its gaudy gears that shatter culturalism's high hopes for utopia?

The 1980s dawned on China with the promise that *zhishi* (knowledge) and *rencai* (talent) would reemerge as the primary capital that drove China's modernization program. Throughout the decade, the popularity of the slogan "Respect knowledge, respect talent" (*zunzhong zhishi, zunzhong rencai*) signaled the exit of Maoism and the reentry of intellectuals as the harbingers of modernity. One cannot tell whether it was Culture Fever that set loose the "fever for 'knowledgeable elements'" (*zhishi fenzi re*) or if it was the dramatic ascendance of intellectuals that triggered the outbreak of Culture Fever.[144] In 1985 when Liu Zaifu raised the thesis of *zhutixing* (subjectivity),[145] Chinese elite were already well prepared to reassert their own subject-position by launching one project after another that echoed the elitist agenda of linking modernity with the empowerment of knowledge and knowledgeable elements. The hegemonic position of ancient scholar-officials seemed once more within reach for the modern elite.

In the mid-eighties, the climate was ripe for the spontaneous collaboration among various elite circles to turn the 1980s into a decade that celebrated highbrow culture and cerebralism. Academic salons mushroomed in urban centers. The Great Cultural Discussion captured and fanned the fever into a brain storm that monopolized the attention of the press and media for more than half a decade. As a timely response to the rekindled nationwide obsession with the power of knowledge and the agency of the intellect, volume one of the first history of "Chinese intellectual talents" (*Zhongguo rencai sixiang shi*) was published in 1986.[146]

There was no doubt that the epochal energy of the 1980s was concentrated on the notion of a modern consciousness (*xiandai yishi*) that would grow out of the fertile soil of the mind. The emphasis on superstructural transformation as the motivating force for modernization was a theme that reverberated throughout the Cultural Discussion. It was the "change of thinking" and the "modernization of concepts" rather than the transformation of the mode of production (for which Li Zehou was a lone missionary) that primarily defined what modernity meant for the elite establishment.[147] The fact that Chinese material civilization lags far behind spiritual civilization seemed to reinforce the culture elite's resolution that it was they, the privileged few, who should lead the masses, peasants, and workers (the populace that was engaged in the material social practice) in the nation's leap toward the twenty-first century.

The Cultural Discussion marked the apex of the elite's decade-long efforts of reinstating the image of the post-Mao intellectual. The icon of a cultural worker (whether he or she advocates scientism, neo-Confucianism, pro-enlightenment movement, hermeneutics, or Marxism) who is engaged in intense mental labor as the spokesperson for the truth of knowledge finds its replica in many familiar fictional characters of the mid-1980s: Lu Wenting in *At Middle Age* and Zhang Yonglin in Zhang Xianliang's *Lühua shu* (Mimosa) (1984) and *Nanren de yiban shi nüren* (Half of a man is a woman) (1985). The representation of the intellectual in all those instances is well trimmed around the edges, free of any blemishes and self-critical impulses. This is a cultural worker whose pursuit of scientific or philosophical knowledge and moral high order is so relentlessly intense that anything that stands in its way has to be dispensed with: Lu Wenting, a superwoman, upright and uncompromising, morally as immaculate as the white doctor's suit she wears daily, sacrifices her private life completely to her medical career and to the welfare of the public; Zhang Yonglin is carved out of a sublimated Hegelian totality within which the conflicting demands of the flesh and the spirit encounter and dissolve each other. Flatteringly portrayed as altruistic and morally characterized as a human being larger than life itself,[148] the intellectual emerges in the guise of what Liu Xiaobo called "deified superhumanity."[149] The making of such a formula, as Liu charged in his condemnation of Chinese intellectuals' engagement in self-promotion, is in essence no different from that which produced the cult of proletarian hero during the revolutionary years.[150] The same pietistic agenda yields the same extreme logic: The rise of the sacred presupposes its self-conscious demarcation from the profane. Only this time, the bipolar poles are reversed. It is the intellectuals who are now put on the pedestal, and the masses, at their feet once more.

The self-image preying on the mind of Chinese intellectuals in the past and throughout the 1980s is by no means that of a populist but the dignified figure of a solitary spokesperson for society. The deterioration of the elite's sociopolitical consciousness known as *youhuan yishi* into a deeply rooted disdain for the unlettered was a phenomenon that resurfaced during the 1980s and could be in part accounted for by the elite's long repressed backlash against Maoism. The rise of one social class is usually accomplished at the expense of the other. This was true during the Cultural Revolution when intellectuals were labeled as the "stinking old nine" and sank to the bottom of the social ladder. The 1980s not only revoked Mao's historical verdict on class struggle, it also reversed the power relations between the two historically antagonistic classes. It was now the intellectuals who rode the waves. The peasants were once again blamed for China's submersion in feudal mentality and economic backwardness.

Throughout the decade, the herculean stature of intellectuals formed a stark contrast to the diminished image of peasants. Fang Lizhi, one of the most vocal champions of the cause of intellectuals, considers the elite the only legitimate guardian of China's spiritual civilization. He is repeatedly candid about the need for the self-inflated image making of intelligentsia: "China truly lacked an intellectual consciousness, or one might call it, scientific consciousness. A concrete example of this lack is manifested in the fact that intellectuals do not form a power that can influence society and influence the overall situation [of China]."[151]

Liu Zaifu goes a step further by proclaiming that the process of Chinese modernization involves not only the reconsolidation of the historical agency of intellectuals but also the carrying out of their mission to "disseminate modern knowledge" and to "bring the enlightenment of modern consciousness to peasants," whose feudalistic cultural psychology, reincarnated in the absurd figure of Ah Q, desperately "needs to be remolded."[152] The contrast between the suprahuman portrayal of intellectuals and the increasingly degraded description of peasants and those on the lower social strata culminate in Liu Zaifu's most recent coinage of the derogatory term *moren* (*der letzt mensch*), the "trivial man," in diametrical opposition to *chaoren*, the "superman." *Moren* includes all

of those who are "ignorant and kind" but who have "no distinct personal integrity and not much character either." Not yet "finishing the
evolution of humanity," this underclass shares certain "regressive spiritual elements" and dwells in a "spiritual world that is on the verge of
drying up."[153] Not surprisingly, Ah Q, Xianglin's wife, Sister Silly in
Honglou meng (Dream of the red chamber), Wu Song's victimized
brother Dalang in *Shuihu zhuan* (Water margins), and even the revolutionary hero Lei Feng—all the illiterates and semi-illiterates—fall neatly
into this category. Under the threat of the quick reproduction of such
"soulless" species, the mission of Chinese intellectuals is designated by
Liu Zaifu as "blocking the mass emergence of *moren*, and most important, preventing them from turning into the subject of society (*shehui
zhuti*)."[154] Such blatant discriminatory class consciousness is by no
means immune to harsh criticism—Liu Xiaobo's outburst enjoyed its
own moment of shocking revelation during the Cultural Discussion. But
the dominant voice of the decade chimed in with Fang Lizhi and Liu
Zaifu in revalorizing intellectualism and disdaining the populace.

Chinese intellectuals will remember, and consecrate in retrospect, the
1980s as a utopian decade of their own making. At the dramatic consummation of their enlightenment cause at the Tian'anmen Square in
June 1989, who could have foretold that the moral and cultural influence of Chinese intellectuals at home would die an uneventful death in
the immediate wake of their world-televised celebrity? Who could have
predicted in 1989 that it was not communist authoritarianism but
capitalist consumer culture that would mark the sudden downward turn
of their fortune and announce the demise of high culture fever so quickly?
The 1990s dawned in China with the ironic truth: Commercialism could
turn yesterday's cutting edge into tomorrow's museum piece.

It is the best of times and the worst of times. The gaps between the
haves and have-nots will no doubt widen continually in the 1990s. Commodities, or shall I say, plain old cash, rather than knowledge and a college diploma, have now come to define one's standing in society. The intellectuals are the biggest losers for the time being. The alarming day
may yet come when Chinese MTV devours the mind of the young generation with its hypnotic sexuality and usurps the cultural hegemony of
the fine print completely. It would be a fascinating sight to witness a five-
thousand-year-old empire tap the energy and beat of popular culture and
embrace high art and trash with equal zest. Perhaps the best way to com-
memorate the 1980s is by looking forward to the emergence in Deng's
China of a popular culture that will deliver us the masses' responses,

frivolous or contemplative, to the pulse of a rapidly changing society. Let us recognize, if not celebrate thoughtlessly, the self-expressions of common folks who are the biggest players of the 1990s as they fly involuntarily from the iron hold of the double hegemony of the past—the historical rule of the Confucian state and the pure ideology of socialism on the one hand, and the "knowledgeable elements" on the other.

THREE

Heshang and the Paradoxes of the Chinese Enlightenment

Heshang (Yellow river elegy), a six-part miniseries, was first broadcast on China's Central Television in the year of the dragon in 1988. The irony of the timing could not have been lost on the Chinese audience, whose responses to the documentary's condemnation of the totem symbol of the dragon and the thousand-year-old "yellow culture" ranged from indignation to heated debate and unreserved acclaim. Broadcast nationwide twice between June and August that year, *Heshang* stirred up a tornado of controversy.[1] Truly, as one critic observed in awe, the miniseries was "a rare spectacle in the thirty years' history of Chinese television."[2] By 1989 when the collection of critical essays *Chongping "Heshang"* (Reassessing "Yellow River elegy") was published, Chinese intellectuals' critique of the TV series had already crystallized into a clear outline. *Heshang*'s scriptwriters were criticized for propagating a view of politics and history that advanced historical fatalism, geographical determinism, the "fallacious backward ideology" of grand unification (*dayitong*), Eurocentrism, total westernization, elite culturalism, the postulate of a nonsocialist new epoch, and the theory of the ultrastability of Chinese feudal society.

Those critiques provide a convenient summary of the content of *Heshang*. Divided into six episodes—"In Search of a Dream" ("Xunmeng"), "Destiny" ("Mingyun"), "A Glimmering Light" ("Lingguang"), "A New Epoch" ("Xinjiyuan"), "Sorrows and Crises" ("Youhuan"), and "Azure" ("Weilanse")—the documentary delivers a message loud and clear: Old China can only revive its dying culture by modernization and westernization. The deepening sense of crisis that pervaded the six episodes echoed Zhao Ziyang's devastating proclamation at the Thirteenth Party Congress in October 1987: "China is now in the *primary* stage of socialism." Su Xiaokang, in his retrospective account of how he started writing the script in early 1988, remembers those days as "ominous," "restless," and "anxiety ridden."[3] The year of 1988, in fact, evoked the superstitious Chinese fear of epochal disasters, which, according to folk belief, never fail to recur at every twelve-year cycle of the dragon year. After all, 1976 shook the entire country with a succession of events of unparalleled magnitude: Zhou Enlai's death, the earthquake at Tangshan, and Mao Zedong's demise. A cycle later, an airplane crash in Chongqing, widespread pestilence in Jiangsu, and the inflation in early 1988 were unpropitious enough to conjure another bout of widespread apocalyptic anxiety in both the cities and countryside.

Heshang's irresistible power resides precisely in its capture, in stark aquatic imagery, of the intensifying crisis consciousness that a failing urban reform inevitably triggered. The apocalyptic mood of late 1987 and 1988 found its most convincing embodiment in the recurrent images of the turbulent floods of the Yellow River. And, from the reformist vantage point, what other image but the open expanse of the Pacific Ocean—a symbol of the indigo myth of modernity—can provide an ultimate exit for the river and, metaphorically, for those "descendants of the dragon" in search of a new dream?

This is the finale, rich in its implications, that greets us on the television screen in episode six: The Yellow River flows into the ocean and meets surging billows of azure blue. The panoramic view of the collision of the turbid and the transparent, which inspired the Tang poet Wang Zhihuan with such aesthetically engaged tranquillity, is turned into a haunting image of ambivalence in the final climactic moments of *Heshang*.[4]

Does the physical landscape of the encounter tell the story of the voluntary submission of the river to the ocean, as many CCP ideologues have charged? Or as Su Xiaokang contended in the documentary, does it embody the historical necessity of the life force of a nation moving from enclosure to openness? The first reading, which imbues the merger with the symbolism of annexation, brings to the fore the issue of the power relationship of the river versus the ocean, in which the former is seen to represent China, and the latter, Western imperialism. Such an interpretation cancels any possibility of treating both the river and the ocean as images of space that speak of the irrevocable passage from the confined to the immeasurable, and thus of the subversion of boundary, whether national, ideological, or psychological. Indeed, the finale of *Heshang* often makes one wonder whether a spectacle of such magnitude is framed in power symbolism that calls for the compulsive identification of the dominated and the dominator, or whether it is framed in space symbolism in which the issue of hegemony gives way to that of developmental process.

Heshang provides no easy solution to these questions in either its verbal or visual construction of what the Yellow River stands for. In fact, much of the power of the documentary derives from its shifting movement between these two sets of symbolism, which provokes conflicting moods of pessimism and optimism in narrator and audience. Yet despite the deprecatory tone that characterizes its initial portrayal of the river, the documentary seems to end in a dramatic reversal to conclude on a note of optimism. What greets our eyes on the screen at the end is no longer the raging river personified as the capricious or ruthless tyrant, but instead, the image of a heroic and triumphant Yellow River that surges toward the estuary in an ambivalent victory: "It is the anguish of the Yellow River, it is the hope of the Yellow River, that contribute to the greatness of the Yellow River. . . . The Yellow River has arrived at the mouth of the ocean—a magnificent but painful juncture. It is here that the mud and slit carried turbulently along for thousands of *li* [one *li* equals about one-third of a mile] will be deposited to form a new mainland" (*Heshang* 283–84).[5]

The Yellow River, characterized earlier as "China's sorrow" and an "unpredictable" destroyer as old as China's debilitating civilization itself, suddenly emerges as a life force that not only signifies "hope" but also promises the forming of a "new mainland." The ambivalence that underlies the symbolism of the Yellow River gives away the mood of the 1980s, an era caught in the tension between ideological enclosure and an infinitely expanding psychological space. Ironically, the vision of *Heshang*, which is riddled with ambiguities, impressed most of its critics as relentlessly unambiguous and coherent. Indeed, even those who attacked the documentary most vigorously have taken at face value its claim to be a genuine reflection on China's cultural traditions (*wenhua fansi*). Although many critiques ridicule the scriptwriters' poetic immersion in history and their aesthetic impulse to clothe and capture the chaos of the phenomenal world in a number of stable images, few do justice to the ideological ambivalence that informs the mode of thinking of modern and contemporary Chinese intellectuals—the enlightened elite, who are ironically no less nostalgic for power symbolism than their historical Confucian counterparts whom they roundly condemn.

It is the paradoxical vision of such a conflict-ridden intelligentsia that makes *Heshang* an intriguing ideological discourse and a work whose complexity continues to evade critics who find gratification in undertaking various ventures that justify either the cause of dogmatic Marxism or that of historiography. One such undertaking, earnestly pursued by both ideological zealots and academic historians, is the identification of the problematic citations and entries that Su Xiaokang culled from historical data to support his thesis.[6] As a narrative that is closer to a popular account of the philosophy of culture (*wenhua zhexue*) than to history itself, *Heshang* falls easy prey to the meticulous inspection of those erudite scholars whose concept of historical narrative is confined to that of chronicle. A less tedious, if less successful, critical enterprise revolves around the rigorous yet somewhat futile arguments over a set of familiar and sometimes clichéd issues: the vice and virtue of agrarian versus maritime civilization, the revolutionary significance of the peasant revolts that punctuated Chinese history, the fallacy of geographical determinism in history, the historical materialist versus the idealist view of history, doubts as to whether the Yellow River embodies the only source and center of ancient Chinese civilization, and the reasons why modern China failed to provide a fertile cradle for the rise of capitalism.

Although one could argue that these issues are crucial to our understanding of China's historical and recent past, they fall short of providing a vantage point for the examination of the documentary as a historical narrative in its own right. To do full justice to the controversial stance of *Heshang*, one needs to go beyond the familiar issues and address a different set of questions that reveals both the power and the limitations of its ideological discourse. I argue that both the potency and the limits of *Heshang* derive from its paradoxical approach to the concept of history, cultural symbolism, and the relationship between nationalism and enlightenment.

THE HISTORICAL PAST: UNAWAKENED DREAM OR A NIGHTMARE?

At first glance, *Heshang* seems self-consciously revolutionary in its destruction of the privileged status of China's historical past. It reiterates the message that "history is burden" through visual representations of those traumatic historical moments that contributed to the poverty and downfall of a once-glorious empire. In contrast to the desolate image of historical ruins and barren loess plateau, the future is projected through a simplified vision of the modern, embodied in specious outer-space imagery and metropolitan vistas of skyscrapers and Japanese bullet trains. The contrast between the old and the new is defined in terms of irreconcilable conflict. It seems only logical that the documentary condemns the characteristically Chinese orientation toward the past as the repository of a paradigm of society's ideal form. The chilling sight of the endless rows of Qin Shihuang's terra-cotta warriors effortlessly evokes the association of tyranny and history. The message is clear: Only by liberating human intelligence from the stifling sense of history will the Chinese people creatively confront the problems of the present. The past conceived as such is viewed as the antithesis rather than as the basis of what Chinese intellectuals revere and value in their own present.

But one may ask, What perspective do they revere? What interest do Chinese intellectuals now serve that leads them to bring the historical past to the bar of judgment? At first glance, the conscious claims of *Heshang* seem to answer these questions. Su Xiaokang and his generation of enlightened intellectuals attempt to provide us with a new perspective in place of the vision of the imperial past. And in catering to the needs of the present and future, they argue that imperial nationalism, which defined the interest of old China, must be replaced by a genuine cultural enlightenment. A close examination of the documentary, however, gives the lie to such claims.

For Frederic Wakeman, one of the most telling lines in the production is Su Xiaokang's nostalgic comment on the passing of a dream: "Our dream of a thousand-year empire ended at the time of Emperor Kangxi" (186).[7] The perspective discredited here is certainly that of the imperial past, and the national self-interest condemned is none other than the dreaming of an everlasting sovereignty. However, those with an attentive ear can hardly miss the subtle discrepancy that exists between the intellectual and emotional content of this telling lament. Although the narrator attempts to ridicule the delusions of patriotic dreamers, conflicting emotions riddle the intentionally sarcastic voice with unrelieved sentimentalism. The preaching of the futility of dreaming such a dream is unmistakably accompanied by a deeply seated, albeit unconscious, nostalgia for the golden past. Even at those moments when Su Xiaokang preaches most eloquently the elimination of such nostalgia, his vision for the future is helplessly and unconsciously embedded in the same rhetoric of imperialistic nationalism. At its heart, *Heshang* often betrays the cause of enlightenment and lapses into the nationalist discourse it is struggling so hard to free itself from. In fact, such suggestive passages run through the entire script, and when examined together they reveal a mentality that *Heshang* itself deplores and castigates with rhetorical persuasiveness:

> Why did the industrial civilization that signals [the coming of] *immense wealth* fail to emerge in Chinese society? (230, emphasis mine)

> Yet the Four Great Inventions did not fare so well in their homeland. The first Chinese who kindled the rocket-like firecrackers that would eventually conquer outer space was nonetheless not *the first human being who flew toward the cosmos.* (217, emphasis mine)

> Although as early as the eleventh century Shen Kuo had described the compass and magnetic field in his *Meng Xi bitan,* China never emerged as *a strong ocean empire.* (217)

> Why did China fail to maintain *the great lead it used to have . . . ?* Why did China fail to maintain its *cultural and political domination* over the world? (216)

> If Hainan Province were to be successful [in its economic projects], it would establish a liaison with the fourteen coastal cities. And together they will form *a gigantic economic dragon* on the Pacific. . . . This historical miracle would definitely bring new tints to Chinese culture. (278)

The modern elite are, after all, dreaming the same dream as their forebears of the dynastic past: wealth, power, and hegemony. The obsession of the old Confucian official-gentry with the domination of the Chinese empire is merely replaced by the same overriding interest in the power of the modern nation-state. It is a power that is presented as an abstracted monolithic structure external to its relationship with society and the individuals that make up the nation. What *Heshang* forcefully calls for—the agenda of enlightenment by means of cultural introspection—is time and again eclipsed by a stronger, perhaps unconscious drive for what it rejects—the revival of the glorious past in the future. Though they propose a creative historical amnesia, Su Xiaokang and his fellow iconoclasts never successfully sever their deep emotional ties to what dynastic history symbolizes. The dragon metaphor that they mock and repudiate in the first episode of the series comes back to haunt them with its potent symbolism in the final episode. One cannot help asking why the vision of an extended coastal economic zone should find its embodiment in nothing other than a cultural symbol that was relegated by the documentary to an ignominious historical past. Once stripped of its imperial garment, the symbol of the debilitated totem animal, we are surprised to find, is paradoxically but conveniently transformed into a symbol of modernity. The reference to the "gigantic economic dragon" introduces a dramatic reversal of what Su Xiaokang preached earlier. It marks one of the most illuminating moments of ideological paradox in *Heshang*.

The project of the liberation of the present from the burden of history is thus contradictory. When the construction of new mental categories is embedded within the old nationalist and imperial discourse, such a project is doomed to contradict itself. Those who call for oblivion remain captive to the ideological preconceptions that they fail to recognize as their own. What empowers the discourse of *Heshang* also serves to constrict it. History is both the dream and the nightmare from which neither the Chinese people nor the intellectuals themselves have awakened. Little has changed since the May Fourth Movement. Su Xiaokang and his generation of intellectuals inherited not only the iconoclastic tradition of their predecessors, but also the superiority-inferiority complex that characterizes the May Fourth generation's reflection of China's past.

Since iconoclasm was generated by the external force of imperialism in the case of May Fourth, the enlightenment program could quickly reverse itself and be transformed from a discourse of genuine self-reflection into a counterimperialist and eventually nationalist discourse. The cause of such an enlightenment, which called for the liberation of the individual from the tyranny of tradition, easily reverted to the political and collective cause of reviving the nation (*minzu*) and, ironically, of preserving the national essence. It seems inevitable that in the context of enlightenment as such, any introspective look into China's historical past engenders an ambivalent attitude that makes Chinese intellectuals at once proud of and hostile toward their own cultural and national heritage, while defiant toward and subservient to the imported Western culture at the same time. It is this emotional complex, which I designate as the "superiority-inferiority complex," and other critics designate as "an unbalanced mentality," that doomed the New Culture Movement from the beginning and compelled even the most enlightened reformers to give up the agenda of enlightenment for the cause of patriotism.[8]

The creative tension between intellectual emancipation and nationalism continues to characterize the struggles China is engaged in to this day in shaping and articulating its own modernity. It has become a predictable pattern, as Vera Schwarcz demonstrates in her work, that the official commemoration of May Fourth always seeks to highlight the role of nationalism in defining, or more specifically redefining, the movement, whereas in contrast the aging veterans of 1919 come to remember and consecrate May Fourth as primarily an enlightenment movement.[9]

It is worth noting that no one seems more anxious to revive the image of the movement as such than post-Mao intellectuals. Both Li Zehou and Liu Zaifu turned to May Fourth in their discussions of the ongoing controversy over traditionalism and modernism that made up the cultural platform before June 4, 1989. Not surprisingly, May Fourth appeared to both of them as having failed to fulfill its cultural missions. What intrigues me the most, however, is not their lament over the unfulfilled vision of their spiritual forebears, but rather their observation of an inexplicable emotional complex of Chinese intellectuals. Li Zehou mentions in passing the problem posed by such a "complex structure of cultural psychology."[10] Liu Zaifu goes a step further by defining it in terms of *tianchao qingjie*, "the complex of the Dynasty of Heaven,"[11] an equivalent to superiority complex, or in terms of Liu's subjectivity theory, a fixation with the concept of "cultural subjectivity."

The implications of the discovery of such a complex are manifold. Most significantly, the dichotomous paradigm of enlightenment versus patriotism can no longer be viewed as stable. Whereas the sentiment of patriotism is relatively unambiguous, the quest for enlightenment cannot be characterized so easily. Inasmuch as its advocates often fall prey to the two conflicting cultural orientations—the inferiority-superiority complex—such a quest is doomed to be self-defeating, since eventually it will fail to close the gap between its inner motivation and its professed goal. What "drowned out the quieter imperatives" of enlightenment is therefore not only the "pressure for political conformity," but no less importantly, albeit more subtly, the pressure of the cultural unconscious.[12] It is illuminating that even an enlightened scholar such as Li Zehou provides no exception to this rule. Despite his advocation of the importance of enlightenment in reevaluating May Fourth, he fell prey to a thematic formula that had misguided a generation of reform intellectuals in the 1920s and that Su Xiaokang reproduces with little variation in *Heshang*: "Although *the wealth and power of our nation (modernization)* still emerges as the primary agenda for Chinese people, the relationship between enlightenment and national survival is after all very different."[13]

What appears ominous, and indeed ironic, is not so much Li's reminder that the agenda of contemporary China is no different from that of imperial China. It is the equation he sets up between *fuqiang* and *xiandai hua*, "wealth and power" and "modernization." If the quest of modernity is motivated by the compulsion to recover the status of the "Dynasty of Heaven," then modernity is ultimately identical to the political and economic hegemony of a nation. Li Zehou's vision of enlightenment thus remains as confined as that of his May Fourth predecessors.

Su Xiaokang, now an exile in the United States, in retrospect came to deplore his idea of "saving the nation through cultural reform" (*wenhua jiuguo*), viewing it as a dream after all.[14] However, little did he realize that the dream was marred not because he mistakenly scapegoated traditional culture for the failures of the socialist system, but because the slogan itself implies an ideological construct that is fundamentally self-contradictory, therefore impossible to fulfill. The claims of enlightenment that are predicated on the autonomy of the individual inevitably contradict the utilitarian and collective interests of nationalism. The schema often reiterated in the European Enlightenment—the assertion that the private and the public interest coincide—confronts its most powerful antithesis in the May Fourth Movement, in the aborted attempts of the Chinese enlightenment philosophers to come to terms with an enlightenment that is forced upon them by the threat of imperialism, and in their attempts to solve the contradiction between the interest of the individual and that of the nation-state.[15] The failure to recognize the often hostile relationship between these two entities inevitably results in the making and aborting of the same dream.

By the same token, insofar as the agenda of enlightenment is generated from a nationalist sentiment that pursues the vision of China as a global power, the reform intellectuals will continue to rely on an interpretive scheme of the past that privileges the first term in such bipolar concepts as superiority and inferiority, wealth and poverty, dominator and dominated, and inventor and emulator. The dynamic relations between Chinese culture and its Western counterpart will continue to be pared down to a comparison of their relative power, defined only in terms of competitiveness. And the Chinese people will forever be haunted by those moments of the past that sustain their vision for a future that perpetuates not only the myth of immense wealth and the draconic stature of its economy, but also the cultural and political domination of the Chinese nation—conceptual categories that lead them back to the program of nationalism, and thus, ironically, to the historical past they are told to forget. Until enlightenment is generated from the genuine impulse of self-examination, until China's intellectuals resolve their superiority-inferiority complex toward their own culture and history, the project of enlightenment will remain a spurious one, forever submerged by the thousand-year-old discourse of power. The lesson that *Heshang* delivers is dire: The nationalist complex that characterizes the way the elite intellectuals look at China's historical past determines the deep structure of their historical imagination for the future. This is a vicious cycle that Su Xiaokang himself warns against, but which he involuntarily reproduces.

Thus the most transparent moment of *Heshang* ironically coincides with its most opaque moment, a moment crystallized in a one-liner: "It seems that many things in China have got to start over again from May Fourth" (279). The spiritual journey back to May Fourth is both potentially dangerous and liberating. It is a quest whose meaning is as vaguely suggested in *Heshang* as the cultural reform it promises to launch. Perhaps it is the perpetual struggle between the elite intellectuals' nostalgic gaze at the historical past and their conscious efforts to break free of its tenacious hold that contributes to the conceptual complexity and emotional ambivalence that infuses the one-liner.[16] One wonders where this suggestive look at May Fourth might lead Su Xiaokang and his elite colleagues and what kind of obsession with the burden of history prompted the unrelenting satirist of history to keep turning back to it. Will this retrospective look send them back into the circular maze of tradition and modernity, nationalism and enlightenment, a route that many eminent May Fourth reformers, Hu Shi and Lu Xun among them, have traced? Or can one hope that the nostalgic look at the history of May Fourth may yet lead contemporary intellectuals to a very different path?[17]

THE FALLACY OF ULTRASTABILITY?

Su Xiaokang's fascination with May Fourth brings us to one of the most controversial theses underlying the documentary: the concept of Chinese history as the unbroken chain of periodic alternation between order and disorder. Su Xiaokang's desire to break this cycle of continuity leads him to envision May Fourth as a potential moment of historical discontinuity that is nonetheless never fully consummated.

If we take the theory of ultrastability at face value and divorce it from the sociopolitical and psychological context that is intimately and unconsciously woven into the wide spectrum of meanings such a theory evokes, we will inevitably agree with the principal charge that *Heshang* propagates an essentially idealist concept of the historical field. In fact, it is an easy task to blame the scriptwriters for their conceptual fallacy of reducing the changing historical process to a formal and coherent totality. What Su Xiaokang and Jin Guantao deliver is an unambiguously synchronic view of history. They argue that insofar as there is movement in Chinese history at all, there is no development, only cyclical recurrence. It does not take much historical understanding to comprehend the simple truth that history knows nothing that is identical. Why then did Su Xiaokang and his team take such pains to construct the illusion of identity to account for the mechanism of a historical process that is in reality characterized by the deep structure of change and heterogeneity?

We may never find a convincing answer to this question. Yet if we insist on examining *Heshang* from the standpoint of the traditional historian, we will continue to miss the ideological implications of the documentary. We need first of all to remind ourselves that it was not produced for the college history curriculum, but for mass consumption. It was not written as a historical text, but rather as a historical narrative of popular interest, presupposing the fictive character of the reconstruction of the events it purports to represent and explain. The promotion of historical action rather than the transmission of pure knowledge serves as the focal point of reference to the emotive content of *Heshang*. Although Su Xiaokang never clearly indicates whether such an action should be defined in terms of cultural or economic reform, the production of the documentary was meant to arouse the masses to action by effecting a deep structural transformation not only of society and its ethos, but also of individuals and their moral and psychological composition.

The official revival of the Confucian cult in China today and the traditionalists' call for a restructuring of the conceptual categories of Confucianism serve only as examples that bear out the impressionist logic of ultrastability. The fate of Confucianism in modern China chillingly testifies to the hypothesis of a cultural unconscious that is built on the metaphor of recurrence and formal continuity. Instead of ushering in an "unhealthy" and "unprogressive" view of history, as *Heshang*'s belligerent critics charged, the thesis of ultrastability, which seems to assume a theoretically neutral ground, serves paradoxically as a powerful mockery of the ideological stagnation and the return complex that the Confucian revival tellingly revealed.[18] It is the ideological implications underlying the notion of ultrastability that empower its fallacious discourse and turn an otherwise fragile academic exercise of the amateur historian into a poignant political statement in disguise.

The dream of a radical transformation of Chinese culture seems to have eluded generations of reform intellectuals. However, what Su Xiaokang contends in criticizing the ultrastability of the system is not merely the possibility of and necessity for macroscopic change of the sociocultural and political structure of a nation. What lies at the heart of any enlightenment project, *Heshang* included, is first and foremost the transformation of the individual. In criticizing China's ultrastability, Su Xiaokang conveys the possibility and urgency of changing the moral-psychological structure of the Chinese individual. One should be alert to the fact that the official revival of Confucian epistemology has emerged at this historical juncture to fulfill two functions. It serves as a double-edged cultural strategy concocted by the state-party apparatus not only to withstand its imperialistic discourse of the foreign, but also to subvert the agenda of modernity and enlightenment that takes the individual as its point of departure. The deep structural transformation that *Heshang* hopes to witness and contribute to, if not trigger, is a process that has to take place within the consciousness of the newly discovered yet precariously balanced individual. The official project of the Confucian revival is thus potentially dangerous in that it operates in the mode of the "metaphorical identification" of the subject with the state, of the private with the public spheres, of morality with loyalty, and of past with present.[19]

Thus *Heshang* opens with poignant footage of the different forms of ritualistic worship of deities—whether religious, political, or simply communal. The sight of rows and rows of pious worshippers bowing down to the icon of collectivized authority is overwhelmingly powerful and ironic. It echoes the formidable spectacle of the terra-cotta warriors and drives home one of the central motifs that unifies the six-part series, namely, the lethargic dissolution of individual consciousness into the cultural unconscious.

It is in terms of meaning of the potential struggle and liberation of the individual consciousness from the collective unconscious (whether cultural, political, or historical) that the theory of ultrastability has one more lesson to teach. Insofar as the Chinese people do not realize the crucial need for a consciousness of their own responsibility for the calamities of the past, the metaphor of recurrence on which the theory of ultrastability is based is tragically valid. The ethical moment of such a theory is reflected in its silent reminder that only in the full consciousness of such a morally irrevocable responsibility can the Chinese today create a future radically different from the past. The concept of ultrastability thus not only speaks of but also speaks to the ethical and psychological inertia that conveniently blurs the distinction between the victim and the victimizer and between conscious choice and choice by default. It is this same collective inertia of the Chinese people that finds expression in their unreflective condemnation of China's socialist past and in their fetishistic worship of a vaguely conceived modernity.

THE FETISHISM OF CULTURAL SYMBOLS

Inasmuch as the hidden agenda of *Heshang* is that of modernity, Su Xiaokang's reconstruction of the cultural symbols that make up China's discredited past appears as fictive as his reading of the recurrent pattern of Chinese history. It is fictive because the structuring principle underlying the reconstitution of "traditional" symbols is not based on tradition as an autonomous system of representations, but rather on the opposite relationships that Su Xiaokang constructs and perceives between indigenous tradition and Western modernity. To be sure, tradition is always defined in retrospect. However, in this case, its meaning not only derives from but is also evaluated by the perspective of a hostile modernity that seeks to appropriate tradition into its own system of representations. The cultural tradition thus recovered is a new mythology that answers to the problematic of an epistemological discourse in which "modernity" emerges as the dominating, albeit invisible, term. Whether "tradition versus modernity" represents the only typological mode of description for the historical dilemma China faces today is a matter that need not detain us here. It is important for us to recognize, however, that the discourse of tradition retrieved through such an oppositional mechanism appears to be a reconstructed image, intrinsically inferior because it is epistemologically derivative. It is an image that comes into being through the creative shuffling of its previous categories under the new assumptions of the discourse of modernity.

In *Heshang* such a creative reorganization of the past reveals itself in the documentary's awareness of its own artificiality. The theory of ultrastability is but one example of the scriptwriters' fictive understanding and representation of history. The entire project can be described as an attempt to reinvoke, in a poetic manner, the spirit of a past age. And in so doing, Su Xiaokang credited as testimony those literary works, myths, and legends that contribute as much to the eliciting of poetic truth as the documents that academic historians consider authentic primary sources. Thus not only does *Heshang* cite unabashedly Zhuang Zi's fable of He Bo (275–76), the legend of the dark-skinned Judge Bao (264), and many other texts of popular fiction, it also makes extensive and undifferentiated use of film clips from the *Yellow Earth, The 1894 Sino-Japanese*

War, and *Old Well* as historically meaningful data that allow us to gain access to the opaque text known as our collective past.

Perhaps China's historian-critics were less bothered by the appearance of fictional materials in the documentary than by the poetic license Su Xiaokang took in using them to justify and account for historical events.[20] Yet the critics who charged *Heshang* with propagating the "man-made myth" of the tyrannical nature of the Yellow River missed the point entirely. It is precisely from this fictional logic that the value of *Heshang* as truth can be derived. A narrative of such an order calls for a different strategy of reading. A literal interpretation of the fictive representations of the documentary reveals only the conceptual limitations of its critics, not those of its makers. It follows that the rigid distinction between mythic thinking and historical thinking has no place in the kind of philosophical inquiry into history that characterizes the spirit of *Heshang*. A true critic's task is not to condemn the fictive nature of historical reflection, but rather to determine the extent to which such a mythical logic provides an adequate basis for understanding historical trends.

One could nevertheless attribute a certain utilitarian motivation to the fictive nature of Su Xiaokang's historical imagination. In a television series produced for mass consumption, the fabulous and the familiar speak directly to the public, whose interests the intellectual reformers of the documentary seek so eagerly to grasp and appeal to. I wonder if there exists a certain tenuous connection between the salesperson psychology of mass culture and Su Xiaokang's choice of the dragon, the Great Wall, and the Yellow River as the dominant cultural symbols of China's imperial past.

All three images undoubtedly form part of the diction of popular culture. And as such, each is endowed with the power to evoke the irrational reverence of the masses. Su Xiaokang understands that histories ought never to be read as unambiguous and immutable signs of the events that took place, but rather as fluid symbolic structures. And as symbols, the meanings of the wall and the river change according to the significance that they have for our current life. Su Xiaokang is at his best when he can successfully demonstrate the essentially provisional character of such cultural metaphors. When embedded in the discourse of modernity, they are charged with different emotional valences and figurative content. Thus the Great Wall, once a living presence of potent immediacy, is turned into a hollow fetish of the race. What was a justifiable source of national pride now casts a shadow over the minds of those who are busy appropriating tradition in the service of a modernist discourse. Such a reevaluation inevitably triggers the process of demystification.

What intrigues me, however, is not so much Su Xiaokang's attempt to lay bare the fetishistic content of defunct cultural symbols as his turn toward the ocean as the new fetish for the Chinese people. One is tempted to ask: Does there exist a deeper connection between the ocean and the wall than that of the alleged contrast between the modern West and traditional China, and between openness and enclosure? The subtle connection between the two, I argue, rests on their belonging to the same repertory of power symbolism that has obsessed Su Xiaokang and Chinese intellectuals throughout the ages. What empowers the color "azure blue" is exactly what used to empower the national symbol of the Great Wall and the dragon—namely, power in the sense of expansion, glory, and aggression. Take a look at all three cultural symbols presented in *Heshang*: Both the wall and the dragon stand for imperial power, and the river grips Su Xiaokang's imagination primarily because of its indomitable nature.

The Great Wall, it is worth noting, has served the radical discourse of iconoclasm on more than one occasion during different historical crises. It is in the choice of this particular symbol that Su Xiaokang betrays his spiritual bond with those daring cultural critics who antedated his own generation. Lu Xun condemned the Great Wall as a symbol of enclosure and political oppression.[21] Decades later, Huang Xiang, a member of the Enlightenment Society during the heyday of the Democracy Wall Movement, contributed to the demystification of the national symbol with a poem in which a personified Great Wall bewails its tyranny and wishes for its own demise.[22]

The citation of the wall in *Heshang* thus has a history of its own. It serves to remind us of the continuity of the iconoclastic tradition that generations of disillusioned intellectuals nourished and established. The intertextual references in question cannot help but evoke the psychological burden that the iconoclasts' unfulfilled mission impose upon their spiritual heirs. However, whereas one can argue that the intertextual reference to the earlier critiques of the Great Wall bestows an aura of urgency and legitimacy on *Heshang*'s preoccupation with the symbol, Su Xiaokang's alleged critique of what the wall stands for—namely, psychological enclosure—often degenerates into a lament over what it fails to achieve for a people whose mind is set upon dynastic or national glory, an image inseparable from military prowess in the past and wealth in the present: "If one argues that the construction of the Great Wall under-

taken by Emperors Shi Huang of Qin and Wu of Han could still be considered an embodiment of the vigor and valor of our *huaxia* civilization,
then the repairing project of the Wall during the Ming dynasty in the
mid-fifteenth century was nothing but an act of failure and recoil" (201).
From this perspective, the Great Wall is considered a "gigantic tragic
monument" for it "fails to represent power, progress, and glory, but instead, it embodies enclosure, conservatism, *impotent defense, and faint-
hearted nonoffense*" (203, emphasis mine). A similar preoccupation with
the hegemonic logic also underlies Su's obsession with the ocean as an
alternative symbol of power. Such an obsession is most poignantly revealed in the repeated footage of the close-ups of huge masts and jumbo-
sized sails, and no less frequently of the fleet of sails preparing for or engaging in sea battles. The Great Wall in Lu Xun and Huang Xiang's text,
a symbol of oppression and alienation, recedes to the background in Su
Xiaokang's vision of a wall that is far more military than psychological.
The Great Wall and the ocean—defense and offense: This seems to be
the inner, if not the conscious, motivation of contrasting the one with
the other in *Heshang*.

The wall, however, is not the only symbol that Su Xiaokang problematizes but contradictorily speaks for at the same time. One cannot
help but wonder why Su Xiaokang is particularly drawn to the symbol
of the dragon, instead of many other symbols that are also characteristically Chinese.[23] Is it a coincidence that *Heshang* repudiates one set of
power symbols that have malfunctioned only to turn to another set that
promises to better serve the same original purpose?

Yet no matter how deeply and unconsciously Su Xiaokang seems to
have succumbed to the discourse of power, it would be unfair to characterize his entire historical project in this manner. For one thing, *Heshang* is not just a verbal construct. It also speaks to us through the camera. And as a visual representation, it is able to transcend the ideological
enclosure determined by the written text. The visual imagery of the encircling wall and the expansive ocean embodies a different kind of symbolism; the internal logic that associates the azure blue and the Yellow
River on the screen is not so much the symbolism of power as that of
space. It is the suggestive vision of the camera that bestows a completely
different interpretation of Su Xiaokang's choice of the ocean as an alternative to the wall and the river. The boundless ocean in contrast to
the enclosed wall and the well-channeled course of the river serves as
such an eloquent metaphor of the infinite possibilities of imminent emancipation that the power symbolism implicit in the merging of the river

into the ocean seems to be subsumed, for several fleeting moments, into the symbolism of space. Only seen in this light can the ocean be liberated from the symbolism of the fetish and serve as the real source of inspiration for those who now turn toward it in search of an answer.

THE QUEST OF THE INTELLECTUAL ELITE

The ending of *Heshang* thus tells us two different stories: one the conquest of the river by the ocean, the other, the miracle of a spatial breakthrough of the imprisoned. Because visual imagery has a life of its own and is less susceptible than verbal imagery to ideological constraint, the spectacle of the merger invites conflicting interpretations. Inasmuch as the conclusion is seen rather than derived from a logical statement, the last few minutes of the documentary embody the tour de force of a conceptual ambiguity beyond the grasp of verbal logic.

Much of the complexity of *Heshang* consists in such opaque moments of the ideological unconscious. Although Su Xiaokang envisions the possibility of cultural cataclysmic transformations, not only the concrete agenda, but also the real nature of such transformations eludes him. However, this ambivalence about the program of enlightenment does not cloud his vision of the role that intellectuals will assume at this historical moment. One could say that he is less inclined to be aware of what the agenda is than who the logical agenda setter will be. There is little ambiguity over who should assume the new cultural authority. Nowhere can one find a better prescription of such a privileged role than in the last episode: "History, however, created a very unique species for Chinese people—the intellectuals. . . . The weapons that could eliminate ignorance and superstition are held in their hands; they are those who could conduct a direct dialogue with maritime civilization; they are those who would irrigate the yellow earth with the fresh sweet spring of science and democracy!" (280).

Is it perhaps because Chinese intellectuals have historically been so close to the seat of power that the impulse to reinstate their vanguard position comes to haunt them time and again? Why is it that underlying the old and new enlightenment movement is the message that has undergone little change since Confucius' time—that knowledge is power? Is it this unconscious search for the privileged status that continuously eluded the modern and contemporary intelligentsia that led Su Xiaokang to lament that "Chinese intellectuals could be nothing more than mere losers in the political arena?"[24]

Seen in the context of power politics, the project of *Heshang* appears less politically altruistic than its makers consciously professed. I argue that their project of modernity and enlightenment simultaneously integrates within itself the project of restructuring power in society and in the CCP and, by implication, an inherent agenda that seeks to remind and reassure society of their once pivotal and hegemonic role in shaping the destiny of China.

It is worth noting that Deng Xiaoping's modernization program theoretically provides Chinese intellectuals with an opportunity to fulfill such a prominent role. Modernization depends upon the expertise of technocracy and an intellectual elite who draw the blueprint for a modernizing China. In reality, however, they are well aware that their political fortune rises and falls with every shift of power within the Party. Throughout modern Chinese history, intellectuals have always held a precarious tenure under an unpredictable administration divided by contending political factions. Under Deng's regime, it is clear that the promise of professional autonomy for the intellectuals is a measure of expedience and based on the principle of utilitarianism. The political assets they have accumulated so quickly since the late 1970s could be dissolved easily. It is perhaps their awareness of the contingent nature of their power base that leads intellectuals like Su Xiaokang to lament. It is also perhaps due to the acute awareness of their own vulnerable position that a program about cultural enlightenment like *Heshang* is often riddled with obscure moments that reveal the intellectuals' deeply rooted obsession with power.

The flickering revelation of the ideological unconscious in *Heshang* portrays an anxiety-ridden elite torn between several conflicting objectives. The contradiction between what they consciously attempt to achieve and what unconsciously binds them often eclipses the possibility of a genuine cultural transformation proposed in the documentary. It points to the internal limitations of a Chinese enlightenment that is based on cultural utilitarianism, on how the past can best serve the present, on an obsession with the bygone hegemony of imperial China, on a kind of cultural determinism that seeks to reduce the pluralistic manifestations of Western civilization to a monistic totality, on its advocates' preoccupation with their own image making, on their subscription to cultural fetishism, and on a pan-Chinese nationalism. It is Su Xiaokang's weakened national self-image and his unresolved emotional ambiguity toward China's historical past that clouds the reformist vision of *Heshang*. Until Chinese intellectuals recognize the precedence of individual and human welfare over national agendas and geopolitical power, the tragic homogeneity of Qin Shi Huang's terra-cotta warriors will continue to prevail and the reformer-intellectuals will forever mistake their superiority-inferiority nationalist complex for genuine self-reflectivity.

FOUR

Mapping Aesthetic Modernity

When I find myself in time of trouble
Mother Mary comes to me.
Speaking words of wisdom,
Let it be.

Thus begins Liu Suola's story "Lantian lühai" (Blue sky, green sea) (1985).[1] The momentary sentimentality that the Beatles' lyric arouses in the preamble of this modern tale soon bites the dust as the narrator, an impious pop singer, renders the reverential "let it be" with a shrug of her shoulders, into *qutamade,* Mandarin Chinese slang meaning "fuck his mother." But of course, any sensitive Chinese reader would share Liu Suola's sacrilegious sentiment long before the punch line is delivered. The evocation of Mother Mary at the beginning of the lyric is already in itself a blasphemy of the first degree in a communist country where only a decade ago every household was devoutly engaged in the ritual practice of invoking the name of the beloved Chairman Mao in times of trouble.

"Blue Sky, Green Sea," like many other tales labeled Chinese "modernist" (*xiandai pai*) during the 1980s, is loaded with disdain for the sacred. But while the experimentalists, the generation succeeding the so-called modernists, could vaunt such irreverence with total abandon, the "modernists" display their impiety with a touch of irony and agony, no matter how lackadaisical they may sound in their ungodly *qutamade.* The dilemma for Liu Suola's narrator, and for the generation of writers who came of age during the Cultural Revolution, does not simply evanesce with the displacement of the indigenous autocratic Father by the magnanimous Virgin Mother of foreign origin. In the mid-1980s, Liu Suola's generation was acutely aware that the ground underneath their feet had caved in completely. Neither the aborted socialist utopia nor imported spiritual convictions could deliver them from an abyss that was nonetheless fascinating in the depth of its hollowness.

Depth in nothingness. This clearly sets Liu Suola apart from the young experimentalists whose experience of the cave-in is indistinguishable from their dabbling in the superficial and disingenuous. Liu Suola's characters, however cynically they reject redemption, have souls that await epiphany. Atheists by default, not by choice, her generation is deprived of religion but waiting for Godot nonetheless. What explains her capacity to respond to the profound religious experience that the Beatles conjure up in "Let It Be" but the very depth of her nihilism? What impassions her narrator's denial of religion (whether Mother Mary or Mao Zedong) but her intense yearning for the religious? No matter how hard they tried, Liu Suola and the Chinese *xiandai pai* could never trivialize their blasphemy as effortlessly as the experimentalists. She and her fellow travelers uttered curses as part of the religious ritual dedicated to the true believers.

Did such aesthetic sensibility touch a sympathetic chord in post-Mao China, where some true believers were still mourning their disillusionment? The continual attack by Party ideologues on the so-called modernist writings and the outbreak of the debate over pseudomodernism (*wei xiandai pai*) in 1988 attested to the pulling of many heart strings that an aesthetic modernity in labor had precipitated.[2] This chapter will register the travail that Chinese writers and literary critics went through as they attempted to articulate the zeitgeist of the post-Mao era—an elusive "modern consciousness" (*xiandai yishi*) that awaited conflicting interpretations from the CCP and the iconoclastic literary elite.

THE HERMENEUTICS OF XIANDAI YISHI

Who owns the copyright to the neologism is by no means settled. Both the Party and the elite have laid claim to it and appropriated the term for their own ideological agendas. Contrary to conventional wisdom, the term *xiandai yishi* incorporates more than just the consciousness of resistance to the so-called official ideological consciousness. The linking of resistance and "modern consciousness" is in fact a much later reinvention of the original term that departs quite dramatically from its earlier semantic culture. As many Marxist ideologues would remind us, the seeds of modern consciousness were sown as early as 1978, when the Third Plenary Session of the Eleventh Party Congress launched the campaign of "thought emancipation" and initiated the agenda of modernization.[3] It was, in short, a term that the Party owned and propagated at the very start.

Thus, in contrast to the derogatory term *xiandai pai* (*xiandai* means "modern," and *pai*, "school"), which contains the negative reference to Western modernism, the catchy phrase *xiandai yishi* was endowed when it first surfaced in post-Mao China with the positive connotation of a keen epochal consciousness that highlighted two keynote concepts of modernity, change and progress. It was not until the mid-1980s that the public's appraisal of these two terms—the one negative, and the other positive—began to undergo an inverse transformation. The term *xiandai pai* gradually lost its ideological stigma as the debate over the nomenclature of Chinese modernism ended in deadlock. A process of revalorization turned the dismissive term into a tame appellation for the Yuppie "modernists" (Liu Suola and Xu Xing). In the meantime, the term *xiandai yishi* fared worse. The popular consensus on the positive value of modern consciousness fell apart as soon as creative writers participated in the naming of the modern. They made it clear that *xiandai yishi* had to record the throb and cadence of an aesthetic modernity that more often than not ran counter to the logic of social modernity.

The history of the term "modern consciousness" took a winding course with nary a dull moment. In the late 1970s and the early 1980s, the semantic core of "modern consciousness" was composed of invigorating definitions such as "self-reflexive consciousness and reform consciousness," an ideological content specified by the Party as the new historical consciousness of postrevolutionary Chinese socialism.[4] After 1984, when significant breakthroughs in urban reform appeared more difficult to achieve, the interpretation of "modern consciousness" underwent a gradual transformation. Frustration with the slow structural change of the system engendered a desolate consciousness of alienation and deprivation among the elite in urban centers. Inundation of the cultural market by translations of Western works ranging from Freud to the existentialists and the *nouveau roman* further heightened an awareness of the inverse drive within *xiandai yishi*.

By the mid-1980s, the semantic boundary of "modern consciousness" was overrun by such a growing number of ambiguous categories (rebellious consciousness, consciousness of freedom, self-consciousness, sense of loss of the self, the exploration of the unconscious, the palpitation of desire, a restless and unrestrained mood, the perturbations of the soul, consciousness of subjectivity, crisis consciousness, critical and pluralistic consciousness) that both the Party and realist writers—who formed a strange but consistent coalition in cultural politics—felt compelled to reclaim their interpretive authority by redefining, and in the process domesticating, the neologism.[5] Seminars sponsored by the official organ were held to delimit the meaning of "modern consciousness," distinguish the so-called genuine from spurious ingredients, and purge those categories labeled "nonmodern" (*fei xiandai*). Among those problematized categories were root-searching (which allegedly ran counter to the zeitgeist of leaping forward), absurdity, subjectivity, nihilism, loneliness, depression, and decadence—categories that the Party long held suspect because of their alleged origin in the West. Insinuations about the dangers of spiritual pollution lurked in Party-sponsored showcases with titles such as "How to Interpret *Xiandai yishi*."[6] Many symposia held during 1985 and 1986, regardless of the ideological bent of their organizers, grew out of the acute awareness of the emerging agonistic competition between the Party and writers to name the semantic properties of modern consciousness.

This controversy over *xiandai yishi* may reinforce the old myth about the overdetermined historical antagonism between those two rivals. But although such a long-standing rivalry seems to play up the irreconcilability of the two hermeneutic systems of modern consciousness, I argue that the Party and writers of modernist bent shared in common certain stipulations that each laid down as essential to its own definition of *xiandai yishi*. Statements that *"xiandai yishi* is more than just a temporal concept" (i.e., modernity) and that "not all the consciousness of the past" should be excluded from the rubric of modern consciousness[7] could have been made by the Party, by the guardians of Confucianist tradition, or (ironically) by the *xungen* school of writers, whose search for cultural roots, a symptomatic quest that emerged during their ambivalent encounter with modern consciousness, earned for them the unwelcome title of "traditionalist."

What does it entail if both the practitioners (the root-searching writers) and the opponents of aesthetic modernism (the Party and realist writers) can find a contingent point of departure for dialogue? The mere possibility that the official ideology could find repercussions in literary discourse—in this particular case, in the cultural ideology of the *xungen* school—suggests that those who take for granted the oppositional relationship between Chinese writers and the CCP can no longer ignore the fact that neither body is made up of stable or homogeneous constituents. Just as the Party succeeded in co-opting many reform-minded writers (Wang Meng was one of its most famous recruits), so the totalized category of "writers" is subject to further differentiation. Even those endowed with "modern" sensibilities quarrel among themselves about the meaning of Chinese aesthetic modernity. For instance, whereas younger iconoclasts like Liu Xiaobo problematize the *xungen* writers' return to mythical origins as antimodern, the latter insist that it is modernity itself that constitutes the horizon for their arousal of mythical pasts. Modern consciousness may signify an uncompromising break with the past for one guild of writers but signify for another the "dialectical relations of sublation" between tradition and modernity.[8] It is hardly justifiable to conclude that Chinese writers, no matter how rebelliously they pose against Party ideology, want to outlaw, simply for the sake of playing oppositional politics, officially sanctioned categories such as "reform consciousness," "exploratory consciousness," "open-door consciousness," and "scientific consciousness" from the semantic proper of *xiandai yishi.*[9] In fact, the official standpoint that modern consciousness is not only globally determined but, more importantly, culturally specific echoes the poetics of root-searching literature (namely that world literature is first and foremost national literature) to such an extent that the formulaic dichotomy of a conservative Party versus the radical writer no longer holds.

Although the occasional border crossing of the official and unofficial line of interpretation often blunted the offensive edge of the controversy over the definition of *xiandai yishi,* the emergence of the problematic of modern consciousness in the mid-1980s was symptomatic of literary critics' attempt in the late 1980s to draw boundaries between sharply defined pairs of bipolar opposites: the indigenous and the alien, the emulative and the original, and in symbolic terms, the spurious and the genuine. The controversy over the definition of "modern consciousness" anticipated the terms of the later debate—the authentic versus the pseudo—that were to underlie the controversy over pseudomodernism in 1988.

THE AESTHETIC MODERN AS IDEOLOGY

No matter how similar the terms of debate, the 1988 controversy over pseudomodernism was not simply a rehash of the earlier one over *xiandai yishi.* In a span of two years, the inquiry surrounding modernism (*xiandai zhuyi*) shifted its focus from "Do we want modernism?" to "Do we have authentic modernism?" Modernism's career in post-Mao China took two dramatic turns, one predominantly ideological (What cause does modernism serve?), which could be dated as early as 1979, and the other formal (Is this modernist discourse ours [Chinese] or theirs [Western]?) that culminated in the 1988 debate of pseudomodernism. Since the premise that one can clearly differentiate the ideological from the formal smacks of crude binarism, I should qualify my argument by adding that the so-called Chinese modernism's formal turn in the late 1980s by no means tossed aside those problematics that its earlier tour into the ideological terrain amassed. Thus the pseudomodernism debate in 1988 was not simply preoccupied with formal issues but also with the critique of the "unhealthy" ideological content that a "spurious" modern consciousness generated and internalized. The critique of Chinese modernism in 1988 was in fact targeted both at its formal aesthetics and at its alleged exaltation of the ideology of irrationality and decadence.

The ideological project of "modernism" did not start with the controversy over *xiandai yishi*. Long before the Party felt the need to rechart and legitimize its own version of modern consciousness, academic scholars at major research centers had envisioned the entry of modernism into socialist China as an outbreak of ideological epidemic rather than the unfolding of a pure aesthetic project. In March 1979, the Institute of Foreign Literature at the Academy of the Social Sciences in Beijing raised the issue of "How to Assess Foreign Bourgeois Literature." In December 1980, a literary quarterly, *Research on Foreign Literature,* set in motion a forum on "Western Modernist School" that generated approximately thirty articles in a year and a half. Those early debates about modernism were invariably framed in terms of the critique of class consciousness. In such an ideological climate, the dilemma for Chinese writers was unimaginatively described by one critic as the making of a choice between bourgeois literature and socialist literature.

The choice was easy in the early 1980s, when memories of ideological campaigns were still fresh and Party leaders were keener than ever to police the mind. The stigma of bourgeois liberalism could turn any undisguised promotion of Western modernism into a case of high treason. Modernity, "in whatever age it appears, cannot exist without a shattering of belief and without discovery of the 'lack of reality' of reality, together with the invention of other realities."[10] Whereas Western modern art brings to bear an emancipatory potential directed against the excesses of technical and bureaucratic rationality, in post-Mao China, the historical burden of "modernist" artists and writers fell on their potential exposure of what was "unreal" about socialist reality and on their discovery and radicalizing of the private space of the subject ("the invention" of the real). Needless to say, this capacity of the aesthetic modern to emancipate had an enduring appeal for Chinese critics. Many had defined and indeed confined "Chinese modernism" in terms of ideological insurgency by naming modernism's challenge to the "mainstream official ideology" its "most fruitful achievement."[11] Sun Shaozhen's famous defense of Misty poetry in March 1981 resorted to rhetoric that clearly illustrated the constraints of the historical imagination of Chinese critics in the early 1980s: "humanism," "alienation," "the 'involuntary' and 'autonomous' subconscious," "singing for individuals," and "struggle against tradition."[12] Although Sun's essay was entitled "A New Aesthetic Principle Is Rising Abruptly" (1981), his critical sensibility was confined within and informed primarily by ideological considerations.

If there is anything that is universal about the Chinese experience of aesthetic modernity, it is this tragic aura of its profound utopian yearning for the unrepressed and its volcanic energy to rebel. One can assume that in post-Mao China, the modern emerged first and foremost as a "dangerous code word in political terms."[13] It is this particular logic of ascribing historical and political agency to aesthetic practices that constitutes the common ground of the ideology of the modern for both Western European and Chinese literature and art.

Thus Chinese critics like Liu Xiaobo and Xu Zidong would endorse the ideological position held by Marcuse and Habermas: Art is "an enclave of negation against the totalizing power of one-dimensional society,"[14] whether the society in question is capitalist as in Western Europe or socialist as in China. Liu Xiaobo defines the aesthetics of "Chinese modernism" in terms of "provocation and quest." Far from being nihilistic, modernist aesthetics in his view poses a conscious "challenge" to a "specific target," which he designates as the "autocratic, dogmatic, uncultured, and disingenuous."[15] Xu Zidong is more moderate in his assessment of the emancipatory project of "Chinese modernism," although there is little doubt that he, too, is preoccupied with the cultural politics of the school rather than with its formal aesthetics. In his vision, modernism fulfilled two conflicting historical missions. On the one hand, its aesthetics took upon itself the task of freeing literature from its subjugation and attachment to politics. But this turn toward aesthetic autonomy not only failed to cancel out, but on the contrary gave birth to, a political burden of a different nature—modernism's second mission, so to speak. Through their encounter with modernist literature and art, China's young generation found an outlet for their spiritual crisis. In this fateful encounter, modernism attracted the cultural and political agenda of individual freedom and enlightenment, and in so doing, it reclaimed a new kind of affiliation, rather than severing its ties, with politics and ideology. The dilemma of "Chinese modernism" can thus be summarized as follows: "The new literature came to deliver its political-cultural—nonliterary—impact precisely by means of its 'pure literary' orientation."[16]

THE FORMAL REVOLUTION

The "pure literary orientation" that Xu Zidong spoke of is not so pure after all if one considers the historical context within which such an orientation first emerged and developed in post-Mao China. As a repository of endangered meanings, contemporary "Chinese modernism" was conscious of its own subversive potential. Precisely because the stakes were so high in the early 1980s, the project of modernism started predictably with defensive and veiled gestures.

One strategy to divert the attention of political authorities was to downplay the equation of modernism and ideology. To achieve this end, critics ushered in a heightened awareness of the formal characteristics of modernism. I do not wish to oversimplify the intricate working of defense mechanisms to which advocates of "Chinese modernism" were susceptible. Whether or not they consciously adopted such a roundabout strategy, it goes without saying that the debate over Chinese modernism did take a significant turn toward the inquiry into formal aesthetics when the politically charged discussion of modernism as a form of bourgeois ideology led to a deadlock in the first half of 1981.[17] Some causal logic must have been at work here. The stranded discussion of modernism as an ideology should have signaled to writers and critics the necessity of bypassing political taboos. If the inquiry into modernism were to continue in any significant form at all, a new critical space would have to be cultivated. The sudden emergence in literary circles in 1982 of the craze to examine modernist techniques could certainly be seen as an epiphenomenon, if not a direct outcome, of the efforts made by Chinese literati to dodge the surveillant gaze of the Party.

There was, of course, no consensus as to whether one should name this phenomenon the aestheticization of the political or "art for art's sake." Critics such as Su Wei detected in the formal turn of "Chinese modernism" an escapist tendency, whereas others viewed it as a strategic retreat.[18] Among the latter, Li Tuo applauded the opening up of the formalistic horizon of literature as a new act of resistance against official ideology. Li's view that any ideological revolution has to start with the subversion of language crystallized in his now famous battle cry against *Mao wenti*, the "Mao [Zedong] Style."[19] With their discovery of the problematic of the aesthetic form, advocates of Chinese modernism had successfully replaced the moot issue "Do we want modernism?" with a new question "Why do we want it?" And their answer—we need modernism because it teaches us innovative techniques—appeased the Party for the time being (even though the ideologues continued to seize opportunities to attack the proponents of modernism, no matter whether the goods it promoted were its form or content) and redirected the subversive energies of "Chinese modernism" to the quest for a new form.

The landmark event that consolidated the new orientation of "Chinese modernism" toward form was the publication of Gao Xingjian's *Xiandai xiaoshuo jiqiao chutan* (A preliminary inquiry into the techniques of modern fiction) in September 1981. The sensational impact on literary circles of this unassuming modernism primer can be gauged by the number of missives that the ensuing debate generated. In addition to the predictable attacks launched by dogmatic ideologues that appeared in official organs such as *Renmin ribao*, all other major newspapers and literary journals convened numerous symposia and seminars throughout the year of 1982 to discuss how Chinese writers could best "borrow and learn" (*jiejian*) from the formal aesthetics of Western modernism.[20] Among the avalanche of publications on the subject at the peak of the debate were three letters that Liu Xinwu, Li Tuo, and Feng Jicai wrote to each other in response to Gao Xingjian's book.[21]

Many of the themes that surfaced in the "three little kites" (a felicitous metaphor for the three writers' exchanges that gained quick circulation among literary circles) were embarrassingly simplistic if we take them out of the historical context of the early 1980s, a juncture when the emergence of modernism as a new aesthetic principle posed a challenge to the legitimacy of realism. That the new trend risked ruffling the feathers of realist writers like Liu Xinwu could well be anticipated. The mastery of modernist techniques suddenly became a prerequisite for sustaining one's membership and in consequence safeguarding one's vanguard position in the writers' guild. Not surprisingly, the veteran writer Liu Xinwu's anxiety about the legitimation crisis of realism found its outlet in his restrained estimation of the influence of the modernist trend in China and in his self-defensive prediction that it was "critical realism" that would serve as the "mainstream" of Chinese literature for some time to come.[22] Liu Xinwu's deep-seated suspicion of modernism revealed as much about his own insecurity in his encounter with the new literary phenomenon as it did about the symptomatic struggle between realism and modernism at the moment when the rise of the latter was considered by many a "historical necessity."[23]

While Liu Xinwu cringed in the face of "the new, the strange, and the grotesque," Li Tuo and Feng Jicai, fervent advocates of modernism, were mired in a dilemma of a different order. By highlighting the formal aspect of the new school, they risked inviting their rival critics to reduce it to a crude formalist logic. Li Tuo and Feng Jicai's appreciation of the aesthetics of form far surpassed Liu Xinwu's naive conception of the aesthetic form as "technical components" that one could "disassemble" (*chaixie*) at will for the purpose of examining them more closely.[24] Yet their talk about the "relative autonomy of the aesthetic form" led eventually to a conclusion not qualitatively different from Liu Xinwu's mechanical understanding of the form as near autonomous and therefore transportable techniques.[25] Although Li Tuo spoke of discovering the literary form specific to the historical content of contemporary China—a vision based on the simple nativist logic "modernism with Chinese characteristics" that all three "little kites" agreed on—he arrived at a contradictory formula, *yang wei zhong yong* (foreign [means] for Chinese utilization), that reiterates the problematic position that dichotomizes form from content by taking the former as nothing more than utilitarian means to be transplanted whenever an occasion arises.[26]

In the end, the 1982 debate over Chinese modernism never succeeded in departing from the utilitarian logic of selective borrowing and creative transformation. Such an epochal imagination, confined within the perspective of "take-ism" (*nalai zhuyi*), an aggressive appropriation of the foreign, would keep reproducing itself throughout the decade of the 1980s. Confronted with the proliferation of foreign signs in post-Mao China, Chinese writers and intellectuals seemed unable to break out of the conceptual paradigm of aggressive appropriation. In the case of the modernism debate, both the defendants and opponents of modernism were caught in the naive belief that they could appropriate the technically progressive aesthetics while evading (Li Tuo and his comrades) or condemning (the gang of Marxist ideologues) its "retrograde" ideological content.[27] The logic of appropriation led to the fallacious dichotomy of form and content (namely, that the form is useful even though the content is not), which in turn gave rise to dubious propositions that realist writers could "absorb" useful techniques of modernism that would "enrich and further develop" instead of subvert realism's own generic logic.[28]

Regardless of the efforts to tame the seditious drive of modernism, the contradiction between realism and modernism could not simply be conjured away by flawed arguments and wishful thinking.[29] The confrontational relationship between these two aesthetic trends loomed as large as ever during the 1982 debate. The discussion of the vices and virtues of realism went hand in hand with those of modernism. Although the modernist debate usurped the former, there was no mistaking that a historical reevaluation of the realist principle in postrevolutionary China had taken place with the same meaningful intensity as the fervor and furor over modernism. An advocate of modernism might shy away from glorifying the subversive role of modernism as a social critique; yet because of their ideological alliance with Marxist aesthetics, realist exponents, in contrast, felt no such inhibitions about promoting their wares on those terms. They never ceased bragging about realism's mission to expose sociopolitical injustice and to "intervene in life."[30]

The competition between modernism and realism went through different phases during the decade of the 1980s. Although a small handful of critics distinguished the two aesthetics in terms of methods of representation—the contrast between the portrayal of the subjective "within" and that of the objective "without" (techniques that explore the interior landscape of the mind versus those that reflect objective reality)—a more commonly designated demarcation of the two was based on a binarism of a different order: that modernism is "theirs" and that realism is "ours."[31]

This ideological position called for one defensive gesture after another from the modernist camp. Some critics dissipated the alien aura of modernism by emphasizing that techniques such as stream of consciousness could be traced to the Tang dynasty in Li Shangyin's poetry. It was "our ancestors" who could make claim to the proprietorship of modernist techniques.[32] Others linked modernism with the arrival of social modernity in China and argued that the modernization of Chinese literature hardly signified total westernization. It was, in short, a global phenomenon historically overdetermined,[33] not attributable to some Occidental origin. Whether it is theirs or ours should thus become a moot issue. But this proposition of the universal validity of modernism could not have sustained its rhetorical potency without forming an alliance with a partner that never failed to prevail, such as nationalism. The double realignment of "Chinese modernism" with universalism on the one hand and with nationalism on the other was considered by many to be the "deep structural standpoint" of the modernist school in post-Mao China.[34] Chinese proponents of modernism, no matter how iconoclastically oriented, reached, with few exceptions, a consensus on the issue of self-positioning. Xu Chi insisted that "our modernist art and literature" is "constructed on the basis of the double affiliation of revolutionary realism and revolutionary romanticism."[35] Li Tuo felt the need to differentiate Western modernism (*xiandai pai*) from Chinese "modern fiction" (*xiandai xiaoshuo*).[36] Both critics acknowledged that Chinese modernism could not but incorporate the unique historical experience of Mao's China. Modernism could therefore reclaim its Chineseness as it underwent this circuitous process of identity quest.

This was a hard-won battle—in retrospect. It was not until the late 1980s that an easier maneuver to tame their rivals began to dawn on the advocates of modernism. Instead of fending off accusations about modernism's Occidental lineage, they learned to expose the origin of Chinese realism as no less foreign than that of modernism itself. The second time around, the hostile proposition of pseudomodernism (1988) triggered the modernists' counterattack on the phenomenon of "pseudorealism"—a scenario that a beseiged modernist camp could hardly envision in 1982.[37] The unfolding of the pseudomodernism debate in 1988 was on some occasions a revisit of the terms of debate already laid down in 1982. But the reconfiguration of the old thesis of modernism versus realism, together with the deconstruction of the pseudobinary of form versus content, gave the later debate momentum that enabled veteran modernist critics to make a qualitative break from the meager vision of modernism as mere craft.

LANGUAGE FEVER: THE SEARCH
FOR AESTHETIC RATIONALITY

No aesthetic or sociocultural trend is completely correct or corrupt. The debate over aesthetic modernism in 1982, no matter how crippled it was by the partial vision of formalism, served as a catalyst for a conceptual revolution in the field of literary criticism, specifically, the emergence of *yuyan* (language) as a new problematic for critical inquiries.

Several factors converged to give rise to the fad of studying language as a system of signs. As social modernity unfolded during the process of progressive rationalization in economic, administrative, and cultural sectors, there emerged a parallel movement in Chinese aesthetic modernity toward a quest for rationality. The magnetism of the concept of rationality for Chinese literary critics grew increasingly stronger as the methodology fever swept over China in the mid-1980s. The Cultural Discussion of 1984–1986 spread a model-conscious mode of thinking. Whether the cultural elite defined modernity in terms of scientific rationality (Jin Guantao), enlightenment of thought (the *qimeng* school), reinvention of tradition (neo-Confucianists), or hermeneutic understanding (Gan Yang), all the participants in the Discussion were anxious to locate paradigms of rationality that would impose a coherent and systematic order upon the chaotic manifold of different experiences of modernity. The new ethos of objectivity in the cultural sector sent waves of stimuli to the literary field. But even long before the mid-1980s, the literati themselves had anticipated the critical turn to the paradigmatic mode of thinking as the depoliticization of literature opened up new interpretive possibilities. The formal revolution of "Chinese modernism" in 1982 was particularly significant in that it reversed the old formula of socialist realism—content determines form—by privileging the latter and thus initiating a new mode of inquiry that highlighted language as the central problematic of literary criticism.

To fully appreciate the revolutionary significance underlying this new agenda of criticism, we only have to recall the prevailing translinguistic myth that traditional Daoist and Zen poetics propagated, namely, "once meaning is grasped, the linguistic sign can be forgotten" (*deyi wangyan*).[38] This cultural myth was reappraised in the new age of methodology as "one without logic and without grammar" by those cultural critics who now considered the traditional elite's efforts of "enervating" the "logic function of language" as one of the major obstacles to China's quest for modernity.[39] What has always been absent from traditional Chinese aesthetics is, in short, "a place for the language-using and language-making agent."[40] This tendency to deny the linguistic signifier its own integrity was further exacerbated in modern China as dogmatic Marxist aesthetics lavished its attention on questions of content at the expense of form. Throughout the 1980s, for Chinese literati at least, the repression of the linguistic sign was a subject as explosive as that of humanity. A Copernican Revolution had taken place around the mid-1980s to trigger the circulation of concepts such as "the ontology of literature" (*wenxue benti lun*) and "literary linguistics" (*wenxue yuyanxue*).[41]

As I suggested, the emergence of this "language fever" (*yuyan re*) in the mid-1980s was on one level the critics' response to the experimentation of creative writers with the formal aesthetics of modernism, and yet on a deeper level, it was undoubtedly an outgrowth of social modernity's obsession with the paradigmatic mode of thinking. Nowhere was this deep structural correspondence to the Culture Fever better manifested than in the rise of a dominant trend of literary criticism oriented toward system theory and structuralist studies, a trend designated as the "panoramic, totalistic, and regulated."[42]

Reason's coming of age in the field of literary criticism in 1985 resulted in a relationship of colonization between cognitive-instrumental and aesthetic rationality. Although critics eagerly announced the liberation of literature from the tyrannical hold of politics and ideology, they were unaware that their interpretive activities produced a different kind of repression: the co-option of aesthetic by instrumental modernity. Instead of multiplying the linguistic sign as creatively as writers, many critics responded to the language fever by committing themselves to a categorical framework that bound their imagination to the interpretation of literature as a differentiated network of system maintenance. The proliferation of journals of literary criticism in the mid-1980s (according to statistics, thirty unofficial journals and thirty official ones) was symptomatic of a logorrhea that wore out even the critics after the initial fever consumed itself. Often their effort to reconstruct the moment of perfect plenitude that a literary work was believed to embody was self-defeating because, by resorting to system theory, control theory, and information theory, they inflated rather than sublated instrumental rationality. What was delivered was less a holistic impulse (aesthetic synthesis that "does not do violence to the particular, the suppressed, the nonidentical")—a utopian vision that Chinese anti-Marxist literary critics would like to claim—than an arbitrary totalizing tendency that grew out of the intensification of the modernization process that privileged cognitive-instrumental reason.[43]

It goes without saying that this methodological revolution of literary criticism took place at a historical juncture that privileged coherence over inarticulateness and system over deviation. Exactly because of this conspicuous correspondence—indeed, collaboration—between aesthetic and social modernity, social historians would look upon the literary critics' fervent search for rationality in the mid-1980s as an encouraging progress syndrome. The fever for well-regulated critical paradigms, when it first started blazing, was a glorious spectacle. Exercise of rigorous logical thinking in the field of criticism was refreshing after centuries of recurrent patterns of intuitive understanding. The triumph of the

Logos over the Dao enjoyed moments, however fleeting, of methodological breakthrough in the mid-1980s. Yet in retrospect, such a drift toward "model consciousness" (*moxing yishi*) amounts to nothing other than a compromise of the aesthetic.

For this reason, literary historians as well as readers (who could not care less about system and control theories) should be heartened by the various efforts made by the root-searching writers and the experimentalists, and by Liu Suola and Xu Xing's *xiandai pai*, to prevent the very collapse of aesthetic into cognitive-instrumental rationality. The linguistic experiment undertaken by each school clearly marked "Chinese modernism" as an oppositional aesthetic that not only ran counter to the telos of social modernity, but that served, more often than not, "as a vehicle of crisis" within the progress syndrome of modernization.[44] More specifically, it was the creative writers' search for aesthetic (ir)rationality that served to subvert rather than complement the instrumental rationality characteristic of social modernity.

In contrast, the critics' project, because of its complicity with the architects of social modernity, was hardly as subversive and invigorating as the creative writers'. The former's much vaunted program of reinventing the aesthetic rationality of postrevolutionary China proved to be highly problematic. They had to clarify the extent to which their vision of a mediated relationship between the subsystems of a literary work is qualitatively superior to the old and largely discredited nonsystematic, impressionistic vision of harmonious totality advocated by Daoist and Zen aestheticians. Was the language fever and methodology fever that transfixed the field of literary criticism at the apex of the culture craze the beginning of a quest for aesthetic rationality or simply the continuation of social modernity's search for scientific rationality?

The answer seemed obvious. A review of the major events of the field reveals that the critics' methodological fever was part and parcel of a deepened reform consciousness that was both empirically and scientifically oriented. Just as the entire society was carried away by its passion to predict as well as to decipher the "route and dispositions" of economic reform, critics' attempts in the mid-1980s to transform the old epistemological structure and open up a new cognitive space were seen by literary historians as a timely response to "epochal demands" defined in terms of the national anxiety of "vindicating in theoretical terms the inevitability, necessity, and reasonability of reform."[45] Symposia held at Xiamen, Wuhan, and Yangzhou invariably focused on the search for the point of convergence between humanist values and scientific rationality—the "unification of the two [contradictory] systems of signs" (the arts and the sciences).[46] Language was highlighted as the strategic point of mediation between science and the humanities.[47] And yet in the historical context of Culture Fever, it was difficult to deepen the examination of the issue of language beyond the mere mechanistic application of descriptive linguistics. Conceived and utilized as nothing more than an "instrument" and "raw materials," language ironically recovered the "position of its own subjectivity" as it was reduced to a mere system of arbitrary signs.[48] Although very few critics at the turn of 1985 would raise objections to the statement that "the shift of literary studies from the experiential model to the scientific one is truly indispensable," yet contrary to what critics themselves insisted, the epochal adventure into the territory of language had not led criticism to a "return to humanity," but to an "alienating world" of insentient indexes.[49]

This was especially true when the interpretive models that the critics utilized were borrowed directly from the natural sciences. System theory more than any other such model provides the meticulous breaking down of a text into various subsystems whose mutual interactions answer to a highly constrained network of "two-way feedback" mechanisms.[50] Such a systematic configuration is programmed into the theoretical model, which then begs the analysis that all literary works manifest such predictable and homogeneous patterns of feedback. The formula is invariably the same. So is the result of interpretation—whether it is a study of the system of Ah Q's personality, an inquiry into aesthetics, or the examination of the value system of modern Chinese literature.[51]

Other models based on the working hypothesis of structural totality (models such as mythological studies, psychoanalysis, and aesthetics) also enjoyed their respective reigns in post-Mao China and produced a significant corpus of pioneering works including Ji Hongzhen's "Wenxue piping de xitong fangfa yu jiegou yuanze" (The system methodology and structural principles of literary criticism) (1984), Lin Xingzhai's "Lun A Q xingge xitong" (A system analysis of Ah Q's personality) (1984), Li Zehou's *Meide licheng* (The path of beauty: A study of Chinese aesthetics) (1981), and Wu Gongzheng's *Xiaoshuo meixue* (The aesthetics of fiction) (1985).[52] The working of scientific rationality is much less dictatorial in these works because their authors do not take for granted the total accessibility of aesthetic experience to scientific inquiries.

Li Zehou's influence is particularly significant in that he opens up the totalitarian system of interpretive reason to the entry of historical consciousness. The panoramic view of Chinese aesthetics from the Paleolithic Age ("totem art") to the Ming-Qing dynasty ("the aesthetics of urban folk cultural practices") does not so much present a mode of thinking characteristic of model consciousness (although Li Zehou's totalizing impulse is evident) as a museum of the "history of the mind" that leads us into the past from which the future can be projected.[53] What fascinates the philosopher is the historical continuity of aesthetics (in *The path of beauty*) and cultural politics (in his trilogy on Chinese thought). Haunted by the recurrence of such aesthetical and cultural problematics throughout premodern and modern Chinese history, Li Zehou launches one inquiry after another into the so-called sediment of the "social content and social ethos" of Chinese people, which in another context he names as the "cultural-psychological" formation of China.[54] Although such a highly structuralist account of the shifts in the constellations of aesthetic-cultural discourses and practices makes little room for genuinely irruptive events that may yet put into question his cherished hypothesis about the consistency of historical narratives—a perspective akin to the functional view of scientific rationality—Li Zehou did unfold, with a historian's diachronic vision, the whole spectrum of a temporal horizon that breaks into the spatial enclosure framed by the instrumental paradigm of system and control theories. What is characteristically a modernist project of spatial decontextualization enters into a productive confrontation with history. The result is exhilarating. The evoking of historical memory, albeit a well-tamed one, constitutes a force that countervails science.

The path of beauty was published in 1981. The book predates the Culture Fever and the ensuing onslaught of instrumental rationality. And yet it provides, preemptively, the best solution to the dilemma of the excessive scientification of humanistic values. Historical studies could accomplish what system theory failed to reckon with—the "immediate" and "contingent" nature of aesthetic activities.[55] With the publication in the early and mid-1980s of Li Zehou's trilogy of Chinese thought, *Zhongguo gudai xixiang shilun, Zhongguo jindai sixiang shilun,* and *Zhongguo xiandai sixiang shilun* (The history of thought of ancient China, The history of thought of pre-May Fourth China, and The history of thought of modern China), the historical macrocosm of his critical perspective established itself firmly as the alternative model to system and control theory while recontaining it at the same time.

Li's formative influence on the younger generation of literary critics can hardly be overemphasized. Although undoubtedly coming into being in response to the new epoch's emphasis on methodical awareness, the works they produced bear palpable imprints of Li Zehou's influence, particularly in the manner they redeem the mechanistic vision of the methodological revolution. I want to mention in particular one such work, "Lun 'Ershi shiji Zhongguo wenxue' " (On "twentieth-century Chinese literature") (1985), a long essay co-authored by Chen Pingyuan, Huang Ziping, and Qian Liqun.[56] As one of the critical works that enables us to speak of the potential intersection of "system consciousness" and "open-door consciousness" understood in symbolic terms, the long essay is a miniature counterpart in literary criticism of what Li Zehou did in aesthetics and philosophy.[57]

As Chen Pingyuan and Huang Ziping indicated, the essay delivers a "macroscopic viewpoint" of a holistic literary system that incorporates the late nineteenth century (*jindai*), the twentieth century (*xiandai*), and contemporary (*dangdai*) Chinese literature.[58] Although all three authors proclaimed their adherence to the standpoint of system theory in their emphasis on the functional coherence of temporal orders (the unity of the past, present, and the future), they hardly de-historicized the subject under study. The tension between taming history methodologically and retrieving the genuine "historical content commonly shared by all" is never resolved in the essay itself, however.[59] Although what is delivered in the end is a reductive "holistic frame that is hidden behind" the literature and the impressionistic portrayal of the "social psychology" of Chinese people—"a strong totalizing consciousness [*zhengti yishi*] characteristic of the theories of methodologies" in general—the critics rescue their essay involuntarily from its categorical enclosure in scientific rationality by means of their proposal of a "retrospective mode of thinking."[60]

What they have in mind is the hermeneutic perspective of reinventing history from the standpoint of the present—"to envision modernity from [the horizon of our] contemporaneity" and thus to trace the "historical origin" of contemporary problematics back to the history of twentieth-century literature. The implicit logic of this "inverted order of narration" (*daoxu*) imparts to the essay an acute historical consciousness that cannot be fully recontained by the instrumental rationality of system theory.[61] And yet the authors themselves seem to have remained unaware of the meeting of the two conflicting views of history in their writings. How they can reconcile the hermeneutic understanding of history—the continual merging of temporal horizons—with the structuralist one—a stabilized temporal scheme—is never mentioned in the essay.

The paradox, however, remains relatively obscure, given the fact that what underlies the treatise proper is dominantly the structuralist concept of history seen as a consistent form and norm. And the unidentified rival theory against which the authors pit their structuralist view is by no means hermeneutic, but the Maoist view of history understood as discrete moments of violent ruptures and permanent revolution. This suggests that Huang Ziping, Chen Pingyuan, and Qian Liqun's conversion to the scientific view of literature is ideologically motivated in the first place. Their revulsion for such concepts as disjunction and revolution cannot be accounted for merely by their reckless acceptance of a system theory that privileges continuity over discontinuity. Theirs is a generation that came of age during the Cultural Revolution, a generation that faithfully enacted the revolutionary doctrine "rebellion is correct, revolution is irreproachable" (*zaofan youli, geming wuzui*). Everything that the Revolution sanctified then has to be desecrated now. The disenchantment with ruptures of history exacerbates the critics' total embrace of the concept of continuity. System theory emerged at the right historical juncture to provide those disenchanted with the myth of discontinuity with a readymade idiom for hidden ideological critique. To the newborn vision of the system consciousness of twentieth-century Chinese literature is attached a repressed critique of the Revolution and all that it entailed: "cataclysmic break," "permutations," "epoch-making changes."[62]

The retrieval of this ideological subtext from the surface text of Chinese critics' fascination with system rationalization in the mid-1980s should serve to remind us that China's postrevolutionary quest for scientific rationality did not simply result from the elite's mindless response to the importation of foreign models. The quest was ideologically rooted in a common historical memory that they tried in vain to suppress. Huang Ziping and the other two critics' insistence on the continuity of the May Fourth literature with premodern and post-Mao literature is symptomatic of the deep psychology of a whole generation of culture elite who square accounts with the violence that Revolution incurred by disclaiming the radical creed of epistemic breaks. However, the swing of the pendulum may bring them, all unaware, to disruption of a different order; the conceptual thinking of "continuity" often ends up committing violence to the particular and the nonidentical. This categorical framework of binary thinking (discontinuity versus continuity) appears to leave a choice ultimately only between an uncritical Maoist affirmation and a radical negation of China's socialist past.

Ironically, it was the memory of that past that both solicited literary critics' initial subscription to system theory and paved the way for their eventual disengagement from it. The half decade's pursuit of scientific rationality undertaken by Chinese literary critics came to an end amid lukewarm discussions about a problematic raised predictably by dogmatic Marxist critics like Chen Yong: how can one best connect system theory and Marxist dialectics?[63] With little effort, the proponents of orthodox Marxism concluded that, methodologically, system theory and dialectics are indeed compatible with each other.[64] Some crowned Marx the "true inventor of modern system sciences."[65] Others argued that both systems of thought share the same operating principles of "totality," "structuralism," "dynamism," "interrelationships," and a "stratified" analytic scheme.[66] A few even claimed that Marxism is superior to system theory because the latter is nothing more than a methodology, whereas the former unfolds an epistemology and extends into a worldview.[67]

The evocation of Marxism must have alarmed those advocates of system theory who trumpeted the autonomy of literary criticism after walking out of the shadow of the cultural past that dictated just the opposite. Memories of the co-option of literature by political ideology haunted discussions of the palpable links between Marxism and system theory, which appeared more and more convincing even to sophisticated literary critics like Ji Hongzhen.[68] Few speculations have been lavished on the uneventful demise of system methodologies in the mid-1980s. I am intrigued, however, by the silences and meaningful gaps that Chinese historians and intellectuals cannot afford to fill. It would certainly be politically unseasonable for them to suggest that the discussions of the hypothetical correspondence between Marxian dialectics and system theory took a heavy toll on the further evolution of the latter's critical impetus, which earlier had initiated literature's overdue divorce from politics and "vulgar sociology" in post-Mao China.[69]

The ideologues' invoking of the socialist past should not be held exclusively responsible for the declining interest in the critics' quest of scientific rationality. The real dilemma that the advocates of system theory had to face was how they could achieve "the synthesis of the two systems of signs," science and *Geisteswissenschaften*.[70] It did not take them long to discover that system theory led them to the same methodological deadlock—a uniformity of critical consciousness that the politicization of literature had earlier mass-produced in Mao's China. Ironically, this was the undesirable impasse that Chinese literary critics had hoped to avoid by means of modern Western methodologies.[71] If the means defeats the end and reproduces what they wish to supersede, critics must undergo a thoughtful reexamination of the vice and virtue of scientific rationality.

Voices critiquing the domination of instrumental reason could be heard from various quarters even at the apex of methodology fever. The call for the return to the experiential, the personal, the emotive, and the evaluative was sporadic at first.[72] Its predictable alliance with the epochal redefinition of literature as a "human science" (*renxue*) toward the latter half of 1985 served to accelerate the blooming of an ontology of literature (*wenxue benti lun*) that emphasizes the self-sufficiency and self-regulation of the internal components within a literary text.[73] Such a view effectively counteracts the aggressive infiltration of scientism into the domain of literature. The growing attention to an aesthetic rationality understood not as an accessory of, but as a means of opposition to, excessive scientific rationality served as the meaningful signal that China's aesthetic modernity was undergoing a gradual differentiation from its social modernity. It should surprise no one, then, that the increasingly focused view of the primacy of aesthetic experience in the field of literary criticism gained its momentum at the juncture when Culture Fever had consumed its utopian energy in 1986.

The rise of the ontological view of literature in post-Mao China was intricately woven into the epochal discourse about subjectivity (*zhuti*). Liu Zaifu, the former head of the Research Institute of Literature at the Chinese Academy of the Social Sciences, was the master theoretician who identified the aesthetic subject as the utopian site for the ultimate realization of freedom from ideology and subjugation. A lengthier treatment of Liu's theory follows in chapter five, "Romancing the Subject." What needs to be examined here is the conventional wisdom that hails Liu Zaifu as the harbinger of Chinese postrevolutionary aesthetics that features the self-positioning of literature—the "return of literature to its own domain"—as its primary agenda.[74]

Many of Liu's theories sound anachronistic half a decade later. In the mid-1980s, however, it was daring to claim that "the principle of subjectivity in literature is . . . [conceived in terms of] reconstructing the subjectivity of human beings" and that such a principle "takes human beings as the center and telos."[75] Liu's humanist voice evoked tremors of empathy from various intellectual coteries. He received accolades from almost every circle of the literary and cultural elite and, no less significantly, the highest honor that an intellectual could garner in China: vehement attacks from Party ideologues. "The Liu Zaifu phenomenon" prevailed for several years until it was usurped by other intellectual trends, among which were anti-intellectualism (such as the "Wang Shuo phenomenon") and the depoliticized antihumanist stance—two symptoms of the market economy that the elitist, humanist veteran Liu could hardly envision, let alone appreciate.[76]

One must not forget that, in the face of new challenges and new fetishes, Liu Zaifu enjoyed the glory of his day. A quick look at the limitations of his theoretical framework does not serve to discredit his influence. It only indicates how his theory has served as a timely means of historical intervention. To the extent that Liu Zaifu's thesis on subjectivity is nothing more than a humanist reinscription of literature and a radical reaction to the materialistic view of literature that failed to recognize human agency, one can understand why he stops far short of mapping out the intricate mechanisms of the aesthetic laws of literature. Liu Zaifu is first and foremost a disciple of the school of "art for life's sake." Although he paid his rhetorical dues to the tenet of "art for art's sake," what he is most concerned about is not the self-positioning of literature but how literature can best intervene in life and politics. A realist at heart, he can hardly shoulder the burden of the formal revolution that he triggered but which only critics and writers of modernist persuasions could orchestrate with virtuosity. Is it surprising then that, in one article after another, he reiterates such humanist slogans as "literature is the lore of human soul, the lore of human personality, and the lore of human spiritual subjectivity"?[77] Even the representative work—*Xingge zuhe lun* (On the composition of [literary] personality) (1986)—that earned him the title of the critic laureate (however fleetingly he might have enjoyed the prestige) falls short of delivering a profound analysis of the aesthetics of characterization.

By defining the dual composition of personality in terms of the dialectic relationship between the good and beautiful and the evil and unsightly, Liu Zaifu remains deeply imprisoned within the epistemological framework provided by Marxian dialectics.[78] As if to attest to the hypothesis that Marxism and system analysis could indeed go hand in hand, the critic exhibits a burgeoning system consciousness caught in a congenial liaison with his dialectical mode of thinking. The combination of both perspectives—the scientific and the dialectic—is responsible for his making of an explanatory machinery ruled ruthlessly by the formulaic repetition of bipolar complementality. The list generated by such a dual compositional principle in the *Xingge zuhe lun* seems interminable. But it is doomed to reproduce itself, because all the bipolar pairs are simply variations of the same motif—endless extrapolations from the parent dialectics of good versus evil. The presence of instrumental rationality once more gained the upper hand. Liu's commitment to aesthetics turned out to be an aborted cause. It soon became obvious that the Liu Zaifu phenomenon was already passé as some writers' (specifically, the experimentalists') quest for aesthetic irrationality quickened its pace from late 1986 onward.

The notion of aesthetic modernity rendered independent of the enlightenment project of the culture elite—a literary phenomenon peculiar to 1987—was a far cry from Liu Zaifu's purposive inquiry into the subjectivity of literature. Throughout the 1980s, before the entry in 1987 of the impious experimentalists who threw sociocultural and historical attachments to the winds, the characteristic as well as the binding dilemma of the Chinese aesthetic imaginary was indeed the intertwining of the aesthetic and the political. Ironically, no matter how hard they theorized about the ontological view of literature, critics such as Liu Zaifu were unable to divorce the aesthetic from its long lopsided relationship with the sociopolitical.

"LITERATURE HAS LOST ITS SENSATIONAL IMPACT ON SOCIETY": THE SEPARATION OF THE AESTHETIC FROM THE SOCIAL

The separation of the aesthetic from the sociopolitical might sound emancipatory in theory. But when the first symptoms of the separation made their appearance circa 1987, both writers and critics found themselves in an awkward position; they had to mourn instead of celebrate the fantasy come true. Freed from the dictates of the social and the political, aesthetic modernity was at the same time relieved of the weight of its oppositional logic. What the emancipation revoked was not merely the shackles of politicization but also the aura attached to the danger and significance of literature as a negative practice, in other words, the utopian vision of aesthetics as the project of ideological subversion. The shift of the raison d'être of literature from a cultural force to a pure aesthetic project would have been a less baffling experience for the elite if it had not occurred at the same time they found themselves suddenly in competition for readership with reportage literature and the myriad products of popular culture—commodities that the market economy delivered to a cultural market now dictated by the principle of profit, not by that of political correctness, and, to the dismay of the elite, not by that of exquisite taste. Needless to say, the odds were against the practitioners of "pure literature."

The consumer market had indeed very little patience for the aesthetics of language and form. In fact, circa 1987 as the experimentalists usurped the limelight of the root-searching writers, their effort of high-lighting language as the ultimate cause of storytelling only served to alienate them from the general reading public. If the issue of cultural sub-jectivity and the revival of traditional aesthetics with which the root-searching writers were preoccupied still enjoyed a certain appeal to China's sinocentric audience, then in contrast, the experimentalists' con-struction of a linguistic utopia—the notion that the subject is a rhetori-cal construct created and dissolved instantaneously with the inaugura-tion and termination of each discursive act—could only court total indifference, if not outright dismissal, from the public.

Some did mourn the loss of the sacred aura of elite literature. Between 1987 and 1988, when the controversy over experimental fiction reached its climax, several catchphrases were thrown into wide circulation, mostly by the elite themselves, deploring the separation of the aesthetic from the social. "Literature lost its sensational impact" is one. "Litera-ture has entered a period of depression" is another.

This phenomenon could indeed be viewed as a symptom that China's modernization had matured or at least sped up its pace toward the end of the 1980s, if we subscribe to Max Weber's hypothesis that "cultural modernity's specific dignity" is constituted by "the differentiation of value spheres in accord with their own logics."[79] In China, the aesthetic and the social had been intertwined throughout history. Yet, although Mao Zedong undoubtedly reinforced the continuum between those two value spheres, the downfall of Maoism after 1979 did not result in the immediate differentiation of the one from the other. The idea that art serves as "an enclave of negation against the totalizing power of one-dimensional society" was not only prevalent in the wounded literature, but also in the root-searching literature whose dedication to the pursuit of a new aesthetic vision did not preclude its participation in the cultural discourse of China's social modernity.[80] Until the appearance of the ex-perimentalists, Chinese writers still believed in the sensational impact of literature over society and in their sacred mission as the vanguard of po-litical and cultural critics.

It was true that, before 1987, art and literature had acquired the character of a public institution and developed the power to regenerate the ethical totality of the nation. Every heat wave of a new literary movement, whether it was the wounded literature, Misty Poetry, reform literature, or root-searching literature, was accompanied by a political or cultural heat wave. Wounded literature and Misty poetry emerged with the fall of the Gang of Four; reform literature came into being in response to the program of Four Modernizations; and root-searching literature arose with the onslaught of Culture Fever. The homogeneity of social ethos characteristic of premodernity had to break down as the sizzling focus of China's reform shifted from issues of ideological revolution to economic activities that in turn split the society, probably for the first time in Chinese history, into heterogeneous social groups whose interests no longer cohered. This process by which science, art, economics, politics, and the law have become distinct value spheres inevitably resulted in a widening chasm between aesthetic discourses and those of sociopolitical morality and, eventually, in the removal of the utopian burden placed on the emancipatory content of aesthetic experience. In 1987, the old mythology that art and literature served as a norm of political agency expired as soon as it achieved its goal to depoliticize itself. The price for this newfound freedom was unexpectedly huge. The traumatic effect of the separation of the aesthetic from the social formed an intriguing contrast to the sensational impact derived from their former union.

At the juncture of 1987, what Chinese writers faced was a dilemma of a different kind. Although modern Chinese literature since the May Fourth era has always been surrounded by an aura derived from its self-conscious practice of an oppositional politics against the autocratic regime, the declaration of aesthetic autonomy from the political at once distanced writers and artists from the masses. The shedding and the eventual loss of the cultic aspect of the aura in question unexpectedly plunged the "post-auratic" art and literature into a legitimation crisis. Having separated themselves from the danger of politicization, writers and artists faced the formidable task of reinventing a raison d'être for their creative activities. But before they had time to absorb their hard-won freedom and readjust to their single status, they found themselves face-to-face with the possibilities of colonization by a new historical nemesis, commercialization. The quest of aesthetic autonomy from the political—a prospect and process that bore close resemblance to deregulation—led ironically to the arrival of free market economy in the newborn marketplace of ideas. It should surprise no one that elite cultural and literary production was no rival to the commodities of mass culture. Consumers' free choice and the capitalist logic of rapid rate of obsolescence guaranteed the total irrelevance of what writers had fought for only a few years ago. Many veteran writers felt the pinch of aesthetic autonomy; they had overcome the politicization of literature only to arrive at the new age of the vulgarization of art and literature.

I suggest that it will take a long time for the Chinese culture elite to recover from the dystopian mood that accompanied the de-auraticization of literature. It is premature for us to speculate on how Chinese highbrow literature can reemerge in the 1990s in the guise of counterculture subverting a rampant consumer culture. Though "post-auratic art" will no doubt have to navigate through perils of a different order, we may celebrate the end of the tyrannical rule of China's thousand-year-old elitism and refrain from immediately condemning the capitalist logic of the fetishization of culture. For the benefit of the Chinese clientele who came from different social strata and literacy constituencies, and who had long been excluded from partaking in China's cultural production and consumption, the differentiation of the cultural market into high, low, and middling classes was, according to one critic, a healthy phenomenon and an inevitable outcome of China's entry into a more sober experience of modernity.[81] The melodramatic outbursts of various kinds of fevers during the first half of the 1980s were only symptomatic of the Great Leap Forward complex, a cultural "primitivism" that would outgrow itself as pluralism took deeper root in Chinese society and as reform consciousness, rather than revolutionary utopianism, finally found its way into the social imaginary of China.

THE CONTROVERSY OVER PSEUDOMODERNISM

The emergence of consumer culture in Deng's China marked the beginning of an era in which commercialism rather than the Mao Style turned out to be Chinese writers' most formidable foe. The liberation of the literary market from the monopoly of elite—an outcome of the segregation of the aesthetic from the social—gave rise to significant permutations in the literary field. Among them were the revival of realism and the controversy over pseudomodernism.

It was predictable that the marketplace of ideas would be inundated by reportage literature whose focus on popular social issues guaranteed generous consumer patronage. In contrast to Liu Binyan's exposé reportage that targeted single incidents of corruption, the revived genre in 1988 took on a macroscopic perspective—which suitably complied with the spirit of system theory—in its methodical exploration of ponderous social issues such as marital problems, the dilemma of population explosion, crises in education, and problems of cohabitation.[82] Although some of the pieces retained the edge of social critique, the genre as a whole had undergone the process of commodification. Reportage pieces began to occupy a noticeable slot even in elite journals, which responded to the commercial tendency no less eagerly than popular magazines. The public's renewed interest in reportage literature reconsolidated the allure of realism, which, despite its underprivileged status since the desecration of socialist realism in post-Mao China, had never lost its popular appeal even during the heyday of "Chinese modernism." In 1988, as it became obvious that the public rejected the introverted turn of experimental fiction, the marketing of realism returned in full force. In October 1988, two renowned literary journals, *Wenxue pinglun* and *Zhongshan* (Bell Mountain), sponsored a joint symposium on "Realism and Avant-Garde Literature" at Taihu. In March 1989, *Zhongshan* added a special feature, "The Grand Exhibition of New Realist Fiction," to its usual coverage of the so-called avant-garde and experimental pieces.[83] The general drift in 1988 proved that the autonomy of the aesthetic was a lost cause as it witnessed its increasing co-option by the social.

It was in this dystopian climate that a more genuine introspection of aesthetic modernity took place among literary critics. The debate over pseudomodernism should therefore be considered not simply as a debate over modernism per se, but as a reaction to the ascendency of social modernity and the loss of the momentum of aesthetic modernity. It was, in short, an inquiry into how elite literature lost its mandate to dictate the terms and agenda of China's cultural scene.

As early as 1985, at the height of "modernism's" sweeping victory over Chinese literature, Wang Meng diagnosed the symptom and fretted over the potential antithetical relationship that the alleged modernists attempted to set up between aesthetics and social mores.[84] But the danger of such antagonism was comprehended only in metaphorical terms. The urgency of the question "Whither should Chinese literature turn and which course should it pursue?"[85] did not engage the critics until the split between the aesthetic and the social materialized. Lest one lose sight of the subtle working of self-interest that accompanied the critics' sense of mission—that they alone could lead in the right direction "a literature now standing at an unfamiliar crossroad"[86]—I suggest that the pseudomodernism debate provided Chinese critics a golden opportunity to reclaim their privileged position as the arbiters of the agenda of the literary revolution. For a long time, it was the creative writers (the Misty poets, the root-searching school, and the experimentalists) who had usurped the limelight of critics in the making of new literary trends and who appeared as the true vanguard of the aesthetic revolution. The critics' debate over modernism in 1982 generated a little interest. But it

soon receded to the background as writers took over the literary platform, giving birth to one formal innovation after another and delivering
"Chinese modernism" in flesh and blood while the critics were caught
up in the query "Do we want modernism?" to no avail. The critics' ensuing experiment with the analytic framework borrowed from system
theory further strengthened the impression that they had lost the title of
trendsetter, a role to which they had been accustomed throughout the
revolutionary period.

Trendsetting, of course, can hardly be achieved without the concurrent ceremony of "trend tagging" in the first place. As Ernesto Laclau
truthfully observed, "The essentially performative character of naming
is the precondition for all hegemony."[87] Huang Ziping, the only critic
acutely aware of the cultural politics underlying the coining of *wei xiandai pai,* was even more concise about the relationship between naming
and discursive hegemony: "Any act of 'naming' is a kind of 'perpetra-
tion of violence.' "[88] The descriptive project of pseudomodernism is
deeply implicated in the baptizer's exercise of the will to power.

Although unconscious of their own hegemonic articulations, Chinese
literary critics should be no strangers to the political implications of
such naming rituals. The Confucian tradition of the rectification of
names has been the favorite game of the ruling elite for thousands
of years. The controversy over the definition of "modern consciousness" in the early 1980s carried on the tradition by providing a contemporary showcase of how the innocuous project of description,
namely, the naming of modernity's dominant features, constituted the
strategic site of power formation. As I demonstrated earlier, the mandate to delimit the cultural agenda of post-Mao China rested in the
hands of whoever (the Party, the realist writers, or the "modernist"
school) won the competition for the interpretive authority to decipher
the meaning of "modern consciousness."

It was only natural that in 1988 the critics' attempt to retrieve their
flagging authority from the hands of creative writers should start with
the ritual of redressing the titular label of "Chinese modernism." Long
before the proposition of pseudomodernism was raised in a small symposium sponsored by *Wenxue pinglun* at the end of 1986 and brought
up for further discussion during an editorial meeting held at the headquarters of *Beijing wenxue,* He Xin resorted to the descriptivist strategy
of debunking Chinese writings labeled as "modernist."[89] The strategy
works this way: By imposing upon the identity of heroes and heroines
in contemporary Chinese literature the Western nomenclature of the ab-

surd and the superfluous being (*duoyuren*), and by concluding that the young generation in China "does not have the right to be cynics" like their Western counterparts—in other words, by declaring that the notion of absurdity is not rooted in the Chinese tradition—He Xin succeeded in turning Chinese modernism into an alien entity, and more specifically, into a "pseudoarticulation" of Western modernism.[90]

He Xin's article resurfaced during the 1988 debate as an important document and provided further ammunition for the advocates of pseudomodernism. Yet in 1985 when the essay was first published, it was not surprising that the faint echo of the problematic of the inauthenticity of the "superfluous character" aroused little attention. It was not until 1988 that the critical space for a frontal attack on "modernist" literature was opened up. And it was not until then that the experimentalists' radical revolution completed aesthetic modernity's total alienation from society, which instigated the critics' much belated scapegoat hunting. Yet it was not the experimentalists but the so-called modernist writers such as Liu Suola and Xu Xing who bore the brunt of the assaults on pseudomodernism.

Many humanist critics unhesitatingly held *xiandai pai* writers responsible for the expropriation of the aesthetic by the social. That those who were repulsed by the avant-gardism of the experimentalists should seize the opportunity to seek vengeance upon *xiandai pai*—their much tamer predecessors—revealed the critics' inability to distinguish those two very different aesthetic moments from each other. Although I disagree with Wang Ning's distinction of the one from the other in terms of such periodizing concepts as postmodernism versus modernism, I share his view that the advocates of pseudomodernism often mistook their real targets—the experimentalists—for the so-called modernists.[91]

Very few critics were perceptive enough to suggest, as Mu Gong did, that the literary scene of contemporary China was "no longer manifested in the clash between 'traditionalists' and 'modernists,' but in the contention among different articulations within 'modernism' itself."[92] Such contention, he noted, was staged by antihumanists against the Sartrean humanists.[93] Without differentiating the one from the other, the proponents of the pseudomodernism argument were often caught in their haste to make a blanket condemnation of any writings that were conscious of their own aesthetic innovations. In so doing, they conflated two different aesthetic moments within "Chinese modernism" itself: the humanist and antihumanist moment.

The lack of differentiation between the humanist and the antihumanist instants within "Chinese modernism" caused much confusion because it gave rise to conflicting definitions of what was considered "pseudo." The issue was further complicated by the fact that, like the writers themselves, the critics who proposed the heady watchword "pseudomodernism" were not a homogeneous group. They, too, were divided along the ideological line between humanism and antihumanism, the former camp embracing the critical tenets of realism, and the latter, those of modernism.

The battlefield was thus crisscrossed by conflicting hostile fire. On the one hand, humanist critics, basing their charge on the alleged Occidental origin of the notion of absurdity and fragmentation, condemned the antihumanist moment in "Chinese modernism" as not indigenous enough and thus "artificial." On the other hand, critics of antihumanist orientation found the humanist articulation within "Chinese modernism" no less "pseudo" precisely because it was not modern and, specifically, not radical and Occidental enough. It is therefore no wonder that writers such as Mo Yan, whose modern and premodern sensibilities are often indistinguishable from each other, was condemned twice as pseudomodern by humanist and antihumanist critics in turn.

Old and middle-aged writers and critics—upholders of humanist values—who experienced the Cultural Revolution as a profound human tragedy simply could not comprehend the existential condition of the new antihumanist hero and heroine who celebrated deprivations and indulged in ennui, anxiety, and absurdity—"agonies," some humanist critics self-righteously concluded, "which did not correspond to the real life [of China]."[94] Antihumanist writings of the younger generation predictably met offhand rejection by humanist critics as categorically alien. The critics denounced and dismissed such writings as sham products imported from the West, hence the label *wei xiandai pai.*

For those critics of humanist bent, the antihumanist rage of the younger generation was tantamount to total libidinal disorientation and blasphemous parody of their own articulation of the wounds and disillusionment that the Revolution had inflicted upon them. Little did they recognize that the utopian ecstasies and pangs that accompanied their memories of the Revolution were as foreign to the younger writers as the latter's apathetical and lackadaisical mood was to the older generation. This is to suggest that in Liu Suola, A Cheng, or Yu Hua's works, the Revolution took a different guise. It was inscribed as an absent cause or as a game of the absurd and the irrational that the heroes and heroines took sardonic pleasure in ridiculing. This was the *authentic* "social-psychological background," to use Huang Ziping's term, from which the "pseudomodernists" emerged.[95] He Xin's didactic address to the young generation that they "do not have the right to be cynics," in conjunction with his earnest call for a new kind of humanist heroism, only betrayed his own ignorance of the coming of age of anti-heroism in post-Mao China.[96]

On the other side of the battlefront, there was discontent of a different kind. Antihumanist critics such as Liu Xiaobo were especially impatient with those so-called modernist works that displayed residual attachment to humanist values. Liu believed that irrationality and inhumanity—the Western representation of the modern—should be taken as the underpinning of China's aesthetic modernity. What he considered "not modern" was the manner by which writers of humanist sensibility—Wang Meng and the root-searching school were cited as particular examples—rationalized themes of the irrational. According to this view, the radicalism of modernism's formal revolution was co-opted by the obstinate persistence of humanist themes: holistic " 'human nature,' 'selfhood,' and 'personality,' core concepts of the 'classical tradition' " at which antihumanists who advocated total westernization lashed out with relentless conviction.[97] Anything that celebrated China's cultural past (the return to Daoist aesthetics and the rediscovery of the tradition of nonaction) was suspected of the "backward looking consciousness" that ran counter to modern consciousness.[98] Many simple formulaic assumptions were made in denouncing the "retrogressive" turn of root-searching literature. For instance, Liu Xiaobo argued that whereas the return to nature in Western literature signified the metaphoric release of repressed desire, the *xungen* writers, in contrast, searched for a nature deprived of the "agitation of the soul, a painless, sanitized, sedate, and pure entity."[99] The implications are clear: A literature devoid of the throbbing of the libido— "the irrational, the instinctual, and the flesh"—was reduced to a pseudo-articulation of modernism.[100]

Toward the end of 1988, the controversy over pseudomodernism began to subside as it became more and more obvious that both the humanist and antihumanist exponents of the problematic of "pseudomodernism" had subscribed to a "treacherous framework of reference," namely, Western modernism, that begged the question of its own validity as the universal criterion for "authentic" modernism.[101] Instead of pursuing the moot question of authenticity, critics sympathetic with Chinese "modernist schools" began to plough a new path through the dust of a bootless debate.

New problematics were raised when the radical thesis of pseudomodernism backfired. First of all, a consensus was soon reached by the elite establishment within the literary guild that the proposition was a specious one in itself. A counterproposal was made to condemn such a critical mode as "supercilious" and "pseudo."[102] The original proposition was seen as the result of a "romantic expectation" envisioned especially by those antihumanist critics who wished that Chinese literature should leap forward prematurely and beyond its bounds.

The most intriguing backlash to the proposition of pseudomodernism was the reverse proposition of "pseudorealism." Both Li Tuo and Xu Zidong emphasized the intricate working of the Chinese cultural unconscious, which, according to them, contained a homogenizing mechanism by which intruding alien phenomena (be they realism or modernism) were transformed beyond recognition. Xu Zidong specified four particular stages by which Western realism underwent the process of sinicization: the tracing of indigenous origins, the logic of voluntary importation, the dissociation of form from content, and the vindication of total homogenization.[103] If, as Li Tuo echoed in the same spirit, the constraints embedded in the "cognitive structure of Chinese people" made them unable to appreciate alien cultural categories as they were,[104] it follows that Chinese writers could never expect to reproduce the latter verbatim.

The proposition of pseudorealism led to the fruitful observation that cross-cultural dialogues between China and the West necessarily entailed creative "misunderstandings" that involve an intricate process by which an indigenous literary culture selectively absorbs and transforms an alien entity to serve its own cultural agenda.[105] The question then is not whether we could have "their" modernism or realism, but rather, what kind of modernism and realism do *we* already have? Once it was understood that Chinese writers had succeeded in "we-izing" (*women hua*) realism in Mao's China, it became obvious that the examination of a so-called sinicized modernism was in order.[106]

The new problematic broke up the stalemate that the pseudomodernism debate engendered. Yet even before Xu Zidong foregrounded the thesis of "our modernism" in 1989, the agenda of nationalizing modernism had been in the making for some time. As early as 1985, Chen Sihe predicted that the time had come for the merging of "modernist phenomena" into "[Chinese] national culture," and in early 1988, Ji Hongzhen ascribed "Chinese modernism" to yet another articulation of the Chinese tradition of "take-ism" in which China instead of the West emerged as the host of the cultural exchange.[107] That is to say, there existed in the Chinese rhetorical flourishes of aggressive appropriation (*nalai*) a deeply seated superiority complex—the "giant consciousness" (*juren yishi*) according to one literary historian[108]—that dictated the sovereignty of China's cultural subjectivity even when it was self-conscious of its debt to the Western discourse. From the start, anxieties about the imperative of overtaking Western modernism were intermingled with discussions of the nativist characteristics of Chinese modernism that reinforced the cultural logic of difference.

On the surface, the critical examination of Chinese modernists has fluctuated between two seemingly conflicting desires: the desire to look the same (hence the catching up with an "authentic modernism") and the desire to look different (the soul-searching for the "Chinese identity"). What remains intact is the Western modernist referential system against which Chinese modernism is to be assessed. Lest it should appear that I am suggesting that Chinese critics were obsessed with Western cultural logic, I wish to emphasize that I am arguing just the opposite: China is only obsessed with itself. The real issue is the power relationship with the West to which Chinese intellectuals are unwilling to subjugate themselves. The two desires are therefore the one and the same—the desire to assert its own subject position and, no less important, the desire to assure that the position is an overpowering one.

The various prescriptions of Chinese modernism in the following quotes illustrate just that. On the one hand, without the fixed pole of Western discourse, Chinese writers and critics would have a hard time defining the identity of China's aesthetic modernity. On the other hand, anxieties over how to empower the indigenous cultural identity eventually loom larger than the mere concern over the justification of the "modernist" label. The cultural politics of demarginalizing the local center overrode that of mindless globalization of China's literary culture.

Wang Ning: "Modernism went through a metamorphosis in China. It is equipped with China's own [aesthetic] form. It absorbs factors of postmodernism and assimilates those elements that preserve traditional realism and romanticism. It keeps pace with Western postmodernism."[109]

Gao Xingjian: "The primary manifestation [of Chinese modernism] was self-assertion, rather than self-denial witnessed in Western modernism. Endowed with Nietzschean tragic pathos, it affirms the value of personality rather than provides an impassive analysis of human nature. It raises objections to traditional feudal ethics and champions the cause of sexual love rather than throws away ethics in contempt and loses appetite for sexual love. It exposes the absurd in reality rather than looks

upon absurdity as existence itself. . . . It propagates the myth of masculinity instead of entertaining doubts about a human nature that takes
the male sex as its given. It plays up the sense of loneliness but does not
march toward nihilism from loneliness. . . . [Western] modernism took
as its point of departure the questioning of the old Western humanism.
In contrast, 'this [our] modernism' rediscovers the once forfeited humanism under the specific conditions of Chinese social reality. It is, in
addition, permeated with the spirit of romanticism. . . . Not only has
'Chinese modernism' not replaced realism, but it has not turned into
Western modernism either."[110]

Xu Zidong: "The ceaseless efforts that Chinese modernist writers
made in their search for the foundation of national culture, [their attempts to] face the psychological crisis resulting from their experience of
the loss of Han culture, and the traditional sense of mission that they
upheld to rejuvenate the national culture—all these [characteristics] constituted the deep-seated position that the 'genuine modernists of our literature' occupied."[111]

To illustrate how "our modernism" differs from theirs, Xu mapped
out the content of Chinese modernism by undertaking specific case
studies. He argued that Wang Meng and Ru Zhijuan utilize the technique of stream of consciousness not for the purpose of making an inquiry into the human subconscious, but to piece together, "by means of
their *rationalized sensibility*," a "topsy-turvy" picture of China's political reality. Han Shaogong (a *xungen* writer) and Can Xue (an experimentalist) resort to metaphors more as an instrument of "political critique" than as a means of metaphysical "reflection on human destiny."
Instead of displaying the indifference of an "outsider," Liu Suola and
Xu Xing's indulgence in sarcasm and black humor is symptomatic of
the "confused and misanthropic mood" of those "superfluous beings"
who agonize over their dislocation in Chinese society. The epochal fascination with "sexual desire" is not an articulation of the crisis of frigid-
ity, but a protest against the "sexual repression and sexual perversion"
prevalent under the age-old puritanical rule of Confucian ethics. Even
the pessimism that accompanies the collapse of value systems in China
and in Western Europe takes different forms: In the former, it takes
shape in the disillusionment with the "revolutionary tradition" in the
wake of a disastrous Cultural Revolution; in the latter, it is found in the
uncertainty about the future of humankind in the face of highly developed technological revolution.[112]

Xu Jingye: "Western poets wrote poetry from the standpoint of a pure
subject-position that was alienated from the whirlpool of society. In con-

trast, modern Chinese poets wrote poetry from the standpoint of class (to a lesser degree), race, nation, or at least from their own 'generational' perspective. The 'self' of the great majority of our poets is endowed with general connotations. This particular situation characterizes the preliminary stage of the development of our modernism."[113]

Li Tuo: "The concept of 'modern fiction' is different from 'modernist fiction.' This distinction is very important for us. We cannot kneel down in front of foreigners after all. We cannot chase after Western modernist literature after all. All our learning, assimilation, and borrowing is for the sake of 'using foreign means to apply to the Chinese case.' "[114]

Huang Ziping, Chen Pingyuan, and Qian Liqun: "In Chinese literature, the anxiety about individual fate is always quickly merged into the crisis consciousness of the whole nation. . . . Liu Suola's 'Ni biewu xuanze' (You have no other choice) (1985)—from its content to semantic structure—shares the corresponding aesthetic characteristics of twentieth-century world literature. Although the anguish in her mind is thoroughly Chinese, it is *modern Chinese,* nonetheless."[115]

Ji Hongzhen: "Emerging from the epochal background of such complicated and unique national sentiment and cultural psychology, Chinese fiction of recent years can hardly produce modernism in the strict sense of the word. . . . Following the clashing currents of modern society, Chinese people have to endure the double repression that the old and new civilizations inflict upon them. The psychic burden resulting from old miseries and new agonies brought about the rupture of the national psyche. The discrepancies between those two large value systems are manifested in the stereotypical [pattern of] bipolar antithesis seen in the works of many middle-aged and young writers. . . . The most typical case is Mo Yan. His works fully embodied the inquiry into the dualism between good and evil that came into being under the painful double pressure that produced the [historical] process in which the [modern] individual's desire is played out in the realm of [premodern] ethical practice. . . .

"Seen from the perspective of individual experience, the sense of loneliness in modern Western literature emerges from the social ecology of a postindustrial society characterized by alienating and apathetic interpersonal relationships. Seen from the collective point of view, loneliness results from the sense of anxiety felt by underdeveloped areas as they witness the destiny of their indigenous civilization waning under the coercive infiltration of modern civilization (i.e., South American literature). Both configurations are markedly distanced from the social life of our own era. For those Chinese people who are self-positioned [by default] in the

collective ethical mode of existence, it is the entanglements of human relations and the onerous weight of human emotions that leave more profound impressions on them. Therefore, in some works, loneliness is not
identical to crisis consciousness. It should be seen as the ideal condition
emerging from the individual's fruitful quest for relative freedom."[116]

Liu Xiaobo: "Not only are the new currents of contemporary Chinese thought founded upon the antifeudal humanism characteristic of
the Age of Enlightenment and the May Fourth period, but [Chinese in-
tellectuals] have to trace and pursue the global perspective and the
newest discoveries of contemporary art. This cannot but lead to the
emergence, in contemporary Chinese new thought, of two mutually opposing but interpenetrated worlds: whereas the spirit of the inner world
is antifeudal, romantic, insurgent, and searching, its external expression
is characteristic of Western modern and contemporary sensibility—
chaotic, nihilistic, and cynical."[117]

All the preceding ruminations on Chinese modernism illustrate that the
burning issue for Chinese literary theorists in the late 1980s was none
other than the desire to look different. What was truly at stake in the debate over pseudomodernism was cultural subjectivity. As China entered
into deeper dialogue with global cultural discourse in the late 1980s,
Western cultural imperialism became a real threat. It was not surprising
then that Chinese intellectuals should feel compelled to readjust the open-
door agenda defined in the early 1980s. The mapping of the local position emerged as a much more urgent business than world citizenship.

The definition of "modernism with Chinese characteristics" as envisioned by the cited theorists presupposes that such a specimen is in fact
the aesthetic manifestation of cultural nationalism—a characteristic
that also marked modern Chinese literature, according to Huang Ziping and his colleagues.[118] Whether China's theorists considered nationalist sentiment a constraint or the motivating force of history, most
contemporary critics such as Ji Hongzhen ("the rupture of the national
psyche"), Xu Zidong ("in search of the foundation of national culture"), and Huang Ziping ("the crisis consciousness of the whole
nation") invariably prescribed the aesthetic in terms of the cultural-
political and delimited the self within the bounds of "historical-
national-humanist consciousness."[119]

But to ascribe Liu Suola's sensibility merely to the palpitation of intellectuals' "anxiety consciousness" is to confuse her with Shen Rong
and realist writers of the May Fourth era. If what is at stake is merely

China's historical subjectivity, how then do we differentiate realism from the new asethetic in Chen Kaige's *Huang tudi* (Yellow earth) (1984), Liu Suola's "You Have No Other Choice" (1985), and the root-searching craze? Should we name it "modernist" or not? In what sense was 1985 the watershed in the history of modern Chinese literature, the year that triggered what Li Tuo designated as the "sudden mutation" in art and literature?[120] What did it mean when younger poets blasted out their "Down with Bei Dao!" during that same year?[121]

It meant the end of the absolute domination of anxiety consciousness deciphered in the old sense of sociopolitical agency. 1985 marked the beginning of the unlocking of the semantic closure of "anxiety consciousness" and the trickling through of the metaphysical content such as "angst" and other malaises born from the younger generation's maladjustment to life.[122] 1985 betokened, in short, the denouement of the enlightenment era in Chinese art and literature and the "end of [Chinese writers'] recurrent return to the enlightenment motif of May Fourth literature."[123] This is not to suggest that the motif in question disappeared, but that it no longer enjoyed its earlier hypertrophic position in contemporary literature with modernist persuasions.

Feudalistic peasants and enlightenment intellectuals—the two complementary stereotypes found in the literature of the May Fourth and early post-Mao era—were replaced in the mid-1980s by cultural yuppies and the underclass of *pizi* (hooligans), accompanied by their humanist brothers, the root-searching heroes. The yuppies and *pizi* lived lightheartedly, played hard, and acted out their desires to abuse life as a meaningless game: "Fuck it," enlightenment and all. The *xungen* writers, in contrast, shuddered at such cynicism. Cultural politics was as endearing to them as to realist writers. Their modern sensibility incorporated a subtle sociopolitical critique and a passionate inquiry into national culture. Predictably, the issue of the historical subjectivity of China continued to dominate the subtext of their inquiry. Yet regardless of this marked difference in the vision of life, *xungen* author A Cheng shared the label of "Chinese modernism" with Liu Suola and her cohort and partook in the epochal configuration of 1985. What bound them together is their acute awareness of the subjectivity of language (*yuyan zhuti*).

1985 emerged as a landmark of modern Chinese literature because for the first time in the literary history of China, a "language-using subject" made its debut in the discursive space long dominated by the collective cultural and historical subject of China. The emerging fictional space cultivated by the linguistic subject subverts the main thrust of the foregoing definitions of the indigenous characteristics of modernism, that "Chinese modernism" is simply the modern version of Chinese cultural nationalism.

There is more to Liu Suola's anxiety and crisis consciousness than her involuntary articulation of the Chinese postrevolutionary cultural syndrome. Even the roots for which the *xungen* writers were searching cannot be unambiguously pinned down as cultural roots per se. Despite critics' identification of Daoist poetics in his writings, A Cheng's quest for a modern aesthetics transcends the specific temporal-cultural boundary of traditional China and the modern West. It is neither traditional Daoist, nor self-consciously Western. Its articulation is simply modern inasmuch as the arbitrary forms of collective consciousness can no longer impose their binding power upon the linguistic idiosyncrasies of one individual writer.

Examples such as A Cheng reinforce the impression that the sheer terms of political and cultural consciousness no longer summarize Chinese writers' and artists' visceral response to the experience of modernity. The artistic agitation in 1985 might truly have been triggered by something more than the well-articulated collective anxieties about China's modernization. Unless we acknowledge the working of the forces that transcend the political-cultural collective, we will be mired in the simple literal definition of "roots" and fail to reckon with the undercurrents of modern consciousness that saturated the *xungen* literature. It is convenient to accept the conventional interpretation of root-searching as symptomatic of "backward looking" ideology. But the term "roots," I remind all literalists, invites alternative explications. If we can deviate from the surface connotation of "tangible roots" and comprehend the term as a visionary metaphor, the so-called root-searching impulse might indeed have "originated from the writers' confusion about the historical locality of *human beings* caught between the past and the future."[124] "Root-searching" could thus be understood as a metaphor for the writers' "sudden urge to make a choice of the [existential] locale" for humankind in general.[125] Such a quest could be for anything but the exclusively defined historical subject of China.

Whether we agree with this novel definition of "root-searching," 1985 witnessed the expansion of the content of the cultural unconscious beyond national consciousness. Only in this sense can we demarcate "Chinese modernism" from realism and map out the historical position of the former as an antagonistic force against the latter, especially in the very beginning of modernism's entry into post-Mao China as an initiation ritual.[126] And yet the dichotomy between the two was by no means as stable as Xu Zidong and most Chinese critics have assumed. "Chinese modernism" is anything but pure. It is a stew—realist stock and romanticist sentiments recontained within the bubbling modernist sensibilities. It is only natural that the curious motley of such new cultural content should burst out of the constraints of the tradition of representation in search of its articulation in a new system of linguistic signs. The uproar against Liu Suola and against the loss of the "genuine" aura of literature during the onslaught of pseudomodernism had much to do with the humanist critics' rebellion against the new linguistic subject that performs a mood, or at worst, a posture, rather than represents a concept.

Most critics were bogged down by the either-or mentality. They conceived of the work of art either in terms of higher meaning (auratic representation) or in terms of nonmeaning (word play). Why the performatory instinct of the linguistic subject is necessarily disingenuous,[127] or more specifically, at odds with the representational persona of the historical subject, is an intriguing issue that has yet to be carefully examined.

Liu Xiaobo, the iconoclastic critic who complained that "Chinese modernism" failed to wage an aesthetic revolution radical enough to meet Western standards, raised only half of this important question when he defined the failure of Chinese modernists in terms of a discrepancy between their internal moral order (preoccupation with themes of enlightenment) and their external means of expression (postenlightenment aesthetics).[128] To highlight such a discrepancy indeed constitutes the first step toward a deeper understanding of what "Chinese modernism" is all about. The diagnosis of the discrepancy itself is insightful. But the critic's prescribed cure is not. Mired in the Chinese epistemological tradition that privileges unity and conceptualizes discrepancy and contradiction as nothing other than lacks to be redressed, Liu Xiaobo prescribed an antidote that sounds as conventional as the Daoist and Zen poetics of harmony that he condemned with a sense of holy mission: "How to *overcome* this discrepancy forms the primary task that contemporary Chinese writers should undertake in their exploration of the artistic form."[129]

Liu Xiaobo's formulation was problematic in many ways. The moral order of Chinese modernism he spoke of was hardly a homogenized one, yet he was completely oblivious to the ambiguous anti-enlightenment moment in the writings of *xiandai pai*. Contrary to his argument, Liu

Suola and Xu Xing's characters were intrigued (if only unconsciously) but hardly constrained by the "social and moral" configuration of "humanism" and the "liberation of personality," themes with which both the May Fourth literature and the Enlightenment were preoccupied. The real irony of Liu's position resides in his holistic impulse to bridge the alleged rupture between antithetical pairs—the internal (the "orderly") and the external (the "disorderly"), content and form—an impulse that reveals his unconscious subscription to an aesthetics deeply confined within a totalistic vision that prescribed the continuum of opposites, a vision that is categorically unmodern. What did our iconoclast evoke but what he had always sworn to expose and castigate: the repressed "illusory harmony" that the traditional Chinese vision of *tianren heyi* (the unity of Heaven and [hu]man) promotes?[130] The return of the repressed in Liu Xiaobo's treatise demonstrates that in modern and contemporary China, militant antitraditionalism is often an ostentatious intellectual guise and a prelude to an ironic inversion to traditionalism.

Liu Xiaobo's example teaches us one lesson: The relationship between the performative (form) and the representational (content) in "Chinese modernism" cannot be summed up in mere antagonistic terms. Neither should the historical task of contemporary Chinese writers be stipulated, as Liu Xiaobo suggested, as the taming of such antagonism. The study of the interrelationship between the semiotic moment and the energetic moment (meaning seen as "pure energy" emanating from the sign) in aesthetic experience will shed light on the making of a quiet revolution in contemporary Chinese literature: the expansion of the boundaries of the subject.[131] The "modernists" themselves hardly dictated the making of any choice between the collective subject and the individual subject or between the historical subject and the linguistic subject. On the contrary, the true characteristics of "Chinese modernism" consist precisely in the cohabitation of all those seemingly contradicting subjectivities. And furthermore, should we worry even if the rupture between the two subjects within each set proves to be as real as Liu Xiaobo feared? Here Xu Zidong provides the most appropriate answer: "The 'avant-gardists' among 'Chinese modernists' in fact often resorted to the aesthetic weapons of the twentieth century (absurdity, loneliness, black humor, and so forth) to search for the cultural goal of the nineteenth century (freedom and the liberation of the individual). This is an unpredictable situation that they were unwilling to acknowledge. But this is *exactly where the value of their work lies.*"[132]

This merging of nineteenth-century telos with twentieth-century aesthetics delivers one message: Chinese aesthetic modernity penetrated the inner sanctum of the symbolic enclosure of a self-sufficient subject irrevocably domesticated by tradition. The opening up of that unified space signified the end of the violent and inauthentic unity that traditional works of art and literature always delivered, a kind of unity that was made possible at the price of suppressing and excluding that which was disparate or could not be integrated. The emancipation of such totalized aesthetic space necessarily entails its fragmentation. A new form of aesthetic synthesis in contemporary Chinese literature has come into view in which what is diffuse and irreconcilable coexists with the all-inclusive—in short, unreason weds reason. Although the liaison of twentieth-century aesthetics with the nineteenth-century cultural goal may seem an unlikely combination, it has percolated through the psyche of the new literary elite without doubt—the unspectacular triumph of the historical logic of Chinese modernity.

The time has finally come for Chinese writers to reckon with rupture thoughtfully if they are heartfelt about their own critique of the cultural experience of totality and harmony that traditionalists took for granted. Modernity, after all, is a trickster rather than a mediator. It tears rather than mends. Metaphorically, it thrives in cacophony rather than in symphony. What can we make of the emotional discord of Sen Sen, Liu Suola's reluctant hero in "You Have No Other Choice," who tries to negotiate his own feelings on the joyful occasion of winning an international award for music composition? How should we interpret his tears of ecstasy but to celebrate them as the token of the split impetus of modern sensibility that represents one sentiment but performs the opposite?

"Unconsciously, he [Sen Sen] turned off his own music, and put the [Mozart] tape into the tape recorder. All of a sudden, a sound refreshing and wholesome, a sound filled with sunshine deeply enveloped him. He never felt so liberated before. He felt as if he were in a pure holy land. All the foul impurities were gone. He was ecstatic. He opened the windows, took one look at a sky as pure as jade, and stretched out his hands to feel the flow of nature. Suddenly, he cried."[133]

"BLUE SKY, GREEN SEA" REVISITED

Like Sen Sen, Liu Suola's generation is irresistibly fascinated with rupture and contradiction. We know that from the title of her story "Blue

Sky, Green Sea" and from the preamble that subverts the spiritual tranquillity of "Let It Be." From the reverent evocation of spatial panorama
opened up to infinite possibilities (sky and ocean) to the blasphemous
denial "fuck it," she pulls us straight into the generation's dichotomous
heart. In carefully juxtaposed moments, the heroine's soul mate, Manzi,
preaches, "Why are you so serious, fake it!";[134] her listener, a dedicated
guitar player, "danced to her words" happily, but then goes ahead and
plays his guitar with such piety that his fingers are drenched in blood.
The story throbs with the recollection of youthful idealism—the heroine's dreamy adolescence merging into her memory of Manzi—but
yearns for self-forgetfulness at the same time. A decadence guilty of its
own extravagance heads halfway toward the humanist moral: Without
eternity, everything is meaningless. Liu Suola has definitely lost her cool
in "Blue Sky, Green Sea" to a sentimentalism that Wang Shuo would
overcome in his celebration of the underclass of *pizi*. The idea of an
empty self freely giving itself contingent content—a playfulness that
Wang Shuo is good at—proves to be an illusion for Liu Suola when there
is still too much at stake: soul, pure heart, love, and faith in the redemptive power of music. The loss of such a binding content in a cruel,
cruel world is what her self-conscious, cynical heroine has to bear. She
bears it, alas, with too many tears. The story, like the heroine's imaginary song about the "iceman made of water" who was melted in a pool
of his own tears, invites moans and groans more than sneers, still much
less a genuine bohemian vision.[135]

"Blue Sky, Green Sea" serves as an example of how a modern Chinese subject emerged out of the token discrepancy between linguistic
signs (occasional curses and scattered images of rebellious gestures) and
the representative (romantic and humanist yearnings for meanings). This
is a subject that can neither reconcile herself to the aborted utopianism
in the wake of the Revolution nor bring herself wholeheartedly to embrace absolute nihilism. She is not a "superfluous being," as He Xin in-
sinuated. Her reluctance to bid farewell to the haunting past results in
an aborted cynicism in the end. Liu Suola's heroine belongs to the community made up of an entire generation preoccupied with the making of
its own "emotional history."[136] That history unfolds itself in the strange
spectacle of a performative bohemia confronting and inevitably contradicting the representational haven of anchored meanings.

Witness again the more dramatic presentation of such a spectacle offered by another well-known yuppie "modernist," Xu Xing. The elusive
theme underlying his "Wuzhuti bianzou" (Variations without a theme)

(1985) emerges as the quest for "something that is sublimated in my soul," a remote but sacred yearning that awaits the sprouting of a "bitter seed" that the hero would carefully "hide away in the most concealed mountain streams."[137] The actual performance of the hero, however, contradicts the sublime sentiment completely. It is carried out in a soulless display of endless ejaculations of "fuck it" and themeless jazzy wisecracks: "Human beings are a twenty-five cents' plate of stir-fried 'three threaded varieties' "; " 'Truth,' 'goodness,' and 'beauty' are a chewing gum" (43). The hero is caught, like Liu Suola's characters, in an unconscious urge to find meaning in life—to "wait for the flowering" and eventual "fruit bearing" of that precious seed hidden away in the deep woods (37)—and in his contradictory impulse to subvert "morals, humors, profundities—fuck your shit!" (44). But we know, no matter how offhandedly he concludes that everyone is but "a big fucking, stinking egg" (41), he cares more than he allows himself to let on. His linguistic game of turning things inside out is an acting-out, for he partakes in the holy mood of a quest that leads him to envision a mirage most tantalizing to an idealist dreamer: "That farthest mountain enwrapped in twilight, against which the sun rested. What is there beyond the mountain? Is it sea? prairie? or a big golden field of apricot gardens?" (64).

So what is it—this rupture between the linguistic and the representational? Is it artificially orchestrated? Is the language of Liu Suola and Xu Xing's hero and heroine purely theatrical? Are they intentionally rough around the edges and yet actually obsessed with purposes and goals of life in high seriousness?

The answer is found in the fascination of Liu Suola and Xu Xing's generation with a "mother fucking intense measure" (*made lidu*) that Sen Sen spoke of with painful religiousness in "You Have No Other Choice."[138] *Made lidu,* a curse and a tribute in one, serves as a metaphor for the topical energy and beat of the early 1980s, which launched artists and writers on an impossible mission to "absorb the hundred years' aesthetic experience of Europe" in the short span of half a decade.[139] What did such explosive tensions produce but a severe mental disorder? The metaphysical quest for a long repressed "creative subjectivity" could only find its self-expression in the epochal symptom of "psychosis."[140] "You Have No Other Choice" celebrates the evils released from Pandora's box. The struggles of Liu Suola's insane characters in the music college crystallize the quixotic battle waged by desires against constraints—the latter manifested in the omnipresent circular image of "perfect functionality" (*gongneng quan*), the archsymbol of harmonics, that hangs ominously from the blackboard and greets the rebellious young musicians with irrevocable authority.

Trendy or not, the characters who dabble in novel linguistic signs such as "fucking intense measure" cannot seem to get enough of them. Such superfluity should not be confused with superficiality, despite Xu Xing and Liu Suola's critics' complaints. The poetic victory of pure signs only serves to remind the characters of the unattainability of the signified in reality. The acute awareness of the contradiction compels them to pro-liferate more signs that in turn widen the chasm. The more deeply they feel the unfulfilled hollowness within, the more eccentrically they tune their rhetoric. Theirs is a generation who, like Sen Sen, rejects the de-fault performance of the "harmonious and eloquent sound that emanates from the piano" in search of discordance, the electrifying expression that breaks out of the confinement of "rhythms with a melody."[141] The crowning tension and intensity, they have come to discover, can only be achieved when they stop acting human and making euphonious signs and sounds. Thus begin the rituals of making and celebrating strident but genuine rattles and jangles:

> Meng Ye plucked the string of his cello with his fingers, suddenly strummed out several single notes. Then he pushed the string in and out, and hit the body of the cello with his palms several times. All of a sudden, he let out an inhuman cry from his throat. Sen Sen cried out loud: 'Fucking intense mea-sure!' Then he thumped both his hands down on the piano keys. Li Ming cov-ered up his ears and wormed himself into his comforter.
> The hallway was filled with Meng Ye's wolf-like howl.
> The harmony of the world. Madness, Li Ming thought.[142]

Totality and harmony—fuck it all! An inferno gapes before us in all mad-ness, ecstasy, and above all, in such high seriousness of purpose.

ROOT-SEARCHING AND MODERN CONSCIOUSNESS

Given the rhythm of discordance underlying modernist sensibility, I may surprise those who insist upon the backward-looking consciousness of *xungen* literature by attempting the seemingly impossible: to listen, with attentiveness, to the echo of Liu Suola's "wolf-like howl" and inhuman cries—typical sound tracks of a modernity gone mad—in the ostensibly tranquil voice of A Cheng's Granddad in "Shuzhuang" (The tree stump) (1984). It is a voice that is filled with "easy charm and mischievous wit."[143] How could those old pastoral songs that celebrate the "roots [that] are buried deep and strong" and taste "like fine wines" that "have aged gracefully, growing in richness and charm" (242) bear any remote resemblance to the roars and racket of modernity?

The answer to this specific question, I suggest, is to be sought in the larger issue: Where do we position the root-searching school on the map of China's aesthetic modernity? And in the same spirit of inquiry, how do we inscribe the idiosyncratic adventures into the agitating energy field of the modern, of individual writers such as Wang Meng and Mo Yan, to whom neither the designation of "modernist" nor "realist" seems to apply?

At first glance, the ethos of *xungen* literature echoes that of social modernity, namely, the collective striving for a utopian perspective that emerges out of the rationalization of society and the intensification of self-reflection. The root-searching school made their debut during the Cultural Discussion in 1985 as an aesthetic movement that served as a figurative cipher of redemption and rational self-reflexivity. Precisely in its capacity to question both tradition and modernity and dramatize the traumatic encounter between these two nemeses in figurative terms, *xungen* literature is a critical tool no less effectively wielded in the intellectuals' attempt to capture the elusive ambience of the utopian state than the high-minded abstract rhetoric of the participants in the grand debate of "tradition versus modernity."

I have mentioned earlier that one of the tributes that the root-searching writers made to aesthetic modernity was their effort to prevent the very collapse of the aesthetic into cognitive rationality. In reaction to cognitive rationality's fascination with a coherent and systematic order, the aesthetic experience that the *xungen* writers delivered was riddled with gaps and silences. In contrast to those intellectuals who found themselves entrenched in the conceptual constraints of methodology fever and who espoused rationality and order at the expense of paradox and disorder, the *xungen* writers' was a much more ambiguous venture into the heart of modernity, in which they found neither consummating order nor total nihilism. In theory, the utopia of the *xungen* movement resides in the reconstruction of an ethical totality retrieved from the past of communal religiosity—in short, an authentic cultural subjectivity of China, which is subject to essentialist recuperation. But in practice, the root-searching consciousness incorporates a different utopian content, an open-ended capacity for self-reflexivity, which enjoys the potential of bailing itself out of essentialist discourse as such. That is to suggest, the root-searching school is instinctively resistant to any norm that is being centered and privileged in the literary text at a given moment, whether the norm is dubbed tradition or modernity, Nature or Culture, the drive for sinification, or the fascination with Western modernism. The root-searching discourse is therefore on the one hand an encircling discourse, and on the other hand, a discourse that promises itself the implantation of the moment of self-critique.

This ambivalent attitude toward the orderly vision characteristic of social modernity accounted for the literature's immense appeal to modernist critics such as Huang Ziping and Li Tuo. Although the *xungen* writers approached life with religious piety, like their contemporaries the Yuppie "modernists," they share the growing painful consciousness that it is their faithful depiction of the rupture rather than the utopian vision of retrieved totality that renders their aesthetic expression meaningful.

One can indeed speak of the *xungen* school's subtle complicitous relationship with a Liu Suola who thrives on dins and blast, and for whom the Spirit has estranged itself. Going insane, as "You Have No Other Choice" reveals, is one alternative to dealing with estrangement; dying is another. Can we envision any other more logical modernist strategy to evoke the lethal encounter between tradition and modernity than making the death of Granddad in "The Tree Stump" an inevitable price he has to pay for returning from the past to the present?

Granddad seems time immemorial at the beginning of the tale. Described as an unsightly tree stump estranged from the bustling modern scene of the small village, he squats at one end of the main street, a mere remnant (rather than a reminder) of the village's historical past forgotten by all, calling little attention from today's pedestrians. The drama begins when the small mountain town wakes up one day from historical amnesia. Not only does it remember the golden melodies that its merry inhabitants used to sing to each other in prerevolutionary times, but it attempts to reconstruct that lyrical past with a singing contest. The past, once evoked, can no longer rest in peace. Granddad—the king of songsters in his prime—has to emerge from oblivion and answer the summons of cultural renaissance. He participates in a singing demonstration at the request of the villagers, concocting and singing, one after another, the jolly mountaineers' verses that time has relegated to the past. The last vestige of tradition is brought to greet the siren calls of modernity. The symbolic return of Granddad—the past—to the modern stage proves fatal: The old songbird breathes his last after an electrifying performance.

The visit from the specter of the past, symbolized by the festive release of the forgotten lyrics, is hardly innocuous. Neither the playful singing of the antiquated songster nor the villagers' "thunderous round of cheers and applause," modernity's greetings to the repercussions of tradition, obliterate the deep chasm that keeps the past apart from the present. This is a chasm no less tangible than the poetic imagery of "the deep canyon" in the tale, a gulf that separates the solitary mountain travelers whose only means of communication with each other in days bygone is ballad singing. But the joking and the bantering "across the chasm" is fated to die out because "the two people would go their separate ways in the mountains, and that would be the end of that" (236). There is no better metaphor to portray the symbolic encounter between tradition and modernity in "The Tree Stump" than the quick succession of audio-visual imagery of the canyon that A Cheng evokes: the sound vanishes into thin air; each goes its own way; and the deep ravine sits there with dispassionate serenity. Modernity demands that Granddad, the last repository of tradition in the village, sing his own swan song upon his close encounter with the modern. Although the content of the past may be bequeathed to future generations as a living tradition—"From then on this street and these mountains once again resounded with their own songs" (242–43)—the formal embodiment of the past invites its own extinction at the touch of the living present, for all past that is excavated is reduced to skeletons and ashes.

No howls of madness are heard in "The Tree Stump." But a chasm of no less poignant depth opens up before us. It takes the form of the deadly, albeit unruffled, confrontation between a personified tradition and modernity. Readers are spared the possibly unpleasant details about such an encounter. The only visible traces of violence resulting from that encounter—the obscure description of Granddad's debilitated existence as a tree stump—imply rather than depict the dramatic rupture that rendered our once heroic mountaineer into an amorphous lump of dried wood whose only sign of existence is the occasional puff of smoke from his pipe. We learn, however, that the very sight of tradition incarnate, reduced to "shriveled" muscles squatting at the east end of the village street, elicits "shudders" from passersby and sinks their spirit "for a good part of the day" (232). It is from these implications that we can reconstruct the site of the disjunct in which the *xungen* consciousness is deeply rooted.

In contrast to the allegedly ostentatious rupture that one witnesses in the Yuppie "modernism" between its linguistic means and the representational content (a rupture dubbed "artificial" by many unsympathetic critics), the root-searching writers have delivered a more subtle split, to

which older generations struggling to reckon with modernity are especially susceptible. Not surprisingly, *xungen* literature was received fa-
vorably by middle-aged critics. They belong to the same generation as
the root-searching writers who toil laboriously to find an access to the
past, and in so doing, who succeed in refuting the Yuppie *xiandai pai*'s
anarchistic manifesto that modernity can only be conceived as a radical
break from the past. Equally unsurprising is the blanket condemnation
of young critics like Liu Xiaobo who labeled as "regressive" a literature
in which he failed to find "souls throbbing" with desires and pains, a literature he summed up as something "tranquil and pure after sublimation"—in short, an enervated literary sensibility that pales in front of a
true modern sensibility that emphasizes, in his view, "feelings, irrationality, the libido, and flesh."[144]

Here we stumble into the issue of generational logic that holds the
key to understanding the different permutations that took place within
such a sweeping, and eventually, meaningless, configuration of a "Chinese modernism." I suggest that we treat both the Yuppie "modernists"
and the *xungen* school as two distinct, and yet not necessarily incompatible, expressions of Chinese aesthetic modernity—the one saturated
with the younger generation's swashbuckling antihumanist rhetoric (an
expression that would only come to fruition with the succeeding generation of experimentalists), and the other marked by a matured mid-life
nostalgia for such sentimental humanist aspirations as history making and remembrance. With this residual humanist affection for land
and for the myth of self-realization (*ziwo shixian*), the root-searching
movement accomplished what the younger generation of Yuppie "modernists" could not care less about, let alone envision: rescuing modernity
from triviality.

What modernity is delivered from by the root-searchers is the modernist myth that we are empty selves facing infinitely open possibilities.
Here even Liu Suola the pseudonihilist cannot help reminding us just
how dull and pathetic such a trifling with modernity's whimsical choices
may seem. Among the various dilemmas that plague her characters in
"Blue Sky, Green Sea" is the plight of a nameless writer of adventure stories who flounders in the ocean of infinite possibilities while concocting
a crime story. We see him, through our heroine's eyes, pale like a patient,
trembling with fathomless despair, and grumbling in a monotone, "Ten
people already died in the tale. But there are still no bad guys. No police either."[145] More people will be killed in vain so that the fiction writer
can keep putting off decisions about the plot. But is this a symptom of

the writer's creative energy? Or is it merely writer's block? The heroine drifts out of the writer's cabin at the end of the story, wondering if she will ever run into an intersection where—here I caught Liu Suola revealing subliminally what she is unwilling to admit all along—the heroine has to make a choice about which direction to turn.

The choice between tradition and modernity is never an easy one, even for the allegedly backward-looking *xungen* writers. In looking into a past that is connected as prehistory with our present, the literature is the least burdened with the agenda of locating the privileged point of temporality. Even the most past-oriented *xungen* author, A Cheng, is much less vulnerable to the lure of tradition than his critics would fain make us believe. The butt of such criticism, "The King of Chess" (*Qiwang*) (1984), displays the author's distinct salute to modern consciousness as much as his immersion in the ancient Daoist philosophy of nonaction (*wuwei*). Those who accuse A Cheng of glorifying the Dao fall far short of grasping that the dramatic pathos of the tale's central metaphor, the mock-heroic battle of the chess king with his rival, lies not in the fictional enactment of the Dao of chess, but in the symbolic battle of life-and-death that took place *within* the chess king Wang Yisheng himself—the turbulent confrontation of his finite self with his transcendental self embodied in his maddening pursuit of the ultimate truth of chess. This clash of Wang Yisheng's empirical self—a mundane existence confined in a social reality he is powerless to transform—with his transcendental subjectivity, which aspires after infinite freedom in the spiritual realm, unmistakably subverts the Chineseness that underlies a tale about the art of chess.[146] I emphasize that the drama and trauma of the confrontation between Wang Yisheng's two selves, which nearly consumes our hero at the end of the story (he sinks into a physical coma), bespeak aesthetics of the modern. More specifically, the confrontation highlights the contest between the old and the new regime, a familiar scenario that modernity never fails to trigger. What constitutes subjectivity in the modern sense is no longer the Daoist holistic self at peace with itself, but a self that problematizes and splits itself from within. What characterizes the chess king's struggle is eventually written in the vocabulary of ambivalence and contradiction—in terms of modernity rather than the Dao.

A Cheng, of course, is unable to serve as the arbiter of history. Contrary to the claims of critics such as Liu Xiaobo, he is unwilling to make the choice between the Dao and the Now. The ending of the tale brings into relief the ambiguity at issue: "[Yet the mountain people] shaved their heads and took up their hoes. The real meaning of life is contained therein. If one recognizes it, one is lucky, one is happy. Eating and putting on clothes are the most basic human desires. Human beings have been busy with that every day since there was life. But one is not human after all if merely confined within it."[147] This last paragraph of "The King of Chess" delivers one message: The conventional supposition of A Cheng's total immersion in the tame vision of Daoism is subverted by his subtle conclusion that questions, in a whisper, the sufficiency of the Dao as the telos of humanity. Neither the exemplary past of a Daoist haven nor an arrogant present that scatters to the winds the myth of origin provides the ultimate resolution to A Cheng's quest for temporal refuge and to that of his fellow root-searching writers.

All my arguments attest to the seemingly contradictory observation that, contrary to what its name delimits, *xungen* literature is as much rooted in the perspective of the present as Liu Suola and Xu Xing's *Xiandai pai*. In mapping the aesthetic modernity of post-Mao China, even a critic as anti-root-searching as Liu Xiaobo has to agree with the savvy comments made by Mu Gong, "From now on the further development of the ideas of literature in China will no longer be primarily manifested in the contest between 'traditionalists' and 'modernists.' It will be manifested, however, in the debates among the various persuasions within the modernist school itself."[148]

MO YAN AND WANG MENG: MODERNIST RHETORIC AND PSEUDOMODERNIST IDEOLOGY

The positioning of the *xungen* school should make it easier for us to explore another two such "persuasions" of aesthetic modernity in post-Mao China, namely, Mo Yan and Wang Meng. Most critics would insist that both authors have contributed to the making of the aesthetics of subjectivity, one of the prominent indexes of modernism. Wang Meng, in particular, has continually surprised his readers by pushing to an extreme his fictional narrator's rhetorical capacity to subvert his own story. But is this flamboyant subjectivity of the narrator sufficient to lure critics to endorse the writer's self-designation as a modernist?

Before exploring this question, I will first look at a seemingly more obvious specimen of "Chinese modernism," Mo Yan's *The Red Sorghum Clan* (*Hong gaoliang jiazu*) (1986).[149] What Mo Yan exhibits, with breathtaking hyperbole, is an orgy of sensationalism on the edge between life and death where heightened awareness lies. He is fascinated with everything that Liu Xiaobo prescribed as modern—the irrational, the libidinous, and the flesh and blood. And nowhere can this impact of kinetic energy be better delivered than through the juxtaposition of contradictory images: the beautiful and the ugly, the sacred and the obscene, sins and virtue, the pure and the filthy, and the heroic and the depraved. The novel is peppered with opposites that culminate in an undifferentiated continuum of life and death. Every moment and movement toward death—here one recalls the most poignant scene in the novel, where the youthful Grandma slips in and out of consciousness as she lies dying in the sorghum field—is simultaneously an exaltation of life and desire. Each time the narrator evokes the visual plenitude of the crimson red sorghum, he pays ritualistic homage to the potent human blood that both sustains and spills the essence of life. If the quality of modernism is measured by its ability to accost death and to live on contradictions, then Mo Yan clearly meets the criterion.

Yet *The Red Sorghum Clan* is by no means a clear-cut case of classic modernism. Although framed in a temporal limbo somewhere between the past and the present that bears close resemblance to the root-searching literature, the novel retrogresses a step further into the mythological mode of primitive consciousness that the *xungen* school more often problematizes than glorifies. What greets our eyes is not merely the distinct private space of self-conscious subjecthood ("Grandma is the pioneer of the liberation of the individual"), a space that indubitably bears the trademark of modernity, but a borderless opaque territory where totemism and shamanistic magic hold absolute reign ("Red Sorghum is the totem of our Northeast Gaomi Township"). What unfolds in the novel is therefore more than just another variation of modernity's contradictory image making. The question to address is not to what end Mo Yan chooses the conflicting strategy of representation that romanticizes in turn the individual will to power and the tyrannical communal ethos, or whether he succeeds in conjuring up a continuum between the modern and the primitive modes of consciousness. The question to address is whether the courting of death and danger and the mindless release of the libido of all the licentious male and female characters are signs of modernity's beckoning or simply a contemporary retelling of primitivism's eternal triumph?

I should point out that this is not the kind of primitivism that Gauguin or Matisse would have understood as devoid of cultural roots and reduced to a metaphor for the fantastic. It takes in everything that modernity wishes to leave behind: the superstitious, feudalistic, ignominious, and irrational, as well as the legendary and visionary. How are we

going to interpret the narrator's obsessive promotion of such unculti-
vated forces except by attributing it to the author's fascination with the
potent domination of the ultrastable presence of tradition? In *The Red
Sorghum Clan,* brute force is the religion. The moments of domination
are canonized side by side with the moments of rebellion. In this ritualistic worship of violence, the tyrant appears as alluring as the rebel.
Revalorized in the aesthetics of energy, barbarism is finally indistinguishable from the modernist aesthetics of desublimation. Does Mo Yan
himself know what he is celebrating—flagrant power or liberating desire? Or can he tell one from the other?

To those readers who insist that Mo Yan's glorification of the instinctual and the libidinous clearly heralds the dawning of modern sensibility, I cannot envision a better rejoinder than to invite them to revisit
the end of the novel where the narrator suddenly speaks with hurried
but deliberate tendentiousness. In a moment of intense nostalgia, he
brings us back to the privileged locale of the village and the collective
unconscious of the villagers. The city where he grew up is put on trial,
together with all that it is associated with, a civilization condemned as
artificial and enervating simply because it was allegedly nonexperiential.
While debunking urban sensibility, the narrator sanctifies the "mysterious emotions" underlying the savage past, a past that he claims will
emerge as "an almighty *thinking* weapon" with which one can grasp the
unpredictable future.[150] And who can exercise the power to evoke those
mysterious emotions but the ghostly apparition of the Second Wife,
whose legendary death is inseparable from the tales of animal posses-
sion and exorcism—stories that reveal tradition in its most crude and
corrupt reincarnation? It is none other than this woman whose spirit is
reciprocal with that of wolves, wild cats, and demons and who stands
at the opposite end of the modern Grandma, who alone wields the mystical power of summoning the narrator, Grandson, from the city back to
the village. One cannot help wondering why it is the reactivated memory of her scandalous death rather than that of the heroic death of
Grandma, the very emblem of modernity, that emerges in the novel's concluding statement as the ultimate sign, the spiritual authority, to which
Grandson has to bow in awe.

This ending exposes Mo Yan's cultural ideology more powerfully than
any other episode in the novel. Mo Yan believes in the mysterious presence of tradition that promises the second coming of history. The myth
of return is consummated as Grandson, the emblem of the future, answers the call of the Second Wife to go back to the mythological village

of red sorghum and to bathe, as her spirit dictates, in the mystical Mo River for three days and three nights. The bewitching and beguiling voice of the Second Wife reminds one of the Sirens in *Odysseus* and the baptism, the return to the womb. Time immemorial cancels out the temporal flow. Tradition provides the normativity on which an empty and frail modernity is dependent. The novel enacts, on the ideological front, the drama of tradition usurping modernity in full glory.

What I am critiquing, however, is not the mythological mode of consciousness itself, but the danger of the flattening out of such a mode into a model. One only needs to look at the *xungen* writer Han Shaogong's experiment with the same narrative mode in "Ba-ba-ba," a story about an idiot and the idiotic existence of his villagers, to understand how the mythological space of narration can open up a critical space that enables readers to raise the question: Is the collective suicide of the villagers at the end of the tale an act of rebellion or of sheer ignorance?[151] What Mo Yan eventually denies us is that ever intriguing possibility to expose and examine the Janus face of mythology and tradition. Whereas the imaginary of the idiot in Han Shaogong's tale evokes the jarring mirror image of modernity, the imaginary of the red sorghum field is narcissistic—the one is self-subversive, the other, self-indulgent. Whereas Han Shaogong stirs up our irresistible impulse to question the primitivistic logic of undifferentiation, a logic that privileges the mysterious continuum of "the subject and the object," "the physical and the psychological," "being and nonbeing," "fantasies and reality," and "humans, Nature, the supernatural,"[152] Mo Yan holds us spellbound by feeding us the sensory pleasure of the indiscriminate. Eventually, he tells us that thinking is an act of cowardice and an offense against Nature.

The case of Mo Yan teaches us that a work that is replete with imagism, appeals to irrationality, exalts the sexual organ, and experiments with unconventional means of storytelling may still fall short of delivering genuine modern sensibility. This brings us back to Wang Meng, the pioneer of the Chinese narrative mode of stream of consciousness.[153]

To make a long story short, I join Leo Lee in concluding that, in spite of his claim to modernism, Wang Meng is first and foremost a realist writer.[154] This would certainly alarm Wang, who dabbled in Western modernist sleight of hand with such noticeable effort and success. What gives away his realist identity is, however, not how he writes, but what he reveals despite himself even when he is formulating a modernist plot. A good case in point is his much acclaimed *Yi ti qian jiao* (A sneeze that charms a thousand), "the most avant-gardist piece in 1988."[155]

The story contains the skeleton of a plot—a VIP's graceful sneezing posture and his not-so-graceful moral persona. What Wang Meng has in mind is to revoke the aura of verisimilitude and to enact playfully, right under the reader's nose, the process of fiction making and the minute details of the writer's conscious fabrication. To accomplish this task, he resorts to the most convenient solution; he turns his narrator into a professional writer like himself. Despite Wang Meng's attempt to subvert all perspectives of narration, it is this strategy that reveals the Achilles heel of an act of writing that can otherwise claim close allegiance to modernism. The problem at issue is precisely the identifiability of the intellectual and ideological perspective of the fictional narrator and the author himself—a default point of departure that realism takes for granted. Although the author strives to achieve, with great success, utter artificiality elsewhere in the tale, he simply forgets to fictionalize the narrator by making him a caricature of Wang Meng rather than the real Wang Meng himself.

This oversight could very well subvert what Wang Meng sets out to do in the first place. His narrator goes about the usual business of vitiating the boundary between the real and the unreal and with an ironic grimace forbids us to take anything seriously, his own narrative voice above all, but what we actually encounter is not a fictional narrator who jokes around insincerely, but a real author making genuine confessions about what he thinks of magical realism, the *xungen* literature's trendy slogan of "marching toward the world," modernist sensibility, China's new wave cinema, and most importantly of all, realism itself.

No literary school escapes our narrator's biting sarcasm. Not even the term "modern" is immune to his metacritical spirit. His wisecracks are often double-edged, for his targets are multiple. He is at his best when, by debunking three new wave film productions ("Yellow Earth," "Red Sorghum," and "Old Well"), cinematic modernism par excellence, he succeeds in poking fun at the root-searching consciousness at the same time. Is there anything left to be redeemed if nothing is sacred anymore?

For such a pious writer as Wang Meng, the altar is of course never left completely empty. From the very beginning, the self-designated modernist author finds himself caught in the awkward position of having to defend realist sensibility, even in a piece of fiction, as a tantalizing remnant of the day. The awkwardness intensifies as the tale unfolds. Whenever the subject of realism comes up, the narrator is self-conscious of his complicitous coexistence with Wang Meng himself. The ensuing rhetorical dodges and double talks to which the narrator resorts in delivering his metacommentaries on realism constitute the most theatrical moments of "A Sneeze That Charms a Thousand." These are the moments when the narrator senses, all of a sudden, the urgency of speaking in restraint and with measured calculation, even though he has given himself away with total abandon to the mockery of every other literary persuasion. There is obviously more at stake when the narrator faces the task of performing the pundit's routine practice of wisecracking about realism. The truth is, he simply does not have the heart to do it. What appears before us is a flustered narrator who forgets the rules of his own game: Everything he says is to be taken with a grain of salt, his opinions about realism without exception. Why can he not serve us the same hearty fare of a belittled realism as he did a feast of parody on the tricks and knacks of modernist techniques?

The fictional constraint underlying the tale, that he make a jest of every literary convention in turn, is the only means that could force our narrator to taunt realism. And yet his discomfort at having to create the semblance of gibing at the school of "art for life's sake" produces no cracks and good teases, but only quibbles and lapses. We read now and then a sentence buried in the superfluous trappings of adverbial modifiers that continuously qualifies what he has to say ("I was even speculating in suspicion whether realism is truly a bit out of vogue"), or a straightforward confession ("What I, the narrator, am experimenting with is a kind of a realism with an umbrella structure"), a rhetorical question ("Is traditional realism endowed with a kind of irresistible appeal?"), or a seemingly equivocal statement: "Making light of 'form' often amounts to making light of 'content.' But even the assertion that form is form, and form is everything, does not necessarily entail that content should be expelled. Is life, God, and love a form of existence, or is it its true content?"[156]

One hardly needs to recapitulate that at this particular juncture it is content rather than form—realism's aesthetics in a nutshell—that wins the narrator's oblique endorsement. A passage like the foregoing is already revealing enough for us to confirm what I have suggested, that Wang Meng's residual loyalty to realism is not to be underestimated. And yet a still more uninhibited confession about his realist persona is found in a longer passage in which the author-narrator deliberates, with a seriousness out of character with his usual joking self, the value of consciousness versus the unconscious.

Will power and reason dominate. Yet they also regulate and balance every individual. Will power and reason could be turned into tools of oppression, giving rise to various forms of hypocrisy and perversion. However, will power and reason could also be made into a provision, a kind of illumination, an intelligent and joyful guidance, fair and sensible, full of wisdom, which produces varied fruits of beauty and goodness. Therefore, as I face the fathomless undercurrents lying beneath the human consciousness, the turbulent, contending, and incomprehensible flow that has lost its light forever or perhaps just temporarily, a vista as bottomless as the dark canyon one looks down at from the mountain top, I feel terrified and dizzy, as if I would fall into its abyss at any time. I cannot bring myself to a face-to-face encounter with this deep unconscious that is burning, contending, and saturated with desires of the self, which cannot but produce jealousy, terror, ferocity, and entanglement."[157]

In weighing reason against the irrational, in pitting consciousness against the unconscious, the narrator divulges a deep-seated conviction to which die-hard realists alone subscribe: disorder should be shunned as a plague. If the unconscious, the energy field of modernism, where desire traverses in repelling, ominous, and dangerous forms, is greeted with such horror and repulsion by the author-narrator, one cannot help thinking twice about the terms of his self-identification as a modernist.

The cases of Mo Yan and Wang Meng indicate only too well that modernist sensibility is as much an issue about the ideological content of modern consciousness as a well-pronounced formal revolution against the technical conventions of realism. Yet although I challenge the conventional wisdom that salutes those two authors as champions of "Chinese modernism," there is no denying that Mo Yan and Wang Meng represent two distinct streams that crisscross the vast territory of China's aesthetic modernity. Acknowledging these two writers' complicitous relationship with primitivism and realism respectively should help us understand that the dawning of aesthetic modernity in Deng's China does not necessarily result in its radical discontinuity from all the previously sanctioned literary conventions. Only naive advocates of a global development model and an ill-informed Western public would confuse the arrival of modernization in China with its "necessary" break from and revolt against all earlier political (socialist), literary (realist), and cultural (Confucianist) traditions. Just as the neo-Confucian revival constitutes an integral part of China's social modernity, so has realism, perhaps even a little dose of romanticism, become part and parcel of the now passé Chinese aesthetic modernity.

Modernism's career in China was doomed to be short-lived from the very beginning. It would not bloom fully until thirty years later in Taiwan.[158] The ripples of aesthetic modernity in 1930s' Shanghai predictably disappeared into the tidal waves of revolutionary politics. Two leading neo-impressionists, Liu Na'ou and Mu Shiying, died young as victims of political assassination.[159] Dai Wangshu passed away in the early 1950s. Shi Zhecun returned to the realist camp as early as the 1940s. Qian Zhongshu and Shen Congwen gave up creative writing for academic research after 1949. Zhu Guangqian, the most progressive modernist theorist, floundered in each political campaign. And modern poets such as Feng Zhi and Bian Zhilin channeled their creative energy to the introduction and translation of foreign literature, ironically, that of classical works in particular.[160] Modernism's first revolt against realism failed wretchedly.

In the 1980s, the reentry of modernism in Deng's China aroused more expectations and promised a golden harvest whose fruits were to be delivered to both the indigenous and Western market. Marching side by side with social modernity, it reappeared as a historical necessity challenging the legitimacy of realism. Its victory, an all consuming one for as long as it lasted (between 1984 and 1986), demarcates one of the great watersheds in the history of contemporary Chinese literature. But just as social modernity could promote an aesthetic modernism to suit its own agenda, it could also halt it when aesthetic rationality gained a momentum of its own beyond the reach of instrumental reason. Liu Suola's defiant brand of Yuppie *xiandai pai* and the *xungen* literature's critique of modernity proved in the end too unruly to be reintegrated into the coherent configuration of a purposive rationality that rewards only radical discontinuity and the notion of compulsive progress. Both the philosophy of root-searching and Liu Suola's incrimination of modernity's alienating persona taste too subtle and bitter to the palate of a populace that craves delectable feasts. It seems predictable that as China marches into the 1990s, the fever for social modernity will rage on with redoubled incentive, leaving behind all that in the semantic property of modern consciousness is self-critical of the epoch's obsession with the progress syndrome and rational structure, namely crisis consciousness, rebellious consciousness, reified consciousness, mood of contradiction, ennui, and antihumanist sentiments.

Any ethos that contradicts the telos of modern history in China— whether it was spelled out as the agenda of national survival during the May Fourth period or as the logic of Development in the Deng Xiaoping era—courts its own demise. The quick ebb and flow of aesthetic modernity demonstrates once more that the dangerous pattern of

boom and bust that has left unfinished many historical projects—a curious variation of the loosening-and-crush political culture of Mao's
China—is a heritage of a revolutionary past that dies hard. Perhaps it is
high time that the Chinese learn how to better appreciate the concept of
sublation. Take our interpretation of modernity: although modernity's
inception means canceling the past on the one hand, on the other it signifies the preservation and elevation of tradition in the dialectic process
as a partial element in a synthesis. Seen in this light, the debate about
pseudomodernism should not be so quickly usurped by, but recontained
instead within, the current discussion of "Chinese postmodernism." Just
as tradition is conceived as the prehistory of modernity, so is the unfinished project of aesthetic modernity the past of a postmodern present.
Although the zeitgeist of the twenty-first century promises no serious
comeback of aesthetic modernism, a more profound understanding of
the Chinese postmodern culture in the 1990s would have to reckon with
an aesthetic modernity that rehearsed postmodernity's penchant for heterogeneity by making one hundred flowers bloom without passing down
a single homogeneous manifesto.

FIVE

Romancing the Subject

Utopian Moments in the Chinese
Aesthetics of the 1980s

The dictum "less is more" is an apt paradox for the aesthetics of classical Chinese poetry and prose, in which the frequent absence of a gram-
matical subject—the pronoun "I"—seems to evoke and extend rather
than attenuate the boundless horizon of the authentic self. This is the self
whose interior landscape is indistinguishable from the exterior one on
which the poet-writer's eye lingers.

Much has been written, especially by poet-critics abroad, about the
well-trodden ground of the continuum of the subject and object in traditional Chinese poetics.[1] The Western fascination with this aesthetic
subjectless self has come a long way since Fenollosa's idiosyncratic interpretation of Chinese ideograms and Gary Snyder's experiments with
the aesthetics of the Dao and Zen. A theoretical proposal such as the
"non-Cartesian subject" still continues, to a certain extent, the saga of
the Western appropriation of the romance with the holistic and immediate self.[2] The West has yet to learn (perhaps it would be with mixed
reactions) that the "Oriental" holistic self, in an ironic reversal, is receding further and further away from the social and cultural imaginary
of post-Mao China.

History alone holds the key to the making and interpretation of such
dramatic reversals. After being subjugated to the collective—whether encoded in Confucian familial superstructure for thousands of years in imperial China or reincarnated in the party apparatus of Chinese Maoism-
Marxism-Leninism during the revolutionary years—Chinese writers
and intellectuals have emerged as the fervent advocates of what the

theoretical agenda of the non-Cartesian subject hopes to redress: a subjectivity marked and authenticated by its inward turn. Whereas the elite trumpeted various theories of subjectivity (*zhuti*) during the early and mid-1980s, the common folks on the streets were genuine practitioners of individualism à la mode. Who could have predicted that China would turn out to be a late bloomer of this sort?

Mao Zedong certainly was no clairvoyant when he set out to tame Chinese writers and intellectuals at the 1942 Yan'an Forum Talks, which nipped in the bud any individualistic and aesthetic turn of post-May Fourth literature. Nor could the party ideologues foresee at the climax of their 1950s campaign against the Marxist literary critic Hu Feng (1902–1985) that his famous slogan "the subjective fighting spirit" would reemerge with a vengeance in various incarnations four decades later. And for millions and millions of Chinese who surrendered themselves with such fanaticism to the utopian longings of the Cultural Revolution, disillusionment was soon followed by deep-seated suspicions of all forms of polity (the archsymbol of the public and the collective) and a simultaneous construction of a fetishism of the subject.

The 1980s witnessed the widening of the chasm between the private and the public. The agonistic relationship between these two realms escalated until the cataclysmic outburst of discontent at the Tian'anmen Square in the early summer of 1989. It seemed only natural that the demise of the cult of a single god in the late 1970s precipitated the rediscovery of humanism. The specter that haunted the Chinese earth was not only the "specter of the human,"[3] but also that of the individual subject. The Chinese Marxists' debate over Marxist humanism and socialist alienation in 1983, on the centennial of Marx's death, not only opened the floodgate of postrevolutionary inquiry into the new problematic of human nature (as opposed to class nature), but also swept in its wake Chinese intellectuals' decade-long fascination with the theme of subjectivity.

THE HISTORICAL ENTRY OF THE TRIPLE PLAYERS: LIU ZAIFU, THE ROOT-SEARCHING SCHOOL, AND THE EXPERIMENTALISTS

Power depends upon Yesterday,
Literature always stands facing Today;
it is not necessary to compare its longevity with Power,
for Literature is obliged to command from Today's
        horizon

a panoramic vista of Yesterday
and in that very act
    blots out the vestiges of Power

Bei Dao

Bei Dao's poetic manifesto, which appears on the cover of a recent issue of *Jintian* (Today),[4] a literary journal in exile published by post-June Fourth expatriates, tells us worlds about the antagonistic and agonistic relationship between political "Power" and "Literature" and about how Chinese literati are constantly engaged in mapping out, consciously or unconsciously, their own positionality against a rival who is both real and imaginary, a stable, identifiable, and unified entity in the name of capitalized Power.

The postmodern notion of power that disseminates into an anonymous structural activity for which no totalized subject is responsible remains a First-World myth that is of theoretical interest but of little explanatory value to Chinese theorists wrestling with indigenous cultural politics. Given the visibility and centrality of the power to contest and the underlying binary structure that defines such highly ritualized contestation (yesterday versus today, longevity versus short life, resistance versus domination), Chinese literati are forever intrigued by the possibility of a total abrogation of the other term in the binary pair. With a naivete that characterizes both martyrs and victors alike, they revel in the reversibility of the subject-positions of Power and Literature in China's existing power structure.

Bei Dao's imaginary evocation of the urgency of the single act of reversal—the blotting out of "the vestiges of Power"—is an unambiguous vision that disciples of Foucault and Western postmodernists would hardly deign to invoke. Although such a binary mode of thinking might appear barbarous in an age of poststructuralist dissolution into the amorphous, the Chinese have a large stake in the continual validity of such binary epistemology insofar as it enables contestatory categories such as "resistance" and "agency" to emerge. Indeed, if the power one resists has a source and center to speak of, the construction of an equally efficacious and empowering subject worthy of its opponent is a theoretical imperative.

In this chapter, I deliver the Chinese postrevolutionary narrative of subjectivity. It is a story of resistance and conflict, a story about insurgent, albeit self-deceptive, strategies of *depoliticization* and *interiorization* that theorists and writers adopted to position themselves against the autocratic Father at home. But this confrontational culture of resistance underwent a subtle transformation in dealing with the opponent of a different persona, i.e., the West, identified as both the tutor and opponent of contemporary Chinese elite. In the face of cultural imperialism, the charting of post-Mao China's own cultural territory called for the reverse strategies of the *politicization* of local culture and the *exterior* projection of the image of China's cultural subject. How Chinese writers and theorists characterized their complex relationship with the foreign Father—one that incorporated their desire to copy, appropriate his image, and resist and exorcize it in turn—formed part of the Chinese discourse of subject formation, a decade-long narrative about the postrevolutionary subject caught in the act of making and imagining a subjective space hitherto alien to the Chinese ethos.

The incentive for making such a space was already unwittingly programmed into the movement for the "emancipation of the mind," which the Party launched in 1979 after the fall of the Gang of Four. By 1984, the stage was well set for the dramatic appearance of the catchword *zhuti* (the subject) that would resonate throughout the utopian decade of the 1980s. Liu Zaifu, the master theorist of the discourse of subjectivity, identified human beings as the subject of history and resistance. To combat the enclosure of politics and unfreedom, Liu theorized the aesthetic subject as the privileged site where the ultimate realization of a total human being is to take place—an imaginary site previously prescribed to the proletariat in the Marxist tradition. The debate over the ideological correctness of Liu's theory, whose landmark significance was acknowledged in the coining of the "Liu Zaifu phenomenon," continued during 1985 and 1986 when the school of root-searching literature emerged to usurp attention and carry the burden of reinventing China's cultural subject.

1985 and 1986 marked both the acme and the beginning of the decline of post-Mao China's utopianism. In 1987, escalating socioeconomic and political depression found its repercussions in various circles of artists and writers. It soon became a vogue for critics to harp on the "depression of creativity" and to mourn the loss of the "sensational impact" that postrevolutionary literature used to deliver. The emergence of the experimentalists in 1987 seemed a timely response to the exhaustion of the utopian motif of the early 1980s. Paradoxically, it was on the premise of sociopolitical and cultural dystopianism that the linguistic utopia of the experimentalists was constructed. This is a dehistoricized and dehumanized utopia created and dissolved instantaneously with the inauguration and termination of each discursive act. With a pseudonihilist sneer, the experimentalists proclaimed that the humanist subject is but an imaginary construct. To those who desire China's entry into global culture at all costs, the seemingly antihumanist impulse of the experimentalists is a welcome sign of a leap into postmodernism. But whether China's avant-gardists have indeed deconstructed the subject remains a controversy. It is one of the aims of this chapter to continue the debate and frame it in terms of the epochal discourse of subjectivity, which has come a long way since Liu Zaifu's modest call for an aesthetics of the humanist subject.

Although overseas critics of mainland China tend to be all too conscious of the belatedness of the Chinese theory of subjectivity in the face of contemporary Western antihumanist outcry, I have little intention of making apologies for the two primary foci of this chapter, Liu Zaifu and the practitioners of the genre of root-searching literature. Their respective immersion in the problematic of the aesthetic and cultural subject should be examined in the broader context of the imaginary landscape evoked in Bei Dao's poem—the perennial battle between Literature and Power. At the risk of simplifying the phenomenon of Liu Zaifu's theory of subjectivity and that of the emergence of *xungen* writers' fascination with the will-o'-the-wisp of "cultural subject," I extrapolate that whereas it is the indigenous power against which Liu pits his autonomous aesthetic subject, the power discourse that *xungen* writers confront is the twin discourse of the Han majority from within (*zhongxin huayu*) and the First-World neocolonial discourse from without. The writers' construction of China's cultural subjectivity therefore is a doubly marginal discourse (*bianyuan huayu*).

This preamble should serve to illustrate that much of the creative potency of Chinese theorists and writers during the 1980s was derived from the momentum of resistance and struggle. Were they deprived of their real or imaginary rival—the autocratic regime at home or the cultural imperialists abroad—Chinese intellectuals and writers might confront a scenario that is as threatening as the postmodern spectacle of "open and total availability."[5] The disappearance of constraints and grounding might mean something much worse than mere anarchy to those who are accustomed to living on confrontational reality and on the compulsion to resist. How would the grief-stricken Chinese intellectuals shape their own identity if they were bereft of their original sin—the pangs of sociopolitical conscience?

The binary epistemology of A versus B (a favorite formula that creates many enabling manifestations in Chinese cultural politics, among them

Gan Yang's proposition of the "contestation between tradition and modernity") enables the Chinese subject to position him or herself and to struggle against the oppressive public space. It is important to note that such an oppressive space is identified with either end of the spatial scale: the repressive Mao Style on one end that leaves no room for creative innovation, and the pluralistic space on the other—the new reality of a depoliticized dystopia, whose total space is paradoxically tantamount to anonymity.[6] The invasion of pluralistic Western logic into the indigenous cultural landscape of post-Mao China—a cultural milieu fervently saluted by those Chinese critics who mistook the domination of contingent content for sovereign freedom[7]—signifies the beginning of the dissolution of the natives' individuality. Little did those critics suspect that the mark of the plural is instantaneously turned into an ominous sign of "the depersonalization of the colonized" inasmuch as it breaks down the mechanism of binary discrimination and renders their political project of subject formation superfluous.[8]

This brief excursion about the binary scheme brings us closer to the Chinese geography of resistance that evolves around Liu Zaifu's theory of subjectivity and the cultural ideologies of root-searching literature. One cannot begin to appreciate the deep structural compulsion underlying the construction of the narrative of the subject in either case until one constructs the total plot of insurgency: the target of subversion, the means of resistance, and the objectives of struggle. The different personae of the imaginary rival(s) in each narrative of resistance (the indigenous despot, the foreign devil, or even the merging of both evils) overdetermine the nature of how the subject is aestheticized. Liu Zaifu's absolute autonomous subject parades triumphantly, in contrast to the opaque subject in *xungen* literature, which is harder to fathom and stabilize primarily because its discursive agonist has no single identity.

But the story of resistance in the Chinese narrative of subjectivity does not simply end with the fading popularity of Liu Zaifu and the root-searching literature. My account of that story continues beyond Liu Zaifu and the *xungen* writers, for failure to do so would not only mirror scandalously the binarism characteristic of Chinese literary and critical discourses in general, but also fall short of tracing the sacrilegious sequel to the once-canonical project of subject formation. The sequel in question revolves around the catchy posthumanist and postmodernist problematic of "Is the subject liquidated?"—a problematic of considerable theoretical interest to contemporary critics who either endorse or condemn the emergence circa 1987 of the so-called *xianfeng xiaoshuo* (avant-garde fiction) or *shiyan xiaoshuo* (experimental fiction). Until one reckons with the controversy over this new genre of fiction—is it merely a case of deconstruction (or even postmodernism)?—one cannot hope to delineate the subtle response of the new generation of Chinese fiction writers to the increasingly fuzzy logic of resistance at the threshold of an epistemic break in the late 1980s.

Translating the subtlety in question is difficult given the fact that the discursive hegemony of the First World is no longer seen as an evil to be withstood. For the first time in modern and contemporary Chinese literary circles, there has emerged a school of experimentalists who imagine themselves to be partners with rather than contenders against the First-World authors. This is a transcolonial subject, an imaginary tabula rasa free of inferiority complex and old ideological hang-ups, defiant and vainglorious enough to master and appropriate the language of the First World and to reinscribe him or herself with an unmistakably idiosyncratic signature in a text of self-possessed subject-position.[9] The revolution of the experimentalists is far too complex to be summarized in a few introductory remarks. It suffices to say that one of their most risky and yet most memorable feats is a premeditated dismissal of the familiar paradigm of power versus resistance and the exaltation of the performativity of language games in its place. Uprooting the deeply ingrained national habit that compelled readers to locate the site of power struggle and patterns of resistance in all discursive practices, the experimentalists sneer at the critics and the reading public by leaving them both in an interpretive vacuum.

Despite its disingenuous flirtation with the linguistic medium (and indeed, with everything else), the narrative tableau of the experimentalists foregrounds the utopian moment of a radically different order from the humanistic vision that characterized the utopian discourse of Liu Zaifu's theory as well as of the root-searching literature. Theirs is a linguistic utopia (an order of authenticity possibly higher than Liu's politico-aesthetic mythology and *xungen* literature's cultural-aesthetic utopia) born, paradoxically, at the very moment of their proclamation that language is artifice. The subject, concluded the daredevils, is nothing more than a mere effect of language.

LIU ZAIFU: THE MASTER GRAMMARIAN OF THE SUBJECT

To strike a novelistic posture such as the experimentalists' requires sardonic audacity and, on many occasions, a penchant for the shameless display of a repressed libidinal drive that has not yet evolved beyond adolescence. However, it depends most of all upon the passing of an age whose energy was thoroughly spent on the agenda of the "awakening of humanity" (*rende juexing*). The experimentalists' seemingly blatant antihumanist heresy would indeed have been out of the question in Liu Zaifu's time.

Liu's major theoretical writings—among them, "On the Subjectivity of Literature" ("Lun wenxue de zhutixing") (1985–1986), "Literary Studies Should Take Humanity as Its Cognitive Center" ("Wenxue yanjiu yingyi ren wei siwei zhongxin") (1985), and *On The Composition of [Literary] Personality* (*Xingge zuhe lun*) (1986)—were all written and published between 1984 and 1986, a period still very much preoccupied with the postrevolutionary binary mode of "bestial nature" (*shouxing*) and "human nature" (*renxing*), and on the deep structural level, with that of "alienation" and the "retrieval of the original nature" (*huigui*).[10] Unmistakably incorporated into the subtext of Liu's insurgent writings is the short-lived debate over socialist alienation and Marxist humanism in 1983, a taboo topic that Chinese critics at home preferred to elide in the wake of the Anti–Spiritual Pollution Campaign (1983), which sealed the controversy by stigmatizing the concept of alienation as ideologically suspect. Little has been said about the political subtext of alienation (and by implication, the entire Chinese apparatus of orthodox Marxism-Leninism) in the critiques of Liu's work, both at home and abroad;[11] yet it is not difficult to identify the agonistic text that bears the brunt of Liu Zaifu's theory of subjectivity as none other than the historical materialism that denies the human subject its self-presence and subjugates it to politics and economic determinism. To put Liu Zaifu's case succinctly, it is clearly humanity (*ren*) rather than textuality (*wen*) or the subject that forms the cognitive center of his epistemic project of subjectivity.[12]

That is to say, no matter how radical he may sound for a fleeting moment, he remains susceptible to the constraints inherent in the generation of Chinese Marxists who still cherish a faith in romantic voluntarism—human beings as the principal subject of history and resistance—and, no less fervently, in the ultimate realization of freedom from ideology as the telos of history. Liu Zaifu's implied antagonist bears the categorical imprint of what Bei Dao refers to in his poetic battle cry as the stark presence of political Power. To combat such a domineering power, Liu constructs a sovereign and determining subject who bears all the familiar trademarks of the Cartesian cogito, the Kantian constituting consciousness that confronts a chaotic empirical world, and the unified and self-present Hegelian subject. The subject is, in short, "dynamic," "creative," "self-regulating," "endowed with will power," "enabling capacity," and so on.[13] Liu is not totally unaware of the implications of a less autonomous subject who may submit to a higher authority; he speaks of *guishu dongji*, the subject's "incentive for dependency," on one occasion.[14] But the Althusserian model of a subject completely embedded in and subjugated to unidentifiable ideologies remains undesirable to the Chinese theoretician: Liu Zaifu is preoccupied with the efficacy of resistance, warranted only by a potent subject-position locked in a single combat against a capitalized Ideology, which, because of its unambiguous identification with political Power, can be located, named, targeted, and counteracted in the end.

Herein resides the dilemma of Liu Zaifu's theory. This subject, the outgrowth of the postrevolutionary antipathy to ideology, is given all the attributes of a depoliticized being; it is first and foremost an aesthetic subject for which the "whole process of its aesthetic reception is exactly the selfsame process of its return to humanity." Such an apolitical entity, however, is of no practical value to the project of resistance. Here Liu has little choice but to instill an old ideological content into his new subject: "The subjectivity of a writer can be realized not only by means of his or her consciousness of freedom, but also by a heightened sense of mission," which is later specified by him as nothing less than the traditional elite's *youhuan yishi* (anxiety and crisis consciousness) impregnated with unmistakable sociopolitical overtones.[15] This subject is furthermore empowered with a potency that "manifests itself not only in the creation of culture, but also in the *resistance* to culture."[16] Ironically, the portrait of Liu Zaifu's subject of mastery now relapses into a haunting, albeit a much more refined, combined version of the traditional Confucian scholar and the proletarian hero.

This is not to say that Liu's subject is simply another static and empty ideological vessel to be filled anew. For one thing, this postrevolutionary subject, unlike the Confucianist and the proletarian hero who are characterized by perfect equilibrium, seems rife and ripe with contradictions. But a closer look at them—predictable binary opposites that await and anticipate reconciliation[17]—reveals Liu Zaifu's subject as merely another utopian site for the realization of the complete and total human being, the subject of mastery and the ultimate solution to all conflicts.

Such utopianism, to be perceived in the structural equilibrium of
the subject, finds its culminating moment in Liu Zaifu's explication of
the final stage of the subject's evolution—"self-dissolution" (*wuwo*)—a
contemporary rewriting of "the unity of Heaven and (hu)man" (*tianren
heyi*).[18] Liu's theoretical alliance with the Western philosophy of subjectivity expires at the moment when he cites traditional Chinese philosophy as a sovereign metaphor for his theoretical privileging of identity over
contradiction. Contrary to the Western thinking subject that is pitted
against the object (material or biological nature), Liu Zaifu posits an aesthetic subject whose telos is realized only through its holistic and total
identification with Nature.[19] The moment of identification occurs when
the subject completes its linear progression from self-assertion (*ziwo*) to
self-transcendence (*chaowo*), and finally to self-dissolution [into Nature
itself] (*wuwo*).[20] The process prescribed here is highly paradoxical, since
one can imagine that nothing short of a spontaneous implosion of the
boundary between subject and object can achieve the perfect harmony
propounded in the conceptual nirvana of *tianren heyi*. Yet the threefold
evolution of the subject not only betrays the elaborate process of a purely
logical and hierarchical dialectic (the Hegelian influence is perceivable)
that is opposite to the traceless continuum of the subject-object-less communion, but it also says nothing of how the subject is warranted to know
its end in its beginning—in other words, how it overcomes the contradictions inherent in its three subject-positions and inaugurates the perfect subject who already knows the end of its own evolution.

To compound the quandary, the emphasis on self-dissolution, and by
extension the "forgetting of the self," runs the risk of effacing the subject
that Liu Zaifu takes such pains to construct. Although the subject in Liu's
discourse is aesthetic and its sole function is defined by its *textual* praxis
(its self-dissolution enacts the ultimate practice of aesthetic liberation),
Liu Zaifu's agenda is by no means consistently aesthetic. In fact, one might
even say that it is unavoidably inconsistent. The commitment of a contemporary literary critic, if I am allowed to reiterate this cliché, like that
of his Confucian and Marxist predecessors in traditional and modern
Chinese history, is almost always divided between aesthetics and politics.
The construction of a merely aesthetic subject eventually proves insufficient for a project that derives its momentum from the inquiry into agency.
In the lingo of resistance, one could of course revalorize Liu Zaifu's aesthetic subject as a political signifier: The ideal portrait of the aesthetic
subject's pure openness to things and its unlimited access to freedom is
not merely an illusion but an agonistic text, the rhetorical victory of the

defeated and impotent empirical subject that remains a sociopolitical reality of his time. However, such a subject, metaphorically empowered, remains a linguistic sign. To a theorist who is still very much a historical materialist at heart, such a sign seems empty without the grace and presence of a historical agent endowed with ethico-political consciousness.

Here Liu Zaifu cannot help stumbling into a dilemma. But strange to say, the theoretical interest that informs his theory of subjectivity lies exactly in his dual discourse of the aesthetic subject and the ethico-political subject. The former, depoliticized, the end product of resistance to the Maoist-Marxist subject, is paradoxically deprived of its agency to act and to resist. This perfectly poised subject is self-enclosed in an imaginary wholeness that cancels the possibilities of gaps and moves toward structural closure. To rescue this aesthetic subject from the undesirable paralysis in the praxis, Liu has no recourse but to commit himself to conflicting propositions: "Aesthetics is the ethics of Future" or "it is the general sense of mission, specifically identical to 'anxiety and crisis consciousness,' that makes up the innermost core of the consciousness of subjectivity that the best writers of all ages and all countries are endowed with."[21] These propositions eventually conjure up the image of an ethico-political subject that he resisted at the start. Such a discourse of subjectivity reveals itself as nothing other than an enabling machine in the political sense.

It is Liu Zaifu's implicit emphasis on the praxis of resistance that brings us back to the nebulous subtext of humanism and alienation in his theory of subjectivity. Humanism presupposes an immutable human essence and predicts the return of fallen and fragmented human nature to its original state of purity and totality. According to the humanist version of Marxism, the process of the degradation of the original is marked by the process of alienation (by social structures). And the retrieval of its lack or loss begins with the assertion and recovery of the free subject as the core of moral and political action. The impetus underlying Liu Zaifu's theory of subjectivity resides exactly in this lengthy process of the return to humanity: "The movement of society and history begins on the day when humankind was born. It undergoes the winding and painful journey of the 'negation of humanity,' and finally returns to (wo)man him/herself. . . . It is only at this particular moment that the value of humanity finds its full embodiment, and the authentic history of humankind really begins."[22] Although Liu is politically too seasoned to adopt the term "alienation," the description of the recovery in question is none other than an unequivocal summary of the central thesis of Marxian humanism; in so summarizing, he evokes the entire repressed subtext of the

Chinese Marxists' debate over socialist alienation and Marxist humanism in the early 1980s.

In place of the metaphysical question addressed to the ontological
subject, Who am I? he thus privileges a question of a slightly different
order: Who is human? The subject thrown out of existence during the
revolutionary era is nothing more than an empty, albeit free, human subject of rudimentary instincts unadorned by trappings of metaphysical
self-questioning. The auto-positioning of a Chinese postrevolutionary
subject presents itself to itself not as a consciousness that questions itself "in such a way as to appropriate the alterity or obscurity that trou-
bles it, either from 'without' or from 'within'" in the Hegelian sense.[23]
The problem that the Chinese subject must confront is not existential
anxiety, or "man's ontological position."[24] Instead, it is engaged in
the task of resisting the notorious annexation by the "without" of a
"within" that has not yet been clearly defined, nor is it capable of efficacious self-questioning. The issue here is hardly one of subtle appropriation of, but rather blatant resistance to, an alien, or rather, an alienating public sphere. In fact, the terms of overdetermined antagonism
between the "within" and the "without" characterizes Liu Zaifu's theory as a philosophy of humanity in disguise rather than a discourse of
subjectivity. In Western philosophy, "there can be no concept at all of
subjectivity without a partaking in the metaphysics of [self-] presence"[25]
and in an act of its simultaneous self-enclosure and disclosure; in Liu's
theory, there can be no concept of subjectivity without its automatic reference to the political allegory of dehumanization. Thus the problematic of subjectivity in Liu's theory always risks being upstaged by that
of humanity.

SERENADING THE CULTURAL SUBJECT:
THEORIES AND PRACTICE

Liu Zaifu's theory of the subjectivity of literature exposes and reinforces
yet another unique orientation of Chinese literature since the May Fourth
period: It was literature rather than philosophy that constituted the strategic site of cultural self-introspection in an age submerged in its own epistemic anxiety over its dramatic transition from tradition to modernity.
Why the quest of a new cultural ideology fell upon the literati and critics
rather than philosophers goes beyond the immediate objective of my present inquiry. It is worth noting that circa 1985, the apex of China's Cul-

ture Fever, it was the literary circle that responded to the debate of *zhongxi zhi zheng* (China versus the West) in the most creative manner. While the circle of philosophers initiated a precarious attempt to revitalize Confucianism in the spirit of modernity to combat the infiltration of various systems of imported cultural philosophies, the literati looked elsewhere for a way out of this predictable and sterile mode of discussion. Inspired by Gabriel Garcia Marquez's "magic realism," they presented an agenda articulated in two slogans: "root-searching" (1985–1986), and "Chinese literature marching toward the world" (*Zhongguo wenxue zouxiang shijie*) (1987–1988).[26] Although what was at stake in both slogans was still the thorny issue of China's cultural identity, with the emergence of *xungen* literature, the site of contestation could no longer be solely identified as culture or ideology, but as one traversed by the new problematic of language as well.

Both Liu Zaifu and Li Tuo provide the theoretical justification for this new orientation toward language. They locate the site of the potential structural change of Chinese ultrastable ideological consciousness in the theatrical transformation of the existing system of signification. Liu deciphers the postrevolutionary ritual of removing one's political stigma (*zhai maozi*) in terms of linguistic liberation: Political de-stigmatization "is an issue of liberation from the prison house of biased classification, and in short, an issue of [exposing] the distortion that language imposes upon human beings."[27] Li Tuo is even more explicit in connecting the revolution of language with that of ideological consciousness.[28]

Fiction writing as a pure discursive practice opposed to the ideological one, an undercurrent already visible in *xungen* literature, will eventually surface with experimental fiction (*shiyan xiaoshuo*) in high tide. Indeed, one must agree with Li Tuo's observation that *xungen* literature paves the way for the emergence of experimental fiction precisely in that the former heralds the arrival of a genuine aesthetic revolution that finds the fulfillment of its most radical implications in the latter.[29] The problematic of the linguistic subject (*yuyan zhuti*)—of how language evolves from its age-old subaltern position into the subject-position of Chinese literary texts—is a topic on which I dwell at length in the final section of this chapter. Here, I focus on the responses that philosophers (Gan Yang) and critics (Huang Ziping) made on the one hand and the *xungen* school (both theorists and writers) made on the other to issues of cultural modernity, and more specifically, to the debate of "sinification versus westernization." All three parties, as we shall see, were preoccupied with the task of empowering China's cultural subject, whose claim to sovereignty was endangered as the result of the identity crisis intensified by this debate.

PARADIGM I: CHINA VERSUS THE WEST OR TRADITION VERSUS MODERNITY?

The opposition between China and the West, "sinification versus westernization," evokes the familiar vista of resistance whose complexity is compounded when the antagonistic binary terms, formerly purely indigenous and local, now expand themselves toward the global. They immediately invite a series of dubious propositions and controversies cast in postcolonial idiom from Western sinologists—"Can we speak of China's subalternity as we do of India's?"—and from the home front— "Do we have an 'authentic' or a 'pseudo' modernism and postmodernism?" I have argued elsewhere that China can never be placed against the West, as India was positioned against Europe, in the ready-made Manichean allegory of opposition of the colonized and colonizer, inferiority and superiority, savagery and civilization, object and subject.[30] There is much to be said about why Edward Said's *Orientalism* (the victimization of the "Orient" by the "Occident") did not strike a chord in the Chinese sensibility, and yet why books about futurology were promoted and translated at such a furious pace. The decision to import one particular theoretical model rather than another is never fortuitous but dependent upon how the Chinese position themselves in the global map in the first place and how efficiently, according to their own assessment, the model in question functions in consolidating or substantiating that position—whether it is a tangible or a merely imaginary position. I do not intend to reiterate here what I demonstrated elsewhere: Chinese intellectuals are acutely aware of China's *positional superiority* vis-à-vis the West, which however indubitably it poses itself as the conqueror in the last few centuries, has a historical subject that is nonetheless raw and depthless according to the Chinese standard. China's obsession with the future and subsequently with futurology—the science of the future—is symptomatic of a subject-position that authorizes itself not by looking back in anger nor by too deeply engaging itself in the self-reflection of a present riddled with anxieties and unfulfilled dreams. It is only the "looking forward" stance that enables the Chinese subject-position fully to articulate and reinvigorate itself. This is a stance unambiguously intertwined with the "leaping forward" mentality that invests the future with a premium to be paid in one installment at a recoverable utopian moment of empowerment.

The voicing of such a sentiment—that "we may yet become the master of the future"—has indeed become part of the quotidian reality too familiar to an average Chinese citizen to attract much attention. But to those who are eager to relegate China to the postcolonial category of the subaltern, a typical quotation from a typical critic may yet raise a few eyebrows: "Toynbee, the most far-sighted historian in the West . . . was positive that the sun of the twenty-first century will absolutely not arise from the West. The future . . . will choose China eventually. . . . Of course this unification should not be seen as China's political or military conquest of the world, nor understood as the domination of the Eastern over the Western hemisphere. It should be taken as the choice made by the entire world to identify with Chinese culture. This is the sinification of global culture, the return of History itself."[31] Simplistic as such a high-minded proclamation may sound, the conviction of the observer is not to be trifled with. Here the explicit alignment of the future with China and a cultural hegemony that haunts those who have not forgotten the bygone glories of Imperial China displays the Chinese historical imagination for a utopia that seems once again well within their reach.

Gan Yang's refutation of the binary paradigm "sinification versus westernization" represents one such attempt to envision and theorize that hegemonic moment. Gan's strategy is to discover the agency of change from within and redefine the terms of resistance as tradition (*gu*) against modernity (*jin*)—*gujin zhi zheng*. He would thus deprive the West of its power to dictate the pace and agenda of China's modernization and move the entire arena from the global (*zhong* versus *xi*) back to the local again.[32] For those Chinese intellectuals whose "subjugation" to Western influences is perceived by themselves in purely technical terms at best, the compelling issue is not how to cancel out its subaltern position (it never sank into a colonial subject as such) but rather how to retrieve its earlier subject-position of the "dynasty of Heaven" (*tianchao*).[33] One can indeed denounce such a position as purely imaginary and empty. In fact, its hidden agenda of a sinocentric return seems to guarantee its quick reversal and retranslation into new terms of domination and subalternity (for instance, the agenda of the "Greater China" promises exactly such a configuration).[34]

China's refusal to take up the position of colonial subject presents an intriguing problematic that cannot simply be dismissed in terms

of its cultural spokespeople's inadequate understanding of the theoretical and political radicalism set loose by Said's onslaught on "Orientalism."[35] The examination of the routine practice of "colonialism
under erasure" as a repressed problematic in China Studies[36] therefore is doubly poignant if we include among its practitioners not only
Western sinologists but also indigenous Chinese critics. The necessity
of adopting different interpretive strategies in treating each phenomenon is compelling, for there is a danger of confusing the defensive
gesture adopted by the real aggressor (Western sinologists: we are
not colonizers) with that voiced by the imaginary victim (indigenous
critics: we are not the colonized). The latter speaks from a subject-
position that cannot be readily appropriated into the standard discourse
of colonialism.

Given the contradictory agenda of postcolonialism—to cancel the
subjectivity of the "Third World" by naming it as such—it is no accident
that a small constellation of Chinese cultural and literary theorists have
fought against it as hard, yet perhaps not as consciously, as they did
against the flagrant infiltration of neocolonial discourses. They realized
the urgency of retrieving the problematic of subjectivity from postcolonial discourse. Invariably, the binary paradigm of resistance (China
versus the West) still retains its viability. But the terms of resistance are
now transferred from the spatial and geopolitical to the temporal and
historical. The struggle is no longer seen as the Orient versus the Occident, nor socialism versus capitalism. It is tradition rather than the West
that is now perceived as the real opponent to China's emergent subjectivity. To better appreciate the insurgency of this new geocultural politics
written against the discourse of postcolonialism, I need to quote Gan
Yang at some length.

> The geographico-cultural differences between Chinese and Western culture
> were often exaggerated indefinitely at the expense of eclipsing the much more
> real and fundamental problematic of the cultural difference between "tradi-
> tion" and "modernity," an issue about the necessary *self*-transformation of
> Chinese culture from its traditional phase to modern phase. It is exactly this
> conceptual exaggeration that contributed to our putting the cart before the
> horse, a syndrome that recurred in our cultural discussions throughout recent
> history. . . . That is, we always unconsciously resorted to the generalized com-
> parison and sweeping discrimination between an abstract Chinese culture
> (which is, in fact, traditional Chinese culture, and to put it bluntly, Confucian
> culture in the main) and an abstract Western culture (which is actually the in-
> carnation of a modern Western culture after its "epistemological break") as a
> means to evade, to overshadow, to displace, and even to obliterate, the more

concrete issue of the distinction between the Chinese traditional mode of culture and its modern counterpart. At the same time, we ignored the fact that
within Western culture itself there exists a distinction between the traditional and modern modes.[37]

By redefining China's modernization as the inevitable process of self-
transformation rather than a reaction against colonialism, Gan Yang
breaks the familiar equation between modernization and westernization
and instills into an otherwise static subject—China locked into the fixed
position of the victim—the drive and agency for change.

Gan Yang's proposal crystallizes and predicts the coming of a utopian moment in contemporary Chinese history when the empowerment
of native discourse emerges as the new agenda that supersedes the vulnerable plea made by the veteran theorist Liu Zaifu to "walk out of the
shadow" of Western fathers.[38] The crucial question to address is the
racial identity of the real oppressor that triggers this Oedipal rebellion.
Is he, as Liu suggests, of foreign identity, or as Huang Ziping daringly
announces, nobody else but the "'Father of Revolution' who has
been constructed step by step during each historical movement staged
throughout modern Chinese history"?[39] The identity of the agonist—
the allusion to Mao Zedong and the Maoist ideologues is unmistakably
blatant—leads Huang to argue against the theoretical position that "attributes all of China's sufferings and misfortunes to the invasion of
Western imperialism, while at the same time ignores the crises of tradition in Chinese history itself."[40] The political implications of Huang's
attempt to energize the indigenous discourse are apparent when he goes
on to speak of the "historical desires" of China as a sovereign subject,
while paring down the intrusive capacity of "Western discourse" to a
mere "participatory" (*canyu*) status in the construction of the authentic
"Chinese story." To Zhang Xudong, the plot of this Chinese story consists of nothing other than the excursion of a "premodern subject"
(*qianxiandai zhuti*) set free at the postmodern juncture of the total
linguistic liberation.[41] A closer look at this enfranchised premodern
subject reveals that it delivers a subject-position that is not only
representable but overdetermined from within, a position that finds its
cogent footnote in Zhang Xudong's account of the genesis of contemporary Chinese literature as the belated yet irrepressible self-expression
of China's historical subject—metaphorically represented as the sum total of "national self-consciousness," "a non-Western logic of 'the imaginary' and system of signs," and "a mechanism of *self*-projection and
self-disclosure" generated in "the context of global culture."[42]

One can of course adopt a metacritical position of recontaining the subversive act of those Chinese theorists by unmasking their strategy of privileging the temporal paradigm of resistance (tradition versus modernity) over the spatial one (China versus the West) as the camouflage of an ominous return to sinocentrism. The seductive pull of a relapse into that ideological position must be enormous. It seems to present, at least to the Chinese insurgents, the only ready-made alternative to the postcolonial paralogic that, by bestowing upon the colonialist an absolutely unitary subject-position, paradoxically guarantees its continual dominance over the colonial subject who is sometimes seen as unpresentable on the discursive level and at other times merely "a subject-effect."[43] It goes without saying, then, that at this particular historical juncture, mired in the antagonistic pressure from within and from without, advocates of the new paradigm cannot but choose to adopt a sinocentric posture that serves as a political metaphor while maintaining a radicalized intellectual position that can best be characterized as a metonymical relationship between the local and the global.

This nativist romanticization about the cultural subject as a fixed space of its own, from which it can speak in a sovereign voice, is rendered problematic by the increasing alacrity and ravenous appetite with which the program of global modernity swallows up space. The utilization of this shifting analytic language of the local and the global characterizes the approach of all three theorists to China as a discursive form under permutation rather than some recoverable emotive content. Thus we can say that theorists such as Gan Yang, Huang Ziping, and Zhang Xudong are not unaware of the danger that their very act of attributing China's cultural agency (selfsame and autonomous, an identity-in-itself) to the indigenous is open to essentialist recuperation. In contrast, the *xungen* school (both theorists and writers alike) see the symbolic violation of the Chinese grammar by the discourse of modernity as a threat that breaks down cultural identity rather than as a catalyst for discursive breakthrough. Thus for those root-searching advocates, the theoretical construction of the agency of China's cultural subject is considered inefficacious without a simultaneous reconstruction of an authentic and essentialist China. This is a China that could ultimately be retrieved through the *xungen* school's grand project of identity searching and structure formation. Theoretical distancing (as practiced by Gan, Huang, and Zhang) was no longer feasible. We now turn to the imaginary geography of a China that hems in both its depictors and spectators.

PARADIGM 2: INSCRIBING THE ROOTED CULTURAL AND AESTHETIC SUBJECT

Why do we want to search for our own roots?—Well,
it's because we want to march toward the world!

Li Tuo

"Marching toward the world" (the First World undoubtedly, or at least that part of the periphery—such as Latin America—that partook in the making of modern Western canon) is a tortuously complicated slogan that accommodates both the repressed complexes of superiority and inferiority that Chinese intellectuals have endured since at least the early twentieth century.[44] At first glimpse, Li Tuo's self-questioning and ad-lib answer seems to map out the conventional spatial configuration of modern Chinese history—the West versus China—as the primary geography of action and counteraction within which the *xungen* "heat wave" took place in the mid-1980s. The inward drawn and defensive search for "national literature" seems the most logical salvation in the face of the aggressive marching of "world literature" into Chinese territory.[45] Yet on the other hand, one cannot dismiss the equally significant centrifugal and offensive drive of the root-searching slogan, a daring act of self-exposure and challenge to the First World. However, although symptomatic of the emotional ambivalence with which *xungen* writers view their self-positioning in the postcolonial world, Li Tuo's glib monologue tells only half of the story.

An undue attention to the desire for dialogues and the spatial logic of the literature ("We [*zhong*] 'search our roots' in order to have a dialogue with the world [*xi*]")[46] runs the risk of displacing the deeper structural contradiction that empowers the root-searching literature to serve both as the metaphor for a new cultural ideology and as the vanguard of a new aesthetics. The contradiction in question—the other half of the untold story of resistance—is what Gan Yang identifies as the temporal paradigm of *gu* (tradition) versus *jin* (modernity) or, put in the vocabulary of the *xungen* movement, the cultural unconscious versus modern consciousness. I emphasize that it is on this binary axis of conflict that one can begin to map out the dual attributes of the subject inscribed in the literature as being cultural and aesthetic at once.

To attempt a sweeping generalization about the poetics of *xungen* literature is tantalizing but self-defeating. Not only do authors give shifting valorizations of the symbolic presence of modernity and tradition in their discourses, but the theorists themselves (some of them are *xungen* authors at the same time, such as A Cheng and Han Shaogong) often construct in retrospect a cultural politics of root-searching that finds little echo in the literary genre itself.[47]

Most theorists would concur that this literature represents not simply an innocent return to Nature (such as the wilderness outside of the Central Plains) and Culture (such as traditional myths and forms), but a besieged embryonic modern consciousness that struggles to come to terms with itself, or more specifically, with its inability (sometimes, a refusal) to map itself on the new modern space. Although primitivism and a profound nostalgia for a bygone agrarian society can be found in a large number of works, it is a movement that emerged from and responded to the quick waxing and waning in the mid-1980s of Chinese *xiandai pai* modernism on the one hand[48] and to the larger philosophical debate of tradition versus modernity on the other. In examining *xungen* literature, one has to keep in mind that it serves simultaneously as a metaphor for and as an actual enactment of the formulaic drama that the debate can only conceive in the most abstract terms.

The trope of modernity that underlies the literature becomes even more evident when we consider the new genre's intricate relationship with Western modernism. Never has it rung truer that "it is necessary to return to the ancients in order to go beyond modernism."[49] The historical contribution of the *xungen* movement to contemporary Chinese literature resides precisely in its simultaneous challenge to and containment of modernism. At a juncture when the creative potency of Liu Suola and Xu Xing's *xiandai pai* was nearly spent and the controversy over pseudomodernism revived the question of Western influence and Chinese mimicry (and thus relentlessly touched the nerve of a nationwide inferiority complex), the emergence of root-searching literature provided a therapeutic solution. It presented an immense emotional appeal to many critics like Xu Zidong whose prescription revealed much of the deep emotional ambiguity with which the *xungen* writers related to modernism: "Planting our 'roots' deeply into the 'yellow soul' is the broadest possible path in China for modernism."[50] The resistance to the modern always and already risks being recontained by the tacit "emotional wish-making" that an outlandish modernism could "redeem and rejuvenate Chinese [literary] culture (most preferably overnight)"[51]—wishful thinking that gives the lie to the conventional argument that "'root-searching' represents a backward-looking consciousness."[52]

Paradoxically, however, the metaphor of modernity and modernism appears as the missing term in a vista crisscrossed by the literature's seemingly anachronistic desires for homecoming. Only by understanding that the missing term is not absent but repressed in this literature can we characterize the *xungen* movement as the burgeoning of a new aesthetic that reveals itself as the genuine descendant of modernity precisely in its implicit solicitation and critique of Western modernism.

Even though it seems impossible to leave aside the aesthetic question that is deeply implicated in the cultural politics of *xungen* literature, I shall attempt to focus my discussion by first examining the point at which the issue of root-searching surpasses aesthetics and becomes a cultural issue instead. This point is found in Li Qingxi's (a *xungen* writer-theorist's) perceptive comments on the literature: "Western modernists broadened the aesthetic horizon of Chinese writers. However, they failed to deliver to them an authentic awareness of their own subjectivity. Modernism cannot resolve the soul problem of Chinese people."[53] It is Li Qingxi's identification of this "soul problem" that opens up an entirely different horizon of polemics and strategies of resolution. To put the complicated problem simply, the site of contestation is cultural subjectivity, a seemingly empty vessel that is defined by whatever form of Western cultural ideology is being poured into it at a given moment. How to redress such a provisional, hence empty identity of the cultural subject (*wenhua zhuti*) preoccupies cultural theorists in China today.

One can almost predict their strategy of resistance: the installation of a subject that is interpellated by and subjugated to a higher authority—spelled out specifically by A Cheng as "cultural constraints" (*wenhua zhiyue*). To combat the empty subject, the *xungen* theorists revalorize a subject who is saturated with meanings and determinations of indigenous categories. This is a subject constrained by its parasitic dependence upon the object (namely culture) and whose self-governing capacity and "dynamic drive" (*nengdong xing*) is put into question—a theory of subjectivity that runs counter to Liu Zaifu's imaginary subject of absolute autonomy.

But the task of the *xungen* theorists has just begun with their positing of a tamed subject—a mere effect of the cultural unconscious—who stares blankly into a predetermined space. To deliver the subject from the spiritual paralysis that a total immersion in culture dictates, they have to recover the creative potency of the subject and provide the workings of a dialectics between subjection and subjectivity. Somehow and from somewhere a critical and self-reflexive subjectivity has to emerge, which can examine culture and tradition in such a light that a transcendence of its own constraints may appear as a theoretical possibility.

Many theorists have indeed dwelled on the capability and necessity of the subject's self-transcending movement. The conflict, however, must be tremendous for those who have to turn the subject inward to indigenous culture for inspiration to withstand its continual conquest by the alien, yet who at the same time feel compelled to plead that "today, our search for cultural roots has to face the world's cultural course. . . . We have to endow it [our root-searching] with a kind of self-transcending capacity. . . . Cushioned itself against [our own] history and culture, it faces toward the world and toward the future."[54] One can perceive a double edge to this call for the implantation of a global and futurist perspective in *xungen* literature. The vision of an imaginary readerly feast that extends its invitation to global readership serves as a reminder that the automatic submission to culture and to the past only produces a self-enclosed subject that is incapable of speaking to the world and to the future.

Thus while emphasizing the importance of return to and reacquaintance with traditional culture in its multifarious guises—whether as some exotic spiritual landscape of Han Shaogong's Chu culture, the Zen and Daoist philosophy of sublimation beautified in A Cheng's "The King of Chess," or cultural archetypes that ethnic minorities enact in esoteric rituals—root-searching theorists place a high premium on the rediscovery of the individual subject as a private field of givenness seriously engaged in self-critique and self-reflection.[55] The body is culturally inscribed but the mind and heart are free. Once we understand this subtext for the seemingly contradictory call for self-transcendence, Li Qingxi's following statements are transparent.

> We may say that the artistic value of some of the representative works of "root-searching" literature consists in their manifestation of how the subject *sublimates* itself. Take A Cheng's "The King of Chess" for instance. What we witness in the story is not [the author's] explication of objective reality . . . but rather his entry into the subject's experience of its own subjectivity by means of his other-worldly narrating attitude. . . . What is emphasized is his [the hero's] *transcendence of the real* and of his existential condition.
>
> They [Han Shaogong, Li Hangyu, and A Cheng] themselves do not view "transcendence" as a nihilist posture. Transcendence by itself means the consummation of critique and self-reflection.[56]

It is this built-in capacity for self-reflexivity that empowers an otherwise passive subject enclosed by cultural trappings. The self-critical orientation of such a cultural subject belies the cliché repeated by literary historians and critics of lesser caliber, namely, that the objective of the *xungen* school is to "rejuvenate the Han culture wholesale" and to "close up the gaps brought about by the cultural break [initiated by the May Fourth Movement] that took place on the vertical axis."[57] One needs to be reminded that cultural conservation is a superficial trademark by which the slogan "root-searching" is stigmatized. It tells more about what triggers the movement than what the movement produces in the end. As we have seen, the imaginary function of the cultural subject in *xungen* theories always transcends the role that is originally and immediately assigned to it. Despite its liaison with the cultural, the subject is self-conscious of its repressed desires and the forms of self-distortion as a result of this liaison. At such moments the retroactive look at cultural roots is fraught with ambiguities. The cup it holds up to toast tradition is always half empty. But just as one is tempted to conclude that the *xungen* writers' critique of tradition derives its drive from the historical agenda of modernity, one is confronted with an equally noticeable "collective motion" defined by Li Tuo as the writers' unconscious questioning of modernity.[58] The shifting critique of tradition and modernity can perhaps best account for the intriguing appeal of *xungen* literature to readers of different ideological bent. Most importantly, it supports the thesis that cultural or ideological constraints function not only to limit subjectivity but also to enable it.

The double bind in which those writers find themselves (are they traditionalists or modernists?) can thus be easily inverted into a dual critique of tradition and modernity.[59] If one can speak of a utopian drive underlying the root-searching consciousness, that drive is nothing other than its open-ended capacity—or more precisely, its instinctual resistance to the norm (whether tradition or modernity, a habitual mode of perception, or prescribed political consciousness) at a given moment. It is this much-trumpeted theoretical openness that enables the root-searching writers to adopt high-minded rhetoric such as "cultural reconstruction" and envision the prospect of China strutting onto the stage of world literature.[60]

Such an enabling discourse, one has to assume, cannot be envisioned without the appearance of an equally empowered discursive subject. The question remains: by what concrete means and in what visible form does the empowerment come into being? Invariably, the quest for roots takes the *xungen* writers back to savage uncharted territories, far from the Central Plains. Despite their different experiences with the wilderness, it is nature and nature alone that electrifies and explodes the human subject out of its fragile earthly frame and recharges it with inexhaustible virility that transcends any worldly confinement.

The theoretical construct of the subject that is potent but retrogressive thus finally gets written into the root-searching literature as a kind of pristine subject inscribed in nature, a subject not too radically different from Marcuse's pre-Freudian subject who shares the same instinctual constitution that promises an unrepressed existential condition and a plenitude of prehistorical energy.[61] Yet the notion of primordial happiness, even when it is realized at the final climactic moment in the narrative fiction (for instance, Wang Yisheng's mock-heroic victory in the chess championship game, or the fisherman Fukui's willful immersion in his symbiotic relationship with the river), is only partially applicable to the psychic makeup of a *xungen* subject who often mistakes its last act of resistance to an imaginary rival—an act staking all on a single throw of the dice—for an effortless unfolding of a harmonious continuum. Wang Yisheng's free-flowing style (*daizai qili shufu*) and Fukui's cool and cozy posture (*daizai jiangli zizai*) may be taken as metaphors for transcendence into a state of mind that liquidates the concept of the subject engaging in rivalry with what constrains and confronts *him* (without exception, the root-searching hero is a male). Yet I want to suggest a different interpretation: such a mood and posture echoes, however subtly and imperceptibly, the tragic pathos of the last hero, as the title of Li Hangyu's story "The Last Fisherman" ("Zuihou yige yulaoer") spells out. It should certainly not be confused with the romantic innocence of prehistorical freedom.[62]

Nonetheless, the belief in that freedom persists. That is what makes the *xungen* heroes larger than life itself. What culture constrains, nature sets free. The contradiction in the *xungen* movement between the theory (the constrained subject) and literature (humans as the embodiment of unfettered instincts) foregrounds once again the dilemma of a dislocated cultural subject in search of self-regeneration and of a new enabling ethics for its enervated subjectivity. The theme of return to nature in a large corpus of this literature—to cite a few examples, Zheng Yi's novels, A Cheng's "Shuwang" (Tree king), Zhang Chengzhi's "Beifang de he" (The river of the north)—delivers collectively a new hero of raw masculinity and spiritual cornucopia. He is, in fact, the very personification of nature itself.

The *xungen* writers' experience of nature is, of course, far from being homogeneous. For Zheng Wanlong, who was born in a secluded mountain village near the Heilong River in northeastern China, nature brought back childhood memories of the legends of pioneers, their dreams, expeditions, and creative energy.[63] The rough landscape tells different stories to other "reeducated youth" (zhiqing) such as Zhang Chengzhi, Zheng Yi, Han Shaogong, Kong Jiesheng, and A Cheng, who were sent to China's remote countryside or its barbarous frontiers when they were adolescents during the Cultural Revolution. For Han Shaogong, Zhang Chengzhi, and Kong Jiesheng, the landscape projects a raw emotional valence that echoes the intensity of their conviction and labor in making the political utopia of Mao's China. Nature awakens less passion, on the other hand, in A Cheng, a lone alienated Han youth among the minorities, whose exile brought him to the remote frontier from inner Mongolia to Yun'nan.[64]

One can extrapolate endlessly from the nature cult in many orthodox xungen works. Perhaps this romantic syndrome is a manifestation of the displaced historical desire of the cultural subject denied its agency. In this light, the craving for the sublime may be nothing more than an allegory of the reconstructed National Subject in search of metaphorical means of empowerment. Or perhaps nature as a trope simply opens up the enclosed and oppressive sociopolitical space of quotidian reality in which the postrevolutionary subject still finds him- or herself helplessly fixed. The liberation of human beings from the politics of abstinence invariably begins with the celebration of the elemental forces in human nature. Or the worship of nature as a new religion or ethics may simply inform the imaginary filling of the nation's spiritual vacuum as it arises anew from the ashes of ideological and religious atheism at the bankruptcy of Maoism-Marxism. And finally, how can we make sense of the inherent clichés of which the root-searching romanticism is suspected—"the village is created by God, the city by human beings"—except by attributing that romanticism not to simple primitivism, as Cao Wenxuan suggests, but to the political unconscious of the bygone Yan'an idealism?

When Zhang Chengzhi spoke of the metaphor of a weather-beaten bridge that used to carry the traffic of "an idealism that the generation of our younger brothers and sons would ridicule," a bridge that "linked the past and future, the starting point of our renewed passionate quest," he was inviting the political interpretation of the romantic vision of the xungen literature.[65] Such an interpretation is even more tantalizing in the case of Han Shaogong, who served the cause of the Revolution as a Red Guard, went to Western Hunan as a reeducated youth, and who, according to Wang Xiaoming, clung to a keen sense of sociopolitical mission at the earlier stages of his writing career.[66]

Yet nature certainly appeared as more than just a political symbol to those *xungen* authors whose exiles, whether voluntarily or involuntarily executed in the secluded and distant backwoods and hinterlands, enabled them to have a close encounter with a force that was both savage and nurturing at the same time. The hard material life in the village "molded their souls anew," but it also provided those adolescents an "ideal environment that enabled them to release their libidinal impulses."[67] As the adopted children of nature, those homeless youths were able to find redemption in the boundless resources that a glorious sunset or a single blade of grass can provide. But the imaginary revisiting of wilderness is not simply a mindless nostalgia for an idyllic prehistorical happiness or for some bygone adolescent growing pains. Their retrospective reveling in an innocuously heroic nature is simultaneously accompanied by their disquieting memory of an aborted utopia and of their betrayal by the Revolution. On another figurative level, then, the carnivalesque return to nature is a laborious self-reflection and a poignant testimony of historical guilt. Although disguised beyond immediate recognition, this heavy-handed confessional fervor accounts for the sentimentality of some *xungen* works. Oftentimes their indulgence in the spiritual quest sounds as tedious and onerous as their description of the luscious landscape.

For those *xungen* writers of *zhiqing* origin, especially those who participated in the Revolution as Red Guards, the remembrance of their earlier political incarnation serves to multiply the root meaning of the term *gen*. The roots that they take such pains to excavate include political and aesthetic roots as well as cultural roots identifiable with the "subject of the Nation" or the "archetypal subconscious inherent in the strengthened subjective spirit of the Chinese race."[68] What makes the discharge of the memory of Cultural Revolution in this literature different from that in the earlier genre of wounded literature is the aestheticization of the political. Paradoxically, in the case of Han Shaogong in particular, so long as political connotations of the term *gen* remain repressed in the literature, root-searching cannot but be turned into a contradictory sign of "uprooting." Instead of looking back at and examining the political culture that molded their utopian vision, the journey backwards leads them to ahistorical cultural myths and aesthetics. Anything but their own political roots is reckoned with in all sincerity. Once depoliticized, memory is desensitized. It is reconstructed into an aesthetic imaginary that runs the gamut from the precarious touch of a thinned Daoist style to the episodic and miscellaneous configuration of traditional narrative (*biji ti*).[69]

Although this strategy smacked of escapism for some authors, the aestheticization of the political is considered by many as an unprecedented formal revolution to be celebrated rather than problematicized. Furthermore, one can still—indeed, one should—speak of a cultural politics underlying such a new aesthetics. That is to say, one should attribute the emergent "language consciousness" (*yuyan zijue*) of the aesthetic subject as a by-product of China's postcolonial self-awareness. And yet this desire to prevail over its discursive subalternity and, in Zhang Yiwu's words, to "undermine the object-position of the Third World,"[70] however strong, cannot trigger the making of a new aesthetic consciousness without going hand in hand with the profound national repulsion against the politicization of literature. What is thrown into the dust bin by the *xungen* school is not only the revolutionary rhetoric of socialist realism, but in fact, realism per se. In its place, root-searching writers make various epistemological propositions to construct a new imaginary. Li Yue calls for the return from the noumenal to the phenomenal itself (*benxiang*). Li Qingxi's aesthetic self undergoes the process of self-recovery (*huanyuan*) and returns to the experiential realm of immediacy: only through instantaneous communion with phenomena can cultural time and space be restored to aesthetic time and space—the zero degree, the ontological origin, which is one and the same as the void.[71]

The *xungen* school's emphasis on the aesthetics of "intuition," "transcendence," "the experiential," "the immanent," and "the act of imagination" reflects the influence of the poetics of Zen and phenomenology.[72] Ji Hongzhen characterizes such a holistic approach to literature as deeply mythological, a total rebellion against the reflectionist and even the representational poetics of realism.[73] What emerges out of this valorization of mythopoetic truth is a new possibility for linguistic experimentation, hitherto only half accomplished by the *menglong* school of poetry (Misty poetry) in the late 1970s and early 1980s. It is no small wonder that Li Tuo should arrive at the insightful assessment that *xungen* literature is not only a successor of *menglong* poetry but also the immediate predecessor of experimental fiction—the consummation of the youngest generation's eventual vengeance upon the Mao Style. The intensification of *xungen* writers' experiment with language delivers nothing short of an enriched lyrical subject (*shuqing zhuti*), which knows and can speak of its own truth content.[74] This subject was first assembled by the Misty poets and fully articulated by the root-searching writers, only to be dissolved again in the avant-gardist rage of the experimentalists.

This discussion of the quest for aesthetic roots brings us back to where we started: In what terms can the *xungen* school of writers present itself proudly as the Chinese counterpart of the magic realism of Garcia Marquez—the very avatar of the "world literature" to which all the *xungen* authors consciously aspire?[75] Between Garcia Marquez and Western modernism, the choice seems clear. A return to indigenous sensibility holds the key to a simple logic at work: Discursive distinctiveness is one and the same as discursive distinction. The example of magic realism unloads many other half-truths for the Chinese writer desperately seeking for a global laureate, among which the least problematic is the prescriptive turning away from the center toward the margin—the discarding of orthodox cultural ideologies, the metaphoric foregrounding of Zen and the Dao, the staging of the mythologies of the minorities, and in short, the making of a literary discourse characterized by Li Tuo as *bianyuan huayu* (the discourse of the margin) posing a challenge to *zhongxin huayu* (the discourse of the center).[76]

The mere recognition that the quintessence of Chinese culture can only be found "outside the norm of [China's] Central Plains" is radical enough to characterize the discourse of root-searching as marginal by intention.[77] However, the revolt against the master narrative that *xungen* literature promises remains incomplete and sometimes even refined out of existence, precisely because the utopian moment of fertile self-reflection that this literature inaugurates often creates another self-sufficient cycle that recaptures the subject into a mastering theory of Nature and Culture that encircles and delimits.

Regardless of its potential to provide a critique of tradition, the *xungen* writers' preoccupation with reconstructing cultural myths, the "collective unconscious," and the "consciousness of a communal moral character" continually flirts with a metanarrative that privileges a cultural subject that is not only holistic but capable of appropriating the alien and the deviant.[78] The hero inscribed in such an all-encompassing narrative is rarely genuinely intractable. Both Nature and Culture have the capacity to domesticate him (Yang Wanniu in *Yuancun* [The village afar]), to devour him relentlessly (Liu Cheng in *Shangzhou* [The Shang District]), or to incapacitate and ridicule him (Bingzai in "Ba-ba-ba").[79] The root-searching discourse is one that, in Han Shaogong's words, "can only accomplish its own self-recognition and self-consolidation through its discovery of the referential system of the Other and by means of its subsequent *appropriation and absorption* of such alien elements."[80] Contrary to what Han insists—that such a discourse does not signify self-enclosure—I want to suggest that the presence of the alien, especially when it is assimilated without a trace into the master narrative, can hardly serve as the index to the latter's open-ended nature. In fact, the tremendous appetite of *xungen* literature for attracting the alien and then hemming it in only reveals its invincible encircling instinct. What the literary discourse presents is nothing short of the self-enclosure of a secondary order.

Our earlier discussion of the emphasis of the *xungen* aesthetics on self-transcendence, namely the return to origin, further reinforces the writers' orientation to escape (or to procrastinate indefinitely about) the subject's confrontation with the real and hence to debilitate its will to resist. What root-searching literature provides in the end is an aestheticized version of the textual politics of resistance—what Li Qingxi characterizes as the transcendence of the subject beyond the confrontation of tradition and modernity.[81] Whether the tragic hero chooses to reconcile himself or continue his battle with Nature or Culture, he emerges as a holistic subject, saturated culturally and aesthetically; but in his very susceptibility to sublimation and self-renewal, he is emptied out into an enclosed narrative space reminiscent of comic epic, where the outbound quest almost always brings the hero back unscathed to where he started. Such a discursive (as well as existential) enclosure, even though it reveals a human subject less capable of determining the course of his own life and less reliable as a "repository for ultimate epistemic authority,"[82] continues to sustain the humanist faith in the notion of a retrievable original nature endowed with a stable core of constituting consciousness.

The norm of this subject—that it can still identify itself as the subject of a history self-conscious of its own telos—can of course be seen as arising from a utopian moment in Chinese history. The mid-1980s witnessed the apex of Chinese optimism, the catching-up craze about the Four Modernizations, and the ruling elite's rhetorical faith in political reform before the setback of Hu Yaobang's ouster in early 1987. I have no intention to rely on mechanistic causality to account for the complex sociopsychological formation of the subject in the *xungen* movement. One cannot, however, avoid paying attention to the intense utopian longing—the distinct epochal marker of the first half decade of the 1980s—in the discursive construction of an epistemologically centered subject capable of remembering history (be it personal or cultural) and anticipating the future.

EXPERIMENTAL FICTION: THE SUBJECT UNDER ERASURE?

This hypothesis about epochal logic directs one's interpretive gaze in an equally suggestive fashion toward the more subtle correspondence between the onset of a pessimistic mood about the much-vaunted possibility of a deep structural change in China's political and economic sectors and the theatrical entry into China's literary stage around 1987 of a group of experimentalists who smashed China's age-old humanist tradition of textual practice by exposing the subject as a fictitious construct incapable of purposeful self-narration and stripped of historical agency. Whether one interprets the experimentalists' dissolution of the stable and self-centered subject of the *xungen* genre as a welcome breakthrough or a cataclysmic breakdown, the new subject is neither cultural nor historical. In fact, one cannot even assume that it is human, for it is pared down to the pure position of the subject, or one might say, a mere discursive effect of the narrator. The question one is tempted to address then is, How and for what sake does this seemingly empty subject come into being?

The greatest difficulty for critics, especially for mainland Chinese critics, who wish to decipher the experimental fiction in the same way as any other literary product of the past is not their frustration with a linguistic medium stripped of all representational signs. It is their disorientation in confronting a text that removes from its practice the moment of critique and, by implication, its resistance to an external imaginary agonist.

As noted at the beginning of this chapter, the binary paradigm of resistance predetermines and is reinforced in turn by a critical exercise characteristic of modern and contemporary Chinese intellectuals and critics—a critique programmed, consciously or unconsciously, to seek for the site of contestation in a given text. It is too tantalizing for critics such as Li Tuo and Bei Dao, for whom the allegory of resistance has always formed the core of literary revolutions (or evolutions), not to interpret the emergence of the experimentalists in the same vein. Li Tuo's frequent criticism of the tyranny of the Mao Style suggests, however subtly, his belief in the revolution at the level of the signifier. He is the first literary critic who perceived the experimentalists' effort to "avoid [falling into] the prior system of signification" (*xian jiegou*).[83] Underlying Li's formula is his acute awareness of the complicity of language in making ideology. Indeed, the struggle against Maoist ideology, and in fact, that against any ideological consciousness, be it capitalist or socialist, is to be conducted by delegitimizing the orthodox style of hegemony (the Mao Style in this case) or, put in theoretical terms, "by changing the signifier, or altering existing practices of representation."[84]

This logic of resistance does apply to the discursive practice of the experimentalists. To a certain extent, the making of their novel textual strategy can be seen as an unconscious maneuver to inaugurate a new subjectivity that subverts the fixed and unitary subject (Liu Zaifu's aesthetic subject and the humanist *xungen* hero) that had emerged out of previous social and political conditions. But the subject in experimental fiction serves as an agent of praxis only in the most allegorical sense. The subject, a mere chimera in itself, is only conscious of its revolutionary form, not of its own intentions and content. A subject of intentions is indeed a far cry from what the experimentalists actually delivered: a linguistic subject-position that is fascinated with its own desire for that part of itself that language simultaneously arouses and deconstructs.

Such subjectivity, by the very fact that it is linguistic and provisional, elicits a theoretical position that finally transcends the simple logic inherent in the old-timers' critical agenda of resistance. A small cluster of avant-garde criticism with strong Lacanian overtones emerged in the late 1980s to legitimize the new fiction as a linguistic maze, a pure "energy" field and an "aesthetic game of narration" implemented by young literati devoid of the self-glorifying anxiety and crisis consciousness.[85]

That the new subject can be emptied of any sociopolitical and historical substance and lingo poses different challenges to old-fashioned and young critics. To the former, the new subject's aphasia is symptomatic of an age that is losing its conscience to the temptations of modernization and capitalism. Insisting that the impetus of literary creativity comes from repressed sociopolitical conscience, both Liu Zaifu and Li Zehou deplore the blasphemous attempts of young writers to turn literature into "a playful game."[86] One can imagine that a subject bare of any "sense of mission," reduced to form, and "whose meaning is canceled out" would appear inconceivably irreverent to the revolutionary generation.[87] But the selfsame subject, who continues to subsist in the "representation of its lack,"[88] triggers an equally disquieting crisis and raises questions of a different contestatory edge for the majority of younger theoreticians as well.

The cardinal question, Who comes after the subject is de-positioned? never really emerges from the theoreticians' ill-defined and hurried inquiry into the epochal classification of this alien subject. Taking the crisis of the subject as the only index to postmodernism, young critics in particular are intrigued by the imaginary spectacle of a China finally catching up with the West's most ostentatious cultural logic. The crux of the matter is thus captured in a different set of questions: is this fading subject, in one critic's words, unambiguously postmodern, or is it, as another argues, nothing more than a premodern subject-position liberated by dint of the postmodern linguistic cave-in in post-Mao China?[89]

The controversy over Chinese postmodernism is a topic that indigenous critics feel less inclined, and arguably less theoretically equipped, to pursue than their counterparts abroad. Even as late as in 1989, the issue of postmodernism did not acquire the aura of emergency that had earlier accompanied the epochal debate over the Chinese pseudomodernists (*wei xiandai pai*). Perhaps because critics and writers were still deeply engaged in the problematic of modernism, or perhaps because of the Chinese mentality of leaping forward—a self-propelling evolutionary impulse intensified by their indifference to the issues that postcolonialism addresses—the proposals and counterproposals about Chinese postmodernism in the late 1980s did not attract adequate attention or evolve into a full-fledged controversy. My own position on this subject, which I shall elaborate in the following chapter, was spelled out in reformulating the problematic of Chinese postmodernism as a pseudoproposition.

The spuriousness of such a proposition tells us much about the perverse tendency of a cultural scene that has been accustomed to privileging theory over creative writing since Mao Zedong's talks at the Yan'an Forum in 1942. The impulse to theorize in revolutionary China, even in the post-Mao era, is never innocent. It is self-conscious of its own agenda. The vanguard position that theorists have long occupied in guiding and regulating artistic activities remained in effect until the emergence of the experimentalists, whose preemptive strike against the "prioritizing of theory over literature and art" caught critics and theoreticians in disarray.[90] For the first time in the history of modern Chinese literature, creative writers usurped the position of theorists as trendsetters. In face of this usurpation, the pseudoproposition of Chinese postmodernism cannot be taken merely as an epiphenomenon of the Chinese "leaping forward" mentality, but should also be interpreted as a strategy that theorists adopt to regain their lost ground. The label of postmodernism, however, proves to be too outlandish and unsettling even for the theorists themselves. Most critics who impose the epochal logic upon the new fiction can hardly grasp what they wish to propagate. When Zhang Yiwu and Wang Ning, and even a theoretically-informed overseas critic such as Tang Xiaobing, speak of the relevance of postmodernity in the Chinese context, they either bypass the definition of the term altogether,[91] bestow upon the phenomenon an exaggerated rival consciousness against modernism,[92] or else conjure up something that is nearly indistinguishable from the poststructuralist predilection for pluralism.[93]

I suggest that the most productive way of examining contemporary Chinese cultural logic is to retrieve the issues hidden beneath the camouflage of pseudopropositions such as postmodernism, Orientalism, or civil society. The one problematic that twentieth-century China has been preoccupied with, albeit with inadequate theoretical awareness, is that of its own historical and cultural subjectivity. This is the subtext of the debate over Chinese modernism and the inquiry made by the young proponents of postmodernism. The terms of debate over the experimental fiction should thus be reformulated. The issue at hand is certainly not whether China is capable of producing postmodernist aesthetics, but rather how the subject (if there is one) is reinscribed in the new fiction.

To those Chinese critics who insist that the experimentalists deliver a subject that is decentered and disseminated into a postmodern simulacrum, Zhang Xudong's one-liner—"This linguistic maze delivers not the end, but rather the inauguration of the self"—poses a defiant challenge.[94] It calls into question the very proposition that Chinese literature has now crossed the threshold of postmodernism that is marked by the liquidation of the subject. The ideological implications underlying Zhang Xudong's position are manifold. It introduces a conscious effort on the part of the young generation of elite critics to reconstruct a cultural subjectivity of China that can stand on its own ground and on its own terms. Zhang's anxiety to locate the agency of change from within by returning China from the global to its local context, a problematic crystallized in Gan Yang's proposal of modernity versus tradition, provides us with a different explanatory paradigm when we examine the new fiction.[95]

The role of memory, history, and temporality (issues that postmodern theory shoves aside), which forms the relatively stable core of the subject, are indigenous categories with which the experimentalists love to toy with deceptive lightheartedness. Each of the three leading experimentalists—Ge Fei, Yu Hua, and Su Tong—eventually offers his own storytelling of history as the "textual unconscious" (wenbenzhong de wuyishi),[96] following upon their sardonic attempt to discredit the authenticity of historical consciousness. Although it is fair to say that all

experimentalists share the conviction that subjectivity is always a product of the symbolic in an instance of discourse (here the Lacanian comparison seems irresistible), Ge Fei's experiment with the chimerical reconstruction of memory, Yu Hua's laborious reproduction of the
simulacrum of fictive time, and the Su Tong narrator's compulsive urge
to fill up the lacuna at catalytic discursive points of departure (for example, "I am the son of my father") all contradict the Chinese "postmodernist" critics' hypothesis that history has given way to poetry and
time to space in the new fiction.[97] In Su Tong in particular we witness
the intensification of the spatial memory that root-searching writers explore with such nostalgia. The difference lies in the shifting of emphasis
from the temporality that has been traditionally interpreted as rooted in
the subject to a temporality that is no longer materialized as flow but
self-conscious of its own artificiality because it is now reconstructed by
the narrator as a pure storytelling device.

What is at issue here is not whether the experimentalists have scattered
history to the winds, but how they rewrote the terms by which the previous generation of revolutionaries inscribed the history of the Cultural
Revolution.[98] The young generation's challenge to their predecessors'
simple binary paradigm of history and fiction certainly unnerved those
in whose memories the symbolism of the Revolution still held a religious,
if painful, place. The experimentalists' reinvention of the Cultural Revolution desacralizes it as an ambivalent construct that is both historical
and fictional, tragic and absurd, profound and superficial. This is an
insight that the actual participants of the Revolution and its victims—
including writers of the wounded literature and literature of retrospection—were incapable of generating. The experimentalists are able to
desensitize the Revolution and turn it into an innocuous, albeit conflict-
ridden, signifier all the more easily insofar as they are being swallowed
up in an existential dilemma of a different order. It is here that the importance of generational logic has to be taken into account when one
discusses the experimentalists vis-à-vis the *xungen, xiandai pai,* and
even the writers during the early post-Mao era. The dilemma that the
experimentalists (and the heroes they depict) faced on the eve of the
Tian'anmen Square crackdown—"Perhaps we have nothing, and perhaps we have everything"—is less an epochal attitude than an emotional
plight characteristic of the postrevolutionary generation.[99]

This dilemma leads to a schizophrenic split between desire and action
and between the imaginary and the real. A "tremendous chasm" opens
up between the "condition of [one's material] existence and spiritual

quest": "On the one hand, they [the experimentalists] indulge in the making of transcendental visions and fiction; yet they cannot but lead an extremely mundane existence on the other. The highest degree of spiritual fulfillment in contrast to extreme material deprivation often pushes them to the brink of self-fragmentation."[100]

This is a generation that "gallops freely in the realm of ideas but feels constrained and paralyzed in action"—a subject-position that is not only saturated with but also inaugurated by chimerical desires ("we have everything").[101] This position is at the same time constructed by and made available only at the moment of its accession to the language of desire. It experiences its own emptiness ("we have nothing"), or perhaps even more precisely its own impotence, before its entry into the linguistic order and shortly after initial penetration is accomplished. Perhaps we can recapitulate the narrator-subject's simultaneous self-empowerment and paradoxical atrophy in sociopolitical reality by inverting Fredric Jameson's logic: In the late eighties in China, there has been a mutation in the subject unaccompanied as yet by any equivalent mutation in the object.[102] China on the eve of June 4, 1989, certainly provided a powerful illustration of an indulgence in the mutation of the imaginary. But the first shot fired at the square should revitalize the cliché—the real can be upstaged only for a fleeting moment before it returns to annihilate the imaginary with a vengeance.

The mutation of the subject in the late 1980s took various twists and turns before the climactic intervention from above. Not the least treacherous and insinuating was the experimentalists' carnivalesque self-exile in the imaginary, a realm indistinguishable from the dream state and mirage (Ge Fei and Sun Ganlu), the hallucinatory (Yu Hua), the psychic ward (Can Xue), or the fabulous and fantastic (Ma Yuan). The solipsistic space mapped out in the new fiction canceled out any possible contact with the real and the intersubjective. But paradoxically, this space of pure fiction could brag shamelessly of being "more authentic than the real."[103] Or one might qualify this statement by saying that "readers can certainly be sure that this [fiction] is fictional, but they have no way of proving that it is fictitious."[104] It is thus truly appropriate for one critic to claim that the greatest achievement of the experimentalists resides in their separation of "language" from "reality" and in their bestowing upon each other its own separate poetic jurisdiction.[105]

However, the collapse of the old metonymic formula of "language-representation-reality" in the new fiction does not mean that the subject that emerged out of the new imaginary is nothing but a linguistic scarecrow. Although the experimentalists privilege the new fictional subject as a linguistic construct free of content, the new fiction forms a genre not merely as a result of the writers' shared discursive practice.[106] One can enumerate common thematic interests that all experimentalists share such as the legendary, "the dilapidated spectacle of History," violent death, an unresolved emotional complex involving the father, the paralogic of coincidence, and, not the least important, a sadistic urge to disembowel the human body (especially a beautiful female body).[107] The emergence of this thematic cluster is partially accounted for by the experimentalists' access to, and perhaps their conscious or unconscious imitation of, each other's works. This self-referential quality of the new fiction tends to coagulate its generic logic irrevocably and appears as an ominous sign of reification to which the experimentalists are no less prone than their less adventurous literary predecessors.

Whatever our verdict on whether the experimentalists' subject has been dismissed, retained, or simply disappeared into a potent signifier in the new fiction, this fuzzy subject bears little resemblance to Liu Zaifu's autonomous subject. What we have here are two extreme attempts to romance and authenticate a subject that has been embedded in false consciousness. For Liu Zaifu, the retrieval of lost innocence from the deceitful (and self-delusive?) and irrational political subject is guaranteed by the enthroning of an aesthetically flawless subject, for whom truth and rationality are not only identical but fully intelligible and transparent. In contrast, the experimentalists' quest of authenticity seems effortless but no less earnest. The romance of Liu Zaifu's wholesome subject is replaced by that of a subject without consciousness and sometimes even without voice. But precisely because of its unstable position in the adventitious chain of discourse, and because of the breakdown of its capacity for retrospective totalization, this subject—only a moment in discourse—is better equipped to withstand the enclosure of reification. Perhaps it is on this ground that one can justify Yu Hua's claim that all his writings are "made to come closer to authenticity."[108] The call for authenticity from an experimentalist, however, should not be confused with Liu Zaifu's search for the truth content of the subject. Liu, at any rate, is incapable of appreciating the paralogic that one can only enter the door of authenticity through the "deceptive form" (*xuwei de xingshi*).[109] The authenticity with which the experimentalists are captivated is a form without content, completely unpredictable and unintentional before its momentary materialization in the discursive act. And what better corresponds to such a form of authenticity than an unstructured subject free

of all references (except for self-references), constraints, and commit-
ments, who is, not surprisingly, an ultimate flirt perpetually available
for romance?

But, one may ask, who is truly capable of writing in the name of romance but the *xungen* writers who denounce such triflings as a sham and
shame? Who better deserves the designation of romantic hero than those
who are in search of "the soul of the nation" (*minzu zhi hun*)?[110] This
is the crowning romance of all romances, the high-minded affair with
the cultural subject. "Where did I come from? Whither would I go? And
who am I?"[111] The "I" in Zheng Yi's pious invocation to the mythical
land in his reveries is no longer a simple human incarnation but the invincible and omniscient cultural and national subject, or one might say,
a self-conscious subject narrating the epic of the nation and its history.
So intense is the epic consciousness that the *xungen* writers are doomed
to cultivate, that the literature truly deserves the designation of metafic-
tion (*yuanxiaoshuo*) much more than its impious successor, the experimental fiction.[112]

Eventually, it is the emergence of this problematic of the cultural subject that distinguishes the decade of the 1980s from the May Fourth
period of the 1920s and 1930s. The reenactment of the debate of tradition versus modernity during the 1980s can no longer be easily appropriated into the sociopolitical agenda aimed at bailing China out of
"semi-feudalism and semi-colonialism" that Mao Zedong and the May
Fourth generation once propagated with such compelling passion.[113] The
new problematic of cultural subjectivity predictably calls for the revisiting of the earlier debate. But the terms of the debate are reformulated in
such a fashion that what is at stake now is no longer simpleminded patriotism or even the ever elusive agenda of enlightenment. The drive for
reinventing China that underlies the rationale of the *xungen* literature is
symptomatic of an epistemological reorientation that neither endorses
nor condemns tradition or modernity.

The epistemological turn toward a hermeneutic understanding of the
claims of the present upon the cultural past (or vice versa) is a vision growing out of a more leisurely paced cultural introspection than that which
the previous revolutionary generation could afford. What seemed un-
thinkable during the May Fourth period looms large during the 1980s in
a utopian vision of a different order—the palpable possibility of an alternative modern, not a mere reproduction of Western modernity. It is
only in this context of utopianism that one can comprehend the defiant
accent in Zhang Xudong's statement: "It is the natural-historical langue

of Chinese society that is determining the cultural parole of any invading discourses."[114] There is, of course, much to critique about the Chinese project of subject formation cast in terms of a potentially sinocentric (re)turn. However, notwithstanding its susceptibility to reverse Orientalism, nativist romanticization remains one of the most effective, albeit dangerous, means of resisting the infiltration of postcolonial discourse.

To conclude this exhibition of romantic impulses that characterize projects of subject formation, I note that all three specimens—Liu Zaifu's theory of the subject, the root-searching literature, and the experimental fiction—have underscored with various depths of sincerity the zeitgeist of the 1980s in post-Mao China. In the 1990s, the ideological labor of subject formation has increasingly lost its aura of urgent appeal in the domain of public culture and has receded further into the enclave of elite culture, as a professional activity monopolized by academics. A once potent issue is now undergoing reification. One may also add that there is in all three romances something that the materialist post-Tian'anmen generation of the nineties would want to ridicule. Neither the heroic (Liu Zaifu and *xungen* literature) nor the mock-heroic (the experimentalists) are able to seduce a generation for whom lifestyle rather than sentiment counts. Eventually it is not authoritarianism but commodity fetishism that can kill romance with a sneer and use its corpse for a sales pitch. All the blood shed at the square and all the king's men cannot reverse the course of history. Perhaps China is now entering the age of postmodernity after all. The irony of it!

SIX

The Pseudoproposition of "Chinese Postmodernism"

Ge Fei and the Experimentalist Showcase

The proposition of "Chinese postmodernism" appeared in the elite literary circle around 1988 when the epoch of "progress" experienced escalating sociopolitical crises. Reason that reigned supreme in the midyears of the 1980s grew self-conscious of its own limitations. And the intellectuals' avid aspirations for the consummation of their enlightenment project only bred empty visions. As literary critics mourned plaintively the "depression of creativity" and predicted the coming separation of the aesthetic from the social, a new aesthetic revolution was in the making.

The notion of aesthetic modernity rendered independent of the culture elite's enlightenment project was surely a far cry from Liu Zaifu's inquiry into the teleology of the aesthetic subject. The year 1987 witnessed the emergence of a new aesthetic trend that sent reason and subjectivity—the two instruments of enlightenment—into exile. To be sure, China's so-called modernists such as Liu Suola and Xu Xing had already presented a sampler of an aesthetic experience that conceptualized a humanist subject on the verge of being liberated from all constraints of purposiveness and especially from all imperatives of ideological utility and labor. Anarchists notwithstanding, Xu Xing and Liu Suola's characters were nonetheless driven souls suffering profound agony. To the extent that their rebellion against the normative was self-conscious of its own tendentiousness, it was no less embedded than Liu Zaifu's in the configuration of sociocultural critiques. The aesthetic was still wedded to the social, however alienating that union might have been.

The experimentalists, in contrast, threw all their sociocultural and historical attachments to the winds. Their dramatic entry into the literary
scene toward the latter half of the 1980s was no less shocking to the *xiandai pai* modernists than to classical aestheticians like Liu Zaifu. The irrational assumed a form so overwhelming that it risked canceling out
aestheticism's subversive force of resistance altogether. In upgrading the
ahistorical, in glorifying purposeless violence, and in fetishizing the contingent, the experimentalists articulated a longing for an inward space
completely insulated from the "without." For the first time in the history
of Chinese literature, we witness a raging aesthetic modernity that unfolded itself apart from the sociopolitical configuration of elite culture.

The arrival of such a disjoined moment highlighted the epoch's unrelieved contradiction between its conscious promotion of the Great Leap
Forward and its simultaneous indulgence in an age-old sinocentric vision that gazes back in nostalgia. From the Cultural Discussion to the
controversies over pseudomodernism and on to the *xungen* school's
efforts to reconstruct cultural subjectivity, Chinese writers and intellectuals were irrevocably stuck in the paradox of how to become modern
overnight and return to the sources at the same time. The experimentalists, however, were not concerned with the paradox. Their pledge to
the global postmodernist logic was as mythical as their commitment to
a self-positioning confined in sinocentric terms. Attempting to disengage
themselves from the perpetual reenactment of this dualism between leaping forward and sinification, the experimentalists positioned themselves
somewhere beyond the pseudobinary. Predictably, the rebels' avant-
gardish flair for extravagance courted immediate attention. The school's
unsettling mix of danger and glamour, of eros and death, opened up an
alluring interpretive possibility for those young Chinese critics who had
uncritically absorbed the intellectual agenda of the Western academy.
The catchphrase "Chinese postmodernism" arrived prematurely as a result. It eclipsed a nascent modernism and fulfilled the quest of those indigenous theorists who were engaged in a mental game that placed China
in a continual catching-up race with the West.

The debate over Chinese postmodernism, which came to a halt after
the 1989 crackdown, resumed in 1992 as China, with the blessing of
Deng Xiaoping himself, joined the global "free" market and made a phenomenal leap into the era of postmodernity. But in 1988 and 1989, when
the debate first erupted, the material condition that would give rise to
rampant commodity fetishism was not yet ripe, and the term "postmodernism" was nothing more than an empty signifier circulated within

a small circle of elites. How did the Chinese elites discover the trendy term long before the era of postmodernity dawned in China?

In 1985, postmodernism landed in Beijing with Fredric Jameson who gave a series of lectures on the subject at Beida. The Chinese translation of his lectures, published first in Xi'an as a collection in 1986 and then as separate essays in *Dangdai* (Contemporary) in 1987, had a rippling effect on young mainland literary critics and literati.[1] Most of the proponents of the proposition of Chinese postmodernism circa 1988 and 1989 were graduate students and critics susceptible to theories imported from the West and eager to impose them verbatim on Chinese texts. The sudden influx of Western theoretical discourses in the mid-1980s—Lacan and Freud, the hermeneutic school, structuralists, poststructuralists, Derrida, and so on—was a long awaited feast for Chinese intellectuals after decades of Mao Zedong's theoretical monopoly of Chinese literary studies. We must understand the "rush to theory" among young mainland intellectuals in light of their resistance to the indigenous autocratic Father as much as their subjugation to the foreign fathers.[2]

The changing relationship of Chinese intellectuals to the Western fathers since the Culture Fever is a topic that is continually evolving in the 1990s into such contestatory theses as that of the alternative modern. In the 1980s, however, the configuration of the power relationship between Chinese literary and cultural elite and the hegemonic discourse of the West was defined in terms of their desire to copy rather than to contest it. When the controversy over the experimentalists' hypothetical relationship with Western postmodernism first broke out, the critics were far more concerned with catching up with the latest cultural logic in the West than with engaging themselves in the ideology of the politics of the local. How to justify the postmodernist label formed the focal point of discussion. It was not until the mid-1990s that the resurgence of the debate over experimental fiction would redefine itself around a set of questions that highlighted the Chinese project of taming and challenging rather than reproducing Western postmodernism.[3] For a short while in the late 1980s, almost every critical essay on the experimentalists duplicated the theoretical lingo of Western critics by harping on the theme of the deconstruction of meaning and the end of history.

The pseudoproposition of postmodernism in China is thus part of the syndrome of the Great Leap Forward myth. It is not the label of postmodernism itself, but the series of questions that the labeling succeeds in evading and masking, that forms the central concern of this chapter. Neither am I interested in documenting the short history of the experimentalist movement here. That would require a thorough investigation of the phenomenon of "sinification" and its strategic position in the Chinese debate over modernism and pseudomodernism. What interests me is the insidious way that the phenomenon entangled itself with fragmentary discussion of the experimentalists and their link with postmodernism. I explore the nature of the tenuous link by reading Ge Fei's "Hushao" (Whistling) (1990), a tale he published in Hong Kong, as a way of discussing the complex issue of sinification, self-positioning of the experimentalists, and the critical confusion about the latter's "postmodernist" affiliation.

THE GREAT LEAP FORWARD AND THE FORMATION OF THE PSEUDOBINARY

Both in real life and in cultural studies, Chinese intellectuals and citizens in urban centers alike adhere to a notion of progress that pursues a straight or spiral course at ever escalating speed. This is an earthy approach to the elimination of poverty of all kinds—material destitution and cultural and ideological vacuity. To counter the image of backwardness, one has no other choice but to leap forward. It is a notion that acquired incentive on its own and grew into something bountiful, boundless, and almost irreversible, until its momentary setback on June Fourth in 1989.

An extremely progressive, *aggressive* attitude toward the future is not new or peculiar to China in the 1980s. Underlying the mainland Chinese notion of progress is that ever prevailing Maoist utopianism that propels Chinese to seek for and yet fail to achieve every political dream for the nation. This teleology, rooted in the discursive practices of Chinese modernity, reaches back to the Darwinian meditations of Yan Fu and Kang Youwei. Whether we label it cultural utilitarianism or simply the utopian vision of a Chinese modernity, the rationality has an unmistakably close resemblance to the Maoist Great Leap Forward mentality. We can perhaps designate this irrationally optimistic mode of self-introspection as "characteristically Chinese."[4] The "wounded literature" comes to mind as a good illustration of the irrational emotionalism and political pragmatism that triggered the post-Maoist examination of the Cultural Revolution. Such introspective writing was a pragmatic and instrumental legitimation of Hua Guofeng's regime because, by simple logic, it imputed all evils to the Gang of Four. Sentimental grumblings about fate and the writers' self-indulgent portrayal of their own suffering fell far short of a genuine introspection or inter-rogation of the historical past and every individual's own complicity in the revolutionary politics of victimization. The forward leap that the wounded literature once promised is hardly a qualitative leap in self-evaluation or historical reflection.

It was unexpected frustration of this forward leap mentality that plunged the nation in late 1987 into a deep discontent. In the imme-diate wake of the Party's Thirteenth Congress in October, the entire nation was seized by a late-blooming consciousness of the impending socioeconomic crises, which was intensified by Premier Zhao Ziyang's announcement in the congress that Chinese society was still lingering at the threshold of "the primary stage of socialism."[5] Zhao Ziyang's assessment revealed the illusory nature of the Maoist Great Leap, but it also returned the collective dreamers to where they in fact stood—in a depleted present. For one rare moment in the history of Chinese communism, genuine nihilism pervaded the minds of the young. "A stunning spectacle it was indeed," recalled an observer at Cui Jian's rock concert, after witnessing millions of Chinese, men and women, chiming in involuntarily to the tune of "I Have Nothing at All" (*yi wu suo you*), one of the rock star's most popular songs in the latter half of the decade.[6]

Everyone seems to be a loser in this crude awakening. Intellectuals had envisioned a future in which they would emerge as the privileged center controlling the flow of information and knowledge. In this new epoch, a longed-for and profound shift in class structure would enable intellectual laborers to dominate manual labor so that, just as in the West, technological knowledge would emerge as the major productive force. Obsessive interest in this future during the early and mid-1980s was widespread. The concept of "cultural capital" particularly intrigued in-vestors, who promoted global cultural practices and the distribution of knowledge to other power centers, particularly college campuses and ur-ban salons.[7] Groups of intellectuals engaged in the making of this new utopian discourse. They launched mega-projects such as the "Toward the Future" series edited by Jin Guantao and Gan Yang's journal and translation series entitled *Culture: China and the World*.

The prevailing zeitgeist prior to the Thirteenth Party Congress un-doubtedly privileged the future and viewed the present as a mere tran-sition to be consumed by the masses in their consciousness of a rapidly sped-up future. Nothing is more important to the Chinese elite than the constant reassurance that they, too, are moving with the current,

carrying on a dialogue with the world, and keeping up with the world—
"the world" in this context, of course, being none other than "the
wealthy and powerful" West.

Their recent forward-looking stance, however, is some distance from
the complex earlier modern Chinese attitude about sinification. At first
glimpse, treading the world stage of progress means learning new and
foreign dance steps and leaving behind bound feet and all that. It would
seem that the present rhetorical march toward the future symbolizes
nothing less than a self-conscious parting of ways with China's earlier articulations of its own image. And yet every Chinese cultural renaissance
in this century has ended in a resurgence of traditionalism. The restora-
tion of Confucianism, a slogan raised at the heyday of the Culture Fever,
does not merely reflect the political agenda of the dogmatic Marxists in
power. It reminds us of the recurring collective impulse of Chinese intellectuals to invoke a historical past in which China positioned itself as the
cultural and spiritual center of the world. Both Liang Qichao and Liang
Shuming dwelt at length on the post–World War I myth of Eastern spirituality versus Western materialism and redirected the drive of sinification
from its retrogressive self-immersion to an outbound salvational project.
In the words of Guy Alitto, Liang Shuming's prophecy on the imminent
Confucianization of the West served the same logic as Liang Qichao's
1919 call for the Chinese "to rush to the West's spiritual salvation."[8]

Both Liangs sought to undermine the symmetrical superior versus subordinate binary configuration by which the West mapped its hierarchical relationship to China since the late nineteenth century. And yet no
matter how humiliating China's encounter with the West has been
throughout modern history, the Chinese formulation of the mental geography of China versus the West never fails to incorporate the reverse
configuration that its premodern history serves with such royal conviction: China is self-positioned politically and culturally as the center that
looks out at its exteriors as a margin to be annexed and homogenized.
The unflagging argument for the inverted pattern of hegemony is indeed
very treacherous, if not downright illogical: It is that modern power relations between the West (the center) and China (the margin) are capable
of undergoing an instantaneous inversion simply because history is said
to be capable of reproducing its precedents verbatim.

I might condemn as "reverse Orientalism" this crude salvational appropriation of a degraded West into Eastern spirituality. My question at
this moment, however, is a problematic of a different order. I am curious about this formulation of a pseudobinary China versus the West in

the first place. Fraudulence surfaces immediately in the conceit that China can speak of its own cultural interior as an autonomous territory separable from the capitalized exterior known as the West. Based on the assumption that Western culture is the antithesis of, and hence exterior to, Chinese culture, the imaginary project of the "spiritual sinification of Western culture" proposed by the two Liangs fails to reflect on the dilemma of how China can speak of the desire to project its own position when such a position already contains within it an internalized Occidental discourse.

This dilemma has intensified in the post-Mao era because nationalism in the 1980s has functioned less efficiently to buffer the Chinese against the insidious infiltration of the foreign than it did in the 1920s. The salvational vision of sinification that both Liangs addressed then was pared down to an earnest defensive strategy in the new epoch. One can no longer take the position of the self for granted. No one can retreat to an unadulterated self-image. Unsurprisingly, anxiety about self-positioning (dingwei) has plagued Chinese ideologues, intellectuals, writers, and critics alike since the mid-1980s.

Two recent examples will suffice to demonstrate the formulaic emergence of the issue of self-positioning at every ideological crisis in the post-Mao era. Deng Xiaoping's call for a "socialism with Chinese characteristics" in 1982 stands out as one typical case in point. Ironically, Deng's self-centered ideological repositioning coincides in spirit with the search of Marxist humanists into Zhuang Zi's philosophy as the Chinese original source for the Sartrean concept of alienation.[9] In both cases, the underlying political agenda of sinification lies not in the allegedly Chinese impulse to harmonize, but in a nationalist defense mechanism that seeks to neutralize and eventually to dissolve the alien. I cannot help but side with Gan Yang, who condemned his fellow intellectuals for their conventional, "typical" habits of "view[ing] all imported foreign cultures as fundamentally originating in China."[10]

Underlying the alleged academic interest in the discovery of a comparative idiom of indigenous and foreign discourses is nothing less than the irresistible impetus to self-position, an activity often indistinguishable from (indeed achievable only through) the subjugation of the alien. It is particularly intriguing to witness the resurgence of the issues of self-positioning in Deng's China whenever an emerging ideological crisis brings to the fore the perennial conflict between tradition and modernity, which the ideologues mistakenly translate into the simple terms of China versus the West.

In literary as opposed to ideological terrains, the phenomenon of sini-fication takes a different route. It no longer perceives itself as a mere strategy. The concept of self-positioning is not resolved in the coining of trendy slogans, nor does it circulate undisguised among the literary elite. It is revealed most clearly in the literary critics' penchant for the nam-ing, renaming, and summing up of each particular school, roughly every two years—the Misty poetry, the wounded literature, the literature of retrospection, root-searching literature, modernism, neorealism, and the experimentalists. In fact, even before the emergence of the "literature of roots" in the mid-1980s, a thick profusion of neologisms delineated the spectacle of a China caught up in ecstatic self-exposure. The emotional energy that the long revolutionary years had pent up was unleashed at last. The elites now promoted Chinese poets and writers as commodi-ties to the world cultural market. And they courted almost unabashedly the Occidental gaze without any qualms about globalizing (*shijie hua*) their own cultural discourse.

Yet the seeds of repositioning, the desire to catch up with the literary-cultural fashion of the day, and hence the fetish for renaming the newest trend and reshaping one's identity in accordance, were planted deep in all these indigenous showcases of the literary ingenuity of post-Mao China. Around the time when the concept of root-searching blossomed, a vigorous critical discourse began to grow around the controversy over the self-positioning of contemporary literature. One should pause here for a moment to note the subtle difference between the subtext for "self-positioning" and that for "repositioning." The absent term in the binary diagram of the former is viewed as an antagonistic term (the confronta-tional Other) that points less to the alien (the West) than to the indige-nous agonist (Maoism), especially when it is literature rather than cul-ture that serves as the point of reference. Politicized literature is seen as the orthodox Other to "unfettered writing" (if there is such a thing to start with). In contrast, the absent term (the global and the foreign) on the conceptual axis of "repositioning" is one to be aligned rather than contested with, at least in the 1980s. When the Chinese writer speaks of self-positioning *literature* in the post-Mao era, she or he has in mind combat against the tyrannical Mao Style. In comparison, the spectacle of the intellectuals' concern with the repositioning of *culture* is symp-tomatic of the leaping forward mentality.

Although the theorists are increasingly aware that the self-positioning of Chinese literature is different from the repositioning of Chinese cul-ture, the confusion, complexity, and difficulty of the new theoretical discourse consists precisely in the allegedly mutual (if only imperceptible) arising and stimulation of these two mutations. Thus for the *xungen* writer A Cheng, the locale for the emerging Chinese modern conscious-ness in contemporary literature is to be found in the collective cultural background of the Chinese people.[11] Critic Zhang Yiwu precludes the possibility of any transcultural text of Third-World literature.[12] For both critics, it is inconceivable that a literary self-positioning can occur with-out being accompanied by a cultural repositioning. And regardless of whether the literary trend of root-searching indicates an anticultural drive or return-to-culture approach,[13] its deep structural obsession with the category of culture is irrevocable.

The anxiety for a repositioned literary culture reveals the profound discomfort that writers and critics felt about the shifting duality of its local and global discursive grounds. The catching-up craze toward the latter half of the 1980s could no longer sustain its earlier faith in the po-tential of the local to usurp the global, whose welcome intrusion in-evitably precipitated an identity crisis in the former. All of a sudden, crit-ics became obsessively focused on the discursive impasse of indigenous writers. Everything had apparently become an inauthentic copy of the foreign. Amid the rapid expansion of China's global vision based on the dialogical principle, which includes a craving for a Nobel prize in litera-ture, there grew an increasingly strong consciousness of an emotional need for a fixed center, a kind of a local subject-position. This position, according to some critics, should continue to converse with, but need not fully comprehend, the global discourse.[14] This is a sinified vision. It emphasizes difference rather than the dialectics between the two poles and hence proclaims: "The finer *our* national literature is, the finer it can become as world literature."[15]

Optimism notwithstanding, this reintroduction in the late 1980s of the thesis of sinification and of China's subject-position has sustained in the process a certain ambivalent revalorization of the indigenous. This triggers a process of self-introspection rather less self-assuring than usual. This time around, critics are more acutely aware of the negative implications that such a process may evoke. As one of them puts it, "Thanks to the stimulus provided by modern Western cultural traditions, Chinese culture finally and gradually grew a new kind of spiritual power—namely, its drive toward self-negation and self-revival."[16] His emphasis on an inner, irreversible order between negation and revival is illuminating. Self-positioning defined in such terms (in stark contrast to the earlier ones of the "negation of the alien") can no longer be taken as a mere disguise of the nationalist sentiment of self-aggrandizement. It in-corporates new content into the old familiar process of sinification. Most significantly, it reveals that such a process could be humiliating rather than self-congratulatory.

Does a cultural repositioning (that is, that self-revival will follow self-negation), resuscitate literary culture? Do these two mutations, cul-tural and literary, necessarily go hand in hand? Putting aside the prob-lematic achievement of the root-searching literature, let us examine another literary orientation that refutes the hypothesis of the mutual arising of those two mutations. I refer here to the new school that emerged in the pervasive dystopian climate of the late 1980s: the so-called avant-garde fiction (*xianfeng xiaoshuo*), later renamed "experi-mental fiction" (*shiyan xiaoshuo*), a highly provisional project that self-consciously underwent the process of self-positioning while turning impervious to the issue of cultural repositioning.

GEI FEI, THE EXPERIMENTAL SHOWCASE, AND THE MIRAGE OF POSTMODERNISM

Often portrayed by China's "progressive" critics as a delicious prey of ravenous postmodernism, Ge Fei, the archexperimentalist, is especially fascinated with the marginal moment between the past and the present. These are moments that defamiliarize and, in so doing, shy away from the task of revalorizing the cultural past. Blasted out of the vicious cy-cle of sinification and westernization, they refuse to be recontained in the third territory of repressed truce.

In light of such a self-conscious resistance to categorical affiliations, we can no longer formulate the thesis in familiar terms. There are no grounds for the claim that the sino-purist stance and the forward West-ern outlook are often bedfellows in the literary culture of the 1980s, and that the two seemingly incompatible epistemological outlooks have soft-ened their antagonism to each other, producing literary trends that in-voke the Chinese Will to harmonize.[17] What makes Ge Fei and the ex-perimentalists an anomaly is precisely their irreverence for such an epochal logic of blending and harmonizing.

The incentive to integrate certainly proved to be as strong as ever throughout the 1980s. The craze for the *xungen* literature revealed a strong interest in the mixed breed of modernism and the nativist nos-talgia for old China's cultural myths, ethical totality, and aesthetic ar-chetypes. Even "neorealism" (*xin xieshi zhuyi*), which the avant-garde journal *Zhongshan* advocated in 1989 as a mainstreaming project, reiterates the principle of blending: the neorealist fiction would "not only exhibit the colorful consciousness of our contemporaneity, but also our powerful historical and philosophical consciousness" and "assimilate the technical advantages of the various trends of modernism."[18]

Yet I argue that, regardless of its apparent popularity, this epochal logic of blending was disrupted by occasional efforts of a few astute critics and writers who wished to struggle free from the pseudobinary of China versus the West. What they rejected was not only the confrontational logic of the self versus the other, but also the eclectic logic of blending. In short, the critical impulse and the impasse of the best critical minds in contemporary China are derived from a reflex that propelled them to find a path leading to none of the following worn-out formulae: a return to the Chinese essence, wholesale westernization, or selection of the best from East and West.[19]

This was true of the experimentalists, who made a similar commitment to break out of this triple bind. Many of the best experiments of the experimentalist school, Ge Fei's "Whistling" among them, deliver us into a precarious mood of limbo and a vision short of coming true. Such is Ge Fei's flair for making fugitive impressions that his work constitutes an excellent vantage point for examining the shadow issue of sinification in the Chinese "postmodern" condition.

Surely controversy over whether there can be a Chinese postmodernism in a society far short of meeting the goals of its modernization project seems less meaningful after June 1989. On the eve of the Tian'anmen Square demonstrations, however, the debate uncovered a familiar urgency that the "great leap" advocates understood only too well. The advent of postmoderism in China would renew China's membership in the global cultural discourse. Whether or not the recently assembled subject of modernity could undergo a premature dissolution into a postmodern simulacrum (a subject-image that disseminates itself continually) never dawned on young advocates of Chinese postmodernism. The hottest theoretical issue of 1988, the pseudomodernism question (their query: Is Chinese modernism a sham after all?), was hardly concluded before critics were once again absorbed in the fear of falling behind. The critique of Chinese modernism quickly shifted ground and gave way to a hasty inquiry into the totality of the Chinese postmodernist vision.

In both cases, the crux of the matter again was the paradoxical encounter of the perennial project of cultural reconstruction (*wenhua chonggou*) (a term less ideologically charged than "sinification") and the project of keeping up with and incorporating the empowering discourse of the West. Critics found themselves in a dilemma: Both the absence and presence of postmodernism seized them with unrelieved anxiety. Its absence corrupted their vision of leaping forward; its presence plunged them again into the elusive quest for Chinese characteristics.

To compound the quandary, though the so-called New Theorists (the postrepresentational theorists) identified a small group of avant-garde writers as China's potential postmodernists, the theorists had not yet found a critical idiom. The avalanche of imported critical jargons ranging from Freudian, Lacanian, mythological, phenomenological, and structuralist to poststructuralist and deconstructionist all in one profuse moment is a phenomenon far more ambiguous than Liu Zaifu envisioned.[20] What Liu prescribed with such optimism in 1989 as "the creative transformation" of Western technical terms into the "deep structure of Chinese" remains as problematic as "the dialogue between the world and our [China's] own unique national language."[21] Creative transformation takes time and effort. Dialogue with the power centers of world culture requires more than good intentions and wishful thinking. The postmodern label that a vulnerable New Theory effortlessly imposed on experimentalists will be meaningful only if the following sequence of events unfolds: Debates break out over realism, modernism, and neo-realism; the new aesthetic experience is translated back into a historical relationship with those three schools; and someone asks the question of how an imaginary order of postmodernism figures into the old double bind, that is, the "great leap" mentality and the sinification complex.

Examining the first two issues in the sequence depends upon mapping the positions of realism, modernism, and neorealism in the 1980s. This is a complex groundwork that needs to be laid elsewhere. This chapter concerns itself solely with issue three, the configuration of the double bind. Tangentially, I raise the question of how the so-called Chinese post-modernist vision negotiates with the contradictory demands of a culturally and historically specific era and with an imaginary space of the global postmodern condition. Ge Fei's narrative fiction appears particularly significant because of its irreverence and its irrelevance to the temporal logic of Deng's China, specifically, to the horizon open to the future. It seems to sidestep the question of a futuristic orientation, by which I mean the view that the future is the only possible locus for the construction of a renewed Chinese identity. Ge Fei's contrary episte-mological vision is bound by a backward stance: it is through the self-narration of the reinvented memories of one's own past that the construction of identity is made possible in the first place.

Generally speaking, contemporary Chinese critics have not yet understood that the experimentalists came into being under the conditions of a common discursive position that promises no epistemological or structural unity. They also have not realized that the postmodernism that Fredric Jameson brought to China during his visit at Beijing University in 1985 is a highly contested critical category in the West. One can, of course, argue that there is a link between the Chinese experimentalists and postmodernists since the former's reading experience could very well deliver a postmodernist vision that is not based on the postmodernist experience. Younger Chinese artists and writers are quite adept at conjuring up visions of this sort without being able to testify to their validity in real life.

Because Confucianist and Maoist indoctrination deprived people of authentic experiences (that is, genuine self-expression in verbal, physical, sexual, and epistemological terms), vision making about democracy, fantasy making of the potent sexual self in literature, and the construction of the theory of subjectivity have become tantalizing national hobbies. Given the characteristically Chinese disruption of vision and experience, it is less productive to argue against the likelihood of Chinese postmodernism than it is to question, as I shall, the totality of its vision. In that light, the anxiety of Chinese critics about the construction of a postrepresentational theoretical apparatus is simply an overreaction. The misleading hypothesis that underlying the synchronic grammar of the avant-garde is a totalized epistemological paradigm that may correspond to a single explanatory model lures critics right into the pseudoproposition of Chinese postmodernism.

Thus, although the experimentalists share a common discursive ground, repeatedly defined in terms of their new awareness of the "subject-position of language" (*yuyan zhuti*) (by which they mean a new emphasis on narration itself as opposed to the writer's earlier preoccupation with the subjectivity of the narrator or that of the narrative itself), they in fact present various versions of that old bourgeois subject caught in the act of discoursing about itself.[22] Interest in language games notwithstanding, Ge Fei and Yu Hua, my two representative experimentalists, still adhere to the modernist myth of the subject. Each takes a different guise, however. One is obsessed with the process of self-assembly, the other with that of self-disassembly. To a great extent,

both would endorse without reservation *the first half* of the Althusserian dictum: "History is a process without a telos or a subject."[23] Both
writers rebelled against the teleological culture logic embraced by their
immediate predecessor, the root-searching school. Yet Yu Hua went
even further than Ge Fei in blurring the lines between true and false
statements and in resisting the tyrannical return of a master narrative.[24]
Their fear of enclosure by such a narrative is, however, paradoxically
accompanied by fear of space, big or small. Thus Yu Hua's fictional
space—take "1986" (*Yijiu baliu*) and "One Kind of Reality" (*Xianshi
yizhong*) for instance—is always pared down to the minimum, evoking
a suffocating effect. It is a world emptied of personal and collective
memories (ironically, "1986" claims to deliver a long lapse of twenty
years' time and deals with a lunatic's congealed memory of the Cultural
Revolution), a nightmarish world delineated by the narrator's conscious
refusal to enter a recognizable temporal and physical space.

Ge Fei's pilgrimage takes a different epistemological turn. "Whistling,"
written in 1990, is a good case in point.[25] This date in itself prompts
one to ask what violent intervention the crackdown of June 4, 1989,
brought about in his writing. Yet the surface text of "Whistling," and in
fact most of the writer's early work, seems to frustrate our expectation
that Ge Fei's stories may correspond to historical trauma. In avant-garde
style, the tale conjures up few interpretive traces of the ideological past
or historical present, despite its reconstruction of the historical anecdote
about two Daoist solitaires during the Wei-Jin dynasty (220–420). So
"Whistling," like Ge Fei's other experiments, repeats his effort at exposing the fictionality of history as narrative and becomes another example of his total lack of commitment to what history might bequeath
us. But the fact that the work was published abroad reinforces our vague
anticipation of intimations of a different order. Before making a closer
examination of this tale, we should first take a quick look at Ge Fei's
narrative logic in general so that the nature of the distinct, dramatic departure of "Whistling" from his earlier works can be more readily
grasped and appreciated.

Ge Fei's fictional world can be characterized as a slow process of laboriously and self-consciously extending the present back into the past.
It is the past, specifically at the moment when the narrator remembers
and registers the fragmentary flashes of his personal past, that anchors
the subject-position of Ge Fei's literary persona. In the preface to his
collection *Mizhou* (The lost ferry), which provides glimpses of authorial intention, Ge Fei speaks of an imaginary space that he yearned to
reach through the "recuperation of the ineffable he encountered in real-

ity and in memory."[26] At first glance, the narrator's acute awareness
that his own memory serves as the locus of subjectivity seems to make
him a marginal case in a postmodernist mood that promotes, among
other more controversial programs, the disintegration of the subject. Ge
Fei, however, is as slippery as many of his fellow travelers. Like them,
his preoccupation with the magical pattern of language does not preclude consciousness of the tug of war between sinification and its internalized Other (that is, whatever newest fad, in this case postmodernism,
is being appropriated from the discourse of the West). "Whistling,"
when taken at face value, conjures up in its telling of the disintegration
of memory exactly such a mirage of the postmodern condition of decentered subjectivity.

Despite the marked difference between "Whistling" and Ge Fei's earlier works (the one stresses the deterioration, the other, the arduous reconstruction of memory), like his other tales "Whistling" reflects upon
lacunae of different forms: an empty rice bowl with blue rims, a swallow that disappears, the shadow of a woman whose features are blurred,
smeared traces of characters printed on a time-worn painting, a deserted
chessboard, a little empty path across the wheat field, the bare content
of a whistle, and a gaze that fails to focus. I would argue against those
who insist on identifying the Western artifice of collage in those disconnected images. I propose that Ge Fei is under the heavy influence of the
Chinese aesthetics of the lacuna, and so, for him, the empty space in its
most concrete form is paradoxically abstract to the utmost. The Chinese
lacuna in a landscape painting or in ancient poetry delivers a much more
elusive absence than the postmodernist concept of "a copy without an
original." "Whistling" is a tale that continually tests the limits of nar-
ratable lacunae; in terms of Ge Fei's fictional logic, it asks, Where can
the labyrinth of an interminable memory or gaze lead?

In his earlier works, the narrator's lingering memory and gaze led
to narrative endings that often, paradoxically, promised the beginning
of another story.[27] Quite naturally, Ge Fei's tales grow into each other
and form an extended matrix of self-referentiality. There are exceptions,
to be sure. Both "Mizhou" (The lost ferry) and "Danian" (The new
year) are terminated at a frozen triumphant moment of the unconscious
when the final identification of desire with death occurs. But in most
cases, a typical Ge Fei tale disseminates, lingers on, and stumbles into
another tale.

Several of Ge Fei's stories are metaphors for the slow process of how
memory exhausts itself by waging a war against the encroachment of the
present. "Whistling," written in the aftermath of an extreme situation,

presents the eventual dilemma of a memory growing hollow and barren, emptied of its content before the will to remember commands its performance. A slightly mocking acknowledgment of the redemptive power of Mr. Wuyou's memory in one story (he could recite by rote from books in his own library burned down by villagers) and even sentimental comparisons of memory to poisonous wine in "Meiyou ren kanjian cao shengzhang" (Nobody saw the grass growing) are parts of the author's painstaking construction of the act of remembering as the meaningful center of his fictional world.[28] In this, the early Ge Fei reminds us of Lyotard's speculations about Proust: "The hero is no longer a character but the inner consciousness of time."[29] Not until the appearance of "Whistling" did Ge Fei's "odyssey of consciousness" lose its nostalgic emotional valence and render itself unnarratable.

WHISTLING

It is no accident that Ge Fei turned to a historical legend for the setting of his statement on the ultimate powerlessness of the human faculty of remembering and narrating. According to the official chronicle, Ruan Ji, one of the renowned Seven Sages of the Bamboo Grove, visited the hermit Sun Deng, with whom he tried in vain to start a conversation on the inner alchemy of Daoism. We are informed that "Deng never responded. Ji gave out a long howling whistle and withdrew. Climbing halfway up a mountain, Ji seemed to have heard a sound that echoed through the rocky ravine. It was Deng whistling in response."[30] In another historical legend about Ji Kang, Ruan Ji's fellow traveler, Sun Deng guarded his reticence until Kang took his leave. Upon the latter's departure, Deng broke his long kept silence and predicted Kang's tragic destiny.[31] In both cases, we sense the presence of will and tension in Sun Deng's silence. In the historical text, the silence serves as a powerful sign that discharges a missing content that is translatable and retrievable: Sun Deng's reserved stillness poses a defiant, hence meaningful, challenge to the corrupt time that is deprived of a stable and legitimate center. Every Chinese intellectual knows the rule of conscience: "In times of disorder, one does not serve [the Son of Heaven]" (*luanshi bushi*).

Ge Fei's aesthetic choice in narrating this legend of futile encounter is an interesting issue. He could have opted for a modernist aesthetics. Sun Deng could emerge as an emaciated but dangerous and subversive nonconformist. One could envision the possibility of the birth of a tale that reconstructs the protagonist's idiosyncratic mannerisms and his private identity. But Ge Fei seems more intrigued by the other alternative, that the hermit's silence finds no representation. Sun Deng's willed silence is dissolved in the contemporary tale into a series of impotent gazes into empty space. The tranquil and well-saturated time that a self-conscious recluse might enjoy is fragmented into disconnected shots of perpetual presents. Even the physical space so meaningful to the historical Sun Deng (deep forests teeming with magic herbs and the echoing rocky ravine, locales that form an ever expanding metaphorical discourse in the master narrative of *xuanxue,* the "School of Profound Learning") retreats in Ge Fei's narrative until it is reduced to being the small inner yard of his hut—a space confined to what his purposelessly wandering gaze can travel.

Amid Ge Fei's various attempts to undermine the heroic subtext of the historical past, one encounters a contradictory move. He appears here to be restoring to the tale an order of narration (that is, the internal order of a narrative beginning and ending) only precariously maintained in his earlier works. However, the order subverts its own logic as soon as we realize that what "Whistling" presents is actually a mock imitation of the beginning and the end of the original legend. To achieve such an effect, Ge Fei inverted the role expectations of the two characters. The narrative begins with Sun Deng waiting listlessly for Ruan Ji at a rendezvous (in contrast to the latter courting the former's attention in the historical account) and ends with Deng's failure to whistle in response (in contrast to the long drawn out whistle of the historical Sun Deng): "Looking around himself, Sun Deng stealthily put his thumb and index finger into his mouth—his extreme physical debility and the violent shaking of his teeth made him unable to utter any sound."[32] The final inversion, paradoxically suppressing and heightening its political impact (that is, silence as a political allegory), highlights Ge Fei's mockery of his own initial attempt to deliver solace in the recognizable form of narration.

All the above suggest the following. First, Ge Fei's closest encounter with the postmodern mirage takes its point of departure and derives its ultimate meaning(lessness) from our recognition of its intertextual reference to a historically specific era, the Wei-Jin period. Second, what is rendered meaningless is the high-minded culture of whistling in the Six Dynasties (420–589), the self-conscious positioning of the historical Sun Deng in a universe dominated by the binarism of ancient Chinese political culture (court versus forest, rituals of conversation versus silence, and so on), and his transcendence of such binarism crystallized in the single triumphant act of whistling.[33] Specifically, the subversion of meaning enacted in "Whistling" is achieved through the text's reference to a culturally specific past (Daoism) and to history's valorization of the symbolic valence of the two recluses howling to each other (that is, to whistling as a specific form of metaphysical language during the historical period, and to hermitage as the only private space that resists the enclosure and intrusion of the public, symbolized in this tale by the act of mundane speech).

It is interesting to note that toying with intertextuality can prove a dangerous game, for the notion releases the invisible working of constraints. Even the most radical case of intertextuality, the parody, is not impervious to the trap of legitimizing the concept of metanarrative. How to evoke but at the same time tame the metanarrative (for example, the intertext of the Sun Deng legend) thus posed a challenge to Ge Fei. His ideological move was to remain uncommitted to history itself. The tale is thus not about an episode in history. It is about those moments that lurk in the historical unconscious. To retrieve them requires the narrator's commitment to the ephemeral and to lacunae. Given the threshold nature of the spatial and temporal framework underlying "Whistling," which is neither other-worldly nor worldly, neither historical nor contemporary, one cannot bypass certain questions: What is the subtext in "Whistling"? Does its presence force an alternative reading of history?

More important even than the writer's inversion strategy (which does provide certain clues to both questions) is how he fills the gaps in the historical text. Specifically, how does Ge Fei replenish the interim that elapses between Ruan Ji's attempt to start a conversation and Sun Deng's refusal to respond? The fact that no narrative interval is available in the original historical text makes such a space a fertile ground for a writer who wishes the impossible, which is to escape and embrace history at the same time. Ge Fei accomplishes his goal by recreating what is forgotten and deleted by history. The missing content of the historical legend constitutes the actual point of departure for his narrative. It is here, at this very locale, not at the beginning or the end of the tale, that the writer must attempt to recapture his ambiguous attitude toward his own cultural heritage with a contemporaneity that has already incorporated the foreign.

A lacuna always forms the center of Ge Fei's fictional world: It is empty and thus tantalizingly invites being filled and refilled. We often find his characters facing each other speechless. Empty space between them usually conjures up alluring memories of the past. A scene of the narrator sitting alone silently on a quiet night with a young woman promises a harvest of retrieved and imagined memories. It is a scene that assumes such a presence in his earlier works[34] that its recurrence in "Whistling" seems to promise the same vintage.

But, we must ask, what fills up the lacuna in Sun Deng's life? What does he do, see, and hear during the interval when Ruan Ji appears and leaves as a part of his daily routine? Sun Deng spends a long time deliberating on one single move at a chess game with an imaginary player (the absent or present Ruan Ji, or an unnamed woman). He looks at a painting covered with dust, breaks a teapot by accident, sits down on a rattan chair, opens up a poetry manuscript, stares at a swallow at high noon, wonders if this is the same swallow he saw last fall, listens to the footsteps of a passerby, and hears the snoring of a woman whose identity is ambiguous (she might be his daughter, or just a stranger). All these sights and sounds barely leave a trace on his consciousness, for they are not endowed with ritualistic significance like those sights and sounds in Ge Fei's other stories. Nor are they riddled with repressed anxiety to be re-contained in the unconscious. The whole cycle of the aimless wandering of Sun Deng's gaze simply repeats itself. Occasionally, his purposeless movements are interrupted by a brief and discontinuous dialogue with Ruan Ji. But we hear the narrator commenting: "Sun Deng's words are nothing but ordinary and boring. They do not signify anything in particular."[35] And Ruan Ji's ejaculation echoes the same unbearable lightness of the tale's mood: "It is just as if you made a whistle . . . you did not find much meaning in it."[36] Given the political and metaphysical high culture of whistling during the fifth and sixth centuries,[37] Ge Fei's narrator's listless extrication of whistling from all its ritualistic significance and his casual retranslation of it into an involuntary and meaningless act should ring doubly ironic here.

Sun Deng struggles on one occasion to deliver the narrative content of his memory. But he only vaguely recalls a married daughter who seems to have been gone for a long time. At one flickering moment he tries to assemble her image: an illusory female appearance that approaches him and then disappears upon his instantaneous loss of concentration. For the first time in Ge Fei's fictional world, we encounter a character who does not remember. The spiritual skeleton of the recluse can no longer articulate itself. In this general picture of debilitation, recollection remains unmotivated: "a poetry manuscript that is turning sallow, a cluster of messy and withering petals, a promise that cannot be fulfilled."[38]

No one would deny that this amorphous interlude makes "Whistling" an extremely difficult tale. It is also an utterly unpretentious strategic locale where Ge Fei makes almost inaudible aesthetic, philosophical, and even political statements without the danger of being overheard.

Ge Fei's aesthetic choice is to portray "the very periphery where Deng's will and consciousness is about to reach its own extinction." That would suggest, in the ambiguous double voice of both Sun Deng and the narrator, that what passes in the interim between Ruan Ji's visits be "rendered into a painting."[39] I draw attention to this because it is such a careful steering away from all the fin de siècle diseases of high modernism—angst and depth, the overflow of the unconscious, and boredom—toward the postmodern "commitment to surface" and pure presentation.[40]

However, the aesthetic tempering of the flat surface of Sun Deng's consciousness does not fall into the typical postmodern condition of the superficial. The post-June Fourth Chinese avant-garde face the dilemma of eclipsing the monumental moment on the square without trivializing it. In so doing, they run the risk of flirting with an obscenity. The dilemma creates more lacunae and longer silences in the text. These evoke the haunting presence of a second coming of the political and philosophical in art and literature. The necessary second coming looms as the most tragic and ironic moment for the radical purists, mostly the experimentalists themselves, who had, just prior to June 4, 1989, declared that literature serves neither politics nor philosophy.

The temptation to meet meaning halfway must be tremendous. Ge Fei voices this temptation as soon as he chooses to retell a story set during the Wei-Jin period. How could a writer reinvest a historical motif like Ruan Ji and Sun Deng's meaningful encounter, which presupposes the meaning of their recluse personae in an overtly historical context, without disclosing his willful intent to tame the master narrative of the particular epoch within which the motif is deeply encoded?

The quandary deepens when we seek in vain for traces of the master narrative in the story. The epoch itself is completely left out of Ge Fei's narrative. Without ever making a single comment in "Whistling" on the specific cultural and historical background of the Wei-Jin era, the writer turns Ruan Ji and Sun Deng into fictional characters of the author's own contemporaneity. The portrait of Sun Deng verges suspiciously on caricature. But even an argument suggesting that the text is a parody of Wei-Jin's metaphysical self-absorption and the high-minded iconoclasts who paraded it about cannot stand. This is not merely because Ge Fei has never shown any satirical impulse in his writing career but, more importantly, because he does not need such a heavy-handed device. All he must do to bring into relief manifold innuendoes, political and metaphysical, is repress the master narrative of the epoch in question. In the irreconcilable gap between the contemporaneity of Ge Fei's characters and the historicity of their repressed origin, one locates the Chinese experimentalists' response to the postmodern call for historical amnesia.

History as a text is always susceptible to radical alteration and reinterpretation. Li Peng and his Communist historians practiced this well. So do the experimentalists. This strange complicity between the two opposing groups of agents tells us much about their shared disrespect for the authority of the original (that is, what is being altered). In practice, of course, the former argue for, and the latter mock the truth value of their rewritten texts. But it is the experimentalists who really fear and feel the pain of this rupture with history. Their resistance to the enclosures of history is often paradoxically accompanied by an imaginary trip back into history, even though Ge Fei's narrator in "Yelang zhi xing" (The journey to Yelang) confesses to us openly that the journey is itself "a mistake." Yelang, the ancient city in Guizhou province that he visits in order to experience historicity and thus valorize its legendary character, is, in fact, simultaneously "receding from the ambience of the ancient texts and from my imagination."[41]

In some of Ge Fei's works, and especially in Yu Hua's "1986," the violent rupture of the historical past and the present produces a traumatic effect on the memory of fictional characters. The resulting amnesia is an open sore over which the experimentalists spread different ointments. Yu Hua's lunatic exposes his wounds playfully and gleefully to those who are perhaps even more forgetful than he. Amnesia instantly becomes a physical malady, a showcase of bodily dissemination, eventually even a celebratory carnival. Ge Fei's melancholy narrators search for the elusive point of contact between amnesia and remembrance. With the exception of Sun Deng in "Whistling," Ge Fei invests his faith in the narrator's act of self-narration. He uses it to relieve the pain of a break wrought by enormous force and artifice.

The artificial flavor of such a rupture is perhaps what the experimentalists are striving for, after all. But the concept of rupture alone cannot really help our repositioning of the school in the literary history of post-Mao China. It is just as inconceivable to envision a Chinese version of European modernism without a dose of classical Chinese sentimentality as to imagine an indigenous postmodernism without the contemporary Chinese lingering obsession with the modernist fixation on the issue of identity, personal or historical. Although there may be some ground for us to suggest that the "great leap" mentality justifies the simple logic of rupture and hence the imposition of the label "postmodernist" on the experimentalists, we have to recognize the continuity of their obsession with the modernist problematic of the subject. On the one hand, the experimentalists' text rehearses the disseminating process of its own generic and cultural identity; it imagines its own ignominious fall from the grace of modernism while attempting at every turn to repress even the minimal impression of history on its subversion of meaning. On the other hand, a closer look at such a text reveals the futility of its postmodernist rehearsals to conjure away the issue of identity and history.

For Chinese intellectuals engaged in the modernist philosophy of the subject, it is difficult to appreciate the immediate relevance of the Wei-Jin period to the Chinese experimentalists. In the microscopic framework of the *xuanxue* ontology, the human subject roams in the path of a million changes as an aesthetic self (*qingyi wo*)[42] who not only empathizes with but also "changes in accordance with the law of a million changes."[43] The Wei-Jin emphasis on *caixing*, "the essence of the aesthetic subject," albeit a substance subjugated to the omnipresent subjectivity of the Dao, presents itself as an intriguing footnote on the subtext of the entire Chinese experimentalist movement. Its adherents have consciously sanctioned the autonomy of the "language-using subject," which is their contemporary counterpart to the Wei-Jin period's aesthetic subject. The term "language-using subject" emerged only in the latter half of the 1980s at the expense of the "moral self" and the "cognitive self."

But can one envision an aesthetic or linguistic subject that remains autonomous at all costs? This is the question that should plague the experimentalists with more urgency and ambivalence after 1989. And the answer to this question is no longer as forthcoming as it was in 1987 and 1988. The writer's involuntary posing of this question and his awareness of the impossibility of finding an answer to it form the eventual riddle and interest of "Whistling." Ge Fei's unresolved motivation of evoking and repressing the allusion to the Wei-Jin era, together with the sheer illusory nature of even an imaginary resolution of the riddle, constitute the aesthetic, philosophical, and political subtext of the tale.

YU HUA, GE FEI, SUBJECTIVITY, AND BODY MUTILATION

Despite its elusive affair with the problematic of historical memory, "Whistling" is, after all, a story that departs quite radically from Ge Fei's earlier works. The lengthy discussion above has left aside one central is-

sue that haunted the writer's earlier experiments. This is the issue of subjectivity. The issue serves as a useful yardstick to determine whether the
Chinese experimentalists have transcended the holistic concept of the
modernist subject, as some critics have proclaimed. What comes to mind
immediately are moments of violence that accompany the dissection of
female and male bodies in Yu Hua and Ge Fei's fiction.

Woman has indeed fallen victim to the experimentalists' exploitation
of fresh desires. She always dies twice. First comes a death of the soul in
her doomed encounter with a man in search of his own subjectivity, which
is equated with sexual potency in the Freudian obsessions of the post-
Mao era and, even more specifically, with the volcanic agitation of his
testosterone. Second, she dies a violent death from her sensual body after it is consumed by his desire. She is either raped as in "Fengqin" (Organ), disemboweled for adultery ("The Lost Ferry"), or violated and
strangled for her beauty and then dissected for no purpose as in "Zhuiyi
Wuyou xian-sheng" (In memory of Mr. Wuyou). It is the highest melo-
drama that the male narrator's reconstruction of his own subjectivity in
Ge Fei's fiction must take place against the backdrop of the dissolution
of the female object. It is always the man who remembers, and through
remembrance slowly recovers and remaps his own subject-position. The
woman on several occasions is a mute listener who serves as a catalyst to
the male speaker's recollection, a neutral appearance who has no personal
history, hence a dull voice which can only repeat, "I don't remember what
happened in the past. Recollection is a glass of poisonous wine."[44] On
other occasions, she is a debilitated mother overwhelmed by her son's
masculine image and manly rage ("The Lost Ferry" and "New Year"),
or a garrulous chatterbox whose "memory has gone bad."[45] Women,
young and old, serve Ge Fei only as containers of the phallus and mirrors
of man's search for his own masculine center. It is still the arduous construction of the male subjectivity rather than the halfhearted deconstruction of female bodies that defines the central task of Ge Fei's narrator.

A violently dismembered male body is a rare spectacle in experimentalist literature. The appearance of such a sensational spectacle in Yu
Hua's stories is shocking even for those who can appreciate the philosophy that underlies such savage imagery. As one critic put it, young contemporary Chinese writers have a penchant for sacrilegious practices.[46]
For Yu Hua, unmotivated violence is only blasphemy of a secondary order. What could be more impious than breaking down, with sensual
abandon and in nonsensical style, a holistic subject that theoreticians
and modernist writers in the post-Mao era have just assembled? And

what could be a more dramatic rupture with the generation that pre-
ceded his own than sentencing this mythologized subject to death? And
to go a step further, not only is the subject doomed to die and suffer the
most violent death, but he is denied his funeral. The true humiliation
comes when Yu Hua decides that the noble semblance of the subject
should be shattered to pieces, as happens to Shan'gang in "One Kind
of Reality."

Yu Hua's pranks against the humanism the older generation of writers has held so dear do not end at the autopsy table, although a quick
glance at the process of how Shan'gang's body is savagely dissected delivers such an impression. What is intriguing is not even the lackadaisical manner in which the narrator describes the lengthy process of how
Shan'gang's skin, bowels, lungs, bones, and heart are divided among a
team of apathetic doctors. What is most interesting is the final piece of
information: the testicles are the last to go. Last, but certainly not least.
We have immediately to wonder why even the most thoroughly subversive writer remains so susceptible to the mental trap set by male sentimentality about his masculinity. This impression is strengthened when
the narrator informs us that Shan'gang's reproductive organs were successfully transplanted (while many of his other organs failed to survive
transplantation) into a young patient who immediately impregnates his
wife and is blessed with a son.[47]

This episode leads us to question whether Yu Hua is reaffirming rather
than disseminating the subject. The Chinese paternal myth that "only a
male heir carries on the family line" places such an onerous emotional
burden on the Chinese men and women that it is almost impossible not
to view this episode in light of the author's unconscious celebration of
the ultimate potency of the male organs. In this context, it is natural
to arrive at the following conclusion: Death is turned into a joke, and
Shan'gang undergoes the entire bloody process of dissection in vain. The
dead arises anew and whole from the mess of his scattered parts in the
image of a son. The logic of dissemination collapses at the very moment
when the testicles themselves become a subject.

But Yu Hua may not be so vulnerable after all to those sacred Chinese myths, the five human bonds (*wulun*) among them, which he sets
out to tear apart in "One Kind of Reality" with such surgical precision
and aplomb. The episode in question could invite speculations of a completely different order if we were to insist on drawing a distinction between the symbolism of the phallus and that of the testicles. Once this
distinction is made, the satirical impulse of the tale becomes transpar-

ent.[48] The phallus itself has become a sanctified subject in contemporary Chinese modernist art, films, and literature. Its subjectivity is defined by pleasure-seeking, not the reproductive principle. The Chinese modernists have indeed gone quite a distance when they make the outrageous statement that copulation is fun. And what could be a better postmodernist prank than carrying on the subversion of the notion of reproduction by announcing that the serious business of reproducing the heir can be achieved with testosterone alone, something purely hormonal, without the blessing of what the phallus stands for? The celebration of the testicles in this light is nothing less than the denigration of the subject-position of the phallus.

One can surely argue that the son here reveals himself as nothing more than a simulacrum, a copy without the original, and so without meaning. What is at issue is hardly the autonomy of the sexual self, a political statement that Chinese modernists love to make over and over again, but rather the paring down, so to speak, of the symbolic stature of the sexual self to a pair of testicles. With one bold stroke, Yu Hua attempts to subvert both of Chinese modernism's most sacred and beloved practices: the fetishism of subjectivity and the fetishism of sexuality. The potency of Shan'gang's testicles in the absence of the phallic symbol is thus simply a joke. The tale sneers at the meaning of totality when it entertains the reader by making her witness the pretentious subversion of the initial subject turn into a tall tale of his meaningless rebirth.

Yu Hua bears testimony to my earlier observation that the "totality" of the Chinese postmodernist vision is part of the leaping forward mythology that Chinese critics at home and abroad have so earnestly constructed. As mentioned earlier, with the exception of "Whistling," Ge Fei's fictional world is built on his narrator's capacity to rearrange his subject-position through the reactivation and retention of his memory. Whereas Ge Fei suggests that the post-Mao epochal fascination with the ontology of the subject will probably linger for a little while longer, Yu Hua demonstrates just the opposite. Meanwhile, the disappearance of the sense of history so often featured in the postmodernisms of Western postindustrial societies may take a different course in China. It may simply become, in the hands of potential Chinese "postmodernists," another reminder of the repressed configuration of historical amnesia. The perpetual presence of Sun Deng in "Whistling" and Yu Hua's protagonists in "One Kind of Reality" may be less a postmodern spectacle and more a simple fictional reflection of the natural human condition under a totalitarian regime that willfully obliterates the historical past.

The generic lesson taught by the experimentalists can perhaps be captured in a simple statement: It is futile to stamp Ge Fei and Yu Hua with
the epochal marker of postmodernism. Whether some of their subversive gestures could be labeled postmodernist matters only to those who
are imprisoned within the Chinese leaping forward mentality. What really matters is how to retrieve the set of issues that remain buried in the
fight over the naming ritual.

This brings us back to the presupposition about Chinese postmodernism—a contradictory mirage that is, in Marilyn Young's words,
"simply the latest version of the sinification versus westernization
pseudobinary."[49] I propose that we view the glamorous proposal of a
postmodernism with Chinese characteristics as nothing more than the
critics' misunderstanding of a narrative strategy deployed by China's
youngest generation of writers for specific ends relevant only to the
Chinese context—a belated rebellion against textual repression, a radicalism that by itself is inadvertently an ideological act. The repression at
issue is less political than epistemological, an end result of the consecration in the 1980s of the metanarrative of humanist philosophy that
has reconstituted a symmetrically centered and thus, once again, repressive male subjectivity. No less reifying than the earlier model of proletarian hero to the experimentalists is the enclosing discourse of the
humanistic hero, mass-produced by the generation of root-searching
writers that immediately precedes their own. Keeping in mind the
specific nature of the textual politics of the experimental fiction, we
can proceed to deconstruct the pseudoproposition of Chinese postmodernism in such a way that it is neither meaningful to claim that it is
not postmodernist nor sufficient to assert that it is yet another version
of Western postmodernism in a Chinese frame.

Finally, one cannot resist the temptation to speculate on the political
implications of the experimental fiction. Ge Fei and Yu Hua's foregrounding of a radical linguistic subject may signify something quite different in the political context of post-Mao China (if we could for the
time being put aside the context of literary history). Their language is offensive to Marxist ideologists as well as to realist and modernist writers.
It is easy to forget that the experimentalists take great delight in offend-
ing the political regime even as they react against the aesthetic principles
of realism and modernism. To write about lovemaking, to celebrate sexual desire, and to revel in violence may amount to nothing more than
sensationalism in a Western commodified society. In China, it is a small
victory for freedom of expression.[50] It is a revolutionary way of writing,

not merely because it challenges an old aesthetics but also because it produces fresh desires. What are those desires? They range from writing poetry at the recollection of battlefield ruins, expressing the desire to die, and committing rape and sacrilege, thus wreaking a violent vengeance against the autocratic Chinese politics of discipline and abstinence.[51] The historical moment of the birth of a postmodernist vision in Chinese literature may be yet to come, given that the ruling elite's ironic blessing to Chinese reformers determined literature's necessary complicity in the capitalist mode of production.[52] The romanticism of June Fourth has receded all too fast into a short-lived historical memory. One can anticipate the renewed fervor of Chinese fashion brokers (of ideas and commodities alike) seeking to promote foreign novelties. Resistance, forged in the name of textual or political freedom, has already been relegated to the past. The lessons taught by the experimentalists will lose their resonance and relevance if accelerating growth of special economic zones and coastal cities ushers China prematurely into the age of postmodernity before the end of the twentieth century.

Amid all the hustle and bustle that a barefaced leap to a "free" global market has induced, it is too tempting to dismiss what Ge Fei's experiments delivered. Living in constant danger of making a statement alone may produce a bloom of the most exotic and local kind. How can one afford not to recognize that the survival of artistic vision may depend upon the rigor of intervention (both of a literary and of a political kind), since it is awareness of the haunting presence of such a blockade that compels writers to keep silence and yet to speak through lacunae? Chinese intellectuals have learned time and again that they pay a price for the utopian heroism of leaping forward. They have yet to be inspired by the dull image of Ge Fei's narrator waiting vigilantly to capture his memory as it flashes up at a moment of danger. It is not just any memory of the past he seeks, but that to which we ascribe "a horizon of unfulfilled expectations."

SEVEN

Wang Shuo

"Pop Goes the Culture?"

The age of innocence is gone. Some celebrate the demise of the 1980s. Others, mostly the cultural elite, are busy fighting among themselves to name the postapocalyptic new age. Has China entered the "post-new-era"? The inquiry threw theorists and critics into a fray that at least kicked up some dust in the off-season the once-popular literary establishment now has to endure. The emergence of the neologism, *houxin-shiqi* (post-new-era), is a relief to those who are more acutely aware than ever of the imperative to write post-Orientalist histories from native perspectives.

But perhaps China's cultural subjectivity is just an imagined stake in the new naming game. What we are greeting could be nothing more than a scenario in which Chinese cultural theorists have grown tired of the fruitless debate over an ever elusive Chinese postmodernism. (Need we remind ourselves that the life span of a literary and cultural controversy in post-Mao China rarely exceeds a year?) Yet whether I attribute the coining of the lackluster term "post-new-era" to the critics' high-minded postcolonial politics or to their characteristically impulsive pursuit and abandonment of one trend after another, the casting aside of the buzzword "postmodernity" in favor of a term that smacks of indigenous periodization is a cultural event in itself worthy of attention.

Although the promoters of this new scheme of periodization haggle over the specific trademarks of post-new-era literature, very few literary historians would disagree with me in singling Wang Shuo out as the most conspicuous and articulate epochal marker for the transition of the 1980s into the 1990s. Although some of his best known works were published around 1987 and 1988, the post-topian sensibility that emanated from *Wanzhu* (The masters of mischief) (1987) and *Wande jiushi xintiao* (What I am playing with is your heart beat) (1988) is unmistakably not a product of the 1980s—a decade designated as "the new era," reigned over by intellectuals, and marked by unrelieved humanistic sentiment and the will to de-alienate. In defying intellectualism and paying impious homage to alienation, our author has clearly eclipsed his own decade and overtaken the other almost by chance.

Wang Shuo's deviance from the zeitgeist of the 1980s cannot be captured in sheer thematic terms. He is the first specimen of a "marketized" literature that promotes "bestseller consciousness" (*changxiao yishi*) above all else.[1] It is this conscious appeal to the entertainment and commodity value of storytelling that marks Wang Shuo's distinct departure from the experimentalists, who might sound as playful and impious as Wang Shuo himself. The hooligan writer's profitable mockery of what the new era literature stood for—the experimentalists' high-minded cynicism included—makes untenable the proposition that we juxtapose the experimentalists and Wang Shuo as "two sides of a dialogic within Chinese (post)modernism."[2]

The manifestation of the "Wang Shuo phenomenon" is a street affair. Urbanites usurp the author's favorite catchword *wanr* (play) and greet each other with a halfhearted theatrical awareness: "What are you playing at lately?"[3] The street fashion industry cashed in on the trendy phenomenon; in 1992 Beijing witnessed swarms of discontented youths wearing the soon-to-be-banned "cultural T-shirts" on which were scribbled two large characters, *mei jingr* (depleted)—a pet phrase that Wang Shuo's heroes blurt out at the drop of a hat. Very soon, our author's joint venture into miniseries and film scriptwriting turned "Wang Shuo" into a household word. At the dawning of the 1990s, the "Wang Shuo phenomenon" swept over the nation and evolved into a catchphrase beyond the powers of any intellectual antipathy to rebuff.

A good look at Wang Shuo is therefore more than just another reading of a *houxinshiqi* celebrity writer. It promises a sketch of the brand-new era that survived the dystopian mood of 1989, an era now caught in a high-profile transition from the pristine 1980s into a caricature that vaunts the new cult of pleasure-seeking and foul play.

The story always begins with a turning point.

POST-NEW-ERA: EPOCHAL WARES

Four years after Tian'anmen Square, the Statue of Liberty has returned to China—as the logo for a popular American brand of ginseng tea.[4]

Urbanites found themselves singing snatches from the Little Red Book in karaoke bars.

"Consumption Is the Motivating Force for the Development of Production"—reads the headline of an editorial in *People's Daily*.[5]

Contrary to what critic Li Qingxi would fain believe, *houxinshiqi* may not be a misnomer, but a belated testimony to a historical turning point that has already materialized in China. It is likely that the neologism arose, as Li argues, from a strategic need of the enervated elite establishment to reclaim its waning authority in arbitrating China's cultural agenda.[6] But perhaps the term popped up at the bidding of the new era itself. With or without the blessing of intellectuals, the post-topian era undoubtedly came into being several years prior to the emergence of its formal appellation.[7]

The 1990s in China seems an age of Attitude. Mockeries reverberate. Verbal spews are street theater. It has become a national knack to satirize a society gone mad with consumerism while quietly going along with the greed. If one wants to understand the mores of the post-new-era, the popular "New Ditty on the Ten Kinds of People" delivers an insight or two.

> The first class of citizens are the cadres;
> > Young and old alike, they enjoy idle fortune.
> The second class of citizens are the entrepreneurs,
> > With their portable telephones tucked in their belts.
> The third class of citizens are the compradors,
> > Who help the foreigners make big bucks.
> The fourth class of citizens are the actors,
> > A wiggle of their butts earns them a thousand dollars.
> The fifth class of citizens are the lawyers,
> > Who gouge both defendants and plaintiffs.
> The sixth class of citizens are the surgeons;
> > They cut open your belly, then ask for a bribe.
> The seventh class of citizens are the peddlars;
> > In one night their pockets bulge with coins.
> The eighth class of citizens are the propagandists;
> > Every three or four days they gorge themselves at banquets.
> The ninth class of citizens are the teachers,
> > Whose tastebuds never experience any delicacies.
> The tenth class of citizens are workers, peasants, and soldiers;
> > They bend their backs and bust their asses,
> > learning from Lei Feng.[8]

This ditty contains all the spices required to make an epochal cuisine: wheeling and dealing, cellular phones (*dageda*), big bucks, official corruption, a downgrading of "knowledgeable elements," and a caricature of the model People's Liberation Army (PLA) soldier Lei Feng. In short, cadres, entrepreneurs, and burgeoning new classes such as lawyers rose to the occasion of Deng Xiaoping's 1992 southern excursion talks ("Let's be more audacious. Let's make faster strides!") by leaving behind the once-privileged Five Red Elements—workers, peasants, and soldiers. An overheated economic reform pushed the nation of merchants into a single activity—going into business.

The onslaught of this trading fever, the alleged third tide since the economic reform was launched, has enlisted some of China's most unlikely recruits: the PLA, child-care centers, elementary and middle schools, universities, and research institutes.[9] All of a sudden, the craze to make a second income has become both an obscene spectacle and a parody of the pragmatism of the once ideologically pure. University professors open up bicycle repair shops and take to the streets selling tea-eggs and steamed buns. Elementary school students are cajoled into buying popsicles from teachers who waive their homework assignments in return.[10] Lu Wenfu, the renowned author of *Meishijia* (The gourmet) (1983) and the vice-chairman of the Chinese National Association of Writers, took up the post of board director for a business corporation. Zhang Xianliang, the author of *Half of a Man Is a Woman*, is now managing two big enterprises. Even the PLA has turned itself into an enormous conglomerate with interests in everything from luxury hotels to pharmaceuticals.[11] This single-minded devotion to "revenue increase" is by no means unprecedented. In the 1960s, the nation rose with the same intense fanaticism to meet Chairman Mao's challenge to maximize the revolutionary inventories of the then Red China. "The most important thing is to participate." This motto has proved its popularity once more in the 1990s, when even intellectuals dip their nets in the salty waters of the sea of avarice. The term *xiahai* (cruising for profits) in showbiz, literally "going fishing on the sea," is now tied in wedlock to the once lofty name "literati." The post-new-era idiom *wenren xiahai* (literati angling a stream) has entered the Chinese dictionary of slang, bearing testimony to the elite's salute to the market economy.

WHERE HAVE THE GOOD OLD DAYS GONE?

Not all the intellectuals stood holding a reel and rod by the seashore, of course. Some reacted against the national mania for profiteering. Others deplored the decline of *Geisteswissenschaften* and witnessed in pain the disappearance of the individual in the face of media hegemony, and with it, the withering of the "serious arts and literature."[12] A few level-headed intellectuals neither panicked nor surrendered. Among them were Xu Jilin and Wang Ning, who attributed the vulgarization of culture to the ethos of commercial society—a spectacle to be anticipated rather than be alarmed by. Instead of reacting passively to the aggressive takeover by mass culture, the elite have one other alternative: taking the initiative of coming to terms with the inevitable bifurcation of culture that accompanied modernization by first and foremost readjusting their role in the post-new-era. Citing Zygmunt Bauman as a useful reference for Chinese intellegentsia at bay, one critic called attention to modern Western intellectuals' voluntary transformation from powerful modern cultural "legislators" to the mere "interpreters" of postmodern pluralistic culture.[13] In the 1990s the market certainly usurped the elite as the new legitimate maker of public opinions. In fact, one of the characteristics of modernization is said to be nothing other than "the erosion of the centered position of intellectuals."[14]

Strangely enough, the Party appeared concerned about the plight of their historical nemesis. On more than one occasion, CCP's Propaganda Department spoke of relieving the writers' sense of crisis in an almost sincere tone. Party spokespeople delivered their routine gobbledegook, which during the 1980s would have aggravated its recipients. Yet in the post-new-era, the officials' talk about initiating a "macroscopic adjustment and control of [China's] cultural market" to offset the principle of "economic efficacy" (the golden logic of mass consumption) sounded like beguiling music to those desperate literati who now saw potential governmental intervention as the last resort for the revival of elite culture.[15] Shall we cite this complicitous relationship between Chinese writers and the Party as a rebuttal of the simple Western formula that preaches the absolute antagonism between the two? Or shall we label this phenomenon another instance of the writers' historical amnesia? I say amnesia, for the historically "wounded" modern Chinese writers only need a little cynicism to predict that calls for greater regulation often play into the hands of a habitually censorious Party. It is no small wonder that the Bureau of the Arts and Literature took to heart its task of propagating once more such clichéd lessons as "We have to combine social and economic efficacy," "We have to link the task of building a cultural market with the construction of socialist spiritual civilization," and so on.[16]

The masterminds truly had a great fall. And despite all the wishful thinking, no task forces nor the Party's men can restore the privileged position of literature and the literati again. The educational and instructive function of the arts and literature has bitten the dust at long last. Forget about social efficacy. The 1990s is the Golden Age of Entertainment.

A quick glance at the wares displayed in street booths and privately owned (*getihu*) bookstores will indicate the average citizen's taste. Novels of swordsmen popular in Taiwan and Hong Kong dominated the market between 1985 and 1986; tear-jerking romances written by Taiwan's and Hong Kong's pop female writers Qiong Yao, San Mao, and Yi Shu intoxicated young readers in 1987; translations of foreign novels on sensual love, mystery and crime (D. H. Lawrence, Mishimura Toshiyuki, and Morimura Seiichi) emerged as hot commodities in 1988. The popular appetite for "spiritual opium" and "cultural garbage" grew more voracious in 1989 as soft and hard pornography, novels about violence, and divination handbooks flooded street corners.[17] Only those who are extremely naive would keep insisting that cultural fast food can never replace pure literature.[18]

As intellectuals faced the inevitable destiny of a retreat into the academy, a new cultural space opened up.[19] This is a space populated by rock music, karaoke bars, dance halls, stars and fans, TV soap operas and popular magazines, practitioners of *qigong,* and on its margin a transformed neorealism that no longer challenges or critiques social mores. Neorealist writers Liu Xihong and Chi Li heralded the literary elite's attempt to move the post-1989 culture of consensus in a new direction toward middlebrow literature. After a decade of expansive mood, the pendulum of Chinese neorealism had finally swung back to the latter term in each of the binary schemata: subversion versus containment, signifier versus signified, desire versus law, and aggression versus stability.[20]

On the surface, the post-new-era seems to witness the return of a national nostalgia for a traditional discourse characterized by ethical conformism, the search for meaning, and a congenial yearning for harmony.[21] The early 1990s' TV miniseries *Kewang* (Aspirations) and *Mama zai aiwo yici* (Mom, love me one more time) are symptomatic of such epochal sentimentality. Indeed, mass nostalgia did not stop at a retrospective look at prosaic familial culture. The reactivation of popular memories also brought back a fever that was laid to rest only a decade ago. Imagine the shock of Western democrats when a reproduction in 1991 of the famous revolutionary ode to Mao Zedong "The Red Sun" broke the record of a single videotape sale—5,800,000.[22] Yes, Mao Ze-

dong is back! He is a new deity, or a commodity, or a symbol of nationalism, depending upon who interprets the resurgence of Mao fever.

Nobody who has heard Cui Jian sing "Changzheng lushang de yao-
gun" (Rock 'n' roll on the Long March) has the heart to trivialize the
post-new-era, which is at least not as tepid and compromising as the
neorealists depict it in their works. The 1990s, after all, is a swarm of
contradictions: It sells environmentalism alongside conspicuous consumption, it ridicules Lei Feng while returning the icon of Mao Zedong
to the altar, it places the subdued vignettes of daily life and common humanity side by side with sensational gossip about the underground industries of prostitution, drugs, and gambling.[23] As Wang Shuo's heroes
will tell you with a sneer, this is not a tame era. Behind the spent utopianism lurks the beast in the jungle.

And yet many critics, Zhang Yiwu among them, argue that if there is
such a thing as the aesthetics of the post-new-era, it is constrained within
the limp and familial vista of plebeian culture (shimin wenhua). The literary terrain is, of course, as divided as ever, with veteran elite such as
Bei Cun, the last experimentalist, coexisting with writers such as Wang
Shuo, whose commercial instinct is as strong as his aesthetic one. And
yet the experimentalists are a dying species. And even Wang Shuo, who
has the ability to be quirky and subversive, can only upstage the neorealists for a short while. Wang may be good at honing his pop image
through the multimedia, but it is the neorealists, after all, who can
achieve a mainstream style by speaking to the general reading public.
Critics have reached a consensus by attributing the newborn artistic vision of neorealism to macroscopic changes in the cultural paradigm of
a society in transition. For many, the post-new-era cultural configuration found its mirror-image in a literature that is no longer obsessed with
the impetus for self-renewal, a trademark of the 1980s, but which now
defines its mission as laying bare the common folk's inclination to look
the same, to approve, and to succumb.[24]

But is the post-new-era itself as dull, devoid of metaphors, reconcilia-
tory, and predictable as its neorealist literary representation? What happens to the lures, thrills, and liberating sensations that consumer culture
delivers to the pop imaginary?

Wang Shuo's charm consists in his penchant for telling this other half
of the story—desire and transgression. He reminds us that the raw libido
that society's castaways release and put on exhibit, so repellent to the neorealists, has always been part of social reality. This is not Wang Shuo's
own fiction. In real life, the recessive adolescent energies of Chinese youth

find outlet in rock star worship, disco dancing, necking in dark corners of parks, and in other more insidious activities. And the common people frequent karaoke bars to indulge in self-expression. The post-new-era may throb with vocal and carnal desires and unspeakable obsessions, but it seems beneath the dignity of the bellelettrists (in their middlebrow disguise) to record the pulse of such a desublimated era. Or is neorealism's inadequacy simply a wish come true: Have literati finally struggled free from the orthodox creed of "art for life's sake" and reinvented realism by giving us an inverse image of what the real is like? In place of the reality of sensual gratification, they feed us imaginary moral asceticism.

Very few have bothered to examine the strange discrepancy between the polite and soft post-new-era literature of the neorealists and the dangerous zeitgeist of the age itself. Is it too embarrassing for the elite to acknowledge their own marginal voice? Or is the gap in question simply irrelevant to a hyperactive age in which hundreds of styles and norms bloom at the same time? Wang Shuo scored again as one of the few who sees through the disingenuity in the semblance of decent culture that some veteran elites staggered to put up. There is something profoundly deceitful about writing and reading a literature that reiterates a puritanical wish for the perfection of the human spirit and moral caliber while living in a time that thrives on hedonism and equates style with soul.[25] Wang Shuo's street gangs expose this duplicity by showing off the ultimate art of total abandon.

How do we then respond to the elitist formula that characterizes the plebeian mood of the 1990s as ordinary folks' quiet adjustments and their earnest search for equilibrium? To expose the illusory nature of this mental posture of a nation engaged in self-discipline, we need only to evoke the ready image of an unruly crowd wearing T-shirts emblazoned with Wang Shuoesque jeers, bumping and grinding to a rock 'n' roll beat. Not only do they echo deafening sound and fury, but the shifting ground beneath their feet sends mental balance to the winds. Neorealism's return to the real, much applauded by the critics, would appear to be nothing more than a sham. Never before has it departed more noticeably from a popular culture that seeks noisy pleasures and mocks self-restraint.

THE CULT OF "HOOLIGANISM"

"My writings are targeted specifically at one particular species— intellectuals. I can't put up with their sense of superiority and aristocratic sentiment. They think that common folks are all hooligans, only

they themselves are the conscience of society. Isn't this aggravating? . . .
I particularly want to attack this 'nobody else but me' mannerism."[26]
Indeed, what could be a better dig at intellectuals than our author's
favorite quip, "Don't you play the saint!" (*bie zhuang*). What could be
a better means of contesting such hypocrisy than creating a whole
species of hooligans who chuckle to themselves, "I am a hoodlum!
I am remarkably genuine!" But these snickering, shady characters are
not merely fictional constructs. Like Wang Shuo himself, the hooligans
(*pizi*), the "last proletarians" in the new society,[27] are by-products of
China's market economy. They make a living by swindling, drinking,
gambling, telling tall tales, and seducing women, small crimes that earn
them the title of "masters of mischief," but which are never serious
enough to turn them into outlaws.

Wang Shuo claims that it is the rise of this new species in the post-
new-era that invigorates an atrophied society suffering from an excessive exercise of the intellect. The hooligans live on one instinct—don't
ever mention "cause" or "mission"!—dumping everything associated
with high culture. Knowledge, justice, morality, and nobility are considered nothing more than the means of oppression that intellectuals invented to subjugate the people. In the process of deconstructing the high-
strung discourse of intellectuals, they create a vocal culture of small alley
talk and tall tales. Their verbal onslaught leaves the battlefield strewn
with mutilated eggheads, who die beneath the relentless whipping of our
hooligans' quick tongues and mere malicious gazes.

Wang Shuo's frank confessions about his repulsion from intellectuals
has earned him the epithet of the master "spurner of elite culture."[28]
However, it is hard to tell how much of the folk spirit that saturates
Wang's writings is truly representative of the "plebeian culture" whose
vision he is reported to champion. Perhaps the more important question
for us to ponder is, Who buys and reads Wang Shuo?

The answer should come as a shock even to the writer himself: intellectuals. It is indeed no small irony that Wang Shuo fandom was first
constructed by none other than those who were his designated enemies.
Who but the critics' guild hailed Wang Shuo the new literary genius?
Who but the authorities of film criticism designated 1988 the "Wang
Shuo year"? It is not surprising that Mu Gong categorized hooligan literature as the aristocratic genre written within the mental configuration
of plebeian culture.[29]

Who are the protagonists, after all, but a pack of riffraff who shoulder none of the burdens of material production? These are not just ordinary roughnecks, but a strange mutation of the low and high—the

dregs of society on the one hand, and the spiritual aristocrats among the populace on the other. Striding at leisure down the streets in boisterous company, they flaunt their fat wallets stuffed with ill-gotten gains with an air of complacency that befits the nouveau riche. Wang Shuo's much publicized exposure of China's enervated intelligentsia has given rise to the canonization of an upper crust of the lay population who turn out to be no common folk. All the critics who joined the "Love Wang Shuo" or "Hate Wang Shuo" campaigns have overlooked the invisible contract that our author made with the class he swore to demolish on paper. Theirs is a deeply dependent bond of reciprocal contempt and mutual sustenance. The public is merely promoting a myth by crowning our hooligan writer the spokesman of the Chinese People with a capital P. Wang Shuo is verbally committed only to intellectuals. The hooligans share his passion for the underclass. Ultimately, though, he is merely promiscuous in his love affair with commoners.

The all-consuming intellectual fervor over the "Wang Shuo phenomenon" has one more side effect. Since the real punch of the hooligans is their gift of turning things inside out, I wonder whether this punch meshes with the commercial success Wang Shuo has been enjoying, thanks to his educated readers, and the trendiness of hooligan style. Consumer society is forever appropriating antimainstream fads into the mainstream itself. Wang Shuo is not immune to this process of fetishization. How genuinely rebellious can his sociopathic personalities appear if their audiences are paying for their very act of subversion? In a society that is good at reproducing images, even the electrifying rebel can be turned into a robot for sale.

In the first few years of the 1990s, however, the danger of Wang Shuo reproducing himself, a fiasco that overtook him around 1993, was not yet a reality. No matter how many critics, both at home and abroad, would like to cite him as another casualty of the postmodern sensibility, his early and mid-career works are more than superficial kitsches that flood the Chinese market. Nor did his lackadaisical hooligans emerge as mere walking corpses who risk turning us into jaded readers. Every so often his heroes may blurt out something like "I am spent!" yet theirs is a restless crowd who would find neorealist Chi Li's story title "Either Hot or Cold Is Fine as Long as I Am Alive" an absolute bore.

THE HOOLIGAN CHRONICLE

Like their fictional counterparts, real-life hooligans had uneventful early careers. They were born at the end of the 1950s and early 1960s. Growing up during the lawless period of the Cultural Revolution, they picked up effortlessly a ruffian's character. Most of the hooligans, like Wang Shuo himself, went into the military in their late teens and retired from the service after a short sojourn. Not equipped with any professional expertise, they reemerged as unemployed youths roaming aimlessly in a swiftly changing urban China. Without money or aspirations, they went underground, drifting in and out of luxurious tourist hotels and restaurants, playing poker and pimping, networking with criminal circles, and talking the night away. The money came and went without a trace. Not even a beautiful and innocent Southern maiden—Northerner Wang Shuo has a predilection for women from the South—can soften their rough edges and bring them salvation.

Wang Shuo may have been exaggerating a bit when he told a reporter for the *New York Times Book Review* that "all the impetus for openness and reform comes from hooligans" for "they do business, build factories, and open shops."[30] It may be true that they have engaged in transactions large and small and mostly illegal—thanks to the opportunistic epochal spirit—yet the fortunes they have gathered have been scattered like leaves in the autumn wind without accumulating into real capital that could be recycled into the mechanisms of production. In fact, one can characterize the hooligan's lifestyle as unproductive and totally consumptive.

There is no denying that it was economic reform that opened up an existential space for the hooligans, who joined others fishing in troubled waters. But it was the Cultural Revolution that first apprenticed them to a lawless childhood. Reminiscing about fist fights and scuffles with rowdy elements when he was a teenager, Wang Shuo paid his tribute—which surely scandalized intellectuals—to Mao's revolutionary era, whose virtue, he claimed, consisted in its capacity to liberate children. "Even though the Cultural Revolution was wicked, it broke up the orderliness of everyday life and provided an opportunity for kids to develop their own personalities. It freed them from the bondage of the hackneyed school education. At any rate, we gain our knowledge from society only. In contrast to the real stuff, what we were taught in school is meaningless."[31] Reemerging into the new consumer age, the hooligans insisted on recreating their childhood playground in everyday life. The pure physical play, wedded to an attitude of lightheartedness, was turned into a narcissistic posture that appeared deceivingly seditious.

In a sense, though, the adult hooligans were not real rebels, for there was no purpose for their rebellion. It was just a lifestyle, decadent and cool. And don't take their inflated egotism to heart; behind the high-profile existence of those seemingly self-possessed playboys are empty husks.[32] Hooligans do not live as improvising individuals, only as a collective. A typical hooligan hero like Fang Yan in *What I Am Playing with Is Your Heart Beat* "always spends his time with a crowd, just like a fish who cannot survive without the water."[33] Deprived of their species consciousness, they are at a total loss. They eat, drink, act, and sin as a cluster. There is only a collaborative memory, not individual ones. Fang Yan may suffer amnesia and labor to retrieve from his shady past the physical image and identity of the woman whom he once loved, which sounds personal and confidential when he embarks on the quest and deludes us into believing that we trespass upon the private domain of an existential hero. Yet the blank slate of his personal history, upon which individual faces, both male and female, are all fused together in an obscure mass, is chalked with nothing but "a chain of vivid memories of [the gang] eating together."[34] Private space does not exist; life is never anything but one big woozy group activity from morning till night. Doesn't this sound like an old story—a contemporary variation of traditional Chinese clan-centered existence? Wang Shuo may have underestimated the infiltration of certain traditional values into his fictional world.

Is it any wonder that readers have a hard time distinguishing Wang Shuo's heroes from each other? Can we resist the question whether this kind of lifestyle is as fluid and free as it seems, or whether it is always already subjugated to a group agenda—like plotting a fictional murder for fun—from which, once committed, none of the lone hooligans can withdraw? The pledge of group loyalty is all. Our author's young urban fans who adored the improvisational beat of hooligan affairs may live in the biggest illusion of all. Wang Shuo's fiction may turn out to be a celebration of group bondage, not that of the solitary heretic! Or can one tell which is which in a linguistic game that confuses behavioral boundaries?

It may be a small solace to learn that although real-life individual hoodlums lived in a homogeneous identity, an examination of Wang Shuo's works reveals that the species consciousness of hooliganism itself underwent a slight adjustment in the late 1980s. The racketeers who earlier on dove unscrupulously into various lawbreaking adventures have finally exhausted their interest in making bucks and dough.[35] Looting no longer excites them. Cash bores them. They even feel nostalgic for the ineffable. "Standing in this yard immersed in the sunshine, I am seized with the strong feeling that I have lost something."[36] And to the shock of early converts, shedding tears in existential anguish—which was once a forbidden sin in their early career—even smacks of redemption to the hooligan who is denied access to a locked room that promises the revelation of "something hauntingly familiar."[37] This is the worst scenario of hooliganism: they are losing their instinct for fun and their grip on the carefree spirit. Worst of all, they are getting sentimental.

What is a hooligan when he no longer wears his heart on his sleeve? The ennui of a meaningless life catches up with him. Readers sense the burden of a weighty soul that pretends to be as flighty as usual. To continue the business of trifling with life, new games have to be invented. What is left for a tease has to be something more vulnerable and dangerous than mere norms and snobs.

The masters of mischief set their sights on caricaturing the notion of authenticity, and the gang in *Your Heart Beat* deride self-identity. We now enter the uncharted territory of a hooligan land where mindless charades are returned to a conceptual framework that produces the very meaning that it earlier sent into exile. Indeed, whether the hooligans are brainstorming about a murder that never took place or substituting real life with simulacra, they have acquired a persona that is outrageously elitist and interpretive.

The show goes on. The laughter sounds more hollow.

PHILOSOPHY À LA HOOLIGAN

If one believes in such a thing as the philosophy of late hooliganism, one is getting a step closer to appreciating Wang Shuo's appeal to the youngest generation of Chinese intellectuals. They alone can savor the humor of Wang Shuoesque deconstructionism while taking in the aesthetics of debauchery. As those once little hooligans slowly age in his fictional world, they become more sophisticated in their corruption. The time has arrived for those rascals to philosophize villainy and to deliver their speculations in metaphors.

There is something profoundly contradictory in seeing the masters of monkey business try their hand at cognitive games. If it was a routine practice for them to bedevil highbrows and lead ladies astray in the old days, it is certainly an inverse blasphemy to witness them now mock depth while reproducing it, play with abstractions, and worst of all, disassemble self-identities. All of a sudden, Wang Shuo himself dares take a crack at deconstructing concepts, the intellectuals' stock in trade. And the metaphysical game of decentering the subject—the gist of *Your Heart*

Beat—almost sounds as flashy and unforgivably privileged as the experimentalists' verbal maze!

It is a befuddling transition. Did the writer mature? Or did he betray his earlier vision? For there is no mistake that despite some familiar traces of playfulness, Wang Shuo's visceral depiction of the hooligan lifestyle in his earlier works is now being replaced by a quiet attention to the construction of philosophic intention in his two best known works, *The Master of Mischief* and *What I Am Playing with Is Your Heart Beat.*

Ma Qing, Yu Guan, and Yang Zhong—the three fall guys in *The Masters of Mischief*—begin to lose their cool as their surreal enterprise, "Three T Company" (troubleshooting, tedium relief, and taking the blame), turns into real labor. Yang Zhong is struck in an unwanted platonic affair with a woman whom he was hired to date as a surrogate lover; Ma Qing, in the guise of a surrogate husband, reluctantly bears the verbal abuse of a frustrated young wife; and Yu Guan, despite his good professional intentions, is appalled by a burly client who demands that Yu do him the service of accepting blows on the ear. As male and female patrons visit them with one ludicrous demand after another, the three "service men" get caught in the rules of their own game.

The cool gesture of selling a substitute reality backfires. Yu Guan, the mastermind behind the "Three T Company," barely pulls through the mock ceremony of a fake book award for a vain customer. For a rare moment, the hooligan, "staring listlessly into the space in front of him" while stumbling through one embarrassing ad-lib after another, is almost done in by the phoniness of the gang's own charlatanism.[38] What is most mortifying is that it's not even fun! The assignments get accomplished without gusto. The hooligans emerge as ordinary salarymen who toil for a job that they no longer believe in. Mountebanks or clowns?

The lampooning of a disingenuous world unexpectedly defeats the lampooner. In the end, it is not clear whether they are masters of mischief or simply overzealous martyrs of an insane epoch. With an ironic twist, the now aging hooligans acquire the aura of deconstructive philosophers who, by dumping the real into a trash can, are immediately filled with desire for sterling authenticity—an embarrassing call for the return of lost innocence.

Could all this be true? The cerebral redefinition of the hooligan vision is focused on nothing other than what used to repel "those rebels without cause": a vague yearning for genuineness. Deconstruction is given a purpose, an un-Wang Shuoesque configuration. "What is left after [the hooligans] discard nobility, negate faith, mock ideals, and destroy social order and moral criteria?" asks one critic.[39] The unexpected answer—a returned longing for the pure and the simple that was deconstructed—saves the hooligans like Yu Guan from a complete bankruptcy of human purpose, but in so doing, throws Wang Shuo back into the quest for meaning he once scorned with such charm.

The novella offers us more than one glimpse of the imagined paradise recaptured, if only for a fleeting instant. This benign vista provides no panoramic view of redemption. It is a simple oasis in the desert, a humble refuge for those constantly on the run. In fact, should it surprise anyone that the hooligans' haven and heaven is found nowhere else but in the surrogate home, a small tamed space furnished by a kind mother and a gentle daughter? Ding Xiaolu and her elderly parent (described as a "well-educated," "tranquil," and "dignified" old lady) provide the restless, wandering gang the simple comfort of dumplings and a nightly shelter now and then. This haven subtly echoes the theme of the surrogate that underlies the entire novella. It is a masterstroke to juxtapose the nominal "Three T Company" and its symbolic foil—a surrogate family piously practicing the same professional ethic of "tender loving care" preached by the company. It is obvious that a surrogate in name cannot hold a candle to the surrogate in substance. What Ding Xiaolu and her mother offer the hooligans is not merely a simulacrum of "home sweet home." The real hearth resides in the heart. This final message of the novella—sentimental to the utmost—should astound most Chinese critics who treat *The Masters of Mischief* as a typical parody of genuineness.

It is only natural that the few episodes of gallantry and moments of benevolence should unfold within the unpretentious fictional space of the Ding residence. There is a kind of calm generosity emanating from the gentle Ding Xiaolu that never fails to disarm Yu Guan and subdue even the implacable Yang Zhong. At a moment of such tender subjugation, we witness the untamed Yang Zhong turn into a courteous gentleman who "shakes [Xiaolu's] hand shyly."[40] As if embarrassed, Wang Shuo takes care to ensure that the hooligans' encounter with such tenderness and genuine human concern is almost inaudible.

> "Did you fall asleep for a little while?" Ding Xiaolu whispered.
>
> "Yes, I did," Yu Guan whispered back. "How come you got up so early?"
>
> "I have to go work today. Can't always stay away from work. Do you want to eat something? There is milk out there."
>
> "Your kitty drank the milk."
>
> "Really, that damn greedy cat." Xiaolu smiled. "Can I make you something?"

"Oh no, don't bother. I don't feel like eating. It's fine if I don't eat break-fast. It's not indispensable."

"Your life is too irregular. It's not good for your health."

"I don't want to live to a hundred anyway. I don't care if it's healthy or not."

"Yu Guan, if there is anything . . . Well, I won't say it. I know that you won't ever need my help. I just want to say this, come whenever you want to."

"I know." Yu Guan looked into her eyes and then took his leave. (39)

Such simple friendship and innocent concern can mollify even the rawest spirit. And yet Yu Guan is no ordinary knave to begin with.

Is a cultured hooligan an oxymoron? But there is no mistake that a few of Wang Shuo's middle-aged hooligans have grown into the roles of brainy and melancholy wise men. Thus we find a meditative Yu Guan subverting the pedantry of Professor Zhao—a pundit cast as a despica-ble hypocrite—in this philosophical dialogue:

[YU:]	"You are saying that we suffered pain in our heart?"
[ZHAO:]	"It is obvious, of course. Even if you didn't confess, I could feel it."
[YU:]	"But what if we don't feel pain?"
[ZHAO:]	"It's impossible—it's illogical. You should feel pain. Why not? You can only be saved if you suffer."
[YU:]	"Then let me tell you, sir. We don't feel any pain."
[ZHAO:]	"Really?"
[YU:]	"Surely."
[ZHAO:]	"Then you simply made me feel sad for you. It only reveals to me the extreme degree of your numbness. This is not resurrection but a downfall! You should cry for yourselves."
[YU:]	"But we don't ever cry. We are having a great time."(50)

"Having a great time"? This halfhearted assertion hardly fools the reader. We know that on more than one occasion, Yu Guan and his gang are not having fun. If all that Professor Zhao can brag about is his ema-ciated intellect, the hooligans have little to brag about either. The hilari-ous triumph of the hooligans over intellectuals in the good old days is turned into a Pyrrhic victory in *The Masters of Mischief.*

Deflated hooliganism leads to an aborted antihumanism—there is no denying that the novella delivers fragmentary instances of humanity. Ding Xiaolu's surrogate family aside, the hooligans themselves have tum-bled into an occasional mental and emotional zone that unfolds, for their eyes only, epiphanies of the most worldly kind. The revelation may come as an exhausted Yu Guan witnesses young men and women indulging themselves in a drinking carnival. In a moment of ecstasy, he declares: "God! Chinese folk are truly the best people on earth. They surely don't have many luxurious demands on their minds" (36). The simple and earthy happiness of the crowd, trivial as it may appear, brings profound relief to a tortuously impious soul.

Or the occasion may arise while the heathen is striking another professional pose as a stand-in. All of a sudden, the gate of heaven opens up. A moment of inexplicable fragility dawns on him: Yu Guan turns the paid job of comforting a jilted woman into a real encounter with compassion.

> [YU:]   "I genuinely try to make you feel better. You feel a little pained, don't you?"
> [WOMAN:]   "How can I not feel the pain?"
> [YU:]   "Do not suffer."(46)

Those are redeeming moments of truth in *The Masters of Mischief*. Yet are they simple slips of the pen, or are they signs of an iconoclastic writer seeking reconciliation with the world? Regardless of Wang Shuo's intentions, his dispirited antiheroism can be overtaken by the hooligans' genuine understanding of human happiness and suffering. It is an ephemeral thing, to be sure. But a hooligan literature that reaches such depth of humanity is no mere soapy pop stuff.

There is plenty of room, in fact, to argue that *The Masters of Mischief* is a miniature specimen of the intellectual game of "spiritual wanderers"—known otherwise as our brash dollar-starved hooligans in their earlier incarnations. Nor is the challenge a visceral one any longer. "I dare to waste myself. Do you dare do it?"[41] Such daredevilry soon sounds formulaic and insipid to a writer whose mission in life is to outwit his intellectual nemeses in a perpetual duel. Next enters a query à la existentialism (should we be surprised at his attempt at high culture?): "Who am I after all?"—a spiritual pursuit in which Wang Shuo will gain ultimate proficiency in his longer piece (arguably his masterpiece), *What I Am Playing with Is Your Heart Beat*.

The novel continues the quest that the author began in *The Masters of Mischief*—an inarticulate authorial intention to retrieve the last remnants of meaning from a complete bankruptcy of human purpose. *Your Heart Beat* features a gang of hooligans who have exhausted every means of rejuvenating their jaded minds and oversexed bodies. In a licentious mood of absolute boredom, they cook up the fictional plot of a murder. One member volunteers to be the disappeared victim and another is nominated as the murderer without his own knowledge. The real intended players of the game are, however, neither the "murdered" nor the "murderer," but the rest of the gang who now revel in the prospect of prolonging and proliferating the fun by inventing endless subplots, implicating each other in earnest, camouflaging real targets with lookalikes, setting up blockades to a premature recovery of the "murderer's" memories ten years later, and mystifying a police force that is seriously engaged in the investigation of a case that was supposed to have taken place a decade ago.

Imagine the letdown of the main players when the supporting actor, the framed murderer Fang Yan, the only hooligan who is kept completely in the dark, usurps the place of his hosts. Not only does he take his part seriously, but the lone middle-aged hooligan also reverses his designated role from being an incriminated spectator to the protagonist of the show, actively participating in the unraveling of the mysterious murder. For the first time in his wasted life, Fang Yan feels the urge and challenge to act. Yet his memory fails him. He faces the daunting task of searching for his alibi—a woman with whom he was supposed to be deeply in love ten years ago, but whose face and name he now cannot remember.

This is an upgraded adult version of a Chinese children's game that the adolescent hooligans once played with zest, "Soldiers Catch Highwaymen." The rules of the game change little. The physical chase now evolves into a mental one. Yet the most important prop remains intact—the murder weapon, a sword with a tiny stain of blood on it.

There would be nothing exciting about *Your Heart Beat* if this were simply a novel about physical violence. But no real blood is spilled. The casualties are neither soldiers nor outlaws, but lost identities and memories. The scene of the crime is not any physical locale but a haunting blind spot in the mind. Wang Shuo is leading us into a completely different landscape of the hooligan underground, where deconstructed identities long to be recovered, and unbelievably, where lost love and innocence are mourned.

The detective story progresses amid the twists and turns of the hero's painstaking search for the woman for whom he once felt all-consuming passion. The texture of the entire novel resembles that of memory itself: hallucinatory, fragmentary, and scintillating. We are led from one mental labyrinth to another. First a house remembers the past and narrates its own history in a delirium—voices talking in the darkness, the mechanical sound of a woman dialing, a telephone ringing at night, the maddening sound of the howling wind, and the missing heroine sleeping behind a locked door.[42] Then an old photograph of the woman evokes disconnected pieces of a puzzle that can never be put back together—a small back alley, a dimly lit ice skating rink, a peal of tinkling laughter, a golden field of rapeseeds, the flashes of a camera's bulb, a trickle of rain, and the distant murmur of a woman's voice that seems to come from an adjacent window to the bedroom. "It seems . . . it seems," she repeats (218). Four women appear, disappear, and reemerge in and out of Fang Yan's disjunct life. Gradually merging into each other's images, they all turn into the woman whom our fugitive hero is tracking. The mystery may finally be resolved. But the subjunctive mood keeps the readers in suspense during the long mental chase. This is what it means to play with your heart beat: The excitement that comes from being suspended in midair. The thumping of the heart and the surging of blood. Ultimate bliss for those who live for the moment.

But this is not just another story about life on the run, no matter how wickedly fickle the title may sound. On the contrary, what is at stake in *Your Heart Beat* is everything that the hooligans' nomadic existence ostracized—identity, meaning, and love. The novel eventually has less to say about the venting of raw libido than about the emptiness and barrenness of the cool sexual fetish that the hooligans call life. Wang Shuo, of course, is too devilish to preach. In the end, he chickens out of the ontological dilemma that *Your Heart Beat* so breathtakingly presents to its hero and to all of us who have become his accomplices. When Fang Yan reaches his journey's end, he also gets closer and closer to the danger of recovering his lost memory. And the closer he approaches the truth of his life, the more uneasy his creator must feel. What happens after the reconstruction of his subjectivity is completed? What are the fictional alternatives left open for Wang Shuo at the end of the novel? Make Fang Yan confront the woman whom he once loved? He obviously cannot dump her twice. Nor can he reunite with a love that is passé. A lighthearted encounter won't do after the heavy-handed pursuit. A philosophical engagement with an old flame on the subject of passion is equally uncool. Where is the exit?

Your Heart Beat ends neither with a bang nor a whimper. Caught between his desire to blur the boundaries between surface and depth, philosophy and parody, Wang Shuo has no other alternative but to conclude his novel with the expedient device of "making fiction within fiction." The first-person protagonist merges suddenly into a third-person narrator who claims that he has just finished narrating one-third of a book that he has been reading on a train. Of course, he relinquishes the privilege of continuing the account for he now has lost the patience to finish reading the tedious volume.

And thus we learn that everything is fluid—the four women's identities and the protagonist's own, fiction and truth, and your heart beat and mine—a poststructuralist truism that Wang Shuo tells with exquisite taste and unrelieved seriousness. All this profundity is an accident at best, made possible by Wang Shuo's last act of cowardice. Not only does he willfully sidestep the author's task of giving us a responsible finale, but he stops short of delivering Fang Yan to his own ultimate reality where a dying Baishan, or Ling Yu, or perhaps both of them in one singular identity, are waiting for him to settle old scores on her deathbed. It is safer to make our hooligan live in everlasting flashbacks so that he may continue to imagine that life is chimerical and that all those women haunting him are but specters of the past. A face-to-face collision with the present is a greater risk than the writer and his hero can take. What if there is such a thing as honest feelings and plain humanity at the end of the tunnel? What is at stake if not hooliganism itself? Wang Shuo has a narrow escape from his most impassioned flirtation with meaning ever.

But braking at the final curve does not bring the hooligan crusade for the signified to a full stop in *Your Heart Beat*. Traces of philosophical intent are scattered along the meandering path that may lead to the Second Coming. Love is undoubtedly the one miraculous formula that unfailingly brings quick redemption, and with it, a purpose in life. Wang Shuo knows that only too well. The poisonous encounter between an evil vagrant and an innocent woman is a recurrent theme in his early fiction. Seduction may send the maiden to her grave early, but the hooligan pays the debt by living in guilt for the rest of his life.[43] In this conflict between good and evil, there is no real winner.

Your Heart Beat is subtler in its lament for the lost maidenhood of innocence. First of all, the female presence is more substantial than ever before. Quantitative strength brings about qualitative mutations. She no longer emerges as the weaker sex. Less sentimentally configured, she arises from the pool of tears as a versatile female hooligan who, for the first time, shares with her male counterparts a narrative space heavily inscribed in the code of masculinity. She participates in plotting the murder and prods her men to action at the first sight of their waning willpower. In short, she has outlived her own victim status and remodeled herself into an equal partner of male hooligans. These women—the poised Li Jiangyun comes to mind—excel in philosophical discourse and outplay male intelligence. It is Li who spells out for Fang Yan the metaphysical significance of his quest: "This is simply an excuse. Judging from the degree of your concern and enthusiasm about this case, I can tell that you do not simply want to prove your own innocence. More importantly, you crave to be more aware of who you are. You are so panic-stricken because, all of a sudden, you don't understand yourself. It seems that there is one piece missing. You cannot patch up your own image" (201).

This woman's interpretive power over Fang Yan is a metaphor for her fluent command of his life, past and present. Yes, she knew him inside and out for ten years as one of the many forgotten ghosts in his past. In retrospect, one of the ironic moments in *Your Heart Beat* is her first un-dramatic (re)appearance as a total stranger to our amnesiac hero. Even long before her identity is exposed, Li Jiangyun emerges from the very beginning of Fang Yan's quest as an uncontested authority on him. She holds the key to the interpretation of Fang Yan's personal history and is one of the four hooligans who give birth to the "heart beat" game—a fact unknown to us until the end of the novel.

So there she is, an old friend of Fang Yan's, but thanks to the lapse of his memory, reappearing convincingly as a new acquaintance whose friendship he is now eager to cultivate. Perhaps it is the sense of déjà vu that draws Fang Yan closer and closer to the mystifying persona she projects. The attraction between a man and a woman, which may lead our hero (and us) astray, soon outgrows its deceptive import as a mere di-verting and distracting subplot, for the aura enveloping Li Jiangyun is provocative of ineffable anxieties that transcend mere sexual catalysis. It is reminiscent of the magnetism of existential purport in which are hid-den the clues to Fang Yan's circuitous quest.

Your Heart Beat would be a boring account of a male hooligan's iden-tity quest without the timely insertion of Li Jiangyun and Fang Yan's long verbal exchanges that sustain the cognitive rhythm of the novel. Every dialogue they exchange and every appearance of hers stirs up tantaliz-ing memories that the bewildered hero tries to untangle. Under the spell of Li Jiangyun's irresistible power, Fang Yan is drawn a step at a time closer to the core of the mystique. She dominates him in a feminine style— quietly, unobtrusively, suggestively, half consciously and half uncon-sciously. Bewitching, omniscient, and compassionate all at once, like Fairy Disenchantment in the *Dream of the Red Chamber*, Li Jiangyun leads Fang Yan through the maze and turns page by page before him the book of his life. She takes him to revisit the House of Memory, which releases familiar images and sounds at night that a confounded Fang Yan fails to decipher. To tease his faltering memory even further, she delivers

Baishan—the woman he is searching for—right to his face. Yet once again she triumphs over Fang Yan, who fails to recognize the woman to whom he promised his heart ten years ago. Rarely has one seen a more manipulative and more omnipotent female character in Wang Shuo's fiction than this physically frail Li Jiangyun.

No relationship is devoid of the sexual politics of power. In the case of Li Jiangyun and Fang Yan, the copulation of the male and female hooligan takes place in the form of intellectual jousts during the day and erotic dreams at night. The formula of "boy seduces girl" is reversed here. She is the one who seduces him with her knowledge of his past. Her sparkling mind takes control.

On another occasion when she is restored to her old identity in the name of Liu Yan, the female hooligan sheds her philosopher's skin and dons the costume of a survivor, a rape victim who tells the heartstricken tales of how her teacher, her own father, and endless other scum violated and trashed her. Reduced to tears by such testimonials of innocence and cruelty, our hero Fang Yan is once more subjugated to the female power. Even as the incarnate of unrequited love, the woman triumphs over the mere signs of desire that each of her ruthless men stands for. *Your Heart Beat* is a work that comes closest to reckoning with a sentimentality that the earlier Wang Shuo repressed more successfully.

More than one critic has pointed out the Achilles heel of Wang Shuo's hooligans as none other than their vulnerability to pure, genuine love.[44] Whereas the young hooligans in Wang Shuo's earlier works—*Kongzhong xiaojie* (Air stewardess) and *Yiban shi huoyan, yiban shi haishui* (Half in flame, half in the sea) come to mind—degrade the redemptive potential of love because they fear losing their cool, *Your Heart Beat* stares such hypocrisy right in the face. A subtle and ambiguous critique of the emotionally insecure male hooligans can be found between the lines.

Ji Hongzhen once argued that Fang Yan's search for the lost memory of Baishan (or Ling Yu) serves as a metaphor for his nostalgia for a bygone cultural value.[45] The descriptive modifier "cultural" may be overstating the case. I name this value "genuineness"—an ethical rather than a cultural badge of honor. True love is but one manifestation of this old-fashioned principle that finds no refuge in the hooligan's dissolute world. Love's voluntary extinction is guaranteed. Baishan and Fang Yan's pure puppy love is doomed from the very start simply because there is no room for genuine love in the hooligans' code of behavior. To remain loyal to them, he has to let go of it. And they help him kiss it goodbye by giving her away as prey for a pack of lustful coyotes.

The hooligans sentence the death of romance in typical lighthearted licentiousness. And Fang Yan's complicity in the execution of his love is one of the bloodiest moments in the novel. The slow recovery of memory reaches a final climactic moment when everything repressed comes back to life in a sudden outburst of rich and palpable details. In one scene after another, the sequence of events is vividly reenacted in front of his (and our) eyes: the passionate involvement of the two lovers, their verbal commitment to each other, the gang drinking, gambling, and cynically debunking Fang Yan's emotional purity, his pained struggle to reassert his hooliganhood, and the vicious game in which he reluctantly participates—swapping partners in bed. Throughout the lackadaisical experiment, Fang Yan plays poker intensely while another hooligan brother tries his hand with Baishan in the next room. Neither Fang Yan nor the readers know for sure if the seduction really succeeds. But imagination itself does the fragile hooligan in. From that moment on, amnesia becomes his lifestyle. Fang Yan bids farewell to Baishan and all the memories associated with her. Ritualistically, he mortgages his soul to hooliganism for life.

Metaphorically, the loss of Fang Yan's memory of his beloved is none other than the loss of genuineness, his once tearful and potent innocence, and with it, the loss of that part of his life that he cannot afford to remember without being brought face-to-face with the hair-raising inhumanity of the very existence of the hooliganism he pledged to. To remember all this is an ordeal in itself—perhaps more fatal than the malady of amnesia itself. Can he ever survive the remembrance of things past? Wang Shuo evades this question in the end. Perhaps this is another reason why the author himself cannot afford to tie up all the loose ends in *Your Heart Beat*. There are too many tricky questions a seasoned reader cannot resist asking: Why did Fang Yan lose his memory in the first place? What will be at stake if he remembers? What is it that his blocked memory keeps from emerging? And finally, when his memory returns at long last, why does the moment of taking stock—a moment that he and we have been waiting for—never arrive? These are the inquiries that a metaphysical Wang Shuo begs us to raise, but from which he eventually cops out. What is he scared of? Could it be true that the message of the utter meaninglessness of such moral debauchery is too close to home to be comfortable even for an archcynic? Is it possible that an honest reckoning with all those questions will make us cast a suspicious eye at a lifestyle that he has thus far been preaching successfully?

As a "contemporary cultural fable,"[46] *What I Am Playing with Is Your Heart Beat* is in the end an eloquent rebuttal of the conventional argument that what Wang Shuo provides is fast-food literature that gratifies the palate, not the mind. It may be blasphemous at times, but it by no means unambiguously deconstructs the so-called high culture. His better works play with circular logic in Ji Hongzhen's terms: the desire to subvert the self, the desire to return to the subverted self, and the profound sense of loss at an aborted return.[47] It is time to reposition Wang Shuo where he belongs, between a declining elite and a burgeoning popular culture. Lacking a firm foothold in either culture, the "Wang Shuo phenomenon" that marks the transitional cultural logic at the dawning of the post-new-era will fade fast from the public memory. Future generations will remember him, first and foremost, as a mocker of the elite rather than as an unequivocal cultural populist at heart. Although Wang Shuo never gives up the chance to promote his pop identity—"What I am most interested in . . . is the faddish life style . . . violence and sex"—I suspect that his brazenness may be just a fiction meant to camouflage something that is embarrassingly personal.[48] As his fiction glides from boisterous humor to implied menace and finally to undisguised contempt for intellectuals, I cannot help asking: Is there any fun at all in stabbing someone who means nothing to you? Could it be, at the risk of insulting an author who seems too cool to have a heart, much less a bruised one, that Wang Shuo is merely trying to come to terms with an inferiority complex that derived from his being denied a college education in his wild late teens?

Whom does Wang Shuo succeed in entertaining but the elite themselves every time he goes slumming? His is a parasitic persona whose rise (and perhaps future downfall) is closely intertwined with the destiny of the intellectuals whose literary taste he commands and at times reproduces. Not even his near-total irreverence toward elitism can hide the fact that there are always ideological limits to the popular disrespect for old structures of intellectual authorities. I suggest, as Andrew Ross concluded in his study of American pop culture, that the history of intellectuals will continue to be written into that of popular culture. In the case of China, the history of the late 1980s and early 1990s is clearly crisscrossed by the "linked material power" of "elitism and anti-intellectualism," "vanguardism and populism," and "paternalism and delinquency."[49] Perhaps Chinese intellectuals have mourned prematurely the loss of their participatory legitimacy in the making of the post-new-era culture. And herein lies the true significance of the "Wang Shuo phenomenon": his is a genuine voice of a cultural eclecticism that taps the sources of "indignity" on the one hand and carries on a clandestine affair with hauteur on the other.

We can find no better landmark than Wang Shuo—a shadow and caricature of intellectuals—to draw the 1980s to an end. The decade has come to a full cycle, from the intellectuals' outrage against socialist alienation and their call for return to humanism to the consecration of the fetish of a new kind of antihumanism that Wang Shuo's hooliganism crystallizes.

Whereas in the early 1980s the intellectuals condemned the Party for having alienated the entire country from a liberal humanism, the common folk at the close of the decade resorted to "people power" to denounce high culture as alienating. The irony is too powerful even for Wang Shuo to address and contain. Elite culture, which is the vocation and insignia of the House of Intellects, now emerges for many as the very symbol and vehicle of social, if not socialist, alienation. It is the destiny of Chinese intellectuals to combat alienation twice, first as an ideological malaise, and second as the post-new-epochal reality that follows the deregulation of taste and caste. Indubitably, they won the first battle. Morally, intellectuals rarely suffered any defeat until the battle cries of popular culture beckoned them to surrender.

Like the colleagues associated with the post-1989 literary journal *Xueren* (Scholars), those who reckoned with the antagonism between elite culture and society have rejected the mob, escaped into the ivory tower, and for better or for worse, retreated into political apathy. For the first time in Chinese intellectual history, a tradition of alienation has taken its root in academic culture. In the decades to come, the ivory tower will stand as both a refuge and fortress for veteran Chinese elites. This scenario is not as humiliating as many may envision. Academia, after all, is where they belong. But the story has just begun. With centuries of the tradition of officialdom deeply ingrained in the intellectual culture, Chinese cultural elite are bound to resist the cozy professionalism that American academics embrace. It is still too early to predict in what participatory form high culture will return to greet the post-new-era. But one can be absolutely certain about one thing: This is a rare opportunity for Chinese intellectuals to practice the dream they have had for decades—to gain total independence from societal and political control.

For the time being, however, there is yet no great danger that Chinese intellectuals will look upon the cult of alienation as "a form of escape for the free intellectual from the essential facts of defeat and powerlessness" as C. Wright Mills proclaimed.[50] Powerless they truly are. But Chinese intellectuals endure their alienation from society by posing as wounded heroes. Alienation is hardly a ritual for them but a disgrace to be borne with tenacity. Today in China, the progressive atrophy of the intellectuals' cultural and political muscle has come to dominate the popular footage on the glistening screen of the post-new-era, thanks to Wang Shuo's effort to turn the negative image making of highbrows into a profitable industry. The intellectuals, on the other hand, are not going to unravel their Wang Shuo complex in the near future. Although there are still some who adamantly deny the dissociation of the social (everyday life) from the cultural (high culture) in rapidly changing China and who ponder the twin temptations of "total withdrawal" or "total reintegration," chances are that they are bashing Wang Shuo in public and reading Wang Shuo behind closed doors. All those rituals will only serve to perpetuate the "Wang Shuo phenomenon" for a few years longer.

Deng's China has come a long way since the controversy over socialist alienation in 1983. The intellectuals' dilemma in the 1990s only serves to remind us of the glory of elitism in which the first ten years of the Deng Xiaoping era basked. If this psychological chronicle of the history of the (re)ascension and downfall of China's literary and cultural elite has any final message to deliver to the subject and object of my investigation, the Chinese intellectuals themselves—it is none other than one they kept reiterating at the beginning of the 1980s: Because we are facing a cul-de-sac, we will create a miracle!

Notes

All translations are mine unless otherwise indicated.

INTRODUCTION

1. There had been fervent discussions, especially toward the latter half of 1986, about the difficulties of carrying out the formula of market economy due to the unsuccessful attempts of the economic sector to transform the old system of party supervision over the administration of factories. The call for political reform was seen in policy slogans such as "the division of Party and politics" (*dangzheng fen'gong*) and the "separation of corporate industry from politics" (*zhengqi fenkai*). A sample of such discussions can be found in Zhao Guoquan's "Fazhan shangping jingji mianling wuge fangmian maodun" (The development of commodity economy is facing five aspects of contradictions), *Renmin ribao,* 1 December 1986, overseas edition, 2.

2. Zhao Ziyang, "Yanzhe you Zhongguo tese de shehui zhuyi daolu qianjin" (Marching toward the path of socialism with Chinese characteristics), *Renmin ribao,* 4 November 1987, overseas edition. Emphasis is mine.

3. Carma Hinton and Richard Gordon's latest documentary, "The Gate of Heavenly Peace," critically examines the students' movement. It demonstrates how the more radical students prevailed over the moderate elements in insisting on not abandoning the square. The film quotes the influential leader Chai Ling as saying that "only when the square is awash with blood will the people of China open their eyes." See David Ansen, "Raise a Red Flag," *Newsweek,* Oct. 9 (1995), 75.

4. Paul Rabinow, introduction to *French Modern: Norms and Forms of the Social Environment* (Cambridge: MIT Press, 1989), 15.

5. Chen Pingyuan, Huang Ziping, and Qian Liqun, "Guanyu 'Ershi shiji Zhongguo wenxue' de duihua" (Dialogues on "Twentieth-century Chinese literature"), in *"Ershi shiji Zhongguo wenxue" sanren tan* (Beijing: Renmin wenxue chubanshe, 1988), 58, quoting Qian Liqun.

6. Zhang Yiwu, "Lun 'houwutuobang' huayu: Jiushi niandai Zhongguo wenxue de yizhong quxiang" (On the post-topian discourse: A tendency of Chinese literature of the 1990s), *Wenyi lilun* 6 (1993), 181–87.

7. The critique of anti-leftism, an increasingly important trend after the June Fourth crackdown, is primarily undertaken by mainland Chinese intellectuals who stayed in the U.S. and who maintained close affiliations with the humanities in the American academy. Those critics include graduate students in literature and history programs and cultural and literary critics in exile like Li Tuo. Li takes a much more complicated ideological position than his peers at Princeton who belong to the Princeton China Initiative, an exile group headed by Liu Binyan. Though he is critical of Maoism, Li is more interested in exploring than explaining away the ideological appeal of Maoism to Chinese intellectuals during the 1950s and 1960s. He attempts to reconstruct Maoism as a double discourse of anti-imperialism and modernization and is opposed to the standard practice of setting up an absolute antagonism between Mao's discourse and the discourse of modernity. See Li Tuo, "Ding Ling bu jiandan: Mao tizhi xia zhishi fenzi zai huayu shengchan zhong de fuza jiaose" (Ding Ling is not simple: The complicated role that intellectuals played in the production of discourse under the Maoist regime), *Jintian* 3 (1993), 236–40.

8. On "pan-ideologization," see Yin Hong, Luo Chengyan, and Kang Lin, "Xiandai wenxue yanjiu de disandai: Zouxiang chenggong yu mianling tiaozhan" (The third generation of modern Chinese literary studies: Marching toward success and facing challenges), *Wenxue pinglun* 5 (1989), 72. The three critics advocate "literature's return to its own subjectivity." If they are vague about the definition of such a self-sufficient domain, they are precise in their condemnation of literature's entrapment in ideology.

On the inaccessibility of literature to the people, see Ye Lihua, "Wenxue: 'shichanghua' de qianti yu lujing" (Literature: The premise and strategies of "marketization"), *Wenxue pinglun* 5 (1993), 15. For Ye Lihua, the literature's return to its "original nature" means the creation of literature that is not only accessible to the common people, but also prioritizes the function of entertainment.

On the intellectuals and enlightenment, see the symposium of "Dangdai zhishi fenzi de jiazhi guifan" (The values and norms of contemporary intellectuals), chaired by Chen Sihe. An article bearing the title of the symposium, transcribed by Zhang Xinying, appeared in *Shanghai wenxue* 7 (1993), 69, 70.

9. Wang Meng and Wang Gan, "Piruan? Huapo?" (Exhaustion? Decline?), *Zhongshan* 3 (1989), 159, quoting Wang Meng.

10. Zhang Xinying, "Dangdai zhishi fenzi de jiazhi guifan," 64, quoting Chen Sihe.

11. Li Zehou, "Ershi shiji Zhongguo wenyi yipie" (A glimpse at the twentieth-century Chinese literature), in *Zhongguo xiandai sixiang shilun* (Treatise on the history of modern Chinese thought) (Taibei: Fengyun shidai chuban gongsi, 1990), 330.

12. On the hedonism of the 1990s, see Zhang Jingchao, "Wenxue zhineng shi yizhong youxian de cunzai" (Literature can only be a limited existence), *Wenyi pinglun* 1 (1993), 22–28. Whereas most Chinese intellectuals condemn popular hedonism, Zhang characterizes it as a sign that shows the "considerable progress" that Chinese people have made in their way of living. Hedonism, according to him, signifies the new emphasis on individual lives and on the world of the "here and now" (24).

CHAPTER 1

1. One notable example is the Chinese students' enthusiastic endorsement of the government's bid for hosting the 2000 A.D. Olympic games in Beijing. In October 1993, on the eve of the Olympic Committee's final vote, thousands of college students in Beijing gathered at the Tian'anmen Square to render moral support to the government. According to the BBC reports, security forces were sent to forestall riots with the sole purpose of safeguarding the students. The sacrilegious implications of such a "demonstration" at the square will certainly ring loudly to those who remember the June Fourth Incident in 1989.

2. The slogan that "consumerism is the motivating force for the development of production" has become popular in the wake of Deng Xiaoping's talks given during his much publicized southern excursions in February 1992. See Zhou Guanwu, "Xiaofei shi fazhan shengchan de dongli" (Consumerism serves as the motivating force for the development of production), *Renmin ribao*, 7 June 1992, 2.

3. *Ren a ren* is the title of Dai Houying's novel originally published by Huacheng chubanshe at Guangzhou in 1980, reprinted by Xiangjiang Publishing Company in Hong Kong, 1985.

4. In the *Manuscripts,* Marx speaks of three kinds of alienation. Human beings are alienated from their work (a break between the individual and productive activity), from their own products (a break between the individual and the material world), and from other human beings (species alienation). Attributing alienation to the birth of private property in capitalist society, Marx believed that the total liberation of human beings could only take place at the complete elimination of private property. See *Karl Marx: Early Writings,* trans. Rodney Livingstone and Gregor Benton (New York: Vintage Books, 1975), 279–400.

5. Stuart Schram, *Ideology and Policy in China Since the Third Plenum,* 1978–84 (London: Contemporary China Institute, SOAS, University of London, 1984), 55.

6. See Schram, *Ideology,* 42–56. Also see Bill Brugger and David Kelly, *Chinese Marxism in the Post-Mao Era* (Stanford: Stanford University Press, 1990), 139–70; David Kelly, "The Emergence of Humanism: Wang Ruoshui and the Critique of Socialist Alienation," in *China's Intellectuals and the State: In Search of a New Relationship,* ed. Merle Goldman et al. (Cambridge: The Council on East Asian Studies at Harvard University, 1987), 159–82.

7. Zhou Yang's talk "Guanyu Makesi zhuyi de jige lilun wenti de tantao" (On the inquiry into several theoretical questions of Marxism) was published in *Renmin ribao,* 16 March 1983, with the help of Wang Ruoshui, who then served

as the deputy editor-in-chief of the newspaper. Even long before 1983, Zhou Yang, Mao Zedong's cultural czar of the 1950s, had shown remorse at his earlier views. In November 1979, he apologized at the Fourth Congress of Artists and Writers to those (Ding Ling and Liu Binyan among them) whom he had purged during the 1940s and 1950s. Hu Qiaomu's article, "Guanyu rendao zhuyi he yihua wenti" (With regard to the question of humanism and alienation) was originally published in *Renmin ribao*, 27 January 1984, 1–5; it was reprinted in *Wenyi lilun* 1 (1984), 57–72.

8. Chinese theorists emphasized that Marx dissociates himself from Hegel's belief that every objectification is necessarily an instance of alienation. Articles and books on the distinction between *duixianghua* and *yihua* were abundant during the debate. See Yang Shi, "Yihua yu duixianghua" (Alienation and objectification), in *Makesi zhuyi yu ren* (Marxism and human beings), ed. The Department of Philosophy of Beijing University (Beijing: Beijing University Press, 1983), 175–200; Liu Minzhong, "Makesi yihua lun chutan" (A preliminary inquiry into Marx's theory of alienation), in *Renxing rendao zhuyi wenti taolun ji* (A collection of essays on the problem of human nature and humanism), ed. the Research Institute of Philosophy of the Chinese Academy of the Social Sciences (Beijing: Renmin chubanshe, 1983), 366–82; and Feng Shen, trans., translator's preface to *Yihua yu laodong* (Alienation and labor), by I. S. Narsky (Changsha: Hunan renmin chubanshe, 1987), 8–10. Originally published as *Otchuzhdenie i trud: po stranitsam i proizvedenii* (Moscow: Izd. "Mysl," 1983).

Lukacs himself admitted in 1967 that the term "reification" is "neither socially nor conceptually identical to alienation." For Lefebvre and others, reification is only one of the manifestations of alienation, albeit the most radical one. See Ignace Feuerlicht, *Alienation: From the Past to the Future* (Westport, Conn.: Greenwood Press, 1978), 13.

9. Zhou Guoping and Jia Zelin, "Sulian zhexue zhong de ren he rendao zhuyi wenti" (The question of (hu)man and humanism in Soviet philosophy), in *Ren shi Makesi zhuyi de chufa dian* (Human beings are the starting point of Marxism), ed. The Editorial Committee of Renmin chubanshe (Beijing: Renmin chubanshe, 1981), 242.

10. Wang Ruoshui, "Tantan yihua wenti" (On the problem of alienation), *Xinwen zhanxian* (The battle front of news) 8 (August 1980), reprinted in *Wei rendao zhuyi bianhu* (In defense of humanism)(Beijing: Sanlian shudian, 1986), 186–99.

11. See Adam Schaff, "Makesi yihua lilun de gainian xitong" (The conceptual system of Marx's theory of alienation), *Zhexue yicong* 1 and 2 (1979); Schaff, "Yihua shi shehui wenti he zhexue wenti" (Alienation is a social problem and a philosophical question), *Zhexue yicong* 4 (1981); Schaff, "Yinggai yanjiu yihua lilun" (We ought to study the theory of alienation), *Zhexue yicong* 6 (1981). Also see Gajo Petrovic, "Lun yihua" (On alienation), *Zhexue yicong* 2 (1979).

12. Adam Schaff, *Marxismus und das menschliche Individuum* (Vienna: Europa-Verlag, 1965), 168–69, 178, 180, 254. Gajo Petrovic, "The Philosophical and Sociological Relevance of Marx's Concept of Alienation," in *Marx and the Western World*, ed. Nicholas Lobkowicz (Notre Dame, Ind.: University of Notre Dame Press, 1967), 152.

13. Adam Schaff, *Marxism and the Human Individual,* ed. Robert S. Cohen, based on a translation by Olgierd Wojtasiewicz (New York: McGraw-Hill Book Co., 1970), 108.

14. Ibid., 131, 135.

15. Ibid., 15.

16. Wang Ruoshui, "Tantan yihua wenti," 195.

17. Hu Qiaomu, "Guanyu rendao zhuyi he yihua wenti," *Wenyi lilun* 1 (1984), 70–71. Also see *Rendao zhuyi he yihua sanshi ti* (Thirty questions on humanism and alienation), ed. The Research Institute of Philosophy at the Shanghai Academy of the Social Sciences (Shanghai: Shanghai renmin chubanshe, 1984), 184. Hereafter, I will refer to *Rendao zhuyi he yihua sanshi ti* as *Sanshi ti.*

18. *Sanshi ti,* 196.

19. Schram reported a conversation with Deng Liqun (director of the Propaganda Department of the Party's Central Committee) in 1984. During the conversation, Deng accused Wang of "reasserting the theory of continuous revolution under the dictatorship of the proletariat." Deng went even further by proclaiming that Wang suggested that "a new Cultural Revolution was necessary to overturn the privileged caste of Party officials." See Schram, *Ideology,* 56.

20. Brugger and Kelly, *Chinese Marxism,* 145. Brugger and Kelly argue that although the leftists during the Cultural Revolution did not use the term "alienation," what they combated was something similar to what Wang Ruoshui proposed in his definition of "economical alienation."

21. Zhou Yang, "Guanyu Makesi zhuyi de jige lilun wenti de tantao," 4.

22. Brugger and Kelly, *Chinese Marxism,* 153.

23. *Sanshi ti,* 185–86.

24. Deng Liqun, "'Makesi zhuyi yu ren' xueshu taolunhui chuanda Deng Liqun jianghua: Taolun rendao zhuyi renxinglun henyou haochu" (Deng Liqun's talk at the symposium on "Marxism and human beings": The advantage of discussing humanism and the theory of humanity), originally published in *Renmin ribao,* 12 April 1983, 1; also in *Rendao zhuyi renxing lun yihua wenti yanjiu zhuanji* (Studies on humanism, theories of human nature, and the problem of alienation: A special collection of essays), ed. Center of Newspapers and Research Materials at People's University (Beijing: Renmin daxue, 1983), 5.

25. Albrecht Wellmer, *Critical Theory of Society,* trans. John Cumming (New York: Herder and Herder, 1971), 54.

26. On the fetishism of politics, see Gao Ertai, "Yihua xianxiang jinguan" (A recent observation of the phenomenon of alienation), in *Ren shi Makesi zhuyi de chufa dian,* 83. Gao elaborates upon the definition of the "fetishism of politics" and identifies it with "the fetishism of power." His definition of "political alienation" is innovative. He identifies all the obsequious and humiliating measures of securing one's political well-being during the revolutionary years as a kind of political labor that kept churning out political commodities—one's own soul, relatives, and friends—commodities that one sold for the exchange of political profits. Gao argues that it was power, not money, that served as the equivalent of Marx's exchange value during the fifties and sixties (88).

27. Wang Ruoshui, "Tantan yihua wenti," 196.

28. Ibid., 195.

29. Ibid., 197.

30. Ferenc Fehér and Agnes Heller, "Are There Prospects for Change in the U.S.S.R. and Eastern Europe?" *Praxis International* 5, no. 3 (1985), 323–32.

31. Iring Fetscher, "Hegel, the Young Marx, and Soviet Philosophy: A Reply to E. M. Sitnikov," appendix to *Marx and Marxism* (New York: Herder and Herder, 1971), 342.

32. Erica Sherover-Marcuse, *Emancipation and Consciousness: Dogmatic and Dialectical Perspectives in the Early Marx* (Oxford: Basil Blackwell, 1986), 122.

33. Schram, *Ideology*, 49.

34. Many important issues related to the contemporary critique of the classical production paradigm cannot be fully explored here. One of the most well-known cases is Jean Baudrillard's questioning of the adaptability of the Marxian concepts of labor and production to postindustrial society. The dominant social form of advanced capitalism, according to Baudrillard, is not the commodity, but the sign. His intellectual agenda was clearly defined as freeing the Marxist logic from the confining context of political economy. See his *The Mirror of Production*, trans. Mark Poster (St. Louis: Telos Press, 1975). I do not feel well equipped to plunge into the debate as to whether the category of work and labor should be rejected in the contemporary context. It is, however, important to note that the material basis for the automatic growth of capital has changed dramatically in an age when capital assumes total mobility. Disembodied capital—the nonmaterial perception of production—that took the form of transnational buying and selling seems to replace the old concept of capital that was closely tied to labor and production in a fixed locale. Exchange no longer takes place between capital and labor, but between capital and capital. What this new form of exchange entails is, of course, the changing locus and nature of labor if we do not want to subscribe to Baudrillard's radical thesis of the total disappearance of labor.

35. Sherover-Marcuse, *Emancipation*, 126.

36. On the initiating capacity of the subject, see Wang Ruoshui, "Wo dui rendao zhuyi wenti de kanfa" (My views on the issue of humanism), in *Wei rendao zhuyi bianhu*, 273. On human beings as the subject of praxis and history, see Zhou Guoping and Jia Zelin, "Sulian zhexue," 242, 261.

37. Wang Ruoshui, "Ren shi Makesi zhuyi de chufa dian" (Human beings are the starting point of Marxism), in *Wei rendao zhuyi bianhu*, 201. Also see Zhou Yang, "Guanyu Makesi zhuyi," 8.

38. E. M. Sitnikov, "A Soviet Critique of 'Western' Interpretations of Marx," appendix to *Marx and Marxism*, 320–21. "If the self-awareness of the proletariat is idolized, as Hegel idolized the self-awareness of men in general by imagining it in the form of the absolute spirit of the world, then the entire historical process is identified with the idolized self-awareness of the proletariat and moves spontaneously forward" (321).

39. Most Western political commentators such as Brugger, Kelly, and Schram are more critical of Hu Qiaomu than of Wang and Zhou. All three of them confirm the existence of the three specific forms of alienation delineated by Wang and Zhou in their essays. Brugger, for instance, thinks that the proposition of

socialist alienation is crucial to the working out of "a socialist telos which takes unalienated human nature as its goal" (150). See his "Alienation Revisited," *The Australian Journal of Chinese Affairs* 12 (1984), 143–51.

40. *Sanshi ti,* 186.

41. Hu Qiaomu, "Guanyu rendao zhuyi," 60.

42. Jürgen Habermas, "On the Obsolescence of the Production Paradigm," in *The Philosophical Discourse of Modernity: Twelve Lectures,* trans. Frederick Lawrence (Cambridge: MIT Press, 1987), 75–82. Ludwig Nagl, "Obsolescence of the Production Paradigm?" in *Alienation, Society, and the Individual: Continuity and Change in Theory and Research,* ed. Felix Geyer and Walter R. Heinz (New Brunswick: Transaction Publishers, 1992), 17.

43. Habermas, "On the Obsolescence," 81.

44. Nagl, "Obsolescence," 19.

45. Victor Zitta, *Georg Lukács' Marxism, Alienation, Dialectics, Revolution: A Study in Utopia and Ideology* (The Hague: Martinus Nijhoff, 1964), 150. Georg Lukács, *Geschichte und Klassenbewusstsein: Studien über Marxistische dialektik* (Berlin: Der Malik-Verlag, 1923), 184.

46. Huang Nansen, "Guanyu ren de ruogan lilun wenti" (On several theoretical questions regarding human beings), in *Makesi zhuyi yu ren* (Marxism and human beings), ed. The Department of Philosophy of Beijing University (Beijing: Beijing daxue chubanshe, 1983), 16, 15.

47. Brugger, "Alienation Revisited," 150.

48. I want to point out that both the revisionists and orthodox Marxists made the exclusive claim that there is only one single authentic Marx. For the former, what the young Marx propagated is the only true Marxism; for the latter, the only true Marxism is the scientific Marxism advocated by the mature Marx. The thesis of an integral Marxism was supported by those theorists who proposed the paradigm of socialist alienation.

49. See Zhao Fengqi, "Nansilafu zhexuejie guanyu ren he yihua wenti de yanjiu" (Studies on the problem of human beings and alienation in Yugoslavic philosophy), *Zhexue yanjiu* 1 (1981), 76–78. Also see Zhou Guoping and Jia Zelin, "Sulian zhexue," 241–89.

50. Ru Xin, director of the Philosophy Research Institute of the Chinese Academy of the Social Sciences, defends the historical continuity between the two Marxisms in his "Rendao zhuyi jiushi xiuzheng zhuyi ma? Dui rendao zhuyi de zairenshi" (Is humanism revisionism? Reacquainting with humanism), in *Renxing rendao zhuyi wenti taolun ji,* 25. But Ru Xin was forced to retract many of his earlier views after the campaign was launched against the humanists. His later antihumanist views are found in "Pipan zichan jieji rendao zhuyi, xuanchuan shehui zhuyi rendao zhuyi" (Criticize bourgeois humanism, promote socialist humanism) *Renmin ribao,* 9 January 1984, 5.

51. Zhao Fengqi, "Nansilafu zhexuejie guanyu ren he yihua wenti de yanjiu," 76–78.

52. Zhou Guoping and Jia Zelin, "Sulian zhexue," 266–67.

53. Wang Ruoshui, "Wei rendao zhuyi bianhu" (In defense of humanism), in *Wei rendao zhuyi bianhu,* 222.

54. Wang Ruoshui, "Ren shi Makesi zhuyi de chufa dian," 200.

55. In his essay on "Guanyu 'geming rendao zhuyi'" (Regarding "revolutionary humanism"), in *Wei rendao zhuyi bianhu,* Wang Ruoshui congratulates China on the popular currency of the two catchphrases "Marxist humanism" and "socialist humanism" (236). In "Wo dui rendao zhuyi wenti de kanfa," Wang hails the emergence of the phrase "socialist humanism" as "the most important achievement" produced by the debate (263). There was, however, really no good reason for Wang Ruoshui to be overjoyed at this, because Hu Qiaomu never gave up the thesis that "revolutionary humanism is the precursor of socialist humanism." Because the former term was concocted by Mao, Hu stripped the proposition of socialist humanism of any modern connotations of humanism.

56. Hu Qiaomu, "Guanyu rendao zhuyi," 64.

57. Wang Ruoshui, "Wo dui rendao zhuyi wenti de kanfa," 255.

58. Huang Songjie, Wu Xiaoming, and An Yanming, *Sate qi ren jiqi renxue* (Sartre the man and his humanist philosophy)(Shanghai: Fudan daxue, 1986), 269–70.

59. Wang Shouchang, "Sate de cunzai zhuyi rendao zhuyi tantao" (An inquiry into Sartrean existentialist humanism), in *Ren shi Makesi zhuyi de chufa dian,* 223–34.

60. Wang Ruoshui, "Wei rendao zhuyi bianhu," 231.

61. Zhou Yang, "Guanyu Makesi zhuyi de jige lilun wenti de tantao," 4.

62. Brugger and Kelly cite a source from the *Summary of World Broadcasts* to the effect that Wang Ruoshui criticized Sartre's anti-essentialist stance. See *Chinese Marxism,* 140.

63. Wang Shouchang, "Sate," 239.

64. Alvin Gouldner, *The Two Marxisms* (New York: Oxford University Press, 1980), 34.

65. Herbert Marcuse, "Re-Examination of the Concept of Revolution," in *Karl Marx and Contemporary Scientific Thought* (The Hague: Mouton, 1969), 481.

66. Wei Jingsheng, "Who Should Take the Responsibility?" *China Focus: A Publication of the Princeton China Initiative* 1, no. 10 (November 1993), 1. The abridged essay is taken from the first article that Wei published after his release. It originally appeared in *Open Magazine* 11 (1993), published in Hong Kong.

67. See He Xin's "Lanse de xue" (Blue snow), Wang Meng's "Hudie" (Butterfly), Dai Qing's "Xueqiu" (Snowball), and Zong Pu's "Wo shi shei?" (Who am I?) and "Woju" (Snail shelter).

68. To cite one example of such a commonplace symposium: In early March 1993, three leading theoretical organs in Beijing—*Wenyi bao, Wenyi yanjiu,* and *Wenxue pinglun*—called for a meeting of literary theorists and critics to discuss the issues of humanism. Although criticizing the antihumanist inclination of the ultra-leftists during the revolutionary years, the symposium also listed the ideological "mistakes" committed by some writers in their depiction of human nature. See *Renmin ribao,* 8 March 1993, 5.

69. Zhu Guangqian, "Guanyu renxing, rendao zhuyi, renqingwei he gongtongmei wenti" (On the issues of human nature, humanism, human touch, and shared aesthetics), in *Renxing rendao zhuyi wenti taolun ji,* 182.

70. Liu Xinwu, "Wo shi wo ziji," *Renmin ribao*, 24 January 1986, overseas edition. The romantic celebration of human value and creative subjectivity actually started much earlier in China. It made its debut in 1974 in Wu Meng's underground collection of *Ganyou geyin dongdi ai* (Daring to sing songs that move the earth to sorrow), a volume published by *Qishi niandai Biweekly* in Kowloon. In 1978, with the establishment of an underground poetry magazine, *Jintian* (Today), another circle of poets and critics addressed the issues raised earlier in Wu's collection such as the unresolved contradiction between subjectivity and objectivity and between humanitarianism and class struggle. Reinforcing Wu Meng's conviction that the individual's subjectivity never fails to transcend its hostile objective environment, the *Today* writers first articulated the agony of the collectivized individual in terms of alienation understood as a nihilist feeling of being uprooted from their essence as authentic human beings. See Leo Lee, "The Politics of Technique: Perspectives of Literary Dissidence in Contemporary Chinese Fiction," in *After Mao: Chinese Literature and Society,* ed. Jeffrey C. Kinkley (Cambridge: The Council on East Asian Studies of Harvard University, 1985), 183.

71. Critic Lei Da dwells on the definition of the "paradoxical self" in his "Zhuti yishi de qianghua: Dui jinnian xiaoshuo fazhan de sikao" (The intensification of subjective consciousness: Thoughts on the recent development of narrative fiction), *Wenxue pinglun* 1 (1986), 121–25. Also see Lei Da, "Lun chuangzuo zhuti de duoyanghua qushi" (On the tendency of creative subjectivity toward diverseness), *Wenxue pinglun* 1 (1986), 63–70. According to Lei, "Social conflicts and psychic contradictions of the writer's creative self correspond to each other. The change of social structure is closely related to the change in the psychic structure of the writer's creative self. . . . A writer who genuinely feels the pulse of his epoch will undoubtedly assimilate and reflect social conflicts and paradoxes through the medium of the consciousness of subjectivity" (69).

72. The Association of Chinese Writers and the Chinese Federation of Writers held a joint symposium in April 1993 to discuss the issues of humanism and alienation in conjunction with the publication of Hu Qiaomu's seminal essay "Guanyu rendao zhuyi he yihua wenti." In the symposium some writers suggested, in the spirit of reconciling the official line with their stance of critical realism (in opposition to revolutionary socialist realism), that "writing about contradictions is not tantamount to writing about alienation." See "Wenyi chuangzuo zhong yao genghao fanying shehui zhuyi rendao zhuyi" (Literary and artistic works should reflect socialist humanism better), *Renmin ribao,* 18 April 1984, 3. On "the heat wave of alienation," see Ye Lang, "Kafuka: Yihualun lishiguan de tujiezhe" (Kafka: The interpreter of the historical view of the theory of alienation), in *Rendao zhuyi he yihua wenti yanjiu* (Beijing: Beida chubanshe, 1985), 186.

73. Gao Ertai, "Yihua xianxiang jinguan," 76.

74. Dai Houying, *Ren a ren,* 349.

75. *Rensheng* was published in *Shouhuo* 3 (1982), 4–90. "Wanxia xiaoshi de shihou" was published in *Shiyue* (October) 1 (1981), 77–134. See Bai Hua's analysis of "When the Sunset Clouds Disappeared" in his "Dangqian wenyi

chuangzuo zhong de renxing rendao zhuyi wenti" (The question of human nature and humanism in current literary works), *Wenyi lilun* 1 (1984), 88–89. Bai's
article was originally published in *Wenyi lilun yanjiu* 3 (1983), 27–38.

76. *Rendao zhongnian* was published in *Shouhuo* 1 (1980), 52–92. The Chinese reading public was moved by the moral integrity and humanist spirit that
Lu Wenting, the protagonist of the novella, displays in her capacity as an altruistic doctor. The image of the suffering middle-aged intellectual also touched her
counterparts in real life. Portrayed as flawless and completely selfless, Lu's appeal to Chinese readers consists in the unambiguous totality of her noble character. For a typical analysis of Lu Wenting, see Tang Zhi, "Wenxue zhong de
renxing yu rendao zhuyi wenti: Du Hu Qiaomu tongzhi 'Guanyu rendao zhuyi
he yihua wenti' biji" (The question of human nature and humanism in literature:
Notes on my reading of comrade Hu Qiaomu's "On humanism and the question of alienation"), *Wenyi lilun* 4 (1984), 35. The essay was originally published
in *Wenyi bao* 4 (1984), 31–39.

77. Gao Ertai, "Yihua jiqi lishi kaocha" (Alienation and its historical inquiry), in *Ren shi Makesi zhuyi de chufa dian*, 163.

78. Zong Pu, "Wo shi shei?" in *Zong Pu xiaoshuo sanwen xuan* (Selections
of Zong Pu's short stories and essays)(Beijing: Renmin wenxue chubanshe, 1991),
39. The story was originally published in *Changchun* (Eternal spring) 12 (1979).

CHAPTER 2

1. Zhang Yiwu, "Shide weiji yu zhishi fenzi de weiji" (The crisis of poetry
and the crisis of intellectuals), *Dushu* 5 (1989), 77–82.

2. Liang Zhiping, "Chuantong wenhua de gengxin yu zaisheng" (The re-
newals and rebirth of traditional culture), *Dushu* 3 (1989), 13.

3. On scientific rationality, see Jin Guantao, *Wode zhexue tansuo* (My inquiry into philosophy)(Taibei: Fengyun shidai chubangongsi, 1989), 22.

4. Li Tuo was the main propagator of the notion of the "Mao Style" as early
as in 1989. See his discussion of the notion in Li Tuo, Zhang Ling, and Wang
Bin, "Yuyan de fanpan: Jinliangnian xiaoshuo xianxiang" (The rebellion of language: The trends of the last two years' fiction), *Wenyi yanjiu* 2 (1989), 79–80.
After Li came to the States, he continued to sharpen his arguments on the Mao
Style. He is now working on a manuscript on "Mao Style and Its Political Institutionalization." See note 19 in chapter four.

5. See Chen Lai, "Fulu: Sixiang chulu de sandongxiang" (Appendix: The
three orientations in the outlets of thought), in *Zhongguo dangdai wenhua yishi*
(Cultural consciousness of contemporary China), ed. Gan Yang (Hong Kong:
Sanlian shudian, 1989), 581–87. Also see Chen Kuide, "Wenhua re: Beijing sichao
ji liangzhong qingxiang" (Culture fever: Background, schools of thought, and
two kinds of tendencies), in *Zhongguo dalu dangdai wenhua bianqian, 1978–
1989* (Cultural transformations of contemporary mainland China, 1978–1989),
ed. Chen Kuide (Taibei: Guiguan tushu gufen youxian gongsi, 1991), 37–61.

6. The group of *Culture: China and the World* published a journal under the
same name, printed by the Sanlian Bookstore in Beijing. It also published three
subseries: a series in "The Library of Modern Western Academic Learning," an-

other one in "The Library of New Knowledge," and the third one in "The Studies of the Humanities."

7. Lin Nan, "Local Market Socialism: Rural Reform in China" (paper presented at the annual meeting of the American Sociological Association, Pittsburgh, Pa., August 1992, and at the conference "Great Transformation in South China and Taiwan," Cornell University, October 1992).

8. Han Shi, ed., *Bashi niandai: Gaibian Zhongguo de sanshisanben shu* (The 1980s: The thirty-three books that changed China)(Hong Kong: Tiandi tushu youxian gongsi, 1992), 13–14.

9. Ibid., quoting the concluding speech given by the head of Chinese People's Bank Chen Muhua in an international symposium on "China Faces Future" held on May 8, 1985.

10. Brugger and Kelly, *Chinese Marxism,* 43. Based on their analysis of an article written by Jia Xinmin (a contributor to the founding issue of the journal published by the "Marching Toward the Future" group), Brugger and Kelly implied that although Chinese futurology is "Marxist," it has "lost much of its recognizable Chinese flavor of optimism and triumphalism" (44).

11. Mao Zedong, "Sixty Points on Working Methods," in *Mao Papers,* ed. Jerome Ch'en (London: Oxford University Press, 1970), 64.

12. Wang Lin, "Shi juhao haishi wenhao?" (Was it a period or a question mark?), *Dushu* 5 (1989), 135.

13. In Li Tuo's talk "Literature as Social Practice in Contemporary China," given at the Asian/Pacific Studies Institute of Duke University on March 1, 1993, he discusses the significance of *pizi* as a cluster of "elements" that emerged with the deep penetration of urban reform into the cities during the late 1980s.

14. On residual modernity, see Tang Xiaobing, "Residual Modernism: Narrative of the Self in Contemporary Chinese Fiction," *Modern Chinese Literature* 7, no. 1 (1993), 7–31. On Chinese postmodernism, see Tang's "The Function of New Theory: What Does It Mean to Talk About Post-Modernism in China?" *Public Culture* 4, no. 1 (1991), 89–108. Tang was one of the critics in the early 1990s who wrote about "Chinese postmodernism." See my critique of the pseudoproposition of Chinese postmodernism in chapter six.

15. Gan Yang has been promoting the concept of the "alternative modern" since 1992, if not earlier. He stresses the importance of exploring the mechanism operating in rural Chinese industries. He argues that rural China (*xiangtu Zhongguo*) illustrates the unique pattern of "development without privatization," an economic law that contradicts the rationale of modernity understood solely in Western terms. See Gan Yang, "Wenhua Zhongguo yu xiangtu Zhongguo: Houlengzhan shidai de Zhongguo qianjing jiqi wenhua" (Cultural China and rural China: The prospects and culture of post-Cold-War China)(paper presented at the conference "Cultural China: Interpretations and Communications," Harvard University, September 3, 1992). In his edited volume *China after 1989: An Alternative to Shock Therapy* (New York: Oxford University Press, in press), he devotes a chapter to "The Chinese Alternative to Privatization." In his unpublished proposal for the manuscript, he pinpoints the "uniqueness of the Chinese experience, expecially in comparison with its counterparts in Eastern Europe and the USSR."

16. Tu Weiming spoke of the monolithic versus pluralistic modernity that distinguished the May Fourth and contemporary Chinese experiment with the notion of modernity. See his *Ruxue disanqi fazhan de qianjing wenti: Dalu jiangxue, wennan he taolun* (Questions regarding the prospects of developing the third-stage Confucianism: Lectures, inquiries, and discussions during my trips to mainland China)(Taibei: Lianjing chuban shiye gongsi, 1989), 13.

17. Gan Yang, "Bashi niandai wenhua taolun de jige wenti" (Several questions about the Cultural Discussion of the 1980s), in *Women zai chuangzao chuantong* (We are creating tradition) (Taibei: Lianjing chuban shiye gongsi, 1989), 28.

18. See Chen Kuide, "Wenhua re," 50, and Su Xiaokang, "Dangdai Zhongguo de wenhua jinzhang" (The cultural tensions of contemporary China), in *Zhongguo dalu dangdai wenhua bianqian, 1978–1989*, 24–25.

19. Li Zhongming, "Cong fanziyouhua douzheng dao Lei Feng yangban (II)" (From the antiliberalism purge to the model of Lei Feng: Part 2), *Zhongyang ribao*, 13 March 1987, overseas edition, 2, based on a report in the Hong Kong political journal *Zhengming* (Contending) 3 (1987).

20. For a detailed discussion of the problematic enlightenment program propagated in the TV series, see chapter three, "*Heshang* and the Paradoxes of the Chinese Enlightenment." A slightly different version of the chapter was published in *Bulletin of Concerned Asian Scholars* 23, no. 3 (1991), 23–33.

21. Yan Bofei, "Paoqi wutuobang: Du Hengtingdun *Bianhua shehui zhong de zhengzhi zhixu*" (Let go of utopia: Reading Huntington's "Political order in changing societies"), *Dushu* 2 (1989), 10.

22. Jin, *Wode zhexue tansuo*, 11–14.

23. Ibid., 51–52.

24. Ibid., 53 and 37.

25. Fu Weixun faulted Jin, whom he considered still a believer in scientific Marxism, for not abandoning Marxism completely. See Fu Weixun, "Zhongguo sixiangjie de Shate yu Bowa" (Sartre and de Beauvoir in China's intellectual arena), in Jin Guantao and Liu Qingfeng, *Xingsheng yu weiji: Lun Zhongguo fengjian shehui de chaowending jiegou* (Prosperity and crisis: On the ultrastability of Chinese feudal society) (Taibei: Fengyun shidai chuban gongsi, 1989), 26–27. Brugger and Kelly are more thoughtful in their effort to label Jin. They ascribe Jin's position to scientific Marxism and humanist Marxism respectively. According to them, Jin was able to "make a commitment to scientific rationality *through* . . . commitment to Marxism" (*Chinese Marxism*, 7, emphasis in the original). They relegate Jin (together with Wang Ruoshui) to the camp of Marxist humanists who are aware of the need to "hold the line for a renewed Marxism" against the "invasive forces of the irrational" (158).

26. Brugger and Kelly, *Chinese Marxism*, 61.

27. Jin and Liu, *Xingsheng yu weiji*, 8–13 and 44–51.

28. Ibid., 51–55.

29. Tu Weiming, "Dalu ruxue xindongxiang de hanyi" (The implications of the new development of mainland Confucianism), *Zhongguo luntan* 27, no. 7 (1989), 31.

30. One of the most frequently cited articles was written by Jin Guantao, Liu Qingfeng, and Fan Hongye, "Wenhua beijing yu kexue jishu jiegou yanbian" (Cultural background and the structural change of science and technology), in *Kexue chuantong yu wenhua: Zhongguo jindai kexue luohou de yuanyin* (Scientific tradition and culture: Reasons why modern Chinese science lagged behind), ed. the editorial board from *Ziran bianzhengfa tongxun* of the Academy of the Natural Sciences (Shannxi: Kexue jishu chubanshe, 1983).

31. Jin Guantao and Liu Qingfeng, "Kexue: Wenhua yanjiu zhong beihulue de zhuti" (Science: The neglected thesis of cultural studies), in Jin and Liu, *Xingsheng yu weiji,* 422.

32. Ibid., 428. Emphasis is mine.

33. Jürgen Habermas, "The Undermining of Western Rationalism through the Critique of Metaphysics: Martin Heidegger," in *The Philosophical Discourse,* 113.

34. Yu Wujin, "Lun dangdai Zhongguo wenhua de jizhong beilun" (On some contradictory theses regarding contemporary Chinese culture), *Renmin ribao,* 23 August 1988, overseas edition.

35. Jin, *Wode zhexue tansuo,* 53.

36. Li Zehou, *Zhongguo xiandai sixiang shilun,* 46–47.

37. When I was in China during the latter half of 1987, *Haideng fashi* (Haideng the High Priest) was the most popular series on TV. During conversations with Chinese friends and strangers whom I met on trains and on the streets, I learned that the popularity of Taiji boxing and *qigong* since the mid-1980s had a lot to do with the popular imagination of magic healing and Daoist occultism.

38. The debate involved May Fourth celebrities Hu Shi, Chen Duxiu, and Liang Qichao, representative figures in different ideological camps. Because the cultural agenda of China at that time was inextricably subjugated to the historical imperative of national survival, the terms of debate were inevitably overdetermined by the utilitarian concerns of the reconstruction of social mores (*shehui gaizao*), for which issues of worldview (*rensheng guan*) appeared far more urgent than those of methodology. As a result, the May Fourth debate was cast in arguments voiced between those who advocated a deterministic scientific worldview that claimed to lay bare historical processes and those who clung to an old humanistic worldview self-enclosed in the local ideology of free will, self-cultivation, and intuitive reasoning.

39. Su Xiaokang, "Dangdai Zhongguo de wenhua jinzhang," 21, 23.

40. As early as 1948, Mou Zongsan classified the history of Chinese Confucianism into three different stages of development. He raised the problematic of "Confucianism of the third stage" that included the systems of thoughts represented by Liang Shuming and his peers such as Zhang Junli, Xiong Shili, Feng Youlan, Qian Mu, Tang Junyi, and Xu Fuguan. Mou traced the Confucian tradition of the Dao back to the first stage (the period from Confucius, Mencius, and Xunzi to Dong Zhongshu of Han Dynasty) and the second stage (the neo-Confucian learning of Song and Ming Dynasty). Tu Weiming reiterated the principle of Mou Zongsan's classification while emphasizing that the contemporary revival of neo-Confucianism during the 1980s served as the continuation of the

third stage *ruxue* that Mou's generation pioneered, and that the completion of the third stage *ruxue* depends upon the younger generation such as Cai Renhou, Liu Shuxiang, and himself.

41. For creative transformation of neo-Confucianism, see Tu Weiming, "Rujia chuantong de xiandai zhuanhua" (The modern transformation of Confucian tradition), "Chuantong wenhua yu Zhongguo xianshi" (Traditional culture and Chinese reality), and "Chuangzao de zhuanhua" (Creative transformation), in *Ruxue disanqi fazhan de qianjing wenti*, 3–144.

42. Tu Weiming was prolific in his writings about neo-Confucianism. For a detailed account of his thoughts on Confucianism of the third stage, see "Ruxue disanqi fazhan de qianjing wenti: 1, 2 & 3" (The problems about the future development of the Confucianism of the third stage: 1, 2 & 3), *Mingbao yuekan*, 21, no. 1 (1986), 27–32; 21, no. 2 (1986), 36–38; and 21, no. 3 (1986), 65–68. Yu Yingshi, "Zhongguo jinshi zongjiao lunli yu shangren jingshen" (Religion and ethics in modern China and the spirit of merchants), *Zhishi fenzi* (Intellectuals) 2, no. 2 (1986), 3–45.

43. Arif Dirlik, "Post-Socialism/Flexible Production: Marxism in Contemporary Radicalism," *Polygraph* 6/7 (1993), 149.

44. Song Zhongfu, Zhao Jihui, and Pei Dayang, *Ruxue zai xiandai Zhongguo* (*Confucianism in modern China*) (Zhengzhou: Zhongzhou guji chubanshe, 1991), 377.

45. Ibid., 418–30.

46. Yang Bingzhang, "Guanyu ruxue disanqi he Zhongguo wenhua de qiantu" (Regarding Confucianism of the third stage and the future of Chinese culture), in *Zhongguo dalu dangdai wenhua bianqian*, 163.

47. Song, Zhao, and Pei, *Ruxue zai xiandai Zhongguo*, quoting Zhang Dainian, 355.

48. Between August 31 and September 4 in 1987, The China Foundation of Confucius held a joint international conference with the Research Institute of East Asian Philosophy in Singapore at Qufu. The main theme of the conference was the revalorization of Confucianism as a cultural model for East Asian industrial nations. The Weberian influence was evident. In October 1989, on the 2,540th anniversary of the birth of Confucius, another international symposium on Confucianism was held in Beijing. Ibid., 357–58.

49. Li Zonggui, "'Xiandai xinrujia sichao yanjiu' de youlai he Xuanzhou huiyi de zhengming" (The origin of "studies on modern neo-Confucian thoughts" and the debates at the Xuanzhou Conference), in *Xiandai xinruxue yanjiu lunji* (The collection of essays on modern neo-Confucianism), ed. Fang Keli and Li Jinquan (Beijing: Zhongguo shehui kexue chubanshe, 1989), 1: 333–35.

50. Tu, "Dalu ruxue," 31.

51. In his interviews with Tu Weiming, Xue Yong raised the issue of the potential misuse of Confucianism in mainland China. Tu Weiming also recognized that it was difficult for Confucianism to attain a "healthy development" in China. Though it is understandable that Xue Yong might feel constrained to discuss the issue, Tu's unwillingness to examine the question more thoroughly gives the impression that he wishes to promote a Chinese neo-Confucian revival at any cost. His evasiveness about the problematic implications of the neo-Confucian re-

naissance in the context of mainland Chinese politics is disturbing. See Tu's *Ruxue disanqi fazhan de qianjing wenti,* 57. On the Party's involvement in Confucian revivalism, see Yang Bingzhang, "Guanyu ruxue," 167.

52. Song, Zhao, and Pei, *Ruxue zai xiandai Zhongguo,* 447.

53. Su Xiaokang, "Dangdai Zhongguo de wenhua jinzhang," 27.

54. Su Xiaokang attributes the onset of the Fever to the cultural and spiritual rebellion of Chinese intellectuals against the tyrannical rule of a homogeneous ideology. Ibid., 31. Chen Kuide summarizes the activities of the Cultural Discussion in terms of a pan-culturalism that took form in the intellectuals' critique of the regime under the disguise of an all-out cultural critique. See Chen Kuide, "Wenhua re," 51–55. Both critics presuppose that the Cultural Discussion was targeted at an antagonist—sometimes named as the Party, sometimes as the socialist system, but most of the time, as a vague combination of both.

55. In the following two sections on instrumental and substantive rationality, I will make frequent references to the information given in the following articles: Wang Hongzhou, "Gang-Tai xuezhe dui Zhongguo chuantong wenhua de yanjiu: Jinnianlai guanyu Zhongguo wenhua wenti yanjiu zhongshu" (Researches of Hong Kong and Taiwan scholars on Chinese traditional culture: A summary of the studies of the problems of Chinese culture in recent years), *Renmin ribao,* 30 May 1989, overseas edition, 2; Wang He, "Ruhe pingjia chuantong wenhua: Jinnianlai guanyu Zhongguo wenhua wenti yanjiu zongshu" (How to evaluate traditional culture: A summary of the studies of the problems of Chinese culture in recent years), *Renmin ribao,* 27 May 1989, overseas edition, 2; Li Cunshan, "Zhongguo chuantong wenhua yu Zhongguo xiandaihua: II" (Chinese traditional culture and Chinese modernization: A sequel) *Renmin ribao,* 20 August 1986, overseas edition, 2; Guo Qiyong, "Guanyu jinnianlai Zhongguo wenhua he Zhongxi wenhua bijiao yanjiu de pingjie" (Comments on Chinese culture studies and the comparative studies of Chinese and Western cultures in recent years), *Renmin ribao,* 3 December 1986, overseas edition, 2. A longer version of this article was published in *Dongfang de liming: Zhongguo wenhua zouxiang jindai de licheng* (The dawn in the east: The journey of Chinese culture toward modern times), ed. Feng Tianyu (Chengdu: Bashu shushe, 1988), 464–82. Other articles that helped my understanding of the neo-Confucian revival include "Guanyu Zhongguo chuantong wenhua de xingzhi" (Regarding the nature of traditional Chinese culture"), *Qiusuo* (Quest) 2 (1988); "Gaige yu chuantong wenhua moshi de zhuanhuan" (Reform and the transformation of the models of traditional culture), *Jinyang Xuekan* (Jinyang journal) 3 (1988); "Lun dangdai Zhongguo wenhua de neizai chongtu" (On the internal conflicts of contemporary Chinese culture), *Fudan Xuebao* (Fudan journal) 3 (1988); "Zhongguo chuantong wenhua 'hexie' tezheng de fansi" (Reflections on the characteristics of "harmony" in Traditional Chinese Culture), *Tianjin shehui kexue* (Tianjin social sciences) 5 (1988); "Guanyu Zhongguo chuantong wenhua de zhengti fansi yu chaoyue" (Thoughts on the totalizing introspection and transcendence of traditional Chinese culture), *Xuexi yu tansuo* (Learning and exploration) 4 (1988).

56. A typical argument from the middle ground can be found in Feng Tianyu, "Dai xuyan: Zhongguo wenhua de jindaihua wenti" (Preface: The issues of the

modernization of Chinese culture) in *Dongfang de liming,* 9–10. Feng pointed out that Japan's modernization could not be exclusively attributed to Confucianism because Japan benefited primarily from its creative utilization of Western learning that was introduced into the country in the mid-nineteenth century.

I need to point out that all the major players (advocates as well as critics) overseas and at home in the neo-Confucian revivalism were male intellectuals. I believe that what is at stake in the potential breakdown of Confucian values is not simply tradition or communal values, but patriarchal elitism, and in more specific terms, the privileged status of the gendered power elite—the legitimate guardians and owners of hard-core and orthodox knowledge. This may in part explain why the spokespeople of neo-Confucianism were exclusively male. It is understandable that female scholars were not interested in propagating a state philosophy from which they had nothing to gain for thousands of years. But it surprised me that Chinese women scholars did not seize this opportunity to join the male critics of neo-Confucianism in critiquing the five hierarchical relations (*wulun*) that victimized them for thousands of years.

57. Mou Zongshan, Zhang Junli, Tang Junyi, and Xu Fuguan published their manifesto "Zhongguo wenhua yu shijie" (Chinese culture and the world) simultaneously in Hong Kong's *Minzhu pinglun* (Commentaries on democracy) and the Taiwan journal *Zaisheng* (Rebirth).

58. Han Qiang, "Xiandai xinruxue yanjiu zhongshu (1986–87)" (A synthetic account of the studies of modern neo-Confucianism (1986–87), in *Xiandai xinruxue yanjiu lunji,* 1: 346–49, quoting Zhu Riyao, Cao Deben, Sun Xiaochun, Mao Dan, and Bao Zunxin.

59. Ibid., 347, quoting Bao Zunxin.

60. For mainland Chinese scholars, modern neo-Confucianism is firmly grounded in the moral metaphysics of *lixue,* especially in the "Learning of the Mind" (*xinxing*) represented by Wang Yangming and Lu Jiuyuan's School. See Fang Keli, "Guanyu xiandai xinrujia yanjiu de jige wenti" (Several questions regarding the studies of modern neo-Confucianism), in *Xiandai xinruxue yanjiu lunji,* 1: 2; Li Zonggui, "'Xiandai xinrujia sichao yanjiu,'" 336, quoting Hu Xiao.

61. This response was made by Chen Kuide during my conversation with him at the "Culture China" conference, Princeton University, May 4, 1991.

62. Chen Kuide, "Wenhua re," 48.

63. Introductions about Marcuse, Adorno, and Horkheimer were seen in academic journals here and there. One of the typical presentations can be seen in Zhao Yifan, "Falankefu xuepai lümei wenhua piping" (The Frankfurt School and overseas culture criticism), *Dushu* 1 (1981), 34–43.

64. Max Horkheimer, *Eclipse of Reason* (New York: Oxford University Press, 1947), 174, 183.

65. "Chinese Dissent, Ready to Wear," *Harper's,* February 1993, 23.

66. Liu Xiaobo, "Yinzi: Fanchuantong yu Zhongguo zhishi fenzi" (Foreword: Antitradition and Chinese intellectuals), in *Xuanze de pipan: Yu sixiang lingxiu duihua* (*Choice and critique: A dialogue with the leader of philosophy*) (Taibei: Fengyun shidai chuban gongsi, 1989), 1–11. Liu propagated a "thorough break from traditional concepts" (5). In order to accomplish that goal, Liu

argued that Chinese intellectuals have to take Western culture as the referential framework for their construction of Chinese modernity.

67. Chen Lai is perhaps the first who used the term "hermeneutics" to characterize Gan Yang's thoughts. See Chen Lai, "Fulu," 582–83. Zhang Xudong followed suit in "The Political Hermeneutics of Cultural Constitution: Reflections on the Chinese 'Cultural Discussion' (1985–1989)" (working paper in Asian/Pacific Studies, Asian/Pacific Studies Institute, Duke University, 1994).

68. Feng Tianyu, "Dai xuyan," 6. Feng named several regions, including the mid- and lower-stream of the Yangzi River and the region surrounding the Pearl River, as locales where traces of the "capitalist mode of production" could be detected: textile and pottery industry, mining, and smeltery. Also see Xiao Shafu, "Zhongguo zhexue qimeng de kanke daolu" (The rugged path of the enlightenment [movement] in Chinese philosophy), in *Dongfang de liming,* 17.

69. Xiao Shafu, "Zhongguo zhexue qimeng de kanke daolu," 23–25.

70. Feng Tianyu, "Cong Ming Qing zhiji de zaoqi qimeng wenhua dao jindai xinxue" (From the early enlightenment culture of Ming and Qing to the new learning of the modern era), in *Dongfang de liming,* 52.

71. Habermas, *The Philosophical Discourse,* 58.

72. Fang Yizhi's concept of *jinxin* (to exert one's heart and mind) called for a thorough utilization of the intuitive nature of wisdom—a concept that keeps pace with Mencius' notion of *liangzhi* (innate knowledge), Daoists' *wuzhi zhi zhi* (knowledge that does not know), and the Buddhists' *banruo (prajna).* Fang had the reputation of being half scientific and half religious. He tried to transcend all three traditional systems of thought but remained deeply embedded within them at the same time. For a detailed analysis of his thinking, see Wang Yu, "Du Fang Yizhi 'Dongxi jun'" (Reading "East-West equilibrium"), in *Ming Qing sixiangjia lunji* (A collection of essays on the Ming-Qing philosophers) (Taibei: Lianjing chuban shiye gongsi, 1981), 211–29, especially 212, 218–19.

73. Yu Wujin, "Lun dangdai Zhongguo wenhua de jizhong beilun," 2.

74. Wang Fuzhi, "Tun," in *Zhouyi waizhuan* in *Zhongguo xueshu minzhu jinshi yuyi* (Recent interpretations and translation of the classical Chinese Great Books), ed. the Xi'nan Books Editorial Committee (Taibei: Xi'nan shuju, 1972), 5: 115.

75. See Huang Zongxi, "Yuan jun," "Yuan chen," "Yuan fa," in *Mingyi daifang lu,* in *Zhongguo xueshu minzhu jinshi yuyi,* 5: 3–5, 7–9, 10–11.

76. Huang Zongxi, "Caiji 3," in *Minyi daifang lu,* in *Zhongguo xueshu minzhu jinshi yuyi,* 5: 32.

77. Tang Zhen, "Daming," in *Qianshu* in *Zhongguo xueshu minzhu jinshi yuyi,* 5: 245, 257.

78. Xu tended to comply. Fang tended to critically select. See Zhang Yongtang, "Fang Yizhi yu xixue" (Fang Yizhi and Western learning), in *Zhongguo zhexue sixiang lunji,* ed. Yu Yingshi, Xiang Weixin, and Liu Fuzeng (The collection of essays on Chinese philosophy and thought) (Taibei: Mutong chubanshe, 1976), the Qing volume, 200.

79. Liang Qichao, "Ming Qing zhijiao Zhongguo sixiangjie jiqi daibiao renwu" (The field of Chinese philosophy at the transition between Ming and

Qing dynasty and its representative figures), in *Zhongguo zhexue sixiang lunji,* the Qing volume, 6.

80. Tu, "Ruxue disanqi fazhan de qianjing wenti," 310, 308–9. Li Zehou agrees with Tu on this point. He cites Gu Yanwu's pragmatic spirit as a good example of the learning of *waiwang* (the kingliness without) emphasized by modern and contemporary neo-Confucianists. See Li Zehou, *Zhongguo gudai sixiang shilun* (On the history of ancient Chinese history of thought) (Beijing: Renmin chubanshe, 1985), 278.

81. Xiao Gongquan, *Zhongguo zhengzhi sixiang shi* (The history of Chinese political thought) (Taibei: Wenhua University Press, 1980), 2: 607–10.

82. See ibid., 622, and Yu Yingshi, "Qingdai sixiangshi de yige xinjieshi" (A new interpretation of the intellectual history of the Qing Dynasty), in *Zhongguo zhexue sixiang lunji,* 5: 11–48, originally published in *Zhonghua wenhua fuxing yuekan* (The Chinese cultural renaissance monthly) 9, no. 1. Although Gu Yanwu and Huang Zongxi earned reputations as anti-*lixue* thinkers, Yu Yingshi demonstrates that they both had deep ties with the "Learning of Reason," the neo-Confucian school of the Cheng-Zhu sect.

83. Yu Yingshi, "Qingdai sixiangshi de yige xinjieshi," 29.

84. Some mainland cultural critics of the post-Mao era have begun to comment on the paradoxes of Chinese enlightenment movements that failed throughout modern Chinese history. Yu Wujin's "Dangdai Zhongguo wenhua de jizhong beilun" is one example. Even Liu Zaifu, a representative of cultural elite, dwells at length on the personality split from which the May Fourth generation suffered by being caught in two conflicting cultural models. See Liu Zaifu, "Liangci lishixing de tupo: Cong 'Wusi' xinwenhua yundong dao xinshiqi de 'xiandai wenhua yishi'") (Two historical breakthroughs: From the "May Fourth" New Culture Movement to "modern cultural consciousness" of the new era), *Renmin ribao,* 27 April 1980, overseas edition, 2. This kind of critique was accompanied by a small handful of articles that emerged toward the end of the 1980s to question the concept of utopia. The two critiques—that of enlightenment and that of utopia—were parallel discourses that could lead to the long overdue discussions of the paralogics of Chinese enlightenment. Besides Yan Bofei's "Paoqi wutuobang," an example of such discourse is Wang Meng, "Fanmian wutuobang de qishi" (The revelation of reverse utopianism), *Dushu* 2 (1989), 44–47. Both essays call for anti-utopianism.

85. Gan Yang, "Ruxue zai xiandai Zhongguo de jiaose yu chulu" (The role and prospects of Confucianism in modern China), in *Women zai chuangzao chuantong,* 1, 2.

86. Ibid., 10, 7. Gan Yang quotes from Edmund Burke's *Reflections on the Revolution in France*—"We compensate, we reconcile, we balance"—to suggest that the modern mission and function of Confucianism consists in its compensatory role to help modernity achieve its equilibrium.

87. Ibid., 20–21.

88. Ibid., 6, 21.

89. Chen Kuide, "Wenhua re," 47.

90. Gan's manifesto appears in "Bashi niandai," 70. His proposal of "conservationism"—crystallized in his paper "The Role and Prospects of Confu-

cianism in Modern China"—was delivered at an international conference on "The Questions and Prospects about the Development of Confucianism" held in Singapore in August 1988.

91. Chen Lai mentions briefly Gan Yang's significant departure from the hermeneutic tradition of Gadamer. He emphasizes Gan's negative definition of the concept of tradition. Indeed, in his 1985 article "Bashi niandai wenhua taolun de jige wenti," Gan denies the existence of a tradition (of which Confucianism forms a major part) that stands outside of the hermeneutic enclosure of modernity. Tradition, in other words, is subordinate to modernity. Tradition can never recreate itself from its own standpoint. Only modernity can achieve the task. Very little was said about the subtle transition from Gan's earlier phase of near-total negation of tradition to his middle career of conservationism. See Chen Lai, "Fulu," 583.

92. Gan Yang, "Bianzhe qianyan" (Editor's preface), in *Zhongguo dangdai wenhua yishi*, iii. It is also worth noting Gan's views about the sequence of events that led to the June Fourth crackdown in 1989. The crackdown served to reinforce Gan's antiradicalism and his conviction that revolution is not the best solution to China's dilemma. I had a lengthy conversation with Gan in Chicago in January 1993, during which we exchanged views on a variety of subjects pertaining to the politics of post-Mao China. His antiradicalist stance is expressed most clearly in the draft of a proposal for his manuscript *China after 1989*.

93. Gan, "Ruxue zai xiandai Zhongguo de jiaose yu chulu," 22.

94. Gan, "Bashi niandai," 32.

95. Ibid., 30.

96. Zhang Xudong, "The Political Hermeneutics," 38–39.

97. Gan, "Bashi niandai," 55.

98. For his critique of "anxiety consciousness," see Gan Yang, "Ziyou de linian: Wusi chuantong zhi queshimian" (The ideal concept of freedom: The blind spots of the May Fourth tradition), *Dushu* 5 (1989), 12–13.

99. I am referring to Gan Yang's project *China after 1989*. The draft of his proposal stresses the "uniqueness of the Chinese [economic] experience" in comparison with its counterparts in Eastern Europe and the USSR. Gan reaffirms the perspective of "gradualist reform" as a way of "avoiding radical revolution" (1–2).

100. See the outline of Gan Yang's talk "Wenhua Zhongguo yu xiangtu Zhongguo," 1–5. Also see the draft proposal of his *China after 1989*.

101. Zhang Xudong, "On Some Motifs in the Chinese 'Cultural Fever' of the Late 1980s: Social Change, Ideology, and Theory," *Social Text* 39 (summer 1994), 154.

102. Those who were closely associated with the committee (Chen Lai and Zhang Xudong, for instance) would disagree with me by arguing that Gan Yang's hermeneutic school occupied a central position in the Cultural Discussion. Both gave the school considerable coverage in their articles on the Cultural Discussion while leaving out the *qimeng* school completely. I need to emphasize that although all the discourses created during the Cultural Discussion were elitist, the hermeneutic school was twice-removed from the public because of its strong affiliation with the academy. Furthermore, the school's adoption of unfamiliar

Western theoretical vocabulary of hermeneutics mystified and alienated many participants of the Cultural Discussion. Its position as a cultural discourse both during and after the Cultural Discussion is therefore marginal.

103. The traditional term *qimeng* invokes the beginning act of education in which a child departs from the state of ignorance with first lessons in learning how to read and write. In late Qing, the term incorporated the meaning of being enlightened with the knowledge of modernity.

104. Li Zehou, "Response to Lin Yu-sheng" (paper presented at the round-table discussion of neo-Confucianism at the annual meeting of the Asian Studies Association, Washington, D.C., 26 March 1993).

105. Li Zehou, *Pipan zhexue de pipan: Kangde shuping* (Critiquing the critique of philosophy: On Kant), rev. ed. (Beijing: Renmin chubanshe, 1986), 56–57. Li contrasts Hegel with Kant by emphasizing the former's theoretical focus on the "objective realistic struggles of the human subject." How to study the "subjective psychological composition" of human subjectivity, a Kantian thesis, constitutes, in Li's view, the most important problematic of the contemporary inquiry into the Communist philosophy of humanity.

106. Ibid., 56.

107. Li Zehou, "Manshuo xiti Zhongyong," in *Zhongguo xiandai sixiang shilun*, 419–20.

108. Ibid., 420, 421.

109. For case studies of rural economy, see N. C. Sen, *Rural Economy and Development in China* (Beijing: Foreign Languages Press, 1990), especially 137–206. Also see *Chengxiang xietiao fazhan yanjiu* (Research on the urban-rural coordinated development), ed. Zhou Erliu and Zhang Yulin (Nanjing: Jiangsu renmin chubanshe, 1991). For the proposal of "rural China," see Gan, "Wenhua Zhongguo yu xiangtu Zhongguo," 2.

110. Li Zehou, "Manshuo xiti zhongyong," 424.

111. Ibid., 421.

112. For his discussion of China's cultural-psychological formation, see Li Zehou, *Zhongguo gudai sixiang shilun*, 32–34.

113. Ibid., 34–35, emphasis mine.

114. Li Zehou, "Manshuo xiti zhongyong," 426.

115. At the convention in March 1993, in his talk "Response to Lin Yu-sheng," Li Zehou also emphasized that both "sedimentation" and "cultural-psychological formation" are not closed concepts.

116. Li Zehou, *Zhongguo gudai sixiang shilun*, 319.

117. Ibid., 322.

118. Ibid., 277–98.

119. Ibid., 322.

120. Li Zehou, *Pipan zhexue*, 436, n. 2.

121. Li Zehou, *Zhongguo gudai sixiang shilun*, 322.

122. Li Zehou, *Pipan zhexue*, 423–24, 435.

123. Ibid., 94.

124. Li Zehou, "Manshuo xiti zhongyong," 427–28.

125. Perry Anderson, *Considerations on Western Marxism* (London: Verso, 1979), 82. Emphasis is in the original text.

126. Li Zehou, *Zhongguo gudai sixiang shilun*, 316.

127. Anderson, *Considerations*, 82.

128. Li Zehou, *Pipan zhexue*, 362.

129. A quick look at Li Zehou's blanket condemnation of Western Marxism reveals a curious logic that spells out the subtle correspondence between Western Marxism and Maoism in his system of thought. What upsets Li Zehou the most (the section on Western Marxists is marred with a kind of raw emotionalism rarely seen in his writings) is labeled in a shorthand fashion as "subjectivism," "voluntarism," "individualism," "antagonism" to the concept of "historical determinism" and their failure to recognize the objective laws of the motion of the forces of production (ibid., 358–59). Although Li Zehou stops short of openly evoking the name of Mao Zedong, his attacks on Western Marxists' turning away from economics and politics to the study of superstructures (cultural ideology in particular) and his sharp criticisms of their alleged indifference to the objective laws of society and history unmistakably evoke the memories of the Great Leap Forward and the Cultural Revolution, both of which were attributed to Mao's faith in voluntarism.

130. Ibid., 199.

131. Martin Jay, *The Dialectical Imagination: A History of the Frankfurt School and the Institute of Social Research, 1923–50* (Boston: Little, Brown and Co., 1973), 4, 64.

132. Herbert Marcuse, *Reason and Revolution: Hegel and the Rise of Social Theory*, rev. ed. (Boston: Beacon Press, 1960), 322.

133. Li Zehou, *Pipan zhexue*, 363.

134. Jay, *The Dialectical Imagination*, 280. Li Zehou, *Pipan zhexue*, 363.

135. Li Zehou, *Zhongguo gudai sixiang shilun*, 29.

136. Li Zehou, "Response to Lin Yu-sheng," 7.

137. Li Zehou, *Zhongguo gudai sixiang shilun*, 29.

138. Li Zehou, *Pipan zhexue*, 56–67.

139. Li Zehou, "Response to Lin Yu-sheng," 9.

140. For his discussion of *shehui shijian*, see Li Zehou, *Pipan zhexue*, 258.

141. Ibid., 340, 204.

142. Li Zehou, *Zhongguo gudai sixiang shilun*, 37.

143. In August 1987 when I visited the city with my students on the Duke Study in China Program, we danced in the square in the evenings and marveled at the temple's transformation from a religious shrine to a secular fairground at night. During the day, we could wander into the compound free, but in the evenings, tickets were sold at the main gate for admission.

144. Xu Junyao mentioned "fever for 'knowledgeable elements'" in his "Zhishi fenzi he xiandai shehui: Cong Gelanxi dao xinzuopai de sikao" (Intellectuals and modern society: From Gramci to the New Left), *Dushu* 9 (1988), 23.

145. See the section on "Liu Zaifu: The Master Grammarian of the Subject" in chapter five, "Romancing the Subject."

146. See Lin Jianchu's introduction to the book, "Yibu kaituoxing de zhuzuo: Ping Lei Zhenxiao *Zhongguo rencai sixiangshi (diyi juan)*," *Renmin ribao*, 28 November 1986, overseas edition, 2.

147. Li Cunshan, "Zhongguo chuantong wenhua yu Zhongguo xiandaihua: II," 2.

148. There was a backlash starting in late 1985 on Zhang Xianliang's gender politics and on his portrayal of Zhang Yonglin, the main protagonist in his trilogy. Critiques were focused on *Half of a Man Is a Woman*. A typical review characterizes Zhang Yonglin as a hypocrite rather than a hero. Negative assessments of Zhang Yonglin abound. See Huang Ziping, "Zhengmian zhankai ling yu rou de bodou" (Positively unfold the fight between soul and flesh), *Wenhui bao*, 7 October 1985; Lu Rongchun, "Zhanshi de zitai yanbuzhu beique de linghun" (The posture of a warrior cannot hide a mean soul), *Zuoping yu zhengming* (Literary works and contending views) 2 (1986). Both articles were reprinted in a collection of critical essays *Ping "Nanren de yiban shi nüren"* (On "Half of a man is a woman"), ed. by Ningxia People's Publishers (Yinchuan: Ningxia renmin chubanshe, 1987), 1–3, 62–67.

149. Liu Xiaobo, "Wufa huibi de fansi: You jibu zhishi fenzi ticai de xiaoshuo suo xiangdaode" (An unavoidable introspection: Thoughts triggered by several novels on the subject of intellectuals), *Wenyi lilun* (Theories of literature and the arts) 12 (1986), 177.

150. Ibid., 175.

151. This excerpt was taken from a report on Fang Lizhi's lectures at Beijing University, "Fang Lizhi zai Beida yanjiang luyin jielu" (Summaries of Fang Lizhi's talks at Beida), *Zhongyang ribao*, 3 February 1987, overseas edition. For a critique of Fang Lizhi, see Richard C. Kraus, "The Lament of Astrophysicist Fang Lizhi: China's Intellectuals in a Global Context," in *Marxism and the Chinese Experience*, ed. Arif Dirlik and Maurice Meisner (Armonk, N.Y.: M. E. Sharpe, 1989), 294–315.

152. Liu Zaifu, "Liangci lishixing de tupo," 2.

153. Liu Zaifu, *Renlun ershiwuzhong* (Treatises on twenty-five human species) (Hong Kong: Oxford University Press, 1992), 52–60.

154. Ibid., 60.

CHAPTER 3

1. *Heshang*'s critics included vice president Wang Zhen, overseas Nobel prize celebrities Yang Zhengning and Li Zhengdao, and Taiwan nationalist intellectual Yan Yuanshu. Zhao Ziyang was one of the few upper echelon Party leaders who endorsed the series. He reportedly gave Singapore's premier Lee Kuan Yew videotapes of the documentary as a personal gift. After the second broadcast, major newspapers such as *Renmin ribao, Guangming ribao, Wenyi bao, Zhongguo qingnian bao, Jingji ribao, Beijing qingnian bao,* and *Wenhui bao* sponsored endless discussion sessions on the miniseries and published numerous articles and editorials on the debate over the documentary.

2. Zhong Huamin et al., eds., *Chongping "Heshang"* (Reassessing "Yellow River elegy") (Hangzhou: Hangzhou daxue chubanshe, 1989), 1. Hereafter, I will refer to this edition of *Heshang* as *CPHS*. It is important to note that serious discrepancies exist between the various versions of *Heshang* texts in different publications. The specific entries of *Heshang* cited in this article appeared both in *CPHS* and in the TV documentary.

3. The script of *Heshang* was produced by a team of writers and scholars. In its printed form, the writing of the script was generally credited to Su Xiaokang and Wang Luxiang. In this essay, for convenience of citation, I refer to Su as the principal scriptwriter. Su Xiaokang, "Longnian de beichuang" (The sorrows of the year of the dragon), in *Ziyou beiwanglu* (A memorandum of freedom) (Hong Kong: Joint Publishing Co., 1989), 264.

4. Wang Zhihuan, "Deng Guanque Lou," *Tangshi sanbaishou xiangxi* (Taibei: Zhonghua shuju, 1972), 274. Wang's five-character *jueju*, which contains the famous line "The Yellow River flows into the sea," is a nature poem in which one finds the harmonious blending of the poet's physical eye and his mind's eye. The landscape of the spatial expanse is both physical and mental.

5. The translation is Frederic Wakeman's. See his "All the Rage in China," *New York Review of Books,* 2 March 1989, 3, 19. Prior to this finale, the tyrannical personification of the river as a "wreaker of havoc" is heard throughout the documentary, especially in the fifth episode, "Sorrows and Crises." See *CPHS,* 248–66.

6. From August to November 1989, *Renmin ribao* launched an editorial project entitled "One Hundred Mistakes in *Heshang.*" The project cites specific errors and conceptual fallacies that the scriptwriters of the documentary are said to have committed.

7. Wakeman, "All the Rage in China," 21.

8. Xiao Xu, "*Heshang* lunzheng qingkuang zongshu," in *CPHS,* provides an overview of the various critiques of *Heshang.* Wang Gaoling and Wu Xin argue in one critique that what the documentary reflects is nothing other than a deep-rooted feeling of frustration brought about by an unjustifiable "competitive consciousness" of the intellectuals who seek to recapture the global hegemonic position that China once occupied.

The most detailed account of the tensions between enlightenment (*qimeng*) and saving the nation (*jiuguo*) that tore apart, and finally compromised, the May Fourth intellectuals is provided by Vera Schwarcz, *The Chinese Enlightenment: Intellectuals and the Legacy of the May Fourth Movement of 1919* (Berkeley: University of California Press, 1986). Whereas Schwarcz argues that "enlightenment became first and foremost a means through which Chinese intellectuals defined themselves" (292), I would supplement her argument by pointing out that enlightenment became first and foremost a means through which Chinese intellectuals *empowered* themselves.

9. See Schwarcz, *The Chinese Enlightenment,* 240–82. It is worth noting that since June 1989, the Chinese government has renewed the slogan of *aiguo zhuyi* (patriotism) with such unprecedented fervor that the slogan appears on almost every important political occasion. Most notably, the 1990 annual May Fourth commemoration was marked by an important speech given by Jiang Zemin, "Aiguo zhuyi he woguo zhishi fenzi de shiming" (Patriotism and the mission of our intellectuals), *Renmin ribao,* 4 May 1990. The title of Jiang's speech spells out the thematic consistency that the party officials have always voiced in combating their resurgent nemesis—the alternative interpretation of May Fourth—namely, enlightenment.

10. Li Zehou, *Zhongguo xiandai sixiang shilun,* 19.

11. Liu Zaifu and Lin Gang, *Chuantong yu Zhongguo ren* (Hong Kong: San-lian shudian, 1988), 255–79.

12. Schwarcz, *The Chinese Enlightenment,* 283.

13. Li Zehou, *Zhongguo xiandai sixiang shilun,* 45. The emphasis is mine.

14. In his own critique of *Heshang* after his escape from China, Su Xiaokang confessed that the documentary suffered many conceptual biases, one of which he characterized as "blaming the culture instead of the system for China's problems." See "Zai Bali xiangqi Caishikou: Liuwang ganhuai" (Thinking of Caishikou at Paris: Recollections in exile), *Baixing* 202 (16 October 1989), 3.

15. For discussion of the European Enlightenment, see Lucien Goldmann, *The Philosophy of the Enlightenment,* trans. Henry Maas (Cambridge: Massachusetts Institute of Technology Press, 1973), 27. According to the rationalist tradition of the Enlightenment, if every individual rationally pursues his or her own self-interest and happiness, the general interest of society will be fulfilled at the same time.

16. As if to resolve the unsettled ambiguity of this one-liner, the production team of *Heshang* chose May Fourth as the subject of its sequel. Unfortunately the sequel project was aborted in the turbulent year of 1989. See Yan Zisha, "*Heshang* jiemeipian Wusi liuchan ji" (The demise of the twin project of *River elegy*—"May Fourth"), *Baixing* 201 (1 October 1989), 36–37.

17. Su Xiaokang himself was not totally unaware of the problematic legacy of the movement. He once remarked, "The New Culture Movement, a possible symbol of the rising sun, marched right into a labyrinth on the very same day of the fourth of May." See Fang Xian'gan, "*Heshang* de quanpan xihua de zhuzhang" (The views on total westernization in *River elegy*), in *CPHS,* 126, quoting Su Xiaokang's discussion of the May Fourth Movement. Seen in this light, Su Xiaokang's proposal that Chinese history start over again from May Fourth could signify the recovery of the original motivating force of the New Culture Movement, in other words, the agenda of enlightenment, before it is subsumed into the program of patriotism.

18. The classical Chinese writing tradition is dominated by the retroactive stance of writers and critics alike. Not only do Chinese literati feel the anxiety of continuing the great heritage of the Five Classics—their gaze is always turned backwards to the past in awe and nostalgia—but in the same vein, this complex of "return" is also manifested in one of the major characteristics of traditional evaluative criticism. Premodern commentators rely upon a small repertory of ancient texts as their aesthetic criterion, by means of which they make their assessment of both classical and contemporary literary and historical texts. Throughout the literary history of imperial China, one finds critics who obsessively return to those canonical texts whose orthodox and sacred stature encounters little challenge. Working in the name of "evaluation," they are particularly fond of tracing the source of influence of a new style to an older one, and in extreme cases, of identifying the moment of origination.

19. Hayden White, *Metahistory* (Baltimore, Md.: Johns Hopkins University Press, 1973), 128. White characterizes China as a "theocratic despotism" that operates on the "metaphorical apprehension of its civilizational projects." In

such a historical field, formal distinctions between separate entities are eliminated and absorbed into the subjectivity of the sovereign who alone assigns and distributes meaning.

20. Zhang Guangxian argues that the emergence of the dragon as the totem symbol for the Chinese is a fairly recent fiction. He also argues against the association between dragon worship and the Yellow River civilization. See his article "Cong lishi de shijiao ping *Heshang*" (Critiquing *River elegy* from the viewpoint of history), *Guangming ribao*, 23 August 1989, 3. Another critic ridicules Su for relying on the fictional logic provided in the movie *The 1894 Sino-Japanese War* to explain the defeat of the Chinese fleet. See Zhong Huamin, "Zuowei zhenglunpian de *Heshang*" (*River elegy* as a political docu-commentary), in *CPHS*, 9. Still other critics dismiss Su Xiaokang's theory of the mysterious affinity between the color yellow and the yellow skin of the Chinese people.

21. Lu Xun, "Changcheng" (The Great Wall), in *Lu Xun quanji* (The complete works of Lu Xun) (Beijing: Renmin wenxue chubanshe, 1973), 3: 63.

22. For the discussion of the Enlightenment Society, see James D. Seymour, ed., *The Fifth Modernization: China's Human Rights Movement, 1978–79* (Stanfordville, N.Y.: Human Rights Publishing Group, 1980). Also see Schwarcz, *The Chinese Enlightenment*, 300–301.

23. One can conjure up half a dozen such symbols that characterize traditional Chinese culture: lotus flower, stone tortoise, engraved stone steles, jade pendant, the yin-yang circle, the ancestral tablet, and so on.

24. Yan Zisha, "*Heshang* jiemei," 37, quoting Su Xiaokang.

CHAPTER 4

1. Liu Suola, "Lantian lühai," in *Zhongguo dalu xiandai xiaoshuo xuan* (The collection of modern short stories of mainland China) (Taibei: Yuanshen chubanshe, 1987), 1: 123. The story was originally published in *Shanghai wenxue* 6 (1985), 12–29.

2. In examining "aesthetic modernity" in this chapter, I focus on narrative fiction. Poetry, drama, the fine arts, and films are not treated here.

3. Ji Yanzhi, "Zai youyige lishi zhuanzhedian shang: Jinian 'Wu Si' yundong qishi zhounian" (At another turning point of history: In commemoration of the seventieth anniversary of the May Fourth Movement), *Renmin ribao*, 3 May 1989, overseas edition, 2.

4. Yang Yi, *Wenhua chongtu yu shenmei xuanze* (Cultural conflict and aesthetic choice) (Beijing: Renmin wenxue chubanshe, 1988), 304.

5. Li Zhun listed eight categories from "rebellious consciousness" to "perturbations of the soul" in his essay "'Xiandai yishi' he tade canzhaoxi" ("Modern consciousness" and its referential framework), *Wenyi lilun* (Theories of literature and the arts) 9 (1986), 105. The essay was originally published in *Guangming ribao*, 21 August 1986. On consciousness of subjectivity, crisis consciousness, and critical and pluralistic consciousness, see Pan Kaixiong, "*Wenyi bao* yaoqing bufen wenyi lilunjie renshi zuotan 'Wenxue yu xiandai yishi' wenti" (*The newspaper of literature and the arts* invited some representatives of literary criticism for a symposium on the problem of "Literature and modern

consciousness"), in *Zhongguo wenyi nianjian: 1987* (The almanac of Chinese literature and the arts: 1987) (Beijing: Wenhua yishu chubanshe, 1988), 63.

6. One such official showcase was a symposium held by *Wenyi bao* (Newspaper of literature and the arts) in July 1986, only months before the students' demonstration and the most serious setback of reform that ended in Hu Yaobang's ouster and the official onslaught against bourgeois liberalism in early 1987. The title of the symposium, "Literature and Modern Consciousness," however innocuous it may appear at first glimpse, should have sent signals of warnings to those writers whose wish to delink literature and ideology had failed throughout modern history. Symposia of this kind conjure up memories of censorship campaigns and perpetuate the commonly held view that there is an agonistic relationship between literature and politics in China. The naming of the symposium implied the target of censure: those writers who dared to redraw the semantic boundary of "modern consciousness" and interpolate the signifying space of the neologism mapped out earlier by the Party.

7. Pan Kaixiong, "Yi xiandai yishi fanying xiandai shenghuo" (Reflecting modern life by means of modern consciousness), *Wenyi lilun* 8 (1986), 11–12.

8. Wu Yuanmai, "Guanyu xiandai yishi he wenyi de sikao" (Reflections on [the relationship between] modern consciousness and literature and the arts), *Wenyi lilun* 10 (1986), 49. The essay was originally published in *Wenyi bao*, 20 September 1986.

9. Ibid., 50.

10. Jean-François Lyotard, *The Postmodern Condition: A Report on Knowledge*, trans. Geoff Bennington and Brian Massumi (Minneapolis: University of Minnesota Press, 1984), 79.

11. Su Wei, "Wenxue de 'xungen' yu 'huayu' de shanbian: Luelun xifang xiandai zhuyi wenxue sichao dui baling niandai Zhongguo wenxue de yingxiang" (The "root-searching" of literature and the change of "discourse": On the influence of the literary trends of Western modernism on Chinese literature of the 1980s), in *Zhongguo dalu dangdai wenhua bianqian*, 187, 204.

12. Sun Shaozhen, "Xinde meixue yuanze zai jueqi" (A new aesthetic principle is rising abruptly), in *Xifang xiandai pai wenxue wenti lunzheng ji* (The collection of essays on the controversy over the problems of Western modernist literature), ed. He Wangxian (Beijing: Renmin wenxue chubanshe, 1984), 1: 323–33. The essay was originally published in *Shikan* (Poetry magazine) 3 (1981). It is worth noting that Sun Shaozhen's essay and the two other articles—Xie Mian's "Xinren de jueqi" (The rising of new talents) and Xu Jingye's "Jueqi de shiqun" (The rising constellation of poetry)—were later labeled as the "Three Risings" and turned into a major target for the campaign of "Antibourgeois Liberalism."

13. Frederick R. Karl, *Modern and Modernism: The Sovereignty of the Artist 1885–1925* (New York: Atheneum, 1985), xiv.

14. Martin Jay, "Habermas and Modernism," in *Habermas and Modernity*, ed. Richard J. Bernstein (Cambridge: MIT Press, 1985), 126.

15. Liu Xiaobo, "Yizhong xinde shenmei sichao: Cong Xu Xing, Chen Cun, Liu Suola de sanbu zuopin tanqi" (A new kind of aesthetic trend: Commenting on the three works by Xu Xing, Chen Cun, and Liu Suola), *Wenxue pinglun* 3 (1986), 37.

16. Xu Zidong, "Xiandai zhuyi yu Zhongguo xinshiqi wenxue" (Modernism and the new-era literature in China), *Wenxue pinglun* 4 (1989), 27.

17. On roundabout strategies, see Su Wei, "Wenxue de 'xungen' yu 'huayu' de shanbian," 193.

18. Ibid.

19. Li Tuo coined the term *Mao wenti* in early 1989 to conceptualize the dilemma in which culture elite such as Liu Zaifu and realist writers were help-lessly immersed. Li would not have been able to formulate the notion of *Mao wenti* if the language fever had not taken root in the establishment of literary criticism around the mid-1980s. Without the awkward explorations undertaken by his peers and predecessors into the systematizing function of language, and in fact, without their earlier aborted attempts to search for aesthetic rationality through the medium of the linguistic sign, there is no telling whether Li Tuo would have ever aspired to examine the field of ideology and Maoism as a so-cial phenomenon structured semiotically by linguistic codes.

In Li Tuo's view, the ideological constraints that prevented critics such as Liu Zaifu from departing completely from Marxian dialectics were a common bondage from which the generation of Cultural Revolution attempted to strug-gle free in vain. Li bid farewell to the prosaic formulation of ideology as consciousness. What he was interested in examining was not the political legiti-mation of Maoism achieved through the means of violent suppression, but the institutionalization, in various sectors of Chinese society, of the dominant dis-cursive form he called the Mao Style. In short, Li Tuo interpreted Maoism as a system of linguistic signs. The hegemony of Maoism in China was established not through the brutal means of "classic authoritarianism," but materialized in a complex process whereby the Party orchestrated a total "control of public dis-course[s] and representation" by resorting to a "comprehensive network" of in-stitutional practices such as "meetings, study groups, personnel organization, and [a] pervasive file system." Li Tuo was one of the first critics in contempo-rary China who conceptualized language as the site in which the social indi-vidual is constructed. In the works written by Li Tuo and his fellow travelers Huang Ziping and Meng Yue, we finally witness the genuine blossoming of an aesthetic rationality that made possible, for the first time in China, an analysis based on the assumption that all social practices can be understood as significa-tion, a specific semiotic system construed by its own codes and rules. Language, to be understood as a discursive system rather than abstract categories such as "human nature," "ideology," "system rationalization," and "sociohistorical consciousness," emerged as the central category of aesthetic modernity as the decade drew to an end.

Li Tuo's reflections on language in relation to history and to representations of social relations opened the route toward a new understanding of the literary history of post-Mao China. It was the battle over language, according to Li, rather than the battle over ideology (humanism versus alienation, modernism versus realism, or bourgeois liberalism versus socialism), that constituted the de-terminate category that captured the profound historical experience of China's postrevolutionary literature. Having identified the Mao Style as the site of con-testation where different groups strove for the (re)production of meaning, Li Tuo deciphered the history of the entire decade in terms of the struggle of Chinese writers against the hegemony of Mao Style. Those who failed in this epochal struggle (among them, writers of the wounded literature and intellectuals such as Feng Youlan and Ba Jin) reproduced the discourse of Mao while making a false claim to ideologically critique Maoism (Li Tuo, "Mao Style and Its Political Institutionalization," unpublished proposal for research, Duke University, spring 1993, 2). Pursuing this line of argument, Li Tuo proclaimed that, contrary to conventional wisdom, it was not the wounded literature but Misty poetry that truly marked the beginning of the "new-era literature." The linguistic revolution that Misty poets initiated was an authentic revolution because it "provided for the Chinese people a different system of signs while destroying the Mao Style" (Li, "Xiandai hanyu yu dangdai wenxue" [Modern Mandarin Chinese and contemporary literature], *Xindi* (New earth) 1, no. 6 (1991), 40). In the same manner, Li Tuo valorized the other two literary movements that he perceived to be direct descendants of Misty poetry: the *xungen* school in the mid-1980s and the experimentalist fiction in the late 1980s. Instead of joining the other critics in condemning as ideologically regressive the root-searching writers' return to cultural myths, Li interpreted their backward-looking consciousness in terms of the quest for a "cultural code totally different from the Mao Style" (41). Needless to say, the real feast of subversion was prepared and delivered by the irreverent experimentalists, whose obsession with radical linguistic games led to the total bankruptcy of the discursive system of Maoism.

By postulating the "Mao Style," Li Tuo rescued the problematic of language from the practitioners of system sciences by whom language was seen as nothing more than a formal instrument of articulation separable from the issues of agency and ideology. For Li Tuo, language constitutes the locale where the social, historical, and individual intersect. It is, in short, the site of contestation and resistance at the same time. Possibilities of inquiries into the constitutive subjectivity in language were thus opened up for those theorists who wished to examine what orthodox Marxism has traditionally repressed: the question of the subject, of language, and of their articulation with each other in relation to ideology. If "any kind of discourse represents the formation of power that suppresses and excludes. . . [and] controls the thinking of human beings through the process of its suppression and exclusion of other discourses" (39), then not only is resistance bound to begin with the liquidation of the authoritative discourse, but more importantly, the formation of a new subjectivity has to begin with the construction of a new discursive system. Li Tuo's materialist rereading of language as a potential means of subjugating and liberating subjectivity suggests that we look at the formation of subjectivity as a constitutive moment in language using. This view has certainly come a long way from Liu Zaifu's theory of subjectivity that presupposed the structural equilibrium and closure of the human subject. The thesis of the Mao Style was suggestive of the infinite possibilities of the reformulation of subject-positions in the breakdown of previous discursive positionality.

20. Chen Huangmei et al., eds., *Zhongguo xinwenyi daxi: 1976–1982 shiliao ji* (Chinese new art and literature series: Collection of historical materials between 1976–1982) (Beijing: Zhongguo wenlian chuban gongsi, 1990), 900–907.

21. All three letters—Feng Jicai's "Zhongguo wenxue xuyao 'xiandai pai':
Gei Li Tuo de xin" (Chinese literature needs the "modernist school": A letter to
Li Tuo), Li Tuo's "'Xiandai xiaoshuo' bu dengyu 'xiandai pai': Gei Liu Xinwu
de xin" ("Modern fiction" is not equal to "modernist school": A letter to Liu
Xinwu), and Liu Xinwu's "Xuyao lengjing de sikao: Gei Feng Jicai de xin" ([We]
need calm reflection: A letter to Feng Jicai)—were originally published in *Shanghai wenxue* 8 (1982). See all three letters in *Xifang xiandai pai wenxue wenti
lunzheng ji,* 2: 499–519.

22. Liu Xinwu, "Zai 'xin qi guai' mianqian: Du *Xiandai xiaoshuo jiqiao
chutan*" (In the face of "the new, the strange, and the grotesque": Reading *The
preliminary inquiry into the techniques of modern fiction*), in *Xifang xiandai pai
wenxue wenti lunzheng ji,* 2: 528. The essay was originally published in *Dushu*
7 (1982).

23. Feng Jicai, "Zhongguo wenxue xuyao 'xiandai pai,'" 505.

24. Liu Xinwu, "Xuyao lengjing de sikao," 519.

25. Feng Jicai, "Zhongguo wenxue xuyao 'xiandai pai,'" 501.

26. Li Tuo, "'Xiandai xiaoshuo' bu dengyu 'xiandai pai,'" 512, 510.

27. Tang Xuezhi, "Yijiu baer nian wenyi lilun yanjiu gaishu" (General account of studies on literary theory in 1982), in *Zhongguo xinwenyi daxi,* 438.

28. Chen Danchen, "Yetan xiandai pai yu Zhongguo wenxue: Zhi Feng
Jicai tongzhi de xin" (Additional discussion of the modernist school and Chinese literature: A letter to Comrade Feng Jicai), in *Xifang xiandai pai wenxue
wenti lunzheng ji,* 2: 566.

29. Arguing against Dai Houying, Geng Yong proclaims that realism did not
form an antagonistic relationship with modernism. He dismisses her arguments
that the rise of modernism necessitated its struggle to break away from the constraints inherent in realism. See Geng Yong, "Xiandai pai zenyang he xianshi
zhuyi 'duikang': Zheli ye bunengbu sheji mouzhong xianshi zhuyi lilun xianxiang" (How modernists "confronted" realism: Here one cannot but speak of a
certain theoretical phenomenon of realism), in *Xifang xiandai pai wenxue wenti
lunzheng ji,* 2: 378–79.

30. Yan Zhaozhu, "Wenxue bentilun de xingqi yu kunhuo: Xinshiqi shinian
wenyi lilun yanjiu saomiao" (The rise and confusion of the ontological theories
of literature: A quick glance at the study of literary theories of the new era during
this decade), *Wenyi yanjiu* 4 (1989), 199, quoting from "Xuanzhuan de wen-
tan" (A revolving literary field), *Wenxue pinglun* 1 (1989).

31. For binarism between modernism and realism in terms of representational methods, see Li Tuo, "Lun 'geshi geyang de xiaoshuo'" (On "Fiction of
various varieties"), in *Xifang xiandai pai wenxue wenti lunzheng ji,* 2: 542–43;
Peng Lixun, "Cong xifang meixue he wenyi sichao kan 'Ziwo biaoxian' shuo:
Shi 'xinde meixue yuanze' haishi jiudiao chongtan?" (Examining the theory of
"self-expression" from the perspective of Western aesthetics and literary trends:
Was it a "new aesthetic principle" or the replaying of an old tune?), in *Xifang
xiandai pai wenxue wenti lunzheng ji,* 1: 350–66.

32. Xu Zidong, "Xiandai zhuyi yu Zhongguo xinshiqi wenxue," 28.

33. Xu Chi, "Xiandai hua yu xiandai pai" (Modernization and modernism),
in *Xifang xiandai pai wenxue wenti lunzheng ji,* 2: 396, 399. Also see Li Zhun's

rebuttal of Xu Chi's argument that modernism went hand in hand with modernization. Li Zhun, "Xiandai hua yu xiandai pai youzhe biran lianxi ma?" (Is there necessarily a connection between modernization and modernism?), in *Xifang xiandai pai wenxue wenti lunzheng ji,* 2: 414.

34. Xu Zidong, "Xiandai zhuyi yu Zhongguo xinshiqi wenxue," 31.

35. Xu Chi, "Xiandai hua yu xiandai pai," 399.

36. Li Tuo, "'Xiandai xiaoshuo' bu dengyu 'xiandai pai,'" 507–13.

37. Both Li Tuo and Xu Zidong raised the counterproposition of "pseudo-realism." See Li Tuo, "Yetan 'wei xiandai pai' jiqi piping" (Further discussions of "pseudomodernism" and its criticism), *Beijing wenxue* 4 (1988), 5, 8. Also see Xu Zidong, "Xiandai zhuyi yu Zhongguo xinshiqi wenxue," 32. According to Xu, the appropriation of European realism in Mao's China underwent a career similar to that fared by modernism in post-Mao China: origin-tracing (i.e., *Shi Jing* [The book of songs] cited as the earliest Chinese origin of realism), voluntary invitation, selective borrowing of realistic methods, and homogenization.

38. Wang Bi, "Ming Xiang," in *Zhouyi luelie, Wang Bi ji jiaoshi,* ed. Lou Yulie (Beijing: Xinhua shuju, 1980), 2: 609.

39. Gan Yang, "Cong 'lixing de pipan' dao 'wenhua de pipan'" (From "The critique of rationality" to "The critique of culture"), in *Zhongguo dangdai wenhua yishi,* 574.

40. For a more detailed discussion of Taoist poetics, see the author's *The Story of Stone: Intertextuality, Ancient Chinese Stone Lore, and the Stone Symbolism of "Dream of the Red Chamber," "Water Margin," and "The Journey to the West"* (Durham: Duke University Press, 1992), 31–33.

41. The origin of the term *wenxue benti lun* is no longer traceable. It has been widely adopted by literary critics since the mid-1980s. On *wenxue yuyanxue,* see Huang Ziping, "Deyi mo wangyan" (Do not forget the linguistic sign once meaning is grasped), *Shanghai wenxue* 11 (1985), 86.

42. He Xilai, "Yijiu bawu nian *Zhongguo wenxue yanjiu nianjian* qianyan" (Preface to the 1985 almanac of the studies of Chinese literature), *Wenyi lilun* 12 (1986), 9.

43. On aesthetic synthesis, see Albrecht Wellmer, "Reason, Utopia, and the *Dialectic of Enlightenment,"* in *Habermas and Modernity,* 48.

44. Astradur Eysteinsson, *The Concept of Modernism* (Ithaca, N.Y.: Cornell University Press, 1990), 26.

45. He Xilai, "Yijiu bawu nian," 14.

46. Bai Hua, "Guanyu fangfalun wenti de zhengming: Jinnianlai wenyi lilun wenti tantao gaishu zhier" (Regarding the debates and discussions over the problems of methodologies: Sequel to the summary of the inquiries into the problems of literary theories in recent years), *Wenyi lilun* 5 (1986), 47. The article was originally published in *Renmin ribao,* 21 April 1986.

47. Wu Yumin, "Xunqiu renwen jiazhi he kexue lixing jiehe de qidian" (In search of the point of convergence between humanist values and scientific rationality), in "Yuyan wenti yu wenxue yanjiu de tuozhan" (Exploration and development of language problems and literary studies), *Wenxue pinglun* 1 (1988), 62–64.

48. Pan Kaixiong and He Shaojun, "Kunnan, fenhua, zonghe" (Difficulties, differentiations, synthesis), in "Yuyan wenti yu wenxue yanjiu de tuozhan," 65. Wu Xiaoming, "Biaoxian, chuangzao, moshi" (Expression, creation, model), in "Yuyan wenti yu wenxue yanjiu de tuozhan," 60.

49. On the scientific model of literary studies, see Xu Ming, "Wenxue yanjiu yao jinxing siwei biange" (Literary studies have to undergo a thought reform), in "Yuyan wenti yu wenxue yanjiu de tuozhan," 68. On alienation, see Wu Xiaoming, "Biaoxian, chuangzao, moshi," 59.

50. Lin Xingzhai, "Lun xitong kexue fangfalun zai wenyi yanjiu zhong de yunyong" (On the application of system science methodology to the study of arts and literature), Wenyi lilun 2 (1986), 33. The article was originally published in Wenxue pinglun 1 (1986), 48–56.

51. He Xilai, "Yijiu bawu nian," 11. Cheng Jincheng, "Zhongguo xiandai wenxue jiazhi guannian xitong lungang" (The outline of the system of the concept of value in modern Chinese literature), Wenxue pinglun 3 (1989), 26–37.

52. Ji Hongzhen, "Wenxue piping de xitong fangfa yu jiegou yuanze," Wenyi lilun yanjiu 3 (1984). Lin Xingzhai, "Lun A Q xingge xitong," Lu Xun yanjiu 1 (1984) 46–54. Li Zehou, Meide licheng (Beijing: Wenwu chubanshe, 1981). Wu Gongzheng, Xiaoshuo meixue (Nanjing: Jiangsu wenyi chubanshe, 1985).

53. Li Zehou, Meide licheng, 1.

54. On social ethos, see ibid., 27. On cultural-psychological formation, see Li Zehou, Zhongguo gudai sixiang shilun, 32.

55. Chen Feilong, "Wenyi kongzhilun chutan" (A preliminary inquiry into the control theory of arts and literature), Wenyi lilun 3 (1986), 29. The article was originally published in Wenyi yanjiu 1 (1986), 20–24.

56. Chen Pingyuan, Huang Ziping, and Qian Liqun, "Lun 'Ershi shiji Zhongguo wenxue,'" Wenxue pinglun 5 (1985), reprinted in "Ershi shiji Zhongguo wenxue" sanren tan (Conversations between Chen Pingyuan, Qian Liqun, and Huang Ziping on "Twentieth-century Chinese literature") (Beijing: Renmin wenxue chubanshe, 1988), 1–26.

57. On literary studies and "open-door consciousness," see He Xilai, "Yijiu bawu nian," 18.

58. Chen, Huang, and Qian, "Guanyu 'Ershi shiji Zhongguo wenxue' de duihua," 101, 103, quoting Chen Pingyuan, and 30, quoting Huang Ziping.

59. Ibid., 30, quoting Huang Ziping.

60. Ibid., 31 and 77. Chen, Huang, and Qian, "Lun 'Ershi shiji Zhongguo wenxue,'" 25. Chen, Huang, and Qian, "Guanyu 'Ershi shiji Zhongguo wenxue' de duihua," 32, quoting Qian Liqun.

61. Ibid.

62. Ibid., 94–95, 100. Chen Pingyuan and Huang Ziping, "Xiaoshuo xushi de liangci zhuanbian" (The two transformations of the narrative form of fiction), Beijing wenxue 9 (1988), 67. Both Huang Ziping and Chen Pingyuan speak of their revulsion to the revolutionary doctrine in relation to their projections of how they would write the literary history of modern China. Both critics deny the cause of the Revolution by questioning the logic of rupture. In Huang's view, the Revolution's emphasis on ruptures did not bring about real changes in Chinese society. It was symptomatic of a deep structural stability of Chinese society

instead. Chen Pingyuan's ironic critique of the doctrine in question is particularly poignant: Rebellion is not necessarily correct, revolution is not necessarily beneficial" (68).

63. Chen Yong, "Xuyao jiaqiang jichu lilun de yanjiu" ([We] need to strengthen the studies of our foundation theories), in *Zhongguo wenxue yanjiu nianjian: 1985,* ed. Editorial Committee (Beijing: Zhongguo wenlian chuban gongsi, 1986), 4.

64. Wang Yuanhua, "Guanyu muqian wenxue yanjiu zhong de liangge wenti" (With regard to the two problematics of contemporary literary studies), *Wenyi lilun* 8 (1986), 109. The article was originally published in *Wenhui bao,* 11 August 1986.

65. Li Xinfeng, "Shenru tantao fangfalun nuli fazhan wenyixue: Wuhan wenyixue fangfalun xueshu taolunhui zongshu" (Go deeply into the examination of the theories of methodology, develop diligently the science of arts and literature: A general account of the symposium on the Theories of Methodology of Arts and Literature at Wuhan), *Wenyi lilun* 3 (1986), 20, quoting Zhou Lequn.

66. Lin Xingzhai, "Lun xitong kexue fangfalun zai wenyi yanjiu zhong de yunyong," 30–33.

67. Li Dongmu, "Xiandai wenxue yanjiu yu xitong kexue fangfa yizhi" (The studies of modern literature and the transplantation of the scientific methods of system theory), *Wenyi lilun yanjiu* 3 (1985), 29.

68. See Ji Hongzhen, "Wenxue piping de xitong fangfa yu jiegou yuanze."

69. Song Yaoliang, "Wenxue xinsichao de zhuyao shenmei tezheng yu biaoxian xingtai" (The major aesthetic characteristics and the modes of manifestations of the new literary trend), *Shanghai wenxue* 6 (1987), 77.

70. Bai Hua, "Guanyu fangfalun wenti de zhengming," 47.

71. Lin Xingzhai, "Lun xitong kexue fangfalun zai wenyi yanjiu zhong de yunyong," 29.

72. Qian Jing, "Yuqiong qianli mu, gengshang yiceng lou: Ji Yangzhou wenyixue fangfalun wenti xueshu taolun hui" (If you desire to look far into the distance, climb up to the next story: Proceedings of the Yangzhou Conference on the Issues of Methodologies of the Studies of Literature and the Arts), *Wenxue pinglun* 4 (1985), 50–55.

73. Liu Zaifu was the first critic who theorized on the proposition that "literature is *renxue.*" See his "Lun wenxue de zhutixing" (On the subjectivity of literature), in *Shengming jingshen yu wenxue daolu* (The spirit of life and the path of literature) (Taibei: Fengyun shidai chuban gongsi, 1989), 83–144; "Wenxue yanjiu yingyi ren wei siwei zhongxin" (Literary studies should take human beings as its cognitive center), in *Wenxue de fansi* (Introspections of literature) (Beijing: Renmin wenxue chubanshe, 1988), 40–53; and "Zhongguo xiandai wenxueshi shang dui ren de sanci faxian" (The three discoveries of humanity in the history of modern Chinese literature), in *Xunzhao yu huhuan* (Searches and invocations) (Taibei: Fengyun shidai chubanshe, 1989), 33–48. Also see Liu Heng, "Wenxue de youji zhengtixing he wenxue lilun de xitongxing" (The organic totality of literature and the systematical nature of literary theory), *Wenyi bao* 11 (1984), 65–68; and Wu Liang, "Fangfa de yongtu" (Applications of methodolo-

gies), *Wenyi bao,* 31 August 1985. On the "ontology of literature," see Liu Zai-fu, "Wenxue yanjiu siwei kongjian de tuozhan" (The expansion and development of the cognitive space of literary studies), in *Wenxue de fansi,* 1–39.

74. Liu Zaifu, "Wenxue yanjiu siwei kongjian de tuozhan," 3.

75. Liu Zaifu, "Lun wenxue de zhutixing," 84.

76. See chapter seven, "Wang Shuo—'Pop Goes the Culture?'" for a detailed exploration of the "Wang Shuo phenomenon."

77. Liu Zaifu, "Lun wenxue de zhutixing," 88.

78. Liu, "Lun renwu xingge de erchong zuhe yuanli" (On the principle of the dual composition of fictional character), in *Shengming jinshen yu wenxue daolu,* 6.

79. Habermas, *The Philosophical Discourse,* 112.

80. On art and one-dimensional society, see Jay, *Habermas and Modernity,* 126.

81. Yang Yu, "Wenxue: Shique hongdong xiaoying yihou" (Literature: After losing its sensational impact), *Renmin ribao,* 12 February 1988, overseas edition. I do not agree with Yang Yu's assessment of the new aesthetic trends that have emerged since the mid-1980s. But his general comments on the implications of the differentiation of literature into "serious" and popular brands are poignant and worth noting.

82. Li Zehou and Liu Zaifu, "Wenxue yu yishu de qingsi: Li Zehou yu Liu Zaifu de wenxue duihua" (Emotive thoughts in literature and arts: A literary dialogue between Li Zehou and Liu Zaifu), *Renmin ribao,* 14 April 1988, overseas edition.

83. "'Xinxieshi xiaoshuo dalianzhan' juanshouyu" (Introduction to the volume of "The grand exhibition of new realist fiction"), *Zhongshan* 3 (1989), 4.

84. Wang Meng, "Dangqian wenxue gongzuo zhong de jige wenti" (Several problems in literary studies at the present), *Hongqi* 24 (1985), 16–19.

85. He Shaojun and Pan Kaixiong, "Zhen yu wei: Guanyu 'wei xiandai pai' taolun de duihua" (The true and the false: A dialogue on the discussions of "pseudomodernism"), *Zuojia* 10 (1988), 79, quoting Li Tuo.

86. Ibid.

87. Ernesto Laclau, preface to *The Sublime Object of Ideology,* by Slavoj Zizek (London: Verso, 1989), xiv.

88. Huang Ziping, "Guanyu 'wei xiandai pai' jiqi piping" (Regarding "pseudomodernism" and its critiques), *Beijing wenxue* 2 (1988), 9.

89. On the symposium, see "Mianxiang xinshiqi wenxue di'erge shinian de sikao" (Speculations on facing the second decade of the new-era literature), transcribed by Tan Xiang, *Wenxue pinglun* 1 (1987), 44–50.

90. He Xin, "Dangdai wenxue zhong de huangmiugan yu duoyuzhe: Du 'Wuzhuti bianzou' suixianglu" (The sentiments of absurdity and the superfluous being: Random notes on reading "Variations without a theme"), *Dushu* 11 (1985), 3–13.

91. Wang Ning, "Guifan yu bianti: Guanyu Zhongguo wenxue zhong de xiandai zhuyi he houxiandai zhuyi" (Norm and mutations: Regarding modernism and postmodernism in Chinese literature), *Zhongshan* 6 (1989), 157–58.

92. Mu Gong, "Xiang Sate gaobie: Jianping *Xin xiaoshuo pai yanjiu* bian-xuanzhe xu" (Farewell to Sartre: With an accompanying review of the editor's preface to *The study of "nouveau roman"*), *Dushu* 3 (1988), 65.

93. Ibid., 68.

94. "Mianxiang xinshiqi wenxue di'erge shinian de sikao," 48, quoting Zhang Yiwu.

95. Huang Ziping, "Guanyu 'wei xiandai pai,'" 5.

96. He Xin, "Dangdai wenxue zhong de huangmiugan yu duoyuzhe," 12.

97. Mu Gong, "Lun 'wei xiandai pai'" (On "pseudomodernism"), *Mengya* 5 (1988), 63.

98. Liu Xiaobo, "Weiji! Xinshiqi wenxue mianlin weiji" (Crisis! The new-era literature is facing crisis), *Wenyi lilun* 12 (1986), 168–69. The essay was originally published in *Shenzhen qingnian bao,* 3 October 1986.

99. Ibid., 169.

100. Ibid., 173.

101. Huang Ziping, "Guanyu 'wei xiandai pai,'" 4.

102. Zhang Shouying, "'Wei xiandai pai' yu 'xiti zhongyong' boyi" (A rebuttal of "pseudomodernism" and "Western substance, Chinese application"), *Beijing wenxue* 6 (1988), 53, 55, 57.

103. Xu Zidong, "Xiandai zhuyi yu Zhongguo xinshiqi wenxue," 32.

104. Li Tuo, "Yetan 'wei xiandai pai' jiqi piping," 8.

105. Ibid.

106. Xu Zidong, "Xiandai zhuyi yu Zhongguo xinshiqi wenxue," 32.

107. Chen Sihe, "Zhongguo wenxue fazhan zhong de xiandai zhuyi: Jianlun xiandai yishi yu minzu wenhua de ronghui" (The modernism in the developing Chinese literature: With an accompanying reflection on the merging of modern consciousness and national culture), *Shanghai wenxue* 7 (1985), 86. Ji Hong-zhen, "Zhongguo jinnian xiaoshuo yu xifang xiandai zhuyi wenxue [shang]" (Recent Chinese fiction and Western modernist literature: 1), *Wenyi bao,* 2 January 1988, 3.

108. Yang Yi, *Wenhua chongtu yu shenmei xuanze,* 324.

109. Wang Ning, "Guifan yu bianti," 158.

110. Gao Xingjian, "Chidaole de xiandai zhuyi yu dangjin Zhongguo wen-xue" (The late-coming modernism and contemporary Chinese literature), *Wen-xue piping* 3 (1988), 13.

111. Xu Zidong, "Xiandai zhuyi yu Zhongguo xinshiqi wenxue," 31.

112. Ibid., 29.

113. Xu Jingye, "Jueqi de shiqun: Ping woguo shige de xiandai qingxiang" (The rising constellation of poetry: On the modernist trend of our poetry), in *Xifang xiandai pai wenxue wenti lunzheng ji,* 2: 599.

114. Li Tuo, "'Xiandai xiaoshuo' bu dengyu 'xiandai pai,'" 510.

115. Chen, Huang, and Qian, "Lun 'Ershi shiji Zhongguo wenxue,'" 14.

116. Ji Hongzhen, "Zhongguo jinnian xiaoshuo," 3.

117. Liu Xiaobo, "Yizhong xinde shenmei sichao," 41–42.

118. Chen, Huang, and Qian, "Lun 'Ershi shiji Zhongguo wenxue,'" 12.

119. Xu Jingye, "Jueqi de shiqun," 580.

120. Li Tuo, "Yijiu bawu" (1985), *Jintian* 3/4 (1991), 59–73.

121. The slogan grew out of the changing self-perception of the young poets of the post-*Menglong* poetry generation. They no longer perceived themselves as cultural critics and the spokespeople of sociopolitical conscience—a historical role that Bei Dao's generation fulfilled. They denied the conventional definition of the poet's persona as the cultural hero. For them, writing poetry was nothing more than a pure linguistic experimentation. The sentiment of antiheroism reflected in the slogan smacked of an Oedipal rebellion.

122. Li Jiefei and Zhang Ling, "Youhuan yishi yu rende reqing" ("Anxiety consciousness" and human passions), *Shanghai wenxue* 9 (1986), 93.

123. Li Jie and Huang Ziping, "Wenxueshi kuangjia ji qita" (The framework of literary history and other subjects), *Beijing wenxue* 7 (1988), 75. Li Jie considers 1985 the beginning of modern Chinese literature in terms of its correspondence to modern world literature.

124. Li Jiefei and Zhang Ling, "Youhuan yishi yu rende reqing," 93, emphasis mine.

125. Ibid.

126. Xu Zidong, "Xiandai zhuyi yu Zhongguo xinshiqi wenxue," 33.

127. Li Jie, "Lun Zhongguo dangdai xinchao xiaoshuo" (On the new wave fiction in contemporary China), *Zhongshan* 5 (1988), 120.

128. Liu Xiaobo, "Yizhong xinde shenmei sichao," 41.

129. Ibid., 42.

130. Ibid., 40. Liu Xiaobo condemned Li Zehou because of the latter's advocacy of Confucian ethics and the aesthetics of *tianren heyi*. For Liu, beauty resides not in harmony but in conflicts. The cultivation and endorsement of aesthetic and moral equilibrium leads to eclecticism and reveals a premodern state of mind that can only be characterized as "the extreme condition of slavedom." To reconstruct Chinese national character, Liu insists that we negate thoroughly the three primary theoretical paradigms underlying traditional culture: the Confucian democratic model of *minben* (for the people), the model personality of Confucius and Yanhui, and the concept of *tianren heyi*. See Liu Xiaobo's chapter on "tianren heyi" in his *Xuanze de pipan*, 135–234.

131. On the semiotic and aesthetic moment in aesthetic modernity, see Albrecht Wellmer, *The Persistence of Modernity: Essays on Aesthetics, Ethics, and Postmodernism,* trans. David Midgley (Cambridge: MIT Press, 1991), 55.

132. Xu Zidong, "Xiandai zhuyi yu Zhongguo xinshiqi wenxue," 30. Emphasis is mine.

133. Liu Suola, "Ni biewu xuanze," in *Ni biewu xuanze* (Beijing: Zuojia chubanshe, 1986), 84. The story was originally published in *Renmin wenxue* 3 (1985), 4–29.

134. Liu Suola, "Lantian lühai," 137.

135. Ibid., 175.

136. Huang Ziping, *Xingcunzhe de wenxue* (The literature of those who survived) (Taibei: Yuanliu chuban shiye gufen youxian gongsi, 1991), 40.

137. Xu Xing, "Wuzhuti bianzou" in vol. 1 of *Zhongguo dalu xiandai xiaoshuo xuan,* 64 and 37. The story was originally published in *Renmin wenxue* 7 (1985), 29–41.

138. Liu Suola, "Ni biewu xuanze," 12.

139. Wang Lin, "Shi juhao haishi wenhao?" 135.

140. Huang Ziping, *Xingcunzhe de wenxue,* 40. Liu Suola, "Ni biewu xuanze," 63.

141. Ibid., 57 and 12.

142. Ibid., 16.

143. A Cheng, "The Tree Stump," in *Spring Bamboo: A Collection of Contemporary Chinese Short Stories,* ed. and trans. Jeanne Tai (New York: Random House, 1989), 241. The story was originally published in *Renmin wenxue* 10 (1984), 229–43.

144. Liu Xiaobo, "Weiji!" 169 and 173.

145. Liu Suola, "Lantian lühai," 177.

146. For a detailed discussion of transcendental subjectivity and modernity, see J. M. Bernstein, *The Philosophy of the Novel: Lukács, Marxism, and the Dialectics of Form* (Minneapolis: University of Minnesota Press, 1984), especially the chapter on "Transcendental Dialectic: Irony as Form, 185–227.

147. A Cheng, "Qiwang," in *A Cheng xiaoshuo xuan* (Collected stories of A Cheng) (Hong Kong: Tuqi youxian gongsi, 1985), 57. The story was originally published in *Shanghai wenxue* 7 (1984), 15–35.

148. Mu Gong, "Xiang Sate gaobie," 65.

149. All five chapters of Mo Yan's *The Red Sorghum Clan* were published in 1986 in quick sequence: "Hong gaoliang" (The red sorghum) appeared in *Renmin wenxue* 3; "Gaoliang jiu" (Sorghum wine) in *Jiefangjun wenyi* 7; "Goudao" (Dog ways) in *Shiyue* 4; "Gaoliang bin" (Sorghum funeral) in *Beijing wenyi* 8; and "Qisi" (Strange death) in *Kunlun* 6.

150. Mo Yan, *Honggaoliang jiazu* (Taibei: Hongfan shudian, 1988), 493. Emphasis is mine.

151. Teng Yun, "Luanhua jianyu mi renyan" (Chaotic blossoms casting a spell on our eyes), *Renmin wenxue* 4 (1986), 124.

152. Fang Keqiang, "A Q he Bingzai: Yuanshi xintai de chongsu" (Ah Q and Bing Zai: The reconstruction of primitive mentality), *Wenyi lilun yanjiu* 5 (1986), 10–11.

153. The powerful and agitated overflow of consciousness in the early experimental works by Wang Meng and Zong Pu corresponded to the sudden release of the creative self and to the dramatic expansion of subjectivity at the turn of the 1980s. The technique, however, soon lost its appeal. Song Yaoliang designated novellas and short stories written in a transformed mode of stream of consciousness as the "fiction of mental mood" (*xintai xiaoshuo*). See Song Yaoliang, "Yishiliu wenxue dongfanghua guocheng" (The Orientalization of the literature of stream of consciousness), *Wenxue pinglun* 1 (1986), 35. The making of the "fiction of mental mood" serves to indicate that the formal revolution of modernism always risks being corrupted by traditional aesthetics. This resistance can be defined as the attempt of old and middle-aged Chinese writers to revitalize the aesthetics of the harmonious blending of scene and mood (*qing* and *jing*) to stabilize, and sometimes to hold in check, the torrential flow of consciousness by bringing it back into a clearly outlined thematic framework and subjecting it to the cultural constraint of a collective consciousness. Although beginning as a revival of Chinese aesthetics, the process of sinicizing stream of

consciousness not only introduces the return of the traditional appreciation of the static beauty of harmony as opposed to the dynamic irregularities characteristic of contradiction, but it also indicates the resurgence of traditional ethos that downplays the role of the individual and suppresses the subjective voice. On the one hand, the remaking of the Chinese mode of stream of consciousness indicates the change of the fictional subject from a superficially paradoxical self not yet endowed with a profound reflexive capacity to a self of psychic depth that has outgrown the torrential mode of thinking. On the other hand, however, the new mode of philosophical introspection signals the co-option of subjectivity by traditional epistemology.

154. See Leo Lee, "Beyond Realism: Thoughts on Modernist Experiments in Contemporary Chinese Writing," in *Worlds Apart: Recent Chinese Writing and Its Audiences,* ed. Howard Goldblatt (Armonk, N.Y.: M. E. Sharpe, 1990), 69. Also see his "The Politics of Technique," 163–73.

155. Wang Meng and Wang Gan, "Wenxue zhege mofang: Duiha lu" (The magic cube of literature: An interview), *Wenxue pinglun* 3 (1989), quoting Wang Gan, 43.

156. Wang Meng, "Yiti qianjiao," *Shouhuo* (Harvest) 4 (1988), 91, 102.

157. Ibid., 94.

158. A comparative study of modernism in Taiwan in the sixties and the Shanghai modernism in the thirties, especially with regard to the genre of poetry, is worth undertaking in another project. For discussions of the modernist movement in Taiwan, see Yvonne Sung-Sheng Chang, *Modernism and Its Nativist Resistance* (Durham: Duke University Press, 1993).

159. See Yan Jiaqi's preface to *Xin'ganjuepai xiaoshuo xuan* (The collection of neo-impressionist fiction) (Beijing: Renmin wenxue chubanshe, 1985), 1–38.

160. Wang Ning, "Guifan yu bianti," 157.

CHAPTER 5

1. The concept of the subject (*zhuti*) is not an indigenous Chinese concept. Inasmuch as it is deeply implicated in the concept of modernity, it was imported from the West when Chinese intellectuals started exploring the issue of modernity and modernization. I do not intend to trace the discursive origin of *zhuti* in modern and contemporary China in this essay. Nonetheless, a working definition of subjectivity may be in order here, even though most readers probably have an intuitive understanding of the term. In the Western philosophical tradition, what we understand today as "the subject" is the Cartesian Subject conceived as a specific and autonomous reality. This entity is "granted an exorbitant privilege in that there is in the end no Being nor being except in relation to him, for him and through him." See Michel Henry, "The Critique of the Subject," in *Who Comes after the Subject?,* ed. Eduardo Cadava, Peter Connor, and Jean-Luc Nancy (New York: Routledge, 1991), 157. The essential predicates of the Cartesian Subject— "identity to self, positionality, property, personality, ego, consciousness, will, intentionality, freedom, humanity, etc."—are all "ordered around being present (*étant-present*), presence to self." See Jacques Derrida, "'Eating Well,' or the Calculation of the Subject: An Interview with Jacques Derrida," in *Who Comes*

after the Subject?, 109. According to David Kolb, modern subjectivity exists "as a subject when it imposes order. To impose a self-originated order on other things is an act of will. Modern subjectivity's self-affirmation expresses its power to control the conditions of representation." See Kolb, *The Critique of Pure Modernity: Hegel, Heidegger, and After* (Chicago: University of Chicago Press, 1986), 141. As a result, the postmodern crisis and critique of the subject is at the same time the crisis and critique of representation. Hegel defines the philosophical subject as "that which is capable of maintaining within itself its own contradiction." The subject always succeeds in reappropriating to itself the exteriority of its own predicate. In other words, the contradiction would be "its *own* . . . that alienation or extraneousness would be ownmost, and that subjectivity . . . consists in reappropriating this proper being-outside-of-itself." See Nancy, introduction to *Who Comes after the Subject?*, 6.

2. I am referring specifically to the special issue of *Discours social/Social Discourse* on the "Non-Cartesian Subject," volume 6, nos. 1–2 (1994), in which an abridged version of this chapter was published. The editors Darko Suvin and Kojin Karatani were interested in the implicit "dialogue between 'non-Cartesian' cultures such as China and Japan with the 'First World.'" In their "Call for Papers," they phrased the problem of the non-Cartesian Subject as "What forms of Subject are possible outside the individualist (Tocqueville) Self, and how does such a single but externalized and *interacting* Subject relate to various existing or potential collective Subjects?" (emphasis mine). Western intellectuals' revolt against the Cartesian subject took various forms. Starting from the poststructuralist "decentered subject," they initiated one debate after another on the status of the subject, debates that covered many disciplines: Lacan on psychoanalysis, Derrida on philosophy, Althusser on politics, and not in the least, literary criticism. To reverse the conceptual drive underlying the Cartesian Subject, many poststructuralist theorists denied the subject any possibilities of human agency. The proposition about the demise of the subject gave rise to counterarguments such as those by Paul Smith, who theorized about the return of the subject to its role as an active historical agent. See Smith, *Discerning the Subject* (Minneapolis: University of Minnesota Press, 1988). The special issue of *Discours social* represents one such attempt to reinvigorate the Western tradition of the subject by inquiring into other forms of the subject in non-Western cultural traditions.

3. Wang Ruoshui, "Wei rendao zhuyi bianhu," 233.

4. Bei Dao, the cover of *Jintian* (Today), 3/4 (1991).

5. David Kolb, *The Critique of Pure Modernity*, 154. Kolb compares the logic of our age with the metaphysical tradition of the past in which one can speak of some higher being or principle of reason that both guaranteed and supported the availability of other beings. Our age witnesses the disappearance of such higher beings. Nothing is there to command the availability of things. "In the world of total availability no one being grounds all the rest." They are just "in plain view." "The meaning of reality is pure available presence."

6. Nan Fan and Huang Ziping, "Xiaoshuo, shenmei qinggan yu shidai" (Narrative fiction, aesthetic sentiments, and [our] time), *Beijing wenxue* (Beijing literature) 11 (1988), 71–74. In this dialogue with Nan Fan, Huang Ziping prob-

lematizes the total and naive acceptance of pluralism by Chinese writers and critics. According to him, "the term 'pluralism' has been turned into the most efficacious charm that covered up our laziness and cowardice—whenever we come across a cultural phenomenon that is difficult to adumbrate, we simply put the matter in a nutshell by saying, 'This is pluralism'" (72). Here Huang Ziping is aware of the omnipresence of pluralism as another form of hegemony.

7. Tang Xiaobing, "The Function of New Theory: What Does It Mean to Talk about Post-Modernism in China?" *Public Culture* 4, no. 1 (1991), 89–108. Tang applauds the arrival of postmodernism in China as an aesthetic intervention in politics and social life. The postmodernist "obsession with intertextuality and the floating signifier leads to a happy rediscovery of the deconstructive force of the Chinese language" (106). But is the authoritarian Mao Style the only thing deconstructed by a "Chinese postmodernism?" To that list, one might add the cultural subjecthood of China, or in Gates' terms, the core identity of the colonized. Perhaps the "deconstructive force" of postmodernism is not so innocent politically as Tang assumes.

8. Henry Louis Gates, Jr. "Critical Fanonism," *Critical Inquiry* 17, no. 3 (1991), 459. Gates points out the problematic nature of the natives' advocacy for pluralism in the postcolonial age. He sees in the invasion by Western pluralistic cultural logic the beginning of the dissolution of the individuality of the colonized. "The colonized is never characterized in an individual manner; he is entitled only to drown in an anonymous collectivity."

9. With the exception of Can Xue, all the experimentalists are male writers.

10. Liu Zaifu's "Lun wenxue de zhutixing" was originally published in *Wenxue pinglun* (Literary review) 6 (1985) and 1 (1986). "Wenxue yanjiu yingyi ren wei siwei zhongxin" was originally published in *Wenhui bao*, 8 July 1985. *Xingge zuhe lun* was originally published in Shanghai by Shanghai wenyi chubanshe, 1986.

11. Critiques of Liu Zaifu usually bypass the implications of Marxist humanism and socialist alienation in his work. Only a few critics such as He Xilai and Song Yaoliang mention in passing the relationship between Liu Zaifu's formulation of subjectivity with the problematic of Marxist humanism. He Xilai's statement drives home the gist of the matter most explicitly: we "cannot simply draw an equation between Liu's 'subjectivity of literature' and Hu Feng's 'subjective fighting spirit. . . . The presentation of the problematic of 'subjectivity of literature' . . . is a philosophical reformulation of [Marxist] humanism in the realm of literature." See He Xilai, "Guanyu wenxue zhutixing wenti de tantao" (The inquiry of the questions regarding subjectivity), *Renmin ribao*, 11 August 1986, overseas edition. Also see Song Yaoliang, *Shinian wenxue zhuchao* (The main literary currents of the decade) (Shanghai: Shanghai wenyi chubanshe, 1988), 273. And see Liu Kang, "Subjectivity, Marxism, and Culture Theory in China," *Social Text* 31/32, 114–40. Although Liu Kang promises to trace Liu Zaifu's "appropriations of Marxist categories in reconstituting subjectivity in Chinese culture," he bypasses the theoretical category of Marxian humanism but dwells at great length on the Hu Feng connection ("subjective fighting spirit"). The relevance of the debate over socialist alienation to Liu Zaifu's theory seems to have totally escaped his attention.

12. One should also be reminded that although most indigenous Chinese critics characterize the literary history of the 1980s in terms of the dual track of human-centeredness (*renben*) versus text-centeredness (*wenben*), certain literary phenomena of the 1980s are hardly reducible to such a clear-cut competitive dichotomy. *Xungen* literature, for instance, marks the emergence of a third category—the cultural unconscious—that merges into an uneven admixture of a burgeoning textual reflexivity and an overflow of ontological self-consciousness. To further complicate the picture, a fourth category, the hyperspace of Nature, which looms large in the literature, transcends the futile differentiation between the conscious and unconscious. A simplistic binary scheme will even fall short of framing Liu Zaifu. The same Liu Zaifu who foregrounds the liberation of humanity as the most effective means of resistance against the tyranny of political ideology also recognizes perceptively that the "cultural [ideological] tyranny of the Gang of Four is one and the same as the 'tyranny of literary style'" (*wenti zhuanzheng*). See Liu, "Lun bashi niandai wenxue piping de wenti geming" (On the formal revolution of the literary criticism of the 1980s), *Wenxue pinglun* 1 (1989), 10. In acknowledging the "hidden constraints" that linguistic signs place upon cognitive activities, he anticipates Li Tuo's later slogan of "the Mao Style" and thus breaks down the prescribed binary conflict between the science of humanity (*renxue*) and the science of signs and textuality (*wenxue*). For the discussion of *renben* versus *wenben*, see Fei Zhenzhong and Wang Gan, "'Renben' yu 'wenben': Yige xinde wenxue piping fanchou sikao" ("Human-centeredness" and "text-centeredness": Contemplation on a new category of literary criticism), *Zhongshan* 2 (1988), 186–93, 116. Also see Song Yaoliang, *Shinian wenxue zhuchao*, 230.

13. Liu Zaifu, "Lun wenxue de zhutixing," 83, 93.

14. Ibid., 105.

15. On the process of aesthetic reception, see ibid., 117–18. On *Youhuan yishi*, see ibid., 112–13.

16. Liu Zaifu, "Lun bashi niandai wenxue piping de zhuti geming," 13. Emphasis is mine.

17. See Liu Zaifu, *Xingge zuhe lun*, for an elaborate account of his dialectic of complementary bipolarity.

18. One can detect a theoretical correspondence between Li Zehou's forthright explication of *tianren heyi* and his implicit endorsement of the classical formula through his explication of the *wuwo* theory. However, although Liu stresses the aesthetic value of such a formula, he seems to be more occupied with transforming the substantive rationality underlying the concept of "unity of Heaven and (hu)man" into the instrumental rationality based on the Marxist humanization of nature.

19. See Lawrence E. Cahoone's critique of Adorno and Horkheimer and the Western theory of subjectivity. It is the subjectivist conception of the self that allows them to link the assertion and development of the self to the renunciation of nature and myth. Adorno and Horkheimer read the subjectivist concept of self and nature into all of Western history as the goal and principle of that history. Lawrence E. Cahoone, *The Dilemma of Modernity: Philosophy, Culture, and Anti-Culture* (Albany: State University of New York Press, 1988).

20. Liu Zaifu, "Lun wenxue de zhutixing," 108–12, 140–41.

21. Ibid., 127, 112.

22. Ibid., 91.

23. Sylviane Agacinski, "Another Experience of the Question, or Experiencing the Question Other-Wise," in *Who Comes after the Subject?*, 9. In Western tradition, subjectivity consists in reappropriating the being-outside-of-itself. The subject proposed by Hegel is "that which is capable of maintaining within itself its own contradiction." Thus there is a common understanding that "the logic of the subjectum is a grammar of the subject that re-appropriates to itself, in advance and absolutely, the exteriority and the strangeness of its predicate" (Nancy, introduction to *Who Comes after the Subject?*, 6).

24. Liu Kang, "Subjectivity, Marxism, and Culture Theory," 9.

25. Smith, *Discerning the Subject*, 46.

26. On Chinese magic realism, see Lu Gao, "Mohuande haishi xianshide? Du 'Xizang, xizai pishengkou shang de hun'" (Magic or realistic? "Tibet, souls tied to the knot of the leather rope"), *Xizang wenxue* 1 (1985). On the two slogans, see Yu Bin, "Minzuhua wenti yu Zhongguo dangdai wenxue de fazhan" (The problem of nationalization and the development of contemporary Chinese literature), *Wenxue pinglun* 6 (1990), 52. Literature about Chinese literature and world literature was abundant during the second half of the 1980s. See *Zouxiang shijie wenxue* (Marching toward world literature), ed. Zeng Xiaoyi (Hunan: Hunan renmin chubanshe, 1985); Meng Yue, "*Zouxiang shijie wenxue*: Yige jiannan de jincheng" (*Marching toward world literature*: A difficult journey), *Dushu* 8 (1986), 50–57; and Zheng Wanlong, "Zhongguo wenxue yao zouxiang shijie: Cong genzhi yu 'wenhua yanceng' tanqi" (Chinese literature wants to march toward the world: Commenting on the planting of roots and "cultural sediments"), *Zuojia* (Writers) 1 (1986), 70–74.

27. Liu Zaifu, "Lun bashi niandai wenxue piping de wenti geming," 7.

28. Yu Xiaoxing, transcriber, "Haiwai Zhongguo zuojia taolunhui jiyao" (Records of the forum of Chinese writers overseas), *Jintian* 2 (1990), 99, quoting Li Tuo. For a detailed discussion of Li's thesis of *Mao wenti*, see chapter four, "Mapping Aesthetic Modernity," note 19.

29. Yu Xiaoxing, "Haiwai Zhongguo zuojia taolunhui jiyao," 94–96, quoting Li Tuo.

30. See Jing Wang, postscript of "The Mirage of 'Chinese Postmodernism,'" *Positions: East Asia Cultures Critique* 1, no. 2 (1993), 379–82, where an earlier version of this chapter was published.

31. Wu Huanlian, "Cong xuanze shengming dao xuanze Zhongguo: Tan 'Zhanwang ershiyi shiji'" (From choosing life to choosing China: Notes on "A comprehensive survey of the twenty-first century"), *Dushu* 3 (1989), 18–19.

32. "Tradition versus modernity" is a problematic raised in Gan, "Bashi niandai," 32.

33. This term was coined in Liu Zaifu and Lin Gang's *Chuantong yu Zhongguo ren*, 255–79.

34. The agenda of those who are remapping the "Greater China" changed over the years. Depending upon whom you are talking to—the Taiwanese, the mainland Chinese, Hong Kongers, or the Chinese diaspora—the agenda of the

Greater China may be defined in economic, cultural, or political terms. Originally, "Greater China" summarized the vibrancy of the economic interactions in
the economically, culturally, and linguistically compatible area of the triangle of
the People's Republic of China, Taiwan, and Hong Kong and Macao. In the
1990s, the Taiwanese are now less enthusiastic about the proposition of Greater
China in favor of "marching toward the South[east Asia]." Yet for the mainland
Chinese, the agenda points to the ultimate political vision of a reunified China
proper and the China periphery. The continual expansion of the mental map of
Greater China conceived by mainland intellectuals in the 1990s is thus not surprising. To echo overseas Chinese philosopher Tu Weiming's proposition of
"Cultural China," recently some of them started touting an even more ambitious
slogan: "A Greater China Cultural Sphere." According to this mapping, China
is situated at the center of the sphere. The first layer of the sphere is made up of
Taiwan, Hong Kong, and Macao; the second layer, the Chinese diaspora; the
third, other countries in East Asia and Southeast Asia. See Zhang Fa, Zhang
Yiwu, and Wang Yichuan, "Cong 'xiandaixing' dao 'Zhonghuaxing': Xinzhishixing de tanxun" (From "modernity" to "Chineseness": In search of a new
pattern of knowledge), *Wenhua yanjiu* 2 (1994), 16.

    35. See Tang Xiaobing, "Orientalism and the Question of Unversality: The
Language of Contemporary Chinese Literary Theory," *Positions: East Asia Cultures Critique* 1, no. 2 (1993), 389–413. In this essay, Tang tries to account for
the "signifying absence" of the Chinese response to Said's *Orientalism*. Although
there is not much indication that Tang actually laments such an absence, there
is little doubt that he reflects a general tendency shared by many scholars (com-
parativists in particular) in China studies: an uncritical adoption of the problematics ("Orientalism" is one, "postmodernism" is another, and "subaltern
studies" is in the danger of becoming another) defined by Western academics as
the overriding categories with which critics or historians examine or even rewrite
the history of China.

    36. See Tani Barlow, "Colonialism's Career in Postwar China Studies," *Po-
sitions: East Asia Cultures Critique* 1, no. 1 (1993), 224–67. In this essay, Barlow traces the postwar sinologists' evasion of the problematic of colonialism in
their treatment of the Chinese history of the Treaty-port era.

    37. Gan, "Bashi niandai," 33. Emphasis is mine.

    38. Liu Zaifu, "Gaobie zhushen: Zhongguo dangdai wenxue lilun 'shijimo'
de zhengzha" (Bidding farewell to all gods: The "fin-de-siècle" struggle in contemporary Chinese literary theory"), *Ershiyi shiji* (Twenty-first century) 5 (June
1991), 125–34. In this essay Liu complains that contemporary Chinese literary
theorists formulate their problematics under the shadow of foreign theorists.
"The squabbles in Chinese theoretical circles are very often in fact foreigners'
squabbles . . . rather than authentic academic debates among Chinese theorists
themselves" (126–27).

    39. Hu Ang [Huang Ziping], "Yu 'taren' gongwu: Weiji shike de xiezuo
zhiyi," (Dancing with the Other: Writings at the moment of crisis—note 1),
Jintian 1 (1992), 209.

    40. Ibid., 208.

41. Zhang Xudong, "Lun Zhongguo dangdai piping huayu de zhuti neirong yu zhenli neirong" (On the thematic content and truth content of contemporary Chinese critical discourse), *Jintian* 3/4 (1991), 5.

42. Ibid., 3. The emphasis is mine.

43. Gayatri Chakravorty Spivak, "Subaltern Studies: Deconstructing Historiography," in *Selected Subaltern Studies*, ed. Ranajit Guha and Gayatri Spivak (New York: Oxford University Press, 1988), 12–13. Spivak interprets the attempt of retrieving subaltern consciousness in terms of the "charting of what in post-structuralist language would be called the subaltern subject-effect" (12).

44. The quote is from Lin Weiping, "Xinshiqi wenxue yixitan: Fang zuojia Li Tuo," (A conversation session on the literature of the new era: An interview with writer Li Tuo), *Shanghai wenxue* 10 (1986), 96, quoting Li Tuo.

45. The list of imported foreign works that exerted considerable influence over Chinese readers and writers is indeed a long one. They include Camus's *The Stranger* and *The Plague*, Salinger's *The Catcher in the Rye*, Heller's *Catch-22*, Beckett's *Waiting for Godot*, Eliot's "The Waste Land," García Marquez's *One Hundred Years of Solitude*, Borges's short stories, Sartre's *The Flies* and *Nausea*, Kafka's *The Castle* and "The Metamorphosis," Baudelaire's poetry, and many Russian novels. See Cao Wenxuan, *Zhongguo bashi niandai wenxue xianxiang yanjiu* (The study of the trends of Chinese literature of the 1980s) (Beijing: Beijing daxue chubanshe, 1988), 12–13, 15–16.

46. Cao Wenxuan, *Zhongguo bashi niandai*, 240.

47. A Cheng's "Qiwang" and Han Shaogong's "Ba-ba-ba" (Da-da-da) (1985) are considered the most representative works in the *xungen* genre. As theorists, both played an important role in initiating the intense theoretical debate over the slogan in the mid-1980s. Han Shaogong's "Wenxue de 'gen'" (The "roots" of literature), *Zuojia* 4 (1985), 2–5, served as the manifesto of the *xungen* movement, and A Cheng's "Wenhua zhiyuezhe renlei" (Culture constrains humankind), *Wenyi bao*, 6 July 1985, laid the foundation for the argument of cultural conservationists that "searching for roots" signifies the glorification of cultural tradition. The discrepancy between what the *xungen* theories propagate and what the narrative fiction actually delivers is intriguing. Whereas most theorists insist on cultivating their literary sensibility by nurturing themselves in tradition, what is reflected in the fiction gives the lie to such uncritical solidarity with tradition. As the critic Li Jie points out, most *xungen* writers' attitude toward tradition and cultural constraints is highly ambiguous. One can even speak of the collective critique in such works of China's homogeneous traditional culture. Li Tuo's observation is helpful in accounting for such a contradiction. He redefines the terms of contradiction between the theory and practice of the *xungen* genre as follows: "[There is] not a single work in the *xungen* genre [that] does not harbor the contradiction between its critique of traditional culture and its recovery of certain aesthetic traditions. This contradiction confused many people." So the pattern of conflict is seen less in terms of tradition versus antitradition, and more in terms of cultural values versus aesthetic values. See Lin Weiping, "Xinshiqi wenxue yixitan," 96, quoting Li Tuo. Also see Li Jie, "Lun Zhongguo dangdai xinchao xiaoshuo," 117–18.

48. On the relationship of *xungen* literature to *xiandai pai,* see Yu Bin, "Minzuhua wenti yu Zhongguo dangdai wenxue de fazhan," 53–54. Yu attributes the appearance of the *xungen* heat wave to the depression of Chinese modernism in the mid-1980s. He further reminds us (quoting another author) that "today's *xungen* converts were exactly those who advocated the imitation of Western modernists yesterday" (53).

49. Luc Ferry and Alain Renaut, *French Philosophy of the Sixties: An Essay on Antihumanism,* trans. Mary H. S. Cattani (Amherst: The University of Massachusetts Press, 1985), 118.

50. Xu Zidong, "Xiandai zhuyi yu Zhongguo xinshiqi wenxue," 33.

51. Ibid., 34.

52. Ji Hongzhen, "'Wenhua xungen' yu dangdai wenxue" ("Culture/root-searching" and contemporary literature), *Wenyi yanjiu* (Inquiry of literature and art) 2 (1989), 70, quoting Liu Xiaobo's argument in "Weiji! Xinshiqi wenxue mianlin weiji."

53. Li Qingxi, "Xungen: Huidao shiwu benshen" (Root-searching: Returning to the phenomenon itself), *Wenxue pinglun* 4 (1988), 16.

54. Gu Hua, "Cong gulao wenhua dao wenxue de 'gen'" (From ancient culture to literary "roots"), *Zuojia* 2 (1986), 76.

55. "The reacquaintance with traditional culture is in essence a reacquaintance with the human subject itself." See Li Qingxi, "Xungen," 15, quoting Ji Hongzhen.

56. Ibid., 17, 19, emphasis mine.

57. Cao Wenxuan's depiction of A Cheng and Han Shaogong's ideological agenda—that of rejuvenating the Han culture—seems questionable (*Zhongguo bashi niandai,* 243–44). Hu Xiaobo shares the view that the *xungen* writers are reactionary. Both fail to see the discrepancy between *xungen* theories and its practice. Han Shaogong's idiot antihero in "Ba-ba-ba" is considered the contemporary version of Lu Xun's Ah Q: the caricature of a corrupt and bankrupt tradition, or one might say, the consummate image of an ailing national character. Critic Zhu Wei speaks of the gaps between A Cheng's "original intention" to manifest the "harmony of Heaven and (hu)man"—a beloved tradition in Chinese cultural philosophy—in "Shuwang" (The tree king) and his actual presentation of the intensifying confrontation between heaven and man. See Zhu Wei, "Jiejin A Cheng" (Approaching A Cheng), *Zhongshan* 3 (1991), 167.

58. Li Tuo, "Yijiu bawu," 71.

59. Most critics in China have come to the conclusion that the new cultural consciousness of *xungen* writers includes both "historical and national consciousness" and "modern consciousness" (*xiandai yishi*). See Cao Wenxuan, *Zhongguo bashi niandai,* 248; Yu Bin, "Minzuhua wenti yu Zhongguo dangdai wenxue de fazhan," 53; Chen Sihe, "Dangdai wenxue zhong de wenhua xungen yishi" (The "root-searching" cultural consciousness of contemporary literature), *Wenxue pinglun* 6 (1986), 27; also see Chen Sihe, "Zhongguo wenxue fazhan zhong de xiandai zhuyi," 86; Li Qingxi, "Xungen," 15, quoting A Cheng; Song Yaoliang, "Wenxue xinsichao de zhuyao shenmei tezheng yu biaoxian xingtai," 76.

60. On cultural reconstruction, see Ji Hongzhen, "'Wenhua xungen' yu dangdai wenxue," 70. On the vainglorious stance popularized by the proponents of

the *xungen* theorists—that "Chinese literature is marching toward the world"—see Li Rui, "'Houtu' ziyu" (The soliloquy of "solid earth"), *Shanghai wenxue* 10 (1988), 70. Li Rui is one of the few writers who problematizes that stance: "I did not know if Chinese literature ought to or would march toward the world. Neither did I know if the world is truly in need of Chinese literature as anxiously as what Chinese people wishfully thought it should be."

61. Herbert Marcuse, *Eros and Civilization* (Boston: Beacon Press, 1955).

62. Here I disagree with Li Qingxi's interpretation of the metaphysical lessons rendered by Wang Yisheng's philosophy of life and Fukui's choice to remain the last fisherman on the Ge river. He perceives the two heroes as the incarnations of the "*free* personality that transcends reality." In another footnote where he explains the meaning of "self-transcendence," he adopts the critical vocabulary of phenomenology by saying that what the *xungen* writers deliver is the "return to the original state of life"—a prehistorical and precultural point of departure that is immanent, pure, and blissful. See Li Qingxi, "Xungen," 20.

63. Zheng Wanlong, "Wode gen" (My roots), *Shanghai wenxue* 5 (1985), 44.

64. Wang Xiaoming, "Bu xiangxinde he bu yuanyi xiangxinde: Guanyu sanwei 'xungen' pai zuojia de chuangzuo" (What I do not believe and what I am unwilling to believe: Regarding the works of three "root-searching" authors), *Wenxue pinglun* 4 (1989), 31.

65. Zhang Chengzhi, "Wode qiao" (My bridge), *Shiyue* 3 (1983), 240. Emphasis is mine.

66. Wang Xiaoming, "Bu xiangxinde he bu yuanyi xiangxinde," 24–28.

67. Ibid., 25. Gong Ping, "Zhiqing ticai de xinzhuti" (The new themes of the topos of "re-educated youths"), *Zhongshan* 2 (1988), 206.

68. Han Shaogong, "Wenxue de 'gen,'" 5. Song Yaoliang, *Shinian wenxue zhuchao*, 15.

69. Ibid., 289. A Cheng's *Biandi fengliu* series (Flowing with the wind wherever it goes) and Jia Pingwa's *Shangzhou* series (The Shang district)—published in the mid-1980s—fall into this narrative category.

70. Zhang Yiwu, "Disan shijie wenhua zhong de xushi" (The discourse of the Third-World culture), *Zhongshan* 3 (1990), 156.

71. Li Qingxi, "Xungen," 22–23.

72. Li Qingxi in particular indicates that the narrative mode of *xungen* literature contains the aesthetics of phenomenology, (ibid., 22).

73. Ji Hongzhen, "'Wenhua xungen' yu dangdai wenxue," 72.

74. You Yi [Meng Yue], "Yetan bashi niandai wenxue de 'xihua'" (Revisiting the problem of the "westernization" of the literature of the 1980s), *Jintian* 3/4 (1991), 35.

75. Li Jie, "Lun Zhongguo dangdai xinchao xiaoshuo," 117.

76. Yu Xiaoxing, "Haiwai Zhongguo zuojia taolunhui jiyao," 96, quoting Li Tuo.

77. Li Hangyu, "Liyili women de 'gen'" (Sorting out our "roots"), *Zuojia* 9 (1985), 78.

78. On the collective unconscious, see Fei Zhenzhong and Wang Gan, "'Renben' yu 'wenben,'" 189. On the consciousness of a communal moral character, see Li Qingxi, "Xungen," 21.

79. Zheng Yi, "Yuancun" (The village afar), in *Yuancun* (Taibei: Haifeng chubanshe, 1990), 25–161. Jia Pingwa, *Shangzhou* (Beijing: Beijing "Shiyue" wenyi chubanshe, 1987). The story was originally published in *Wenxuejia* 5 (1984). Han Shaogong, "Bababa," *Renmin wenxue* 6 (1985), 83–102.

80. Han Shaogong, "Wenxue de 'gen,'" 4. The emphasis is mine.

81. Li Qingxi, "Xungen," 17.

82. Cahoone, *The Dilemma of Modernity,* xiii.

83. Li Tuo, Zhang Ling, and Wang Bin, "Yuyan de fanpan," 78.

84. Smith, *Discerning the Subject,* 35.

85. Li Tuo, Zhang Ling, and Wang Bin, "Yuyan de fanpan," 75, 76, 80.

86. Li Zehou and Liu Zaifu, "Wenxue yu yishu de qingsi," 2.

87. Liu Xinwu's complaints and condemnations of the younger writers' experiment with language are typical of the opinions of the older generation of critics. See Liu's "Zhongguo zuojia yu dangdai shijie" (Chinese writers and the contemporary world), *Renmin ribao,* 11 March 1988, overseas edition.

88. Mikkel Borch-Jacobsen, "The Freudian Subject, from Politics to Ethics," in *Who Comes after the Subject?,* 64.

89. On the postmodern subject, see Zhang Yiwu, "Lixiang zhuyi de zhongjie: Shiyan xiaoshuo de wenhua tiaozhan" (The end of idealism: The cultural challenge of experimentalist fiction), *Beijing wenxue* 4 (1989), 11. On the premodern subject, see Zhang Xudong, "Ge Fei yu dangdai wenxue huayu de jige muti" (Ge Fei and some motifs of contemporary literary discourse), *Jintian* 2 (1990), 83.

90. Wang Furen provides an insightful analysis of the tendency of Chinese literati to prioritize theory over literature and art in his essay "Zhongguo jinxiandai wenhua he wenxue fazhan de nixiangxing tezheng" (Modern and contemporary Chinese culture and the characteristics of the inverse reaction of cultural developments), *Wenxue pinglun* 2 (1989), 14.

91. Zhang Yiwu, "Lixiang zhuyi de zhongjie," 11.

92. Wang Ning, "Guifan yu bianti," 160–61.

93. See Tang Xiaobing, "The Function of New Theory," especially 106–8.

94. Zhang Xudong, "Ge Fei yu dangdai wenxue huayu de jige muti," 83.

95. Zhang Xudong, "Lun Zhongguo dangdai piping huayu de zhuti neirong yu zhenli neirong," 3.

96. Meng Yue, "Su Tong de 'jiashi' yu 'lishi' xiezuo" (The writing of Su Tong's "Family chronicle" and "History"), *Jintian* 2 (1990), 84.

97. Yu Hua talks about his computation of fictive temporality in his own analysis of the temporal scheme of "Ciwen xiangei shaonu Yangliu" (This kiss was dedicated to Willow). He experiments with different arrangements of temporal logic—split time, overlapped time, and temporal disorder (mapped out mathematically as 1 2 3 4 / 1 2 3 4 / 1 2 3 / 1 2)—in the story to vindicate his fictional logic: "The meaning of time consists in its capability of restructuring the world instantaneously." See Yu Hua, "Xuwei de zuopin" (Hypocritical work), preface to *Shishi ru yan* (Worldly affairs are like clouds) (Taibei: Yuanliu chuban gongsi, 1991), 19–20.

98. On the claim that the experimentalists have scattered history to the winds, see Zhang Yiwu, "Lixiang zhuyi de zhongjie," 6–7. Also see his "Xiao-

shuo shiyan: Yiyi de xiaojie" (The experiments of fiction: The deconstruction of meaning), *Beijing wenxue* 2 (1988), 77.

99. Li Jie, "Lun Zhongguo dangdai xinchao xiaoshuo," 138.

100. Ibid.

101. Zhao Mei, "Xianfeng xiaoshuo de zizu yu fufan" (The self-sufficiency and superficial drift of the avant-garde fiction), *Wenxue pinglun* 1 (1989), 33.

102. "There has been a mutation in the object unaccompanied as yet by any equivalent mutation in the subject." See Fredric Jameson, *Postmodernism* (Durham, N.C.: Duke University Press, 1991), 38.

103. Zhang Yiwu, "Xiaoshuo shiyan," 77. Yu Hua attributes all his efforts of writing fiction to his wish to "get closer to authenticity." See Yu's "Xuwei de zuopin," 5.

104. Li Jie, "Lun Zhongguo dangdai xinchao xiaoshuo," 129.

105. Wu Liang, "Qidai yu huiyin: Xianfeng xiaoshuo de yige zhujie" (Anticipations and responses: A footnote on the avant-garde fiction), *Zuojia* 9 (1989), 62.

106. I disagree with Wu Liang's proclamation that "experimental fiction is a chain of serendipitous literary events that are independent of each other" (ibid., 59). Hong Feng's stories, for instance, find so many intertextual markers in Ma Yuan and Yu Hua that they almost guarantee the working hypothesis of conscious imitation. "Bensang" (The funeral), a story told in a prosaic monotone, can justify its affiliation with the new genre much less on discursive than on thematic terms (namely the death of the father). Hong Feng, "Bensang," *Zuojia* 9 (1986), 2–21.

107. On dilapidated spectacle of history, see Chen Xiaoming, "Lishi tuibai de yuyan" (The language of degenerated history), *Zhongshan* 3 (1991), 146–47.

108. Yu Hua, "Xuwei de zuopin," 5.

109. Ibid., 7.

110. Zheng Yi, "Xunzhao minzu zhi hun" (In search of the soul of the nation), in *Yuancun*, 7.

111. Ibid.

112. Zhao Yiheng, "Yuanyishi he dangdai Zhongguo xianfeng xiaoshuo" (The metaconsciousness and contemporary Chinese avant-garde fiction), *Jintian* 1 (1990), 81.

113. Mao Zedong, "Zhongguo geming he Zhongguo gongchandang" (The Chinese Revolution and the Chinese Communist Party), in *Mao Zedong xuanji* (Selected writings of Mao Zedong), ed. The CCP publication Committee for the *Selected Writings of Mao* (Beijing: Renmin chubanshe, 1967), 589–94.

114. Zhang Xudong, "On Some Motifs in the Chinese 'Cultural Fever,'" 154.

CHAPTER 6

1. Jameson's lectures on postmodernism at Beida were published in the collection *Houxiandai zhuyi yu wenhua lilun* (Postmodernism and culture theories), trans. Tang Xiaobing (Xi'an: Shanxi Normal University Press, 1986) and reprinted in Taibei, 1989.

2. On young mainland critics' rush to theory, see Zhang Yingjin, "Re-envisioning the Institution of Modern Chinese Literature Studies: Strategies of Positionality and Self-Reflexivity," *Positions: East Asia Cultures Critique* 1, no. 3 (1993), 816–32. I use "fathers" advisedly. Although feminism was occasionally introduced by women critics in mainland China, it never entered the mainstream critical discourse of an elite dominated by men.

3. The gradual articulation of this position—one that stresses the ideology of the alternative postmodern and modern—brought to the fore the issue of cultural locality and subjectivity. The posing of this problematic is especially significant in the 1990s as Chinese mass culture becomes more and more susceptible to the homogenizing process of globalization. In fact, one could argue that it is the imminent invasion into the Chinese market of American exports such as ABC's *Dynasty* that made the intellectuals' agenda of the Chinese alternative—an imaginary localism—meaningful and compellingly persuasive. Zhu Wei's analysis of Chinese intellectuals' complex toward Occidentalism is insightful: "Our attitude toward the West, just like what Han Shaogong showed in his short story 'Da-da-da,' is characterized by this complex: on the one hand, [we] call [them] 'Dad, dad, dad' in the most subservient tone, and then [we] turn around and defiantly curse [them]—'Fuck your mother'—behind their back." See Chen Xiaoming, Dai Jinhua, Zhang Yiwu, and Zhu Wei, "Dongfang zhuyi yu houzhimin wenhua" (Orientalism and postcolonial culture), *Zhongshan* 1 (1994), 130.

4. Liao Tianliang et al. "Renge de kun'e yu jingshen de zixing" (The dilemma of personality and the self-examination of the mind), *Renmin ribao*, 5 November 1988, overseas edition. Liao and Li argue that although the Chinese often speak of the Confucian dictum "I examine myself three times a day," such self-introspection is more often motivated by certain "practical and emotional ends" than by the rational examination of the self. An incomplete self-examination can hardly yield the crisis consciousness that would lead China to a qualitative break from its own past. It is worth noting that in 1988, a pervasive mood of cultural depression was acutely felt by the Chinese residents in the cities. The term "crisis" (*weiji*) recurred in critical essays of all kinds. He Bochuan's *Shan'ao shang de Zhongguo* (China in the hollow of the mountain) (Guizhou: Renmin chuban-she, 1988) became a bestseller immediately after its publication—the first book written on the subject of contemporary China in crisis.

5. Generally speaking, the latter half of the 1980s witnessed a disturbing mood of restlessness. The possibility of reinvigorating Marxism had outlived its historical moment, the ideological debate between traditionalists and modernists had turned into a stalemate, and the contradiction between theory and practice (of which the revival of the 1982 slogan "socialism with Chinese characteristics" was a reminder), had revealed itself as an insurmountable barrier to marching toward the future. Amidst the general dystopian climate, China reexperienced class conflicts between intellectuals, urban workers, and those who had benefited the most financially from the modernization programs, namely, residents of special economic zones and the peasants who lived in the vicinity of cities and coastal areas. Intellectuals now spoke condescendingly of the gaps between peasants' regressive orientation and the epoch's emphasis on enlightenment.

6. Zhou Yan, "Women neng zouchu 'wenhua digu' ma?" (Can we walk out of our cultural depression?), *Dushu* 12 (1988), 5–6.

7. The Chinese *shalong* (salon) mushroomed in big urban centers circa 1985. It provided a space for young and middle-aged intellectuals to exchange their views on a variety of academic subjects such as the economic, legal, and political reforms. It was reported that one of Zhao Ziyang's think-tanks—the Beijing Youth Association of Economic Studies—was actively involved in the sponsoring and hosting of such gatherings. "Xueshu shalong" (Academic salons) *Renmin ribao*, 14 August 1986, overseas edition.

8. Guy S. Alitto, *The Last Confucian: Liang Shu-ming and the Chinese Dilemma of Modernity* (Berkeley: University of California Press, 1979), 116, quoting from Liang Qichao's *Ouyou xinying lu jielu* (Reflections on a European journey).

9. Gao Ertai, "Yihua jiqi lishi kaocha," 184. It is worth noting that literary critics were also preoccupied with locating the Chinese origin of the concept of alienation in premodern literary texts. Some of them proclaimed that in the Chinese tradition, the concept originated in Pu Songling's story of "Cuzhi" in *Liaozhai zhiyi* (Strange tales of a studio). See Huang Ziping's "Guanyu 'wei xiandai pai' jiqi piping," 5.

10. Gan, "Bashi niandai," 37.

11. Li Qingxi, "Xungen," 15.

12. Zhang Yiwu, "Disan shijie wenhua zhong de xushi," 152.

13. Li Qingxi, "Xungen," 22. According to Li, the root-searching movement is not merely an uncritical return to tradition. The cultural revival contains an "anticultural" drive. One of the popular themes in this literature, Li argues, is the description of the antagonism between cultural traditions and the human condition. Not all critics agree with Li's viewpoint. Wang Xiaoming discredits the concept of root-searching as "regressive" and "primitive." Seen from his perspective, the *xungen* mentality represents a retroactive stance and its return-to-culture approach is identified as "antievolutional" (32). See Wang Xiaoming, "Bu xiangxinde he bu yuanyi xiangxinde," 24–35. Other critics such as Chen Sihe interpret the "return" in aesthetic terms. The search for roots is thus viewed as a reinterpretation and reevaluation of "the national cultural archive." See Chen, "Dangdai wenxue zhong de wenhua xungen yishi," 27.

14. Zou Ping, "Zoujin lenggu: Xinshiqi wenxue de weilaishi" (Walking into the cold valley: The history of the future of our literature in the new era), *Shanghai wenxue* 10 (1988), 73.

15. Ji Hongzhen, "Shenhua de shuailuo yu fuxing" (The decline and revival of myth), *Wenxue pinglun* 4 (1989), 109. The emphasis is mine.

16. Li Qingxi, "Xungen," 23.

17. Alitto, *The Last Confucian*, 82–83.

18. Preface to "'Xinxieshi xiaoshuo dalianzhan' juanshouyu," 4.

19. Strictly speaking, the emergence of the so-called New Theory in contemporary China during the late 1980s was less a reality than an earnest wish made by critics themselves. The anticipation of new critical paradigms was brought about by a small handful of essays that discussed the question of language and attempted a systematic analysis of literature as text and as narrative. Underlying

the search for the new paradigm was the rebellion of the new critics against the concept of literature as representation and against the theory of the subject— whether that of society, of history, of culture, or of the author. Few essays, however, accomplished what they promised to deliver. Part of the problem could be attributed to the reliance by the critics upon and their inadequate absorption of the new theories from abroad, the introduction of which was fragmentary at best. There was also anxiety among the critics to keep up the quick pace with which the avant-garde writers conjured up one new vision after another. For a general discussion of the dilemma of the New Theorists, see Xin Xiaozheng and Guo Yinxing, "Xinlilun de chujing" (The situation of the New Theory), *Dangdai zuo-jia pinglun* (Review of contemporary writers) 6 (1988), 4–10.

20. Liu Zaifu, "Lun bashi niandai wenxue piping de wenti geming," 16. It is worth noting that Liu later changed this position and mourned the inability of Chinese critics to walk out of the "shadows of the foreign other." See his "Gaobie zhushen."

21. Liu Zaifu, "Lun bashi niandai wenxue piping de wenti geming," 21.

22. The discovery of language as the new locus for critical studies seems to begin with Li Tuo's call for the Chinese writers' liberation from the Mao Style. See Li Tuo, Zhang Ling, and Wang Bin, "Yuyan de fanpan," 79. For a detailed discussion of the subjectivity of language, see chapter four, "Mapping Aesthetic Modernity." The term "the subjectivity of language" recurred in various critical writings throughout the latter half of the 1980s.

23. Louis Althusser, *Réponse à John Lewis* (Paris: Maspéro, 1973), 91–98.

24. Perhaps it is precisely because of the very tenacity of Yu Hua's resistance to the return of a master narrative that his works try to grasp time and again the deep structure of the self-cornered narrator who is unwilling to discourse himself out of the dilemma. This discursive self-imprisonment repeats itself in Yu's works and forms a tyranny of its own kind. Li Tuo, the critic who discovered and promoted Yu Hua, sensed a "certain danger" in his young protégé and predicted that the latter "would not travel as far as Ge Fei and Ye Zhaoyan in terms of the experimental nature of their works." See Li Tuo, Zhang Ling, and Wang Bin, "1987–1988: Beizhuang de nuli" (1987–1988: Efforts of the sublime), *Dushu* 1 (1989), 57.

25. The date at the end of the story suggests that Ge Fei finished the tale on May 17, 1990. See Ge Fei, "Hushao" (Whistling), *Bafang* 12 (1990), 196.

26. Ge Fei, "Xiaozhuan" (Author's autobiographical sketch), in *Mizhou* (Beijing: Zuojia chubanshe, 1989).

27. Three of Ge Fei's stories—"Xianjing" (The trap), "Hese niaoqun" (A flock of tawny birds), and "Meiyou ren kanjian cao shengzhang" (Nobody saw the grass growing)—in the collection *Mizhou* overlap and form a network of self-referentiality.

28. Ge Fei, "Zhuiyi Wuyou xiansheng," in *Mizhou*, 6.

29. Jean-François Lyotard, "Appendix," trans. Régis Rurand, in *The Post-modern Condition*, 80.

30. Fang Xuanling et al. "Ruan Ji" in "Lie zhuan 19," (Collected biographies 19), in *Jin shu* (The chronicles of Jin dynasty) (Beijing: Zhonghua shuju, 1974) 49, 1362.

31. Fang Xuanling et al., "Ji Kang," in *Jin Shu*, 1370.

32. Ge Fei, "Hushao," 196.

33. For a detailed analysis of the culture of whistling, see Douglass Alan White, unpublished Harvard undergraduate thesis entitled "Ch'eng-kung Sui's 'Poetic Essay on Whistling.'"

34. Ge Fei, "Hese niaoqun," 42–43; "Meiyou ren kanjian cao shengzhang," 66–70; "Bangke" (Shells), in *Mizhou*, 231.

35. Ge Fei, "Hushao," 186.

36. Ibid., 188.

37. The Chinese attitude toward whistling can be summarized in two stanzas from the *Xiao fu* (Rhapsody on whistling): "He [the recluse] finds constraining the narrow road of the world/He gazes up at the concourse of heaven, and treads the high vastness; He transcends the common, and forgets his body/Then, filled with noble emotion, he gives a long drawn out whistle." See Chenggong Sui, "Xiao fu," in *Wen xuan*, ed. Xiao Tong (Taibei: Shimen tushu youxian gongsi, 1976; a reprint of the 1809 edition of Hu Kejia), 18/26b, 266. These two stanzas were translated by Douglass Alan White (see note 33).

38. Ge Fei, "Hushao," 195.

39. Ibid.

40. Jameson, foreword to *The Postmodern Condition*, xviii.

41. Ge Fei, "Yelang zhi xing" (The journey to Yelang), *Zhongshan* 6 (1989), 124.

42. The ontological thrust underlying the "pure conversations" was generated by the reinterpretation of the Great Books—*Yi Jing, Lun Yu, Lao Zi*, and *Zhuang Zi*. The new interpretive model for the classics integrates the Confucian and Daoist philosophical frameworks.

The term *qingyi wo* was coined by Lao Siguang in his interpretation of the significance of the *caixing* school within the Wei-Jin *xuanxue* tradition. See Lao, *Zhongguo zhexue shi* (Taibei: Sanmin shuju, 1981), 2: 145–57. Lao argues that *caixing* is opposed to *xinxing*; the former is identical to the aesthetic persona of the individual, and the latter, to the moral persona. Lao also argues that the Chinese debate over the definition of the self seems to vacillate between these two interpretations at the expense of the third thesis—that of the cognitive self.

43. Wai-lim Yip, ed. and trans., *Chinese Poetry: Major Modes and Genres* (Berkeley: University of California Press, 1976), 169, quoting Kuo Xiang's (d. 312) commentary on Zhuang Zi's concept of change.

44. Ge Fei, "Meiyou ren kanjian cao shengzhang," 68–69.

45. Ge Fei, "Yelang zhi xing," 125.

46. Ye Fang, "Women haineng you shenme?" (What else can we have?), *Wenxue pinglun* 3 (1988), 21.

47. Yu Hua, "Xianshi yizhong" (One kind of reality), in *Shibasui chumen yuanxing* (Traveling far from home at eighteen) (Beijing: Zuojia chubanshe, 1989), 256.

48. Miriam Cooke in Asian and African Languages and Literature at Duke University has discussed with me on several occasions the phenomenon of postmodernism in the context of Third-World literature. I would like to acknowledge her contribution to my analysis of this particular story.

49. I am here quoting from Marilyn Young's discussion notes on my original paper submitted to the "After Orientalism" symposium.

50. I would like to attribute this particular statement to Zhang Xudong of the Literature Program at Duke.

51. The first two references are to Ge Fei, "Mizhou," in *Mizhou,* 104, 108.

52. The Fourteenth Party Congress in Beijing in October 19, 1992, endorsed the economical reform under the banner of free market economy. Not only citizens who swarmed to the Shenzhen Stock Exchange to buy shares, but even administrators at the Central Party School seem to be enraptured by the profit motive.

CHAPTER 7

1. Ye Lihua, "Wenxue," 18.

2. This reading is suggested by David Der-Wei Wang. "Instead of emplotting the cultural transformation of the past decade as one from the stage of innocence to the stage of cynicism, one might want to speculate that the Chinese writers of the 80s were never as innocent as they seemed" (reader's report, 3). I argue that Wang Shuo marked the beginning of the post-new-era that witnesses the commercialization of literature. It is the changing mode of production and the changing socioeconomic culture—the focus of my discussion of Wang Shuo's emergence—rather than the transformation of themes from "innocence" to "cynicism" that distinguishes Wang Shuo from the experimentalists.

3. Zhang Boli, "Wang Shuo: Rebel without a Cause," *China Watch* 1, no. 1 (1993), 8.

4. Joe Klein, "Why China Does It Better," *Newsweek,* 12 April 1993, 23.

5. Zhou Guanwu, "Xiaofei shi fazhan shengchan de dongli," *Renmin ribao,* 7 June 1992, 2.

6. Li Qingxi is dubious about the new proposition. According to him, the transformation from the new era into the post-new-era took place only in the cultural, not in the literary realm. He does not think that the literary configuration of the 1990s was markedly different from that of the 1980s. He believes that the coining of *houxinshiqi* merely reflects the crisis mentality that plagued the literary establishment. Critics were compelled to react to the decline of the literary market by making new theoretical proposals and stirring up controversial public opinions. See Li Qingxi, "Baiwu liaolai de 'houpiping': Yetan 'houxinshiqi wenxue'" (A bored "postcriticism": On the literature of the "post-new-era"), *Wenyi lilun* 2 (1993), 129–30.

7. The fervent discussion of the new term "post-new-era" took place in the latter half of 1992. Leading literary journals such as *Wenyi bao, Zuojia pinglun,* and *Wenhui bao* published one article after another on the subject.

8. Guo Dong, *Benshiji zuihou yihang jiaoyin: Dangdai qingnian wenhua redian xunzong* (The last footsteps of this century: In search of the cultural heat waves of contemporary youth culture) (Tianjin: Tianjin Academy of the Social Sciences Publishing Co., 1993), 141. This ditty was translated by Victor Mair.

9. According to scholars, the trading consciousness of Chinese people emerged in 1984 when fourteen coastal cities were first opened up for trade. The ensuing surplus and mismanagement of business firms and corporations invited governmental intervention in 1985. The second tide occurred in 1988. Statistics have it that the total number of firms reached 370,000 by 1989. In the immediate wake of the Tian'anmen crackdown, the Party once more tightened regulations in business laws in response to the people's indictment of official corruption voiced during the demonstrations. The third tide occurred shortly after Deng's southern excursion talks in February 1992. See Guo Dong and Tian Feng, eds., *Cong xuanyun dao mikuang: Dangdai Zhongguo shida kuangchao toushi* (From bewilderment to craziness: A penetrating look at the ten maniac trends in contemporary China) (Tianjin: Tianjin Academy of the Social Sciences Publishing Co., 1993), 2–8.

10. Cao Qian, "Jiaoshi cuxiao dui ertong buli" (Teachers promoting goods did harm to our children), *Renmin ribao,* 20 June 1992, 5.

11. Joe Klein dubbed the PLA "China's Mitsubishi." See Klein, "Why China Does It Better," 23.

12. Both Wang Xiaoming and Sun Ganlu (one of the experimentalists) are dismayed at the crisis that confronts arts and literature in the 1990s. See their commentaries in the symposium report "Yansu wenyi wang hechu qu?" (Where are serious arts and literature going?), *Wenyi lilun* 3 (1993), 96, 101.

13. Wang Ning, "Zhishi fenzi: Cong lifazhe dao jieshizhe" (Intellectuals: From the legislator to the interpreter), *Dushu* 12 (1992), 114–18. Also see "Yansu wenyi wang hechu qu?" 99, quoting Xu Jilin.

14. "Yansu wenyi wang hechu qu?" 99, quoting Xu Jilin.

15. The Task-Force Section of the Bureau of the Arts and Literature in the Department of Propaganda, ed., "Guanyu shehui zhuyi shichang jingji tiaojianxia wenyi lingyu mianling de xinwenti" (Regarding the new problems that confront the realm of the arts and literature under the economic conditions of socialist market), *Wenyi lilun* 3 (1993), 30. For a good example of how some intellectuals not only welcomed but also called for the intervention of the Party in regulating the literary market, see Wang Zeke, "Shangpin jingji he zhishi fenzi" (Commodity economy and intellectuals), *Dushu* 9 (1992), 145–48. Other critics such as Bao Jiawan echoed another typical concern of the old and middle-aged writers about the social efficacy of literature. See Bao Jiawan, "Shehui zhuyi shichang jingji yu wenyi chuangzuo" (The socialist market economy and the creation of the arts and literature), *Wenyi lilun* 3 (1993), 35–37.

16. "Guanyu shehui zhuyi shichang," 30.

17. For a detailed description of the cultural market in post-Mao China, see Guo Dong and Tian Feng, *Cong xuanyun dao mikuang,* 226–27.

18. Chen Juntao made such a statement in "Chunwenxue bingwei xiaowang" (Pure literature has by no means disappeared), *Wenyi lilun* 3 (1993), 95.

19. Wang Ning argued that literary criticism in China should undergo a process of academicization. See his "Zhongguo jiushi niandai wenxue yanjiu zhong de ruogan lilun keti" (Several theoretical topics in the studies of Chinese literature of the 1990s), *Wenyi lilun* 1 (1993), 176. The proposal can be traced

back to 1992, when a group of scholars at Beijing University initiated the discussion at a symposium on "The Current Situation and the Future of Contemporary Chinese Theoretical Criticism." It was pointed out that one of the central tasks of returning critics to the academy is to ensure that literary criticism maintain its own autonomy independent of the dictates of the market. See Bai Hua, "'Xueyuanshi piping' de tishi" (The proposal of "academic criticism"), *Dushu* 10 (1992), 153. I cannot agree more with Bai's proposal. I would extend it by saying that it is in the academy, not in society nor in politics, that Chinese intellectuals should find their niche. It is high time for the Chinese literary and cultural elite to turn themselves into professional intellectuals. Commercial culture and the culture of professional expertise can coexist in an industrial society as long as one comes to terms with the division of cultural labor and the compartmentalization of the cultural market.

20. Zhang Yiwu, "Houxinshiqi wenxue: Xinde wenhua kongjian" (The post-new-era literature: A new cultural space), *Wenyi lilun* 1 (1993), 184.

21. Critics such as Zhang Yiwu insist on defining the new epochal expressions in terms of the cultural producers' "return" to traditional discourse. He further argues that the "return" symptom in the ideological realm went side by side with the return to older forms of narration. See "'Renmin jiyi' yu wenhua de mingyun" ("The memory of people" and the fate of culture), *Zhongshan* 1 (1992), 171.

22. Guo Dong and Tian Feng, *Cong xuanyun dao mikuang*, 111.

23. The official media coverage of environmentalism stepped up after Qu Geping, the chief of Chinese National Environmental Bureau, returned from the UN-sponsored World Convention of Environmental Protection and Development held in Brazil in June 1992. See Xu Zhenglong, "Fazhan jingji bixu jiangu huanbao" (Economic development must go hand in hand with environmental protection), *Renmin ribao*, 24 June 1992, 3. Many editorials and articles on the same topic appeared in newspapers around the same time.

24. Zhang Yiwu, "Houxinshiqi wenxue," 183.

25. Critics such as Wu Bingjie reiterate this puritanical wish. See his "Shenghuo de biange yu chuangzuo de tiaozheng: Yijiu jiuyi nian zhongduanpian xiaoshuo chuangzuo manping" (The change of life and the adjustment made by creative writings: Random comments on the novellas and short stories published in 1991), *Renmin ribao*, 12 March 1992, 5. According to Wu, the works published in 1991 were generally concerned with the perfection of human spirit, emotions, and mind.

26. Zhang Yi, ed., *Kankan Wang Shuo* (Wang Shuo talking up a storm) (Beijing: Huaxia chubanshe, 1993), 12.

27. Ibid., 10.

28. Mu Gong, "Wang Shuo: Zhishi fenzi wenhua de bishizhe" (Wang Shuo: The spurner of intellectual culture), *Zhongshan* 1 (1991), 152.

29. Ibid.

30. Sheryl WuDunn, "The Word from China's Kerouac: The Communists Are Uncool," *The New York Times Book Review*, 10 January 1993, 3, 23.

31. Wang Shuo, *Wo shi Wang Shuo* (I am Wang Shuo) (Beijing: Guoji wenhua chuban gongsi, 1992), 34.

32. It is conventional wisdom promoted by most critics that Wang Shuo promotes "extreme individualism." See Zhang Dexiang and Jin Huimin, *Wang Shuo pipan* (Critiquing Wang Shuo) (Beijing: Zhongguo shehui kexue chubanshe, 1993), 34.

33. Wang Shuo, *Wande jiushi xintiao* (What I am playing with is your heart beat), *Wenxue siji* (Four seasons of literature) 1 (1988), 189.

34. Ibid., 177.

35. Zhang Dexiang and Jin Huimin, *Wang Shuo pipan,* 20.

36. Wang Shuo, *Wande jiushi xintiao,* 194.

37. Ibid., 212.

38. Wang Shuo, "Wanzhu" (The masters of mischief), *Shouhuo* (Harvest) 6 (1987), 34.

39. Yan Jingming, "Wanzhu yu dushi de chongtu: Wang Shuo xiaoshuo de jiazhi xuanze" (The masters of mischief and their conflicts with the city: The choice of values in Wang Shuo's fiction), *Wenxue pinglun* 6 (1989), 90.

40. Wang Shuo, "Wanzhu," 33.

41. Zhang Dexiang and Jin Huimin, *Wang Shuo pipan,* 39.

42. Wang Shuo, *Wande jiushi xintiao,* 211.

43. The theme of the angel versus the devil is played out in many of Wang Shuo's earlier works such as "Kongzhong xiaojie" (Air stewardess), "Fuchu haimian" (Emerging from the sea), and "Yiban shi huoyan, yiban shi haishui" (Half in flame, half in the sea). The heroine in "One Half" pays with her life for falling in love with the hooligan hero.

44. Zhang Yi, *Kankan Wang Shuo,* 113.

45. Ji Hongzhen, "Jingshen liulangzhe de zhili youxi: Wang Shuo *Wande jiushi xintiao* suojie" (The intellectual game of spiritual wanderers: Decoding *What I am playing with is your heart beat*), *Beijing wenxue* 7 (1989), 36.

46. Zhang Dexiang and Jin Huimin, *Wang Shuo pipan,* 114.

47. Ji Hongzhen, "Jingshen liulangzhe de zhili youxi," 34.

48. Wang Shuo, "Wode xiaoshuo" (My novels), *Renmin wenxue* 3 (1989), 108.

49. Andrew Ross, *No Respect: Intellectuals and Popular Culture* (New York: Routledge, 1989), 5.

50. C. Wright Mills, *White Collar: The American Middle Classes* (Oxford: Oxford University Press, 1953), 159.

Bibliography

A Cheng. "Qiwang." In *A Cheng xiaoshuo xuan*, 7–57. Hong Kong: Tuqi you-xian gongsi, 1985.

———. "The Tree Stump." In *Spring Bamboo: A Collection of Contemporary Chinese Short Stories*, ed. and trans. Jeanne Tai, 229–43. New York: Random House, 1989.

———. "Wenhua zhiyuezhe renlei." *Wenyi bao*, 6 July 1985.

Agacinski, Sylviane. "Another Experience of the Question, or Experiencing the Question Other-Wise." In *Who Comes after the Subject?*, ed. Eduardo Cadava, Peter Connor, and Jean-Luc Nancy. New York: Routledge, 1991.

Alitto, Guy S. *The Last Confucian: Liang Shu-ming and the Chinese Dilemma of Modernity*. Berkeley: University of California Press, 1979.

Althusser, Louis. *Réponse à John Lewis*. Paris: Maspéro, 1973.

Anderson, Perry. *Considerations on Western Marxism*. London: Verso, 1979.

Ansen, David. "Raise a Red Flag." *Newsweek*, 9 October 1995, 74–76.

Bai Hua. "Dangqian wenyi chuangzuo zhong de renxing rendao zhuyi wenti." *Wenyi lilun* 1 (1984): 88–89. Also published in *Wenyi lilun yanjiu* 3 (1983): 27–38.

———. "Guanyu fangfalun wenti de zhengming: Jinnianlai wenyi lilun wenti tantao gaishu zhier." *Wenyi lilun* 5 (1986): 47.

———. " 'Xueyuanshi piping' de tishi." *Dushu* 10 (1992): 153.

Bao Jiawan. "Shehui zhuyi shichang jingji yu wenyi chuangzuo." In "Wenxun." *Wenyi lilun* 3 (1993): 35–37.

Barlow, Tani. "Colonialism's Career in Postwar China Studies." *Positions* 1, no. 1 (1993): 224–67.

Baudrillard, Jean. *The Mirror of Production*. Trans. Mark Poster. St. Louis: Telos Press, 1975.

Bei Dao. Cover. *Jintian* 3/4 (1991).

Bernstein, J. M. *The Philosophy of the Novel: Lukács, Marxism, and the Dialectics of Form.* Minneapolis: University of Minnesota Press, 1984.

Borch-Jacobsen, Mikkel. "The Freudian Subject, from Politics to Ethics." In *Who Comes after the Subject?*, ed. Eduardo Cadava, Peter Connor, and Jean-Luc Nancy, 1–8. New York: Routledge, 1991.

Brugger, Bill. "Alienation Revisited." *The Australian Journal of Chinese Affairs* 12 (1984): 143–51.

Brugger, Bill, and David Kelly. *Chinese Marxism in the Post-Mao Era.* Stanford: Stanford University Press, 1990.

Cadava, Eduardo, Peter Connor, and Jean-Luc Nancy, eds. *Who Comes after the Subject?* New York: Routledge, 1991.

Cahoone, Lawrence E. *The Dilemma of Modernity: Philosophy, Culture, and Anti-Culture.* Albany: State University of New York Press, 1988.

Cao Qian. "Jiaoshi cuxiao dui ertong buli." *Renmin ribao,* 20 June 1992.

Cao Wenxuan. *Zhongguo bashi niandai wenxue xianxiang yanjiu.* Beijing: Beijing daxue chubanshe, 1988.

Chang, Yvonne Sung-Sheng. *Modernism and Its Nativist Resistance.* Durham, N.C.: Duke University Press, 1993.

Chen Danchen. "Yetan xiandai pai yu Zhongguo wenxue: Zhi Feng Jicai tongzhi de xin." In *Xifang xiandai pai wenxue wenti lunzheng ji,* ed. He Wangxian, 2: 557–67. Beijing: Renmin wenxue chubanshe, 1984.

Chen Feilong. "Wenyi kongzhilun chutan." *Wenyi lilun* 3 (1986): 27–31.

Chen Huangmei et al., eds. *Zhongguo xinwenyi daxi: 1976–1982 shiliao ji.* Beijing: Zhongguo wenlian chuban gongsi, 1990.

Chen Juntao. "Chunwenxue bingwei xiaowang." *Wenyi lilun* 3 (1993): 95.

Chen Kuide. "Wenhua re: Beijing, sichao ji liangzhong qingxiang." In *Zhongguo dalu dangdai wenhua bianqian, 1978–1989,* 37–61. Taibei: Guiguan tushu gufen youxian gongsi, 1991.

———, ed. *Zhongguo dalu dangdai wenhua bianqian, 1978–1989.* Taibei: Guiguan tushu gufen youxian gongsi, 1991.

Chen Lai. "Fulu: Sixiang chulu de sandongxiang." In *Zhongguo dangdai wenhua yishi,* ed. Gan Yang, 581–87. Hong Kong: Sanlian shudian, 1989.

Chen Pingyuan and Huang Ziping. "Xiaoshuo xushi de liangci zhuanbian." *Beijing wenxue* 9 (1988): 65–69.

Chen Pingyuan, Huang Ziping, and Qian Liqun. *"Ershi shiji Zhongguo wenxue" sanren tan.* Beijing: Renmin wenxue chubanshe, 1988.

———. "Guanyu 'Ershi shiji Zhongguo wenxue' de duihua." In *"Ershi shiji Zhongguo wenxue" sanren tan,* 27–105. Beijing: Renmin wenxue chubanshe, 1988.

———. "Lun 'Ershi shiji Zhongguo wenxue.' " In *"Ershi shiji Zhongguo wenxue" sanren tan,* 1–26. Beijing: Renmin wenxue chubanshe, 1988.

Chen Sihe. "Dangdai wenxue zhong de wenhua xungen yishi." *Wenxue pinglun* 6 (1986): 24–33.

———. "Zhongguo wenxue fazhan zhong de xiandai zhuyi: Jianlun xiandai yishi yu minzu wenhua de ronghui." *Shanghai wenxue* 7 (1985): 79–86.

Chen Xiaoming. "Lishi tuibai de yuyan." *Zhongshan* 3 (1991): 144–56.

Chen Xiaoming, Dai Jinhua, Zhang Yiwu, and Zhu Wei. "Dongfang zhuyi yu houzhimin wenhua." *Zhongshan* 1 (1994): 126–48.

Chen Yong. "Xuyao jiaqiang jichu lilun de yanjiu." In *Zhongguo wenxue yanjiu nianjian: 1985,* ed. Editorial Committee, 3–4. Beijing: Zhongguo wenlian chuban gongsi, 1986.

Cheng Jincheng. "Zhongguo xiandai wenxue jiazhi guannian xitong lungang." *Wenxue pinglun* 3 (1989): 26–37.

Chenggong Sui. "Xiao fu." In *Wen xuan,* ed. Xiao Tong, 18/26b. Taibei: Shimen tushu youxian gongsi, 1976. A reprint of the 1809 edition of Hu Kejia.

"Chinese Dissent, Ready to Wear." *Harper's,* February 1992, 23.

Dai Houying. *Ren a ren.* Hong Kong: Xiangjiang Publishing Co., 1985.

Deng Liqun. " 'Makesi zhuyi yu ren' xueshu taolunhui chuanda Deng Liqun jianghua: Taolun rendao zhuyi renxinglun henyou haochu." *Renmin ribao,* 12 April 1983. Also published in *Rendao zhuyi renxing lun yihua wenti yanjiu zhuanji,* ed. Center of Newspapers and Research Materials at People's University, 5. Beijing: Renmin daxue, 1983.

Derrida, Jacques. " 'Eating Well,' or the Calculation of the Subject: An Interview with Jacques Derrida." In *Who Comes after the Subject?,* ed. Eduardo Cadava, Peter Connor, and Jean-Luc Nancy, 96–119. New York: Routledge, 1991.

Dirlik, Arif. "Post-Socialism/Flexible Production: Marxism in Contemporary Radicalism." *Polygraph* 6/7 (1993): 133–69.

Eysteinsson, Astradur. *The Concept of Modernism.* Ithaca: Cornell University Press, 1990.

Fang Keli. "Guanyu xiandai xinrujia yanjiu de jige wenti." In *Xiandai xinruxue yanjiu lunji,* ed. Fang Keli and Li Jinquan, 1: 1–13. Beijing: Zhongguo shehui kexue chubanshe, 1989.

Fang Keli and Li Jinquan, eds. *Xiandai xinruxue yanjiu lunji.* Vol. 1. Beijing: Zhongguo shehui kexue chubanshe, 1989.

Fang Keqiang. "A Q he Bingzai: Yuanshi xintai de chongsu." *Wenyi lilun yanjiu* 5 (1986): 9–17.

Fang Lizhi. "Fang Lizhi zai Beida yanjiang luyin jielu." *Zhongyang ribao,* 3 February 1987, overseas edition.

Fang Xian'gan. "*Heshang* de quanpan xihua de zhuzhang." In *Chongping "Heshang,"* ed. Zhong Huamin et al., 123–34. Hangzhou: Hangzhou daxue chubanshe, 1989.

Fang Xuanling et al. "Ji Kang." In "Lie zhuan 19." In *Jin shu,* 3: 1369–74. 5 vols. Beijing: Zhonghua shuju, 1974.

———. "Ruan Ji." In *Jin shu,* 3: 1359–69. Beijing: Zhonghua shuju, 1974.

Fehér, Ferenc, and Agnes Heller. "Are There Prospects for Change in the U.S.S.R. and Eastern Europe?" *Praxis International* 5, no. 3 (1985): 323–32.

Fei Zhenzhong and Wang Gan. " 'Renben' yu 'wenben': Yige xinde wenxue piping fanchou sikao." *Zhongshan* 2 (1988): 186–98.

Feng Jicai. "Zhongguo wenxue xuyao 'xiandai pai': Gei Li Tuo de xin." In *Xifang xiandai pai wenxue wenti lunzheng ji,* ed. He Wangxian, 2: 499–506. Beijing: Renmin wenxue chubanshe, 1984.

Feng Shen, trans. Translator's preface to *Yihua yu laodong*, 8–10. Changsha: Hunan renmin chubanshe, 1987. Trans. from *Otchuzhdenie i trud: po stranitsam i proizvedenii* by I. S. Narsky. Moscow: Izd. "Mysl," 1983.

Feng Tianyu. "Cong Ming Qing zhiji de zaoqi qimeng wenhua dao jindai xinxue." In *Dongfang de liming: Zhongguo wenhua zouxiang jindai de licheng,* ed. Feng Tianyu, 41–71. Chengdu: Bashu shushe, 1988.

———. "Dai xuyan: Zhongguo wenhua de jindaihua wenti." In *Dongfang de liming: Zhongguo wenhua zouxiang jindai de licheng,* 1–11. Chengdu: Bashu shushe, 1988.

———, ed. *Dongfang de liming: Zhongguo wenhua zouxiang jindai de licheng.* Chengdu: Bashu shushe, 1988.

Ferry, Luc, and Alain Renaut. *French Philosophy of the Sixties: An Essay on Antihumanism.* Trans. Mary H. S. Cattani. Amherst: University of Massachusetts Press, 1985.

Fetscher, Iring. "Hegel, the Young Marx, and Soviet Philosophy: A Reply to E. M. Sitnikov." Appendix to *Marx and Marxism,* 331–54. New York: Herder and Herder, 1971.

Feuerlicht, Ignace. *Alienation: From the Past to the Future.* Westport, Conn.: Greenwood Press, 1978.

Fu Weixun. "Zhongguo sixiangjie de Shate yu Bowa." Appendix 2 to *Xingsheng yu weiji: Lun Zhongguo fengjian shehui de chaowending jiegou,* by Jin Guantao and Liu Qingfeng, 1–31. Taibei: Fengyun shidai chuban gongsi, 1989.

Gan Yang. "Bashi niandai wenhua taolun de jige wenti." In *Women zai chuangzao chuantong,* 25–71. Taibei: Lianjing chuban shiye gongsi, 1985.

———. "Bianzhe qianyan." In *Zhongguo dangdai wenhua yishi,* ed. Gan Yang, i–vi. Hong Kong: Sanlian shudian, 1989.

———. "Cong 'lixing de pipan' dao 'wenhua de pipan.' " In *Zhongguo dangdai wenhua yishi,* ed. Gan Yang, 557–79. Hong Kong: Sanlian shudian, 1989.

———. "Ruxue zai xiandai Zhongguo de jiaose yu chulu." In *Women zai chuangzao chuantong,* 1–24. Taibei: Lianjing chuban shiye gongsi, 1989.

———. "Wenhua Zhongguo yu xiangtu Zhongguo: Houlengzhan shidai de Zhongguo qianjing jiqi wenhua." Paper presented at conference "Cultural China: Interpretations and Communications," Harvard University, 3 September 1992.

———. *Women zai chuangzao chuantong.* Taibei: Lianjing chuban shiye gongsi, 1989.

———. "Ziyou de linian: Wusi chuantong zhi queshimian." *Dushu* 5 (1989): 11–19.

———, ed. *China after 1989: An Alternative to Shock Therapy.* New York: Oxford University Press, in press.

———, ed. *Zhongguo dangdai wenhua yishi.* Hong Kong: Sanlian shudian, 1989.

Gao Ertai. "Yihua jiqi lishi kaocha." In *Ren shi Makesi zhuyi de chufa dian,* ed. the Editorial Committee of Renmin chubanshe, 162–216. Beijing: Renmin chubanshe, 1981.

————. "Yihua xianxiang jinguan." In *Ren shi Makesi zhuyi de chufa dian,* ed. the Editorial Committee of Renmin chubanshe, 72–98. Beijing: Renmin chubanshe, 1981.

Gao Xingjian. "Chidaole de xiandai zhuyi yu dangjin Zhongguo wenxue." *Wenxue pinglun* 3 (1988): 11–15, 76.

Gates, Henry Louis, Jr. "Critical Fanonism." *Critical Inquiry* 17, no. 3 (1991): 457–70.

Ge Fei. "Bangke." In *Mizhou,* 227–55. Beijing: Zuojia chubanshe, 1989.

————. "Hese niaoqun." In *Mizhou,* 28–63. Beijing: Zuojia chubanshe, 1989.

————. "Hushao." *Bafang* 12 (1990): 179–96.

————. "Meiyou ren kanjian cao shengzhang." In *Mizhou,* 64–99. Beijing: Zuojia chubanshe, 1989.

————. *Mizhou.* Beijing: Zuojia chubanshe, 1989.

————. "Mizhou." In *Mizhou,* 100–131. Beijing: Zuojia chubanshe, 1989.

————. "Xiaozhuan." In *Mizhou,* i. Beijing: Zuojia chubanshe, 1989.

————. "Yelang zhi xing." *Zhongshan* 6 (1989): 124–34.

————. "Zhuiyi Wuyou xiansheng." In *Mizhou,* 1–10. Beijing: Zuojia chubanshe, 1989.

Geng Yong. "Xiandai pai zenyang he xianshi zhuyi 'duikang': Zheli ye bunengbu sheji mouzhong xianshi zhuyi lilun xianxiang." In *Xifang xiandai pai wenxue wenti lunzheng ji,* ed. He Wangxian, 2: 377–94. Beijing: Renmin wenxue chubanshe, 1984.

Goldmann, Lucien. *The Philosophy of the Enlightenment.* Trans. Henry Maas. Cambridge: MIT Press, 1973.

Gong Ping. "Zhiqing ticai de xinzhuti." *Zhongshan* 2 (1988): 206–7.

Gouldner, Alvin. *The Two Marxisms.* New York: Oxford University Press, 1980.

Gu Hua. "Cong gulao wenhua dao wenxue de 'gen.' " *Zuojia* 2 (1986): 74–76.

Guo Dong. *Benshiji zuihou yihang jiaoyin: Dangdai qingnian wenhua redian xunzong.* Tianjin: Tianjin Academy of the Social Sciences Publishing Co., 1993.

Guo Dong and Tian Feng, eds. *Cong xuanyun dao mikuang: Dangdai Zhongguo shida kuangchao toushi.* Tianjin: Tianjin Academy of the Social Sciences Publishing Co., 1993.

Guo Qiyong. "Guanyu jinnianlai Zhongguo wenhua he Zhongxi wenjua bijiao yanjiu de pingjie." *Renmin ribao,* 3 December 1986, overseas edition. A longer version was published in *Dongfang de liming: Zhongguo wenhua zouxiang jindai de licheng,* ed. Feng Tianyu, 464–82. Chengdu: Bashu shushe, 1988.

Habermas, Jürgen. "On the Obsolescence of the Production Paradigm." In *The Philosophical Discourse of Modernity: Twelve Lectures,* 75–82. Cambridge: MIT Press, 1987.

————. *The Philosophical Discourse of Modernity: Twelve Lectures.* Trans. Frederick Lawrence. Cambridge: MIT Press, 1987.

————. "The Undermining of Western Rationalism through the Critique of Metaphysics: Martin Heidegger." In *The Philosophical Discourse of Modernity: Twelve Lectures,* 131–60. Cambridge: MIT Press, 1987.

Han Qiang. "Xiandai xinruxue yanjiu zongshu (1986–87)." In *Xiandai xin-ruxue yanjiu lunji*, ed. Fang Keli and Li Jinquan, 1: 341–53. Beijing: Zhong-guo shehui kexue chubanshe, 1989.

Han Shaogong. "Bababa." *Renmin wenxue 6* (1985): 83–102.

———. "Wenxue de 'gen.' " *Zuojia* 4 (1985): 2–5.

Han Shi, ed. *Bashi niandai: Gaibian Zhongguo de sanshisanben shu*. Hong Kong: Tiandi tushu youxian gongsi, 1992.

He Bochuan. *Shan'ao shang de Zhongguo*. Guizhou: Renmin chubanshe, 1988.

He Shaojun and Pan Kaixiong. "Zhen yu wei: Guanyu 'wei xiandai pai' taolun de duihua." *Zuojia* 10 (1988): 77–79.

He Wangxian, ed. *Xifang xiandai pai wenxue wenti lunzheng ji*. 2 vols. Beijing: Renmin wenxue chubanshe, 1984.

He Xilai. "Guanyu wenxue zhutixing wenti de tantao." *Renmin ribao*, 11 August 1986, overseas edition.

———. "Yijiu bawu nian *Zhongguo wenxue yanjiu nianjian* qianyan." *Wenyi lilun* 12 (1986): 9–20.

He Xin. "Dangdai wenxue zhong de huangmiugan yu duoyuzhe: Du 'Wuzhuti bianzou' suixianglu." *Dushu* 11 (1985): 3–13.

Henry, Michel. "The Critique of the Subject." In *Who Comes after the Subject?*, Ed. Eduardo Cadava, Peter Connor, and Jean-Luc Nancy, 157–66. New York: Routledge, 1991.

Hong Feng. "Bensang." *Zuojia* 9 (1986): 2–21.

Horkheimer, Max. *Eclipse of Reason*. New York: Oxford University Press, 1947.

Hu Ang [Huang Ziping]. "Yu 'taren' gongwu: Weiji shike de xiezuo zhiyi." *Jin-tian* 1 (1992): 205–12.

Hu Qiaomu. "Guanyu rendao zhuyi he yihua wenti." *Wenyi lilun* 1 (1984): 57–72. Also published in *Renmin ribao*, 27 January 1984.

Huang Nansen. "Guanyu ren de ruogan lilun wenti." In *Makesi zhuyi yu ren*, ed. The Department of Philosophy of Beijing University. Beijing: Bejing daxue chubanshe, 1983.

Huang Songjie, Wu Xiaoming, and An Yanming. *Sate qi ren jiqi renxue*. Shang-hai: Fudan daxue, 1986.

Huang Ziping. "Deyi mo wangyan." *Shanghai wenxue* 11 (1985): 84–88.

———. "Guanyu 'wei xiandai pai' jiqi piping." *Beijing wenxue* 2 (1988): 4–9, 13.

———. *Xingcunzhe de wenxue*. Taibei: Yuanliu chuban shiye gufen youxian gongsi, 1991.

———. "Zhengmian zhankai ling yu rou de bodou." In *Ping "Nanren de yiban shi nüren,"* ed. Ningxia People's Publishers, 1–3. Yinchuan: Ningxia renmin chubanshe, 1987.

Huang Zongxi. "Caiji 3." In *Minyi daifang lu*. In *Zhongguo xueshu minzhu jin-shi yuyi*, ed. Xi'nan Books Editorial Committee, 5: 31–32. Taibei: Xi'nan shuju, 1972.

———. "Yuan chen." In *Minyi daifang lu*. In *Zhongguo xueshu minzhu jinshi yuyi*, ed. Xi'nan Books Editorial Committee, 5: 7–9. Taibei: Xi'nan shuju, 1972.

———. "Yuan fa." In *Minyi daifang lu*. In *Zhongguo xueshu minzhu jinshi yuyi*, ed. Xi'nan Books Editorial Committee, 5: 10–11. Taibei: Xi'nan shuju, 1972.

———. "Yuan jun." In *Minyi daifang lu*. In *Zhongguo xueshu minzhu jinshi yuyi*, ed. Xi'nan Books Editorial Committee, 5: 3–5. Taibei: Xi'nan shuju, 1972.

Jameson, Fredric. Foreword to *The Postmodern Condition: A Report on Knowledge*, by Jean-François Lyotard, vii–xxi. Minneapolis: University of Minnesota Press, 1984.

———. *Houxiandai zhuyi yu wenhua lilun*. Trans. Tang Xiaobing. Xi'an: Shaanxi Normal University Press, 1986.

———. *Postmodernism*. Durham, N.C.: Duke University Press, 1991.

Jay, Martin. *The Dialectical Imagination: A History of the Frankfurt School and the Institute of Social Research, 1923–50*. Boston: Little, Brown and Co., 1973.

———. "Habermas and Modernism." *Habermas and Modernity*, ed. Richard J. Bernstein, 125–39. Cambridge: MIT Press, 1985.

Ji Hongzhen. "Jingshen liulangzhe de zhili youxi: Wang Shuo *Wande jiushi xintiao* suojie." *Beijing wenxue* 7 (1989): 34–39.

———. "Shenhua de shuailuo yu fuxing." *Wenxue pinglun* 4 (1989): 87–92, 109.

———. " 'Wenhua xungen' yu dangdai wenxue." *Wenyi yanjiu* 2 (1989): 69–74.

———. "Wenxue piping de xitong fangfa yu jiegou yuanze." *Wenyi lilun yanjiu* 3 (1984): 10–17.

———. "Zhongguo jinnian xiaoshuo yu xifang xiandai zhuyi wenxue." *Wenyi bao*, 2 January 1988 and 9 January 1988.

Ji Yanzhi. "Zai youyige lishi zhuanzhedian shang: Jinian 'Wu Si' yundong qishi zhounian." *Renmin ribao*, 3 May 1989, overseas edition.

Jia Pingwa. *Shangzhou*. Beijing: Beijing "Shiyue" wenyi chubanshe, 1987.

Jiang Zemin. "Aiguo zhuyi he woguo zhishi fenzi de shiming." *Renmin ribao*, 4 May 1990, overseas edition.

Jin Guantao. *Wode zhexue tansuo*. Taibei: Fengyun shidai chuban gongsi, 1989.

Jin Guantao and Liu Qingfeng. "Kexue: Wenhua yanjiu zhong beihulue de zhuti." Appendix to *Xingsheng yu weiji: Lun Zhongguo fengjian shehui de chaowending jiegou*, 403–30. Taibei: Fengyun shidai chuban gongsi, 1989.

———. *Xingsheng yu weiji: Lun Zhongguo fengjian shehui de chaowending jiegou*. Taibei: Fengyun shidai chuban gongsi, 1989.

Jin Guantao, Liu Qingfeng, and Fan Hongye. "Wenhua beijing yu kexue jishu jiegou yanbian." In *Kexue chuantong yu wenhua: Zhongguo jindai kexue luohou de yuanyin*, ed. the editorial board from *Ziran bianzhengfa tongxun* of the Academy of the Natural Sciences. Shaanxi: Kexue jishu chubanshe, 1983.

Karl, Frederick R. *Modern and Modernism: The Sovereignty of the Artist 1885–1925*. New York: Atheneum, 1985.

Kelly, David. "The Emergence of Humanism: Wang Ruoshui and the Critique of Socialist Alienation." In *China's Intellectuals and the State: In Search of A New Relationship*, ed. Merle Goldman et al., 159–82. Cambridge: The Council on East Asian Studies at Harvard University, 1987.

Klein, Joe. "Why China Does It Better." *Newsweek*, 12 April 1993, 23.

Kolb, David. *The Critique of Pure Modernity: Hegel, Heidegger, and After*. Chicago: University of Chicago Press, 1986.

Kraus, Richard C. "The Lament of Astrophysicist Fang Lizhi: China's Intellectuals in a Global Context." In *Marxism and the Chinese Experience,* ed. Arif Dirlik and Maurice Meisner. Armonk, N.Y.: M. E. Sharpe, 1989.

Laclau, Ernesto. Preface to *The Sublime Object of Ideology,* by Slavoj Zizek, ix–xv. London: Verso, 1989.

Lao Siguang. *Zhongguo zhexue shi.* Vol. 2. Taibei: Sanmin shuju, 1981.

Lee, Leo Ou-fan. "Beyond Realism: Thoughts on Modernist Experiments in Contemporary Chinese Writing." In *Worlds Apart: Recent Chinese Writing and Its Audiences,* ed. Howard Goldblatt, 64–77. Armonk, N.Y.: M. E. Sharpe, 1990.

————. "The Politics of Technique: Perspectives of Literary Dissidence in Contemporary Chinese Fiction." In *After Mao: Chinese Literature and Society,* ed. Jeffrey C. Kinkley, 159–90. Cambridge: The Council on East Asian Studies of Harvard University, 1985.

Lei Da. "Lun chuangzuo zhuti de duoyanghua qushi." *Wenxue pinglun* 1 (1986): 63–70.

————. "Zhuti yishi de qianghua: Dui jinnian xiaoshuo fazhan de sikao." *Wenxue pinglun* 1 (1986): 121–25.

Li Cunshan. "Zhongguo chuantong wenhua yu Zhongguo xiandaihua (xia)." *Renmin ribao,* 20 August 1986, overseas edition.

Li Dongmu. "Xiandai wenxue yanjiu yu xitong kexue fangfa yizhi." *Wenyi lilun yanjiu* 3 (1985): 19–30.

Li Hangyu. "Liyili women de 'gen.' " *Zuojia* 9 (1985): 75–79.

Li Jie. "Lun Zhongguo dangdai xinchao xiaoshuo." *Zhongshan* 5 (1988): 116–38.

Li Jie and Huang Ziping. "Wenxueshi kuangjia ji qita." *Beijing wenxue* 7 (1988): 70–75.

Li Jiefei and Zhang Ling. "Youhuan yishi yu rende reqing." *Shanghai wenxue* 9 (1986): 84–93.

Li Ping. "Wanxia xiaoshi de shihou." *Shiyue* 1 (1981): 77–134.

Li Qingxi. "Baiwu liaolai de 'houpiping': Yetan 'houxinshiqi wenxue.' " *Wenyi lilun* 2 (1993): 129–30.

————. "Xungen: Huidao shiwu benshen." *Wenxue pinglun* 4 (1988): 14–23.

Li Rui. " 'Houtu' ziyu." *Shanghai wenxue* 10 (1988): 29, 68–71.

Li Tuo. "Ding Ling bu jiandan: Mao tizhi xia zhishi fenzi zai huayu shengchan zhong de fuza jiaose." *Jintian* 3 (1993): 222–42.

————. "Literature as Social Practice in Contemporary China." Paper presented at the Asian/Pacific Studies Institute, Duke University, 1 March 1993.

————. "Lun 'geshi geyang de xiaoshuo.' " In *Xifang xiandai pai wenxue wenti lunzheng ji,* ed. He Wangxian, 2: 534–56. Beijing: Renmin wenxue chubanshe, 1984.

————. "Mao Style and Its Political Institutionalization." Unpublished proposal for research, Duke University, spring 1993.

————. "Xiandai hanyu yu dangdai wenxue." *Xindi* 1, no. 6 (1991): 30–43.

————. " 'Xiandai xiaoshuo' bu dengyu 'xiandai pai': Gei Liu Xinwu de xin." In *Xifang xiandai pai wenxue wenti lunzheng ji,* ed. He Wangxian, 2: 507–13. Beijing: Renmin wenxue chubanshe, 1984.

————. "Yetan 'wei xiandai pai' jiqi piping." *Beijing wenxue* 4 (1988): 4–10.

————. "Yijiu bawu." *Jintian* 3/4 (1991): 59–73.

Li Tuo, Zhang Ling, and Wang Bin. "1987–88: Beizhuang de nuli." *Dushu* 1 (1989): 52–58.

————. "Yuyan de fanpan: Jinliangnian xiaoshuo xianxiang." *Wenyi yanjiu* 2 (1989): 75–80.

Li Xinfeng. "Shenru tantao fangfalun nuli fazhan wenyixue: Wuhan wenyixue fangfalun xueshu taolunhui zongshu." *Wenyi lilun* 3 (1986): 17–24.

Li Zehou. "Ershi shiji Zhongguo wenyi yipie." In *Zhongguo xiandai sixiang shilun*, 261–333. Taibei: Fengyun shidai chuban gongsi, 1990.

————. "Manshuo xiti zhongyong." In *Zhongguo xiandai sixiang shilun*, 397–433. Taibei: Fengyun shidai chuban gongsi, 1990.

————. *Meide licheng*. Beijing: Wenwu chubanshe, 1981.

————. *Pipan zhexue de pipan: Kangde shuping*. Rev. ed. Beijing: Renmin chubanshe, 1986.

————. "Response to Lin Yu-sheng." Paper presented at the roundtable discussion of neo-Confucianism at the annual meeting of the Asian Studies Association, Washington, D.C., 26 March 1993.

————. *Zhongguo gudai sixiang shilun*. Beijing: Renmin chubanshe, 1985.

————. *Zhongguo jindai sixiang shilun*. Beijing: Renmin chubanshe, 1979.

————. *Zhongguo xiandai sixiang shilun*. Taibei: Fengyun shidai chuban gongsi, 1990.

Li Zehou and Liu Zaifu. "Wenxue yu yishu de qingsi: Li Zehou yu Liu Zaifu de wenxue duihua." *Renmin ribao*, 14 April 1988, overseas edition.

Li Zhongming. "Cong fanziyouhua douzheng dao Lei Feng yangban (2)." *Zhongyang ribao*, 13 March 1987, overseas edition.

Li Zhun. "Xiandai hua yu xiandai pai youzhe biran lianxi ma?" In *Xifang xiandai pai wenxue wenti lunzheng ji*, ed. He Wangxian, 2: 413–26. Beijing: Renmin wenxue chubanshe, 1984.

————. " 'Xiandai yishi' he tade canzhaoxi." *Wenyi lilun* 9 (1986): 105–7.

Li Zonggui. " 'Xiandai xinrujia sichao yanjiu' de youlai he Xuanzhou huiyi de zhengming." In *Xiandai xinruxue yanjiu lunji*, ed. Fang Keli and Li Jinquan, 1: 333–35. Beijing: Zhongguo shehui kexue chubanshe, 1989.

Liang Qichao. "Ming Qing zhijiao Zhongguo sixiangjie jiqi daibiao renwu." In *Zhongguo zhexue sixiang lunji*, ed. Xiang Weixin and Liu Fuzeng, 5 (The Qing volume): 1–10. Taibei: Mutong chubanshe, 1976.

Liang Zhiping. "Chuantong wenhua de gengxin yu zaisheng." *Dushu* 3 (1989): 5–20.

Liao Tianliang et al. "Renge de kun'e yu jingshen de zixing." *Renmin ribao*, 5 November 1988, overseas edition.

Lin Jianchu. "Yibu kaituoxing de zhuzuo: Ping Lei Zhenxiao *Zhongguo rencai sixiangshi (diyi juan)*." *Renmin ribao*, 28 November 1986, overseas edition.

Lin Nan. "Local Market Socialism: Rural Reform in China." Paper presented at the annual meeting of the American Sociological Association, Pittsburgh, Pa., August 1992.

Lin Weiping. "Xinshiqi wenxue yixitan: Fang zuojia Li Tuo." *Shanghai wenxue* 10 (1986): 90, 91–96.

Lin Xingzhai. "Lun A Q xingge xitong." *Lu Xun yanjiu* 1 (1984): 46–54.

———. "Lun xitong kexue fangfalun zai wenyi yanjiu zhong de yunyong." *Wenyi lilun* 2 (1986): 29–37.

Liu Heng. "Wenxue de youji zhengtixing he wenxue lilun de xitongxing." *Wenyi bao* 11 (1984): 65–68.

Liu Kang. "Subjectivity, Marxism, and Culture Theory in China." *Social Text* 31/32 (1992): 114–40.

Liu Minzhong. "Makesi yihua lun chutan." In *Renxing rendao zhuyi wenti taolun ji,* ed. The Research Institute of Philosophy of the Chinese Academy of the Social Sciences, 366–82. Beijing: Renmin chubanshe, 1983.

Liu Suola. "Lantian lühai." In *Zhongguo dalu xiandai xiaoshuo xuan,* 1: 123–78. Taibei: Yuanshen chubanshe, 1987.

———. *Ni biewu xuanze.* Beijing: Zuojia chubanshe, 1986.

———. "Ni biewu xuanze." In *Ni biewu xuanze,* 4–84. Beijing: Zuojia chubanshe, 1986.

Liu Xiaobo. "Weiji! Xinshiqi wenxue mianlin weiji." *Wenyi lilun* 12 (1986): 165–73.

———. "Wufa huibi de fansi: You jibu zhishi fenzi ticai de xiaoshuo suo xiangdaode." *Wenyi lilun* 12 (1986): 175–82.

———. *Xuanze de pipan: Yu sixiang lingxiu duihua.* Taibei: Fengyun shidai chuban gongsi, 1989.

———. "Yinzi: Fanchuantong yu Zhongguo zhishi fenzi." In *Xuanze de pipan: Yu sixiang lingxiu duihua,* 1–11. Taibei: Fengyun shidai chuban gongsi, 1989.

———. "Yizhong xinde shenmei sichao: Cong Xu Xing, Chen Cun, Liu Suola de sanbu zuoping tanqi." *Wenxue pinglun* 3 (1986): 35–43.

Liu Xinwu. "Wo shi wo ziji." *Renmin ribao,* 24 January 1986, overseas edition.

———. "Xuyao lengjing de sikao: Gei Feng Jicai de xin." In *Xifang xiandai pai wenxue wenti lunzheng ji,* ed. He Wangxian, 2: 514–19. Beijing: Renmin wenxue chubanshe, 1984.

———. "Zai 'xin qi guai' mianqian: Du *Xiandai xiaoshuo jiqiao chutan.*" In *Xifang xiandai pai wenxue wenti lunzheng ji,* ed. He Wangxian, 2: 520–28. Beijing: Renmin wenxue chubanshe, 1984.

———. "Zhongguo zuojia yu dangdai shijie." *Renmin ribao,* 11 March 1988, overseas edition.

Liu Zaifu. "Gaobie zhushen: Zhongguo dangdai wenxue lilun 'shijimo' de zhengzha." *Ershiyi shiji* 5 (June 1991): 125–34.

———. "Liangci lishixing de tupo: Cong 'Wusi' xinwenhua yundong dao xinshiqi de 'xiandai wenhua yishi.' " *Renmin ribao,* 27 April 1989, overseas edition.

———. "Lun bashi niandai wenxue piping de wenti geming." *Wenxue pinglun* 1(1989): 5–22.

———. "Lun renwu xingge de erchong zuhe yuanli." In *Shengming jinshen yu wenxue daolu,* 3–42. Taibei: Fengyun shidai chuban gongsi, 1989.

———. "Lun wenxue de zhutixing." In *Shengming jingshen yu wenxue daolu,* 83–144. Taibei: Fengyun shidai chuban gongsi, 1989.

———. *Renlun ershiwuzhong.* Hong Kong: Oxford University Press, 1992.

————. *Shengming jingshen yu wenxue daolu.* Taibei: Fengyun shidai chuban gongsi, 1989.

————. *Wenxue de fansi.* Beijing: Renmin wenxue chubanshe, 1988.

————. "Wenxue yanjiu siwei kongjian de tuozhan." In *Wenxue de fansi,* 1–39. Beijing: Renmin wenxue chubanshe, 1988.

————. "Wenxue yanjiu yingyi ren wei siwei zhongxin." In *Wenxue de fansi,* 40–53. Beijing: Renmin wenxue chubanshe, 1988.

————. *Xingge zuhe lun.* Shanghai: Shanghai wenyi chubanshe, 1986.

————. "Zhongguo xiandai wenxueshi shang dui ren de sanci faxian." In *Xunzhao yu huhuan,* 33–48. Taibei: Fengyun shidai chubanshe, 1989.

Liu Zaifu and Lin Gang. *Chuantong yu Zhongguo ren.* Hong Kong: Sanlian shudian, 1988.

Lu Gao. "Mohuande haishi xianshide? Du 'Xizang, xizai pishengkou shang de hun.'" *Xizang wenxue* 1 (1985): 15–16.

Lu Rongchun. "Zhanshi de zitai yanbuzhu beique de linghun." In *Ping "Nanren de yiban shi nüren,"* ed. Ningxia People's Publishers, 62–67. Yinchuan: Ningxia renmin chubanshe, 1987.

Lu Xun. "Changcheng." In *Lu Xun quanji,* 3: 63–64. Beijing: Renmin wenxue chubanshe, 1973.

Lu Yao. *Rencheng. Shouhuo* 3 (1982): 4–90.

Lukács, Georg. *Geschichte und Klassenbewusstsein: Studien über Marxistische dialektik.* Berlin: Der Malik-Verlag, 1923.

Lyotard, Jean-François. "Appendix." Trans. Régis Rurand. In *The Postmodern Condition,* trans. Geoff Bennington and Brian Massumi, 71–82. Minneapolis: University of Minnesota Press, 1984.

————. *The Postmodern Condition: A Report on Knowledge.* Trans. Geoff Bennington and Brian Massumi. Minneapolis: University of Minnesota Press, 1984.

Mao Zedong. "Sixty Points on Working Methods." In *Mao Papers,* ed. Jerome Ch'en, 57–76. London: Oxford University Press, 1970.

————. "Zhongguo geming he Zhongguo gongchandang." In *Mao Zedong xuanji,* ed. the CCP Publication Committee for the *Selected Writings of Mao,* 585–617. Beijing: Renmin chubanshe, 1967.

Marcuse, Herbert. *Eros and Civilization.* Boston: Beacon Press, 1955.

————. *Reason and Revolution: Hegel and the Rise of Social Theory.* Rev. ed. Boston: Beacon Press, 1960.

————. "Re-Examination of the Concept of Revolution." In *Karl Marx and Contemporary Scientific Thought,* 477–82. The Hague: Mouton, 1969.

Marx, Karl. *Economic and Philosophic Manuscripts of 1844.* In *Karl Marx: Early Writings,* 279–400. Trans. Rodney Livingstone and Gregor Benton. New York: Vintage Books, 1975.

Meng Yue. "Su Tong de 'jiashi' yu 'lishi' xiezuo." *Jintian* 2 (1990): 84–93.

————. "*Zouxiang shijie wenxue:* Yige jiannan de jincheng." *Dushu* 8 (1986): 50–57.

"Mianxiang xinshiqi wenxue di'erge shinian de sikao." Transcribed by Tan Xiang. *Wenxue pinglun* 1 (1987): 44–50.

Mills, C. Wright. *White Collar: The American Middle Classes*. Oxford: Oxford University Press, 1953.

Mo Yan. *Honggaoliang jiazu*. Taibei: Hongfan shudian, 1988.

Mu Gong. "Lun 'wei xiandai pai.' " *Mengya* 5 (1988): 62–64.

———. "Wang Shuo: Zhishi fenzi wenhua de bishizhe." *Zhongshan* 1 (1991): 152.

———. "Xiang Sate gaobie: Jianping *Xinxiaoshuo pai yanjiu* bianxuanzhe xu." *Dushu* 3 (1988): 64–71.

Nagl, Ludwig. "Obsolescence of the Production Paradigm?" In *Alienation, Society, and the Individual: Continuity and Change in Theory and Research*, ed. Felix Geyer and Walter R. Heinz, 17–26. New Brunswick: Transaction Publishers, 1992.

Nan Fan and Huang Ziping. "Xiaoshuo, shenmei qinggan yu shidai." *Beijing wenxue* 11 (1988): 71–74.

Nancy, Jean-Luc. Introduction to *Who Comes after the Subject?*, ed. Eduardo Cadava, Peter Connor, and Jean-Luc Nancy, 1–8. New York: Routledge, 1991.

Ningxia People's Publishers, ed. *Ping "Nanren de yiban shi nüren."* Yinchuan: Ningxia renmin chubanshe, 1987.

"One Hundred Mistakes in *Heshang*." *Renmin ribao*, August–November 1989.

Pan Kaixiong. "*Wenyi bao* yaoqing bufen wenyi lilunjie renshi zuotan 'Wenxue yu xiandai yishi' wenti." In *Zhongguo wenyi nianjian: 1987*, 63. Beijing: Wenhua yishu chubanshe, 1988.

———. "Yi xiandai yishi fanying xiandai shenghuo." *Wenyi lilun* 8 (1986): 11–12.

Pan Kaixiong and He Shaojun. "Kunnan, fenhua, zonghe." In "Yuyan wenti yu wenxue yanjiu de tuozhan," 64–66. *Wenxue pinglun* 1 (1988).

Peng Lixun. "Cong xifang meixue he wenyi sichao kan 'Ziwo biaoxian' shuo: Shi 'xinde meixue yuanze' haishi jiudiao chongtan?" In *Xifang xiandai pai wenxue wenti lunzheng ji*, ed. He Wangxian, 1: 350–66. Beijing: Renmin wenxue chubanshe, 1984.

Petrovic, Gajo. "Lun yihua." *Zhexue yicong* 2 (1979).

———. "The Philosophical and Sociological Relevance of Marx's Concept of Alienation." In *Marx and the Western World*, ed. Nicholas Lobkowicz. Notre Dame, Ind.: University of Notre Dame Press, 1967.

Qian Jing. "Yuqiong qianli mu, gengshang yiceng lou: Ji Yangzhou wenyixue fangfalun wenti xueshu taolun hui." *Wenxue pinglun* 4 (1985): 50–55.

Rabinow, Paul. Introduction to *French Modern: Norms and Forms of the Social Environment*, 1–16. Cambridge: MIT Press, 1989.

Rendao zhuyi he yihua sanshi ti. Ed. The Research Institute of Philosophy at the Shanghai Academy of the Social Sciences. Shanghai: Shanghai renmin chubanshe, 1984.

Rendao zhuyi renxinglun yihua wenti yanjiu zhuanji. Ed. Center of Newspapers and Research Materials at People's University. Beijing: Renmin daxue, 1983.

Ren shi Makesi zhuyi de chufa dian. Ed. the editorial committee of Renmin chubanshe. Beijing: Renmin chubanshe, 1981.

Renxing rendao zhuyi wenti taolun ji. Ed. The Research Institute of Philosophy at the Chinese Academy of the Social Sciences. Beijing: Renmin chubanshe, 1983.

Ross, Andrew. *No Respect: Intellectuals and Popular Culture.* New York: Routledge, 1989.

Ru Xin. "Pipan zichan jieji rendao zhuyi, xuanchuan shehui zhuyi rendao zhuyi." *Renmin ribao,* 9 January 1984.

———. "Rendao zhuyi jiushi xiuzheng zhuyi ma? Dui rendao zhuyi de zairenshi." In *Renxing rendao zhuyi wenti taolun ji,* ed. The Research Institute of Philosophy at the Chinese Academy of the Social Sciences, 20–33. Beijing: Renmin chubanshe, 1983.

Schaff, Adam. "Makesi yihua lilun de gainian xitong." *Zhexue yicong* 1/2 (1979).

———. *Marxism and the Human Individual.* Ed. Robert S. Cohen. New York: McGraw-Hill Book Co., 1970.

———. *Marxismus und das menschliche Individuum.* Vienna: Europa-Verlag, 1965.

———. "Yihua shi shehui wenti he zhexue wenti." *Zhexue yicong* 4 (1981).

———. "Yinggai yanjiu yihua lilun." *Zhexue yicong* 6 (1981).

Schram, Stuart. *Ideology and Policy in China Since the Third Plenum, 1978–84.* London: Contemporary China Institute, SOAS, University of London, 1984.

Schwarcz, Vera. *The Chinese Enlightenment: Intellectuals and the Legacy of the May Fourth Movement of 1919.* Berkeley: University of California Press, 1986.

Sen, N. C. *Rural Economy and Development in China.* Beijing: Foreign Languages Press, 1990.

Seymour, James D., ed. *The Fifth Modernization: China's Human Rights Movement, 1978–79.* Stanfordville, N.Y.: Human Rights Publishing Group, 1980.

Shen Rong. *Rendao zhongnian. Shouhuo* 1 (1980): 52–92.

Sherover-Marcuse, Erica. *Emancipation and Consciousness: Dogmatic and Dialectical Perspectives in the Early Marx.* Oxford: Basil Blackwell, 1986.

Sitnikov, E. M. "A Soviet Critique of 'Western' Interpretations of Marx." Appendix to *Marx and Marxism,* by Iring Fetscher, 320–31. New York: Herder and Herder, 1971.

Smith, Paul. *Discerning the Subject.* Minneapolis: University of Minnesota Press, 1988.

Song Yaoliang. *Shinian wenxue zhuchao.* Shanghai: Shanghai wenyi chubanshe, 1988.

———. "Wenxue xinsichao de zhuyao shenmei tezheng yu biaoxian xingtai." *Shanghai wenxue* 6 (1987): 75–80.

———. "Yishiliu wenxue dongfanghua guocheng." *Wenxue pinglun* 1 (1986): 33–40.

Song Zhongfu, Zhao Jihui, and Pei Dayang. *Ruxue zai xiandai Zhongguo.* Zhengzhou: Zhongzhou guji chubanshe, 1991.

Spivak, Gayatri Chakravorty. "Subaltern Studies: Deconstructing Historiography." In *Selected Subaltern Studies,* ed. Ranajit Guha and Gayatri Spivak, 3–32. New York: Oxford University Press, 1988.

Su Wei. "Wenxue de 'xungen' yu 'huayu' de shanbian: Luelun xifang xiandai zhuyi wenxue sichao dui baling niandai Zhongguo wenxue de yingxiang." In *Zhongguo dalu dangdai wenhua bianqian 1978–1989,* ed. Chen Kuide, 183–207. Taibei: Guiguan tushu gufen youxian gongsi, 1991.

Su Xiaokang. "Dangdai Zhongguo de wenhua jinzhang." In *Zhongguo dalu dangdai wenhua bianqian,* 1978–1989, ed. Chen Kuide, 21–35. Taibei: Guiguan tushu gufen youxian gongsi, 1991.

———. "Longnian de beichuang." In *Ziyou beiwanglu,* 263–91. Hong Kong: Joint Publishing Co., 1989.

———. "Zai Bali xiangqi Caishikou: Liuwang ganhuai." *Baixing* 202 (16 October 1989): 3–4.

Sun Shaozhen. "Xinde meixue yuanze zai jueqi." In *Xifang xiandai pai wenxue wenti lunzheng ji,* ed. He Wangxian, 1: 323–33. Beijing: Renmin wenxue chubanshe, 1984.

Suvin, Darko, and Kojin Karatani, eds. Special issue on the non-Cartesian subject, East and West. *Discours social/Social Discourse* 6, nos. 1–2 (1994).

Tang Xiaobing. "The Function of New Theory: What Does It Mean to Talk about Post-Modernism in China?" *Public Culture* 4, no. 1 (1991): 89–108.

———. "Orientalism and the Question of Universality: The Language of Contemporary Chinese Literary Theory." *Positions* 1, no. 2 (1993): 389–413.

———. "Residual Modernism: Narrative of the Self in Contemporary Chinese Fiction." *Modern Chinese Literature* 7, no. 1 (1993): 7–31.

Tang Xuezhi. "Yijiu baer nian wenyi lilun yanjiu gaishu." In *Zhongguo xinwenyi daxi: 1976–1982 shiliao ji,* ed. Chen Huangmei et al., 437–42. Beijing: Zhongguo wenlian chuban gongsi, 1990.

Tang Zhen. "Daming." In *Qianshu.* In *Zhongguo xueshu minzhu jinshi yuyi,* ed. the Xi'nan Books Editorial Committee, 5: 244–45. Taibei: Xi'nan shuju, 1972.

Tang Zhi. "Wenxue zhong de renxing yu rendao zhuyi wenti: Du Hu Qiaomu tongzhi 'Guanyu rendao zhuyi he yihua wenti' biji." *Wenyi bao* 4 (1984): 31–39.

The Task-Force Section of the Bureau of the Arts and Literature in the Department of Propaganda, ed. "Guanyu shehui zhuyi shichang jingji tiaojianxia wenyi lingyu mianling de xinwenti." *Wenyi lilun* 3 (1993): 23–30.

Teng Yun. "Luanhua jianyu mi renyan." *Renmin wenxue* 4 (1986): 121–27.

Tu Weiming. "Dalu ruxue xindongxiang de hanyi." *Zhongguo luntan* 27, no. 7 (1989): 30–36.

———. *Ruxue disanqi fazhan de qianjing wenti: Dalu jiangxue, wennan he taolun.* Taibei: Lianjing chuban shiye gongsi, 1989.

———. "Ruxue disanqi fazhan de qianjing wenti: 1, 2, & 3." *Mingbao yuekan* 21, no. 1, 21, no. 2, 21, no. 3 (1986): 27–32, 36–38, 65–68.

Wakeman, Frederic. "All the Rage in China." *New York Review of Books,* 2 March 1989, 19–21.

Wang Bi. "Ming Xiang." In *Zhouyi luelie,* 2: 609 of *Wang Bi ji jiaoshi,* ed. Lou Yulie. Beijing: Xinhua shuju, 1980.

Wang, David Der-Wei. Reader's report to the University of California Press, 1994.

Wang Furen. "Zhongguo jinxiandai wenhua he wenxue fazhan de nixiangxing tezheng." *Wenxue pinglun* 2 (1989): 5–16.

Wang Fuzhi. "Tun." In *Zhouyi waizhuan*. In *Zhongguo xueshu minzhu jinshi yuyi*, ed. the Xi'nan Books Editorial Committee, 5: 115. Taibei: Xi'nan shuju, 1972.

Wang He. "Ruhe pingjia chuantong wenhua: Jinnianlai guanyu Zhongguo wenhua wenti yanjiu zongshu." *Renmin ribao,* 27 May 1989, overseas edition.

Wang Hongzhou. "Gang-Tai xuezhe dui Zhongguo chuantong wenhua de yanjiu: Jinnianlai guanyu Zhongguo wenhua wenti yanjiu zhongshu." *Renmin ribao,* 30 May 1989, overseas edition.

Wang, Jing. "*Heshang* and the Paradoxes of Chinese Enlightenment." *Bulletin of Concerned Asian Scholars* 23, no. 3 (1991): 23–32.

———. Postscript. "The Mirage of 'Chinese Postmodernism': Ge Fei and the Avant-Garde Showcase." *Positions* 1, no. 2 (1993): 379–82.

———. "Romancing the Subject: Utopian Moments in the Chinese Aesthetics of the 1980s." *Discours social/Social Discourse* 6, nos. 1–2 (1994): 115–40.

———. *The Story of Stone: Intertextuality, Ancient Chinese Stone Lore, and the Stone Symbolism of "Dream of the Red Chamber," "Water Margin," and "The Journey to the West."* Durham, N.C.: Duke University Press, 1992.

Wang Lin. "Shi juhao haishi wenhao?" *Dushu* 5 (1989): 133–35.

Wang Meng. "Dangqian wenxue gongzuo zhong de jige wenti." *Hongqi* 24 (1985): 16–19.

———. "Fanmian wutuobang de qishi." *Dushu* 2 (1989): 44–47.

———. "Yiti qianjiao." *Shouhuo* 4 (1988): 41, 90–108.

Wang Meng and Wang Gan. "Piruan? Huapo?" *Zhongshan* 3 (1989): 148–60.

———. "Wenxue zhege mofang: Duiha lu." *Wenxue pinglun* 3 (1989): 38–46.

Wang Ning. "Guifan yu bianti: Guanyu Zhongguo wenxue zhong de xiandai zhuyi he houxiandai zhuyi." *Zhongshan* 6 (1989): 154–61.

———. "Zhishi fenzi: Cong lifazhe dao jieshizhe." *Dushu* 12 (1992): 114–18.

———. "Zhongguo jiushi niandai wenxue yanjiu zhong de ruogan lilun keti." *Wenyi lilun* 1 (1992): 176–81.

Wang Ruoshui. "Guanyu 'geming rendao zhuyi.' " In *Wei rendao zhuyi bianhu,* 234–38. Beijing: Sanlian shudian, 1986.

———. "Ren shi Makesi zhuyi de chufa dian." In *Wei rendao zhuyi bianhu,* 200–216. Beijing: Sanlian shudian, 1986.

———. "Tantan yihua wenti." In *Wei rendao zhuyi bianhu,* 186–99. Beijing: Sanlian shudian, 1986.

———. *Wei rendao zhuyi bianhu.* Beijing: Sanlian shudian, 1986.

———. "Wei rendao zhuyi bianhu." In *Wei rendao zhuyi bianhu,* 217–33. Beijing: Sanlian shudian, 1986.

———. "Wo dui rendao zhuyi wenti de kanfa." In *Wei rendao zhuyi bianhu,* 239–74. Beijing: Sanlian shudian, 1986.

Wang Shouchang. "Sate de cunzai zhuyi rendao zhuyi tantao." In *Ren shi Makesi zhuyi de chufa dian,* ed. the Editorial Committee of Renmin chubanshe, 217–40. Beijing: Renmin chubanshe, 1981.

Wang Shuo. *Wande jiushi xintiao. Wenxue siji* 1 (1988): 174–255.

———. "Wanzhu." *Shouhuo* 6 (1987): 24–52.

———. "Wode xiaoshuo." *Renmin wenxue* 3 (1989): 108.

———. *Wo shi Wang Shuo*. Beijing: Guoji wenhua chuban gongsi, 1992.

Wang Xiaoming. "Bu xiangxinde he bu yuanyi xiangxinde." *Wenxue pinglun* 4 (1989): 24–35.

Wang Yu. "Du Fang Yizhi 'Dongxi jun.' " In *Ming Qing sixiangjia lunji*, 211–29. Taibei: Lianjing chuban shiye gongsi, 1981.

———. *Ming Qing sixiangjia lunji*. Taibei: Lianjing chuban shiye gongsi, 1981.

Wang Yuanhua. "Guanyu muqian wenxue yanjiu zhong de liangge wenti." *Wenyi lilun* 8 (1986): 109–14.

Wang Zeke. "Shangpin jingji he zhishi fenzi." *Dushu* 9 (1992): 145–48.

Wang Zhihuan. "Deng Guanque Lou." In *Tangshi sanbaishou xiangxi*, 274. Taibei: Zhonghua shuju, 1972.

Wei Jingsheng. "Who Should Take the Responsibility?" *China Focus: A Publication of the Princeton China Initiative* 1, no. 10 (1993): 1.

Wellmer, Albrecht. *Critical Theory of Society*. Trans. John Cumming. New York: Herder and Herder, 1971.

———. *The Persistence of Modernity: Essays on Aesthetics, Ethics, and Postmodernism*. Trans. David Midgley. Cambridge: MIT Press, 1991.

———. "Reason, Utopia, and the *Dialectic of Enlightenment*." In *Habermas and Modernity*, ed. Richard J. Bernstein, 35–66. Cambridge: MIT Press, 1985.

"Wenyi chuangzuo zhong yao genghao fanying shehui zhuyi rendao zhuyi." *Renmin ribao*, 18 April 1984.

White, Douglass Alan. "Ch'eng-kung Sui's 'Poetic Essay on Whistling.' " Undergraduate thesis, Harvard University, n.d.

White, Hayden. *Metahistory*. Baltimore, Md.: Johns Hopkins University Press, 1973.

Wu Bingjie. "Shenghuo de biange yu chuangzuo de tiaozheng: Yijiu jiuyi nian zhongduanpian xiaoshuo chuangzuo manping." *Renmin ribao*, 12 March 1992.

Wu Gongzheng. *Xiaoshuo meixue*. Nanjing: Jiangsu wenyi chubanshe, 1985.

Wu Huanlian. "Cong xuanze shengming dao xuanze Zhongguo: Tan 'Zhanwang ershiyi shiji.' " *Dushu* 3 (1989): 14–20.

Wu Liang. "Fangfa de yongtu." *Wenyi bao*, 31 August 1985.

———. "Qidai yu huiyin: Xianfeng xiaoshuo de yige zhujie." *Zuojia* 9 (1989): 59–62.

Wu Meng. *Ganyou geyin dongdi ai*. Kowloon: Qishi niandai Biweekly, 1974.

Wu Xiaoming. "Biaoxian, chuangzao, moshi." In "Yuyan wenti yu wenxue yanjiu de tuozhan." *Wenxue pinglun* 1 (1988): 59–61.

———. "Buxiangxinde he buyuanyi xiangxinde: Guanyu sanwei 'xungen' pai zuojia de chuangzuo." *Wenxue pinglun* 4 (1989): 24–35.

Wu Yuanmai. "Guanyu xiandai yishi he wenyi de sikao." *Wenyi lilun* 10 (1986): 49–50.

Wu Yumin. "Xunqiu renwen jiazhi he kexue lixing jiehe de qidian." In "Yuyan wenti yu wenxue yanjiu de tuozhan." *Wenxue pinglun* 1 (1988): 62–64.

WuDunn, Sheryl. "The Word from China's Kerouac: The Communists Are Uncool." *The New York Times Book Review*, 10 January 1993.

Xiang Weixin and Liu Fuzeng, eds. *Zhongguo zhexue sixiang lunji*. Vol. 5: Qing Dynasty. Taibei: Mutong chubanshe, 1976.

Xiao Gongquan. *Zhongguo zhengzhi sixiang shi*. Vol. 2. Taibei: Wenhua University Press, 1980.

Xiao Shafu. "Zhongguo zhexue qimeng de kanke daolu." In *Dongfang de liming: Zhongguo wenhua zouxiang jindai de licheng*, ed. Feng Tianyu, 13–40. Chengdu: Bashu shushe, 1988.

Xiao Xu. "*Heshang* lunzheng qingkuang zongshu." Appendix 2 to *Chongping "Heshang,"* ed. Zhong Huamin et al., 286–99. Hangzhou: Hangzhou daxue chubanshe, 1989.

Xin Xiaozheng and Guo Yinxing. "Xinlilun de chujing." *Dangdai zuojia pinglun* 6 (1988): 4–10.

Xi'nan Books Editorial Committee, ed. *Zhongguo xueshu minzhu jinshi yuyi*. 6 vols. Taibei: Xi'nan shuju, 1972.

" 'Xinxieshi xiaoshuo dalianzhan' juanshouyu." *Zhongshan* 3 (1989): 4.

Xu Chi. "Xiandai hua yu xiandai pai." In *Xifang xiandai pai wenxue wenti lunzheng ji*, ed. He Wangxian, 2: 395–400. Beijing: Renmin wenxue chubanshe, 1984.

Xu Jingye. "Jueqi de shiqun: Ping woguo shige de xiandai qingxiang." In *Xifang xiandai pai wenxue wenti lunzheng ji*, ed. He Wangxian, 2: 568–613. Beijing: Renmin wenxue chubanshe, 1984.

Xu Junyao. "Zhishi fenzi he xiandai shehui: Cong Gelanxi dao xinzuopai de sikao." *Dushu* 9 (1988): 19–24.

Xu Ming. "Wenxue yanjiu yao jinxing siwei biange." In "Yuyan wenti yu wenxue yanjiu de tuozhan." *Wenxue pinglun* 1 (1988): 66–69.

Xu Xing. "Wuzhuti bianzhou." In *Zhongguo dalu xiandai xiaoshuo xuan*. 2 vols. 1: 37–82.

Xu Zhenglong. "Fazhan jingji bixu jiangu huanbao." *Renmin ribao*, 24 June 1992.

Xu Zidong. "Xiandai zhuyi yu Zhongguo xinshiqi wenxue." *Wenxue pinglun* 4 (1989): 21–34, 60.

"Xueshu shalong." *Renmin ribao*, 14 August 1986, overseas edition.

Yan Bofei. "Paoqi wutuobang: Du Hengtingdun *Bianhua shehui zhong de zhengzhi zhixu*." *Dushu* 2 (1989): 5–12.

Yan Jiaqi. Preface to *Xin'ganjuepai xiaoshuo xuan*, 1–38. Beijing: Renmin wenxue chubanshe, 1985.

Yan Jingming. "Wanzhu yu dushi de chongtu: Wang Shuo xiaoshuo de jiazhi xuanze." *Wenxue pinglun* 6 (1989): 87–91.

Yan Zhaozhu. "Wenxue bentilun de xingqi yu kunhuo: Xinshiqi shinian wenyi lilun yanjiu saomiao." *Wenyi yanjiu* 4 (1989): 197–207.

Yan Zisha. "*Heshang* jiemeipian Wusi liuchan ji." *Baixing* 201 (1 October 1989): 36–37.

Yang Bingzhang. "Guanyu ruxue disanqi he Zhongguo wenhua de qiantu." In *Zhongguo dalu dangdai wenhua bianqian, 1978–1989*, ed. Chen Kuide, 155–68. Taibei: Guiguan tushu gufen youxian gongsi, 1991.

Yang Shi. "Yihua yu duixianghua." In *Makesi zhuyi yu ren*, ed. The Department of Philosophy of Beijing University, 175–200. Beijing: Beijing University Press, 1983.

Yang Yi. *Wenhua chongtu yu shenmei xuanze.* Beijing: Renmin wenxue chuban-she, 1988.

Yang Yu. "Wenxue: Shique hongdong xiaoying yihou." *Wenyi bao,* 30 January 1988. Also published in *Renmin ribao,* 12 February 1988, overseas edition.

"Yansu wenyi wang hechuqu?" *Wenyi lilun* 3 (1993): 96–101.

Ye Fang. "Women haineng you shenme?" *Wenxue pinglun* 3 (1988): 16–22, 85.

Ye Lang, "Kafuka: Yihua lun lishiguan de tujiezhe." In *Rendao zhuyi he yihua wenti yanjiu,* 185–201. Beijing: Beida chubanshe, 1985.

Ye Lihua. "Wenxue: 'shichanghua' de qianti yu lujing." *Wenxue pinglun* 5 (1993): 13–18.

Yin Hong, Luo Chengyan, Kang Lin. "Xiandai wenxue yanjiu de disandai: Zouxiang chenggong yu mianling tiaozhan." *Wenxue pinglun* 5 (1989): 60–73.

Yip, Wai-lim, ed. and trans. *Chinese Poetry: Major Modes and Genres.* Berkeley: University of California Press, 1976.

You Yi [Meng Yue]. "Yetan bashi niandai wenxue de 'xihua.'" *Jintian* 3/4 (1991): 30–42.

Yu Bin. "Minzuhua wenti yu Zhongguo dangdai wenxue de fazhan." *Wenxue pinglun* 6 (1990): 46–55.

Yu Hua. "Xianshi yizhong." In *Shibasui chumen yuanxing,* 1–10. Beijing: Zuo-jia chubanshe, 1989.

———. "Xuwei de zuopin." Preface to *Shishi ruyan,* 5–21. Taibei: Yuanliu chuban gongsi, 1991.

Yu Wujin. "Lun dangdai Zhongguo wenhua de jizhong beilun." *Renmin ribao,* 23 August 1988, overseas edition.

Yu Xiaoxing, transcriber. "Haiwai Zhongguo zuojia taolunhui jiyao." *Jintian* 2 (1990): 94–103.

Yu Yingshi. "Qingdai sixiangshi de yige xinjieshi." In *Zhongguo zhexue sixiang lunji,* ed. Xiang Weixin and Liu Fuzeng, 5: 11–48. Taibei: Mutong chuban-she, 1976.

———. "Zhongguo jinshi zongjiao lunli yu shangren jingshen." *Zhishi fenzi* 2, no. 2 (1986): 3–45.

"Yuyan wenti yu wenxue yanjiu de tuozhan." *Wenxue pinglun* 1 (1988): 56–74, 82.

Zeng Xiaoyi, ed. *Zouxiang shijie wenxue.* Hunan: Hunan renmin chubanshe, 1985.

Zhang Boli. "Wang Shuo: Rebel without a Cause." *China Watch* 1, no. 1 (1993): 8–9.

Zhang Chengzhi. "Wode qiao." *Shiyue* 3 (1983): 239–41.

Zhang Dexiang and Jin Huimin. *Wang Shuo pipan.* Beijing: Zhongguo shehui kexue chubanshe, 1993.

Zhang Fa, Zhang Yiwu, and Wang Yichuan. "Cong 'xiandaixing' dao 'Zhong-huaxing': Xinzhishixing de tanxun." *Wenhua yanjiu* 2 (1994): 8–18.

Zhang Guangxian. "Cong lishi de shijiao ping *Heshang.*" *Guangming ribao,* 23 August 1989.

Zhang Jingchao. "Wenxue zhineng shi yizhong youxian de cunzai." *Wenyi pinglun* 1 (1993): 22–28.

Zhang Shouying. " 'Wei xiandai pai' yu 'xiti zhongyong' boyi." *Beijing wenxue* 6 (1988): 53–59.

Zhang Xinying, transcriber. "Dangdai zhishi fenzi de jiazhi guifan." *Shanghai wenxue* 7 (1993): 64–71.

Zhang Xudong. "Ge Fei yu dangdai wenxue huayu de jige muti." *Jintian* 2 (1990): 76–83.

———. "Lun Zhongguo dangdai piping huayu de zhuti neirong yu zhenli neirong." *Jintian* 3/4 (1991): 2–15.

———. "On Some Motifs in the Chinese 'Cultural Fever' of the Late 1980s: Social Change, Ideology, and Theory." *Social Text* 39 (summer 1994): 129–56.

———. "The Political Hermeneutics of Cultural Constitution: Reflections on the Chinese 'Cultural Discussion' (1985–1989)," 1–54. Working paper in Asian/Pacific Studies. Asian/Pacific Studies Institute, Duke University, 1994.

Zhang Yi, ed. *Kankan Wang Shuo.* Beijing: Huaxia chubanshe, 1993.

Zhang Yingjin. "Re-envisioning the Institution of Modern Chinese Literature Studies: Strategies of Positionality and Self-Reflexivity." *Positions* 1, no. 3, (1993): 816–32.

Zhang Yiwu. "Disan shijie wenhua zhong de xushi." *Zhongshan* 3 (1990): 151–57.

———. "Houxinshiqi wenxue: Xinde wenhua kongjian." *Wenyi lilun* 1 (1992): 182–84.

———. "Lixiang zhuyi de zhongjie: Shiyan xiaoshuo de wenhua tiaozhan." *Beijing wenxue* 4 (1989): 4–11.

———. "Lun 'houwutuobang' huayu: Jiushi niandai Zhongguo wenxue de yizhong quxiang." *Wenyi lilun* 6 (1993): 181–87.

———. " 'Renmin jiyi' yu wenhua de mingyun." *Zhongshan* 1 (1992): 165–72.

———. "Shide weiji yu zhishi fenzi de weiji." *Dushu* 5 (1989): 77–82.

———. "Xiaoshuo shiyan: Yiyi de xiaojie." *Beijing wenxue* 2 (1988): 76–80.

Zhang Yongtang. "Fang Yizhi yu xixue." In *Zhongguo zhexue sixiang lunji*, ed. Xiang Weixin and Liu Fuzeng, 5: 179–205. Taibei: Mutong chubanshe, 1976.

Zhao Fengqi. "Nansilafu zhexuejie guanyu ren he yihua wenti de yanjiu." *Zhexue yanjiu* 1 (1981): 76–78.

Zhao Guoquan. "Fazhan shangping jingji mianling wuge fangmian maodun." *Renmin ribao,* 1 December 1986, overseas edition.

Zhao Mei. "Xianfeng xiaoshuo de zizu yu fufan." *Wenxue pinglun* 1 (1989): 31–39.

Zhao Yifan. "Falankefu xuepai lümei wenhua piping." *Dushu* 1 (1981): 34–43.

Zhao Yiheng. "Yuanyishi he dangdai Zhongguo xianfeng xiaoshuo." *Jintian* 1 (1990): 78, 79–88.

Zhao Ziyang. "Yanzhe you Zhongguo tese de shehui zhuyi daolu qianjin." *Renmin ribao,* 4 November 1987, overseas edition.

Zheng Wanlong. "Wode gen." *Shanghai wenxue* 5 (1985): 44–46.

———. "Zhongguo wenxue yao zouxiang shijie: Cong genzhi yu 'wenhua yanceng' tanqi." *Zuojia* 1 (1986): 70–74.

Zheng Yi. "Xunzhao minzu zhi hun." In *Yuancun*, 6–7. Taibei: Haifeng chubanshe, 1990.

———. "Yuancun." In *Yuancun*, 25–161. Taibei: Haifeng chubanshe, 1990.

Zhong Huamin. "Zuowei zhenglunpian de *Heshang*." In *Chongping "Heshang*," 4–10. Hangzhou: Hangzhou daxue chubanshe, 1989.

Zhong Huamin et al., eds. *Chongping "Heshang*." Hangzhou: Hangzhou daxue chubanshe, 1989.

Zhou Erliu and Zhang Yulin, eds. *Chengxiang xietiao fazhan yanjiu*. Nanjing: Jiangsu renmin chubanshe, 1991.

Zhou Guanwu. "Xiaofei shi fazhan shengchan de dongli." *Renmin ribao*, 7 June 1992.

Zhou Guoping and Jia Zelin. "Sulian zhexue zhong de ren he rendao zhuyi wenti." In *Ren shi Makesi zhuyi de chufa dian*, ed. the Editorial Committee of Renmin chubanshe, 241–89. Beijing: Renmin chubanshe, 1981.

Zhou Yan. "Women neng zouchu 'wenhua digu' ma?" *Dushu* 12 (1988): 5–10.

Zhou Yang. "Guanyu Makesi zhuyi de jige lilun wenti de tantao." *Renmin ribao*, 16 March 1983.

Zhu Guangqian. "Guanyu renxing, rendao zhuyi, renqingwei he gongtongmei wenti." In *Renxing rendao zhuyi wenti taolun ji*, ed. The Research Institute of Philosophy at the Chinese Academy of the Social Sciences, 181–88. Beijing: Renmin chubanshe, 1983.

Zhu Wei. "Jiejin A Cheng." *Zhongshan* 3 (1991): 157–72.

Zitta, Victor. *Georg Lukács' Marxism, Alienation, Dialectics, Revolution: A Study in Utopia and Ideology*. The Hague: Martinus Nijhoff, 1964.

Zong Pu. "Wo shi shei?" In *Zong Pu xiaoshuo sanwen xuan*, 34–41. Beijing: Renmin wenxue chubanshe, 1991.

Zou Ping. "Zoujin lenggu: Xinshiqi wenxue de weilaishi." *Shanghai wenxue* 10 (1988): 72–76.

Index

Absolute Spirit, 21, 292n38
Absurdity, 33, 35, 42, 169–70
Academy of Chinese Culture, 40, 49–50, 70
A Cheng, 166, 180–81, 214, 218, 241, 329n47; and Cultural Revolution, 219, 331n69; and subjectivity, 173, 174, 215, 216; and tradition vs. modernity, 182–83, 185–86. *See also* Root-searching literature
Adorno, Theodor, 76, 77, 105, 106, 302n63, 326n19
Aesthetic modernity, 4, 42–48, 137–48, 177–94; and alternative modern, 46–47, 297n15; and Cultural Revolution, 137, 313n19; and formalism, 144–48, 313–14n19; and ideology, 141–44; and linguistic-representative rupture, 177–80, 183; and May Fourth Movement, 48, 298n16; and modernization, 42, 43, 45, 192, 315–16n33; and Mo Yan, 46, 166, 171, 181, 186–89; and nationalism, 147–48; and nihilism, 137–38; 1930s, 193; and play, 44–45; and postmodernism, 233, 252; and rationality, 42–44; and stream of consciousness, 147, 189, 322–23n153; and subjectivity, 42, 160, 172–74; and utopianism, 42, 143, 159; and Wang Meng, 46, 167, 170, 181, 186, 189–92. *See also* Experimental fiction; Language fever; Modern consciousness; Pseudomodernism de-

bate; Root-searching literature; *Xiandai pai*
Ah, Human Beings! Human Beings! (*Ren a ren*) (Dai), 10, 32
"Air Stewardess" ("Kongzhong xiaojie") (Wang), 282, 341n43
Alienation: economic, 12, 14, 16–17, 291n20; Marx on, 10, 12, 13, 24, 289n4, 290n8; political, 12, 16, 291n26; and postmodernism, 239, 335n9; and post-new-era, 285–86; of thought, 12, 19. *See also* Socialist alienation
Alitto, Guy, 238
Alternative modern, 46–47, 64, 73, 90, 235, 297n15, 305n99, 334n3. *See also* Cultural subject; Greater China; Greater East Asia
Althusser, Louis, 58, 203, 324n2
Anarchism, 13–14, 233
Anderson, Perry, 105
Antihumanism, 26, 29, 77, 184; and experimental fiction, 184, 199, 202; and pseudomodernism debate, 165–67; and Wang Shuo phenomenon, 276–77
Anti-imperialism, 1, 288n7
Anti-Spiritual Pollution Campaign, 11, 15, 19, 25, 202
Anxiety consciousness. *See* Crisis consciousness
Aspirations (*Kewang*), 266
At Middle Age (*Rendao zhongnian*) (Shen), 34, 114, 296n76

Designer: Nola Burger
Compositor: BookMasters, Inc.
Text: Sabon 10/13
Display: Sabon
Printer: BookCrafters, Inc.
Binder: BookCrafters, Inc.

5672